'The time for more coaching of students in HE has come. This book is a welcome response to challenges in Higher Education learning and teaching. It shifts the focus from what students learn to how they could do it. Coaching approaches transform teaching and learning into provision that is tailored to each student, their unique goals, backstories, and circumstances.'

Klaus-Dieter Rossade, *Professor and Executive Dean, Faculty of Wellbeing, Education and Languages Studies, The Open University, UK*

'This timely book is an inspiring resource for higher education, offering practical tools, case studies, and thoughtful insights to foster a coaching culture that supports both staff and student development. It serves as a powerful advocate for person-centered methodologies and relationships, addressing critical topics like ethics, equality, and wellbeing with depth and care.'

Jelena Matic, *Senior Educational Developer and Creator of the Coaching in Higher Education Network*

'This volume gives great insight into the growing culture of coaching at The Open University (UK), where the mission is to be open to people, places, methods and ideas. It absolutely makes sense to take a person-centred approach to enable individuals to realise their own solutions in higher education.'

Paul Miles, *Learning Lead for Leadership and Management, Organisational Learning, The Open University, UK*

Coaching and Mentoring Students in Higher Education

Coaching and Mentoring Students in Higher Education provides student support and learning development professionals with a comprehensive, evidence-based guide for delivering coaching and mentoring interventions with students.

Focused on the context of higher education, it shares practitioner and research insights from a range of coaching and mentoring programmes and considers their transferability to the international higher education sector. It is a collection of practitioner research based on literature reviews, qualitative and quantitative evaluation of student feedback and scenario case studies. Each chapter offers practical tips and recommendations for colleagues in the sector looking to implement coaching and mentoring as a mode of support. Inviting readers to reflect upon their learning at key stages throughout the book, it addresses many key issues for higher education providers – including student engagement, retention and mental health and wellbeing.

This essential volume contributes to the growing body of scholarship looking at coaching and mentoring support at university and the impact on retention and student outcomes, and is key reading for senior leaders, strategic managers and student-facing staff alike.

Enya-Marie Clay was previously a personal learning adviser at The Open University, UK. Enya has trained as a career leader and has worked in further education as a careers lead and librarian.

Jennifer Hillman, Ph.D., is a senior manager in the Academic Development team for Associate Lecturers at The Open University, UK.

Dave Lochtie is an operations manager for Ann Craft Trust. Dave previously served as a senior operations manager for the Personal Learning Advice Service at The Open University, UK.

Coaching and Mentoring Students in Higher Education

A Practitioner Guide to Developing Independent Learners

EDITED BY
ENYA-MARIE CLAY, JENNIFER HILLMAN
AND DAVE LOCHTIE

Routledge
Taylor & Francis Group
LONDON AND NEW YORK

Cover image: Rudzhan Nagiev via Getty Images

First published 2026
by Routledge
4 Park Square, Milton Park, Abingdon, Oxon, OX14 4RN

and by Routledge
605 Third Avenue, New York, NY 10158

Routledge is an imprint of the Taylor & Francis Group, an informa business

British Library Cataloguing-in-Publication Data
A catalogue record for this book is available from the British Library

ISBN: 978-1-032-78041-2 (hbk)
ISBN: 978-1-032-78040-5 (pbk)
ISBN: 978-1-003-48601-5 (ebk)

DOI: 10.4324/9781003486015

Typeset in Dante and Avenir
by codeMantra

Contents

Acknowledgements *ix*
List of Contributors *xi*
List of Figures and Tables *xviii*
Foreword *xxi*
Jill Andreanoff

Introduction: Coaching and mentoring students in higher education 1
Enya-Marie Clay, Jennifer Hillman and Dave Lochtie

1 Confidentiality and the ethics of coaching and mentoring students 31
Jenny Lynden

2 Coaching and mentoring through an equity lens 70
Jo Blissett and Enya-Marie Clay

3 Working with students: Contracting and chemistry 114
Chrissie Farley, Joshua Samuels-Hylton and Emma Vance

4 Coaching and mentoring for wellbeing 149
Fareeha Karim and Leanne Lindsey

5 Coaching, mentoring and the learning development toolkit 187
Jennifer Hillman and Mary-Jayne Wilton

6 Peer mentoring in higher education 220
Catherine Comfort and Chris Kubiak

7 Developing coaching skills in student support practitioners 245
Jane Dudeney and Georgina Durley

8 Coaching supervision: Supporting staff development and wellbeing 268
Julie Stock, Helen Williams and Richard Peat

Postscript: What might the future hold for coaching and mentoring in higher education? 294
Martin Ousley

Appendices *302*
Index *315*

Acknowledgements

As editors, we each have strong connections to the work of a coaching and mentoring service for students at The Open University (OU), UK which was a four-year pilot project between 2021 and 2024. We would like to begin by expressing our gratitude to colleagues working within the wider Personal Learning Advice (PLA) Service team. Their generosity, expertise and genuine care for students have helped to shape and refine the approaches discussed in several chapters of this book.

We are also grateful for the leadership and collegiality shown to us by others who have believed in the transformative power of coaching and mentoring and supported the equity-centred work of the PLA team. Our particular thanks go to Deborah Peat, Sara Ebbett, Billy Khokhar and members of the service leadership team and steering group.

Outside of the organisation, Jill Andreanoff has written a foreword which has helped us to frame the contributions in this book. We have also benefitted from rich conversations and staff development workshops with Natalie Lancer. The Olympian and former 800 m British Champion Shelayna Oskan-Clarke became a valuable friend of, and generous advocate for, the work of the PLA Service.

We recognise and acknowledge the work of other OU colleagues and teams who have provided us with data to help refine the service and shaped our evaluation of it. This includes Paul Edwards as well as the Data and Student Analytics team. We are particularly grateful to faculty colleagues who have championed our coaching and mentoring work – including Daphne Chang and Hannah Lavery – in addition to the very many associate lecturer colleagues who have collaborated with us to support students.

The ideas in this volume have been enhanced by rich conversations at a number of conferences and events and we are grateful to workshop participants at the 2022 Advance HE EDI Conference, the 2023 RAISE conference and several internal research and scholarship events. We are thankful to Alicja Syska and Katharine Jewitt who read and commented on the work in the draft, as well as the anonymous reviewers who helped us to refine the original book proposal.

This volume draws upon a wide range of literature and features a variety of reproduced or adapted materials and we would like to thank all of the referenced authors, works and publishers, particularly Jonathan Passmore, Helen Webster, Peter Hawkins, Aisling McMahon, Christine Champion, Alison Maxwell and Kate Pinder, as well as brap and the International Coaching Federation.

We are especially grateful to the students who contributed their time and energy to the development of the service, individually and collectively as part of The OU Student Association. More broadly, this book would not have been possible without the extraordinary students we work with at The OU. It is to them that this book is dedicated.

Proceeds from editorial royalties will be donated to the Open University Students Educational Trust supporting students in financial need.

List of Contributors

Jo Blissett is a dedicated careers advisor, human resources and learning development professional with over 14 years of experience in higher education. Throughout her career, Jo has specialised in delivering coaching and mentoring programmes designed to support student growth, academic success and personal development. In her current role as a Personal Learning Adviser at The Open University, Jo provides personalised one-on-one coaching to a diverse student body. Her recent work has focused on supporting neurodivergent students, including those with dyslexia, dyscalculia, autism and ADHD, as well as students managing mental health challenges. In addition to her coaching work, Jo has played a key role in designing and leading group workshops aimed at building study confidence and fostering academic achievement. Her passion for inclusivity extends to her academic pursuits and she is currently working towards a Master's degree in Inclusion, with a focus on supporting autistic adults. Driven by a commitment to equitable education, Jo is passionate about creating supportive learning environments where students from all backgrounds can thrive. Her mission is to empower every learner to overcome barriers, unlock their potential and achieve their goals. She recently co-authored an article on coaching through an 'equity lens' for the Journal of Learning Development in Higher Education.

Enya-Marie Clay is a dedicated learning development professional committed to promoting and widening access to lifelong learning and supporting others to achieve success and fulfilment in whatever form that takes for them. With over ten years of experience in education, she is a level five-qualified coaching professional and a level seven-qualified careers leader with interests in equitable practice and creative approaches. Since 2021, Enya has been a Personal Learning Adviser at The Open University where she has contributed to the development of the service as well as presented at conferences, created workshops for staff and students and delivered 1:1 coaching and mentoring. Prior to this, she worked in various roles in both further and higher education specialising in student support, learning development and Equality Diversity and Inclusion. Enya holds an MLitt in English Literature and a BA (Hons) in History with a research interest in the ethics of memory and representation in children's literature and education. She has also volunteered in roles that promote community engagement in creative writing and literature for wellbeing and personal growth.

Catherine Comfort (Ph.D.) is a senior lecturer, fellow of the HEA and the academic lead for access, participation and success within the Faculty of Business and Law at The Open University (OU). Her career at The OU has and continues to focus on ensuring an equitable experience for all our distance learners, particularly those who face barriers to study. She is particularly keen to ensure we listen to what students tell us rather than what we think they need. As part of her work, she has run a successful peer-mentoring scheme on a Level One Business Module. Her research interests include the benefits of mentoring for young people and students. Prior to joining The OU in 2014, Catherine worked in business consultancy, market research and central and local government. She is also a volunteer mentor with a local authority mentoring scheme.

Jane Dudeney is a training and development specialist in academic services at The Open University, UK. Jane has a particular interest in fostering personal and professional growth, particularly in areas of mindset and self-awareness, as well as developing support staff to have empowering conversations with students. She has recently led projects to support building a culture of learning in an environment of change, focusing mainly on coaching and mentoring strategies. A qualified coaching practitioner and teacher, Jane has previously contributed to a publication on learning and teaching in the post-compulsory sector around mental health and wellbeing, drawing on her experience in further education. Currently, Jane is working with others to promote a coaching culture within her organisation alongside pursuing a Master's degree in Human Resource Management.

Georgina Durley has worked in education for over 12 years in a mixture of further and higher education. She is currently a senior manager for a group of guidance practitioners who offer support to students navigating complex barriers to study. She is qualified in offering guidance herself and practised in guidance before managing the service. Georgina has experience in working in safeguarding, careers and recruitment services, coaching and guidance and this experience is utilised in her contributions to Chapter 7 of this volume.

Chrissie Farley is a qualified 1:1 coach and educator with over 20 years' experience in widening participation management, advocacy and facilitation across London and Sussex. She has overseen the delivery of a broad range of student-centred interventions that include fostering access, community, engagement and progression for care-experienced students, young adult carers, students estranged from their families and forced migrants – driving meaningful outcomes across all levels of education. As a first-generation graduate from an IMDQ1 area who herself 'lost' a year of study due to a severe lack of confidence at university, Chrissie is passionate about advancing inclusion in education and creating opportunities for lifelong learning for everyone.

Jennifer Hillman (Ph.D.) is a senior manager in the Academic Development team for Associate Lecturers and Practice Tutors at The Open University, UK. Jennifer trained as a historian and was a Max Weber and British Academy Postdoctoral Fellow for two years before taking up a lectureship at the University of Chester. Jennifer has been teaching and supporting learning in higher education (HE) for over 15 years in both lecturing and professional services roles at York, Queen Mary University of London, Cumbria and Blackpool and the Fylde College. Jennifer is interested in how coaching can support teaching and learning in HE and is committed to scholarship in this area. More broadly, Jennifer believes in the importance of diversity and representation in HE and her own experiences of studying and living with obsessive compulsive disorder has informed her person-centred approach. Jennifer is a senior fellow of the Higher Education Academy.

Fareeha Karim is a second-generation English-Pakistani Muslim who has been dedicated to higher education (HE) since 2017. Fareeha's personal experience of living with foster children and young adults, many of whom were from ethnic backgrounds, has deeply informed her approach. She has provided invaluable coaching and mentoring to help them adjust to life in the UK and access the education and hobbies they desired. Her passion for empowering ethnic minority communities and fostering their self-actualisation drives her work within HE and the broader community.

She has held various roles along the Information, Advice and Guidance continuum and since 2022 has focused on coaching and mentoring students from ethnic backgrounds and with various intersectionalities. Through her contributions to higher education policies and publications, Fareeha aims to make a positive and meaningful impact on students' wellbeing throughout their academic journey.

Chris Kubiak (Ph.D.) is the Co-Director of The Open University's assessment programme and a senior lecturer in the School of Health, Wellbeing and Social Care (HWSC). His research work has focused on practice-based learning in care settings, peer mentoring and home help for older people. More recent research has focused on learning opportunities for carers and medical simulation. During his tenure as Associate Head of School for Learning, Teaching and Innovation in HWSC, he initiated the establishment of a peer-mentoring programme for level one students. He remains a strong advocate for the importance of supportive relationships in fostering student success.

Leanne Lindsey is a British Black Caribbean woman with over 15 years of experience delivering careers advice, coaching and mentoring. As a qualified careers advisor, she has provided comprehensive careers Information, Advice and Guidance to young people and adults across secondary, further and higher education. Additionally, as a qualified life coach, she has delivered coaching within the public, private and non-for-profit sectors. Leanne is deeply passionate about making coaching accessible and inclusive, focusing on supporting communities strategically disadvantaged by institutional, social and economic barriers. Her work is driven by a commitment to ensuring that everyone has equitable opportunity to realise their full potential and maintain optimum wellbeing.

Dave Lochtie (SFHEA) is the operations manager for the Ann Craft Trust, a leading authority in safeguarding adults at the University of Nottingham. He was formerly the senior operations manager for the Personal Learning Advice Service at The Open University. He is a Co-Chair of the Association for Peer Learning and Support that promotes best practice in student-led learning. He is a qualified teacher and co-author of *Effective Personal Tutoring in Higher Education* and *The Higher Education Personal Tutor's and Advisor's Companion*. He has worked in student services management roles at the University of Derby and University of New Orleans, as well as serving as a director, trustee and governor of the University of Roehampton and Bournemouth University Students' Union.

Jenny Lynden (Ph.D.) is a British Psychological Society (BPS) Chartered Psychologist, a chartered coaching psychologist, a member of the Division of Health Psychology, a registered test user (Occupational, Ability and Personality) and an accredited member of the International Society for Coaching Psychology. Jenny is also an accredited coaching supervisor listed on the BPS Register of Applied Psychology Practice Supervisors. Jenny is a senior lecturer and staff tutor in Psychology in the School of Psychology and Counselling at The Open University and co-lead of the Faculty of Arts and Social Sciences Coaching Cultures Project. Jenny uses an integrative coaching model, including solution-focused, positive psychology and cognitive behavioural coaching approaches and specialises in supporting faculty staff and students in higher education to flourish. Jenny has authored peer-reviewed papers in international journals on applications of coaching psychology across workplace and educational contexts: https://www.open.ac.uk/people/jml364

Martin Ousley FRSA MISCP is a Coaching Psychologist with over 20 experience in a variety of coaching roles and currently working in private practice as an integrative coach/counsellor. Prior to returning to private practice he was as a Personal Learning Adviser for the Open University for four years working with students on a one to one and group basis to help them overcome a variety or personal and societal barriers in regard to educational and career opportunities. He is also a qualified Coaching Supervisor, Teacher and Trainer and has supervised and mentored other coaches throughout his career. He has worked in adult education for over 30 years in both further and higher education as well as coaching roles in the private sector.

Richard Peat is a qualified careers advisor, life coach, coaching supervisor, teacher and assessor having worked for over 30 years within education in a range of advice, guidance, coaching and teaching roles. He has experience across the whole education sector having worked within every level of education from primary school up to postgraduate higher education. Recent work has focused on providing education, guidance and coaching support to people on the neurodiverse spectrum (including dyslexia, dyscalculia, autism and ADHD) and those with mental health conditions or other learning disabilities. The main ethos of his work is to ensure that the people he works with are actively encouraged and support in achieving their own personal goals and potential. During his contribution to this book, he has been working within The Open University as a Personal Learning Adviser,, coaching students with significant barriers to educational progression and achievement and then as senior manager within the team. He continues to work within education.

Joshua Samuels-Hylton is a qualified coach, teacher and academician with over 15 years of higher education experience. He has worked as a Social Sciences lecturer and has also been commissioned as an academic consultant at several universities, throughout the UK, Europe and the Caribbean. Josh has an inimitable passion for teaching, learning development and empowering students to raise their aspirations and actualise their true potential. Thus, he works diligently to assist students in the cultivation of skills, habits, attitudes and the requisite knowledge needed for long-term academic success. Diversity and inclusion hold great importance to Josh. Consequently, he strategically engages with efforts to reduce gaps in access, success and progression to best increase representation and visibility in the achievement of equitable outcomes.

Julie Stock is a learning manager in Organisational Learning at The Open University (OU), UK. Specialising in compliance training, coaching and mentoring, Julie has had various roles across the University, but in her early 30s moved into the world of HR, and specialising in learning and development. Julie has been a coach for about 15 years, setting up The OU's Coaching Service nine years ago, which she continues to manage. Julie is also a mentor and coach supervisor. Julie's current interests in coaching are around personal effectiveness, wellbeing and positive self-reflection. Julie is a Co-Chair of the Eastern Region Forum of the Staff Development Forum, sponsored by Advance HE. Julie has a Master's in Human Resource Management and is a Chartered member of the CIPD. Julie is also a Master Strengthscope Practitioner and Insights Discovery Practitioner.

Emma Vance is a Scottish educator and qualified level five coach with over 20 years of experience in widening participation, employability, outreach and student support in further and higher education. As a coach-mentor at The Open University, Emma specialises in helping students navigate academic challenges and personal struggles, emphasising mental health and wellbeing. Committed to holistic support, Emma seeks to create educational environments responsive to the diverse needs of today's students, believing that integrating academic guidance with mental health support fosters belonging and resilience throughout the learning journey.

Helen Williams started her career as a Geography teacher in secondary schools in Bradford just over 20 years ago. Following this, she worked in a consultancy, coaching and management capacity within a local authority, the NHS and Teach First. Committed to life-long learning in the service of supporting and developing others, she holds an MA in Special Educational

Needs, PGDip HR Management, PGCert Healthcare Leadership and an ILM Level Five Certificate in Mentoring and Coaching.

Mary-Jayne Wilton has worked at The Open University (OU) since 2017 in guidance, coaching and mentoring roles and managing student support teams. She also works as an EDI consultant at Impact People and Change for clients including Nottingham Trent University. Prior to joining The OU, her background and qualifications are in coaching, learning and development practice, careers advice and employability support. Mary has also worked as a support worker and then director for POW, a charity supporting sex workers and those at risk of sexual exploitation. Additionally, she has been a trustee for Y-NOTTS, a charity responsible for awarding developmental and educational grants to young people aged 16–25. Areas of particular interest are the language of inclusion and belonging, anti-oppressive and inclusive practice and finding innovative and effective ways to engage and diversify organisations with new perspectives, ideas and stories.

List of Figures and Tables

Introduction

Table 0.1 Key differences between coaching and mentoring 5
Figure 0.1 Overview of the Personal Learning Advice Service coaching and mentoring activities 10
Figure 0.2 Timeline of the Personal Learning Advice Service pilot project 13
Table 0.2 Student experience survey responses 2023–2024 17

Chapter two

Figure 2.1 Overview of the PLA framework 72
Figure 2.2 PLA coaching and mentoring through an equity lens 73
Figure 2.3 Overview of PLA coaching and mentoring practice 78
Figure 2.4 Example core competencies/key skills used within the PLA coaching and mentoring continuum – adapted from the International Coaching Federation (2022) 79
Table 2.1 Mapping UD principles to service/practitioner activity 88
Table 2.2 Activity: insider/outsider reflection table 97
Table 2.3 Insider/outsider, responses and perceptions 98
Table 2.4 Example practitioner reflection, focused on empowering action 104
Table 2.5 Stop, start, continue plan 107

Chapter three

Table 3.1 Nine stages of the contracting process and the parties involved 117
Figure 3.1 The tripartite relationship between coach, coachee and university 118
Figure 3.2 A spectrum illustrating the flow between expert power and individual agency in helping relationships – adapted from (Webster, no date) 119
Figure 3.3 The four typical roles involved in supporting a student in higher education 120
Table 3.2 Template to support contracting when coaching and mentoring students 128
Table 3.3 Re-contracting in action 133

Chapter four

Figure 4.1 A flowchart for managing referrals 170

Chapter five

Table 5.1 The synergies between learning development, coaching and mentoring 189

Chapter seven

Table 7.1 Comparison of open and closed questioning styles 259

Chapter eight

Table 8.1 The application of the Seven-Eyed model (Hawkins and McMahon, 2020) to the supervision of staff coaches in HE 270
Table 8.2 The application of the Seven-Eyed model (Hawkins and McMahon, 2020) to the supervision of student coaches in HE 278

Table 8.3 The CLEAR supervision model applied in peer supervision in the PLA Service 281
Table 8.4 Considerations for procuring external supervision for student-facing staff 283
Table 8.5 Shared Ways of Working in supervision 286
Table 8.6 Session plan for supervision sessions 288

Foreword

Jill Andreanoff

I was absolutely delighted and honoured to be asked to write the foreword for this exciting new resource promoting and encouraging the use of quality coaching and mentoring in the higher education (HE) sector. I have long been an advocate for good practice coaching having personally seen the benefits of robust interventions in many of the HE institutions (HEIs) I have worked in, so any publication that makes a convincing case for introducing these initiatives or provides guidance for how to do so is very welcome.

Unfortunately, despite publications like this, many HEIs still pay 'lip-service' to coaching and mentoring without committing to the full investment of time, training and resources needed to fully reap the benefits. Assumptions are often made by senior leadership teams that the participants (because they are well-educated individuals, often with an excellent teaching career) have the expertise to provide coaching. They fail to recognise that coaching is a skill that needs to be continually practised to be honed and mastered and that not every individual is suited to this role despite how successful they may be in their day job. Skills such as active listening and effective questioning techniques may not be inherent or even needed for their day-to-day role. Add to this, the fact that staff are often asked to undertake the coaching of students or fellow staff as an addition to their usual duties, without proper training or supervision, is no surprise that many schemes fail due to this lack of insight and investment.

This useful resource highlights with case studies, providing some excellent and helpful examples, of how these skills can be incorporated into other HE student-facing roles. It uses common dilemmas and scenarios faced by practitioners, highlighting practical examples of how appropriate solutions can be found through coaching and how to best utilise coaching supervision.

Since publishing my own book in 2016 endorsing the exemplary practice in HE, in hindsight (and with some regret) I realised there were gaps in the content. This publication has very successfully not only filled those gaps but also has provided some excellent insights and practical tips to aid those wishing to enhance the student experience and achievement. Using staff as coaches and mentors does present challenges, such as overcoming the power dynamics of the student/staff relationship, but this resource enables the reader to address them and many others too.

Coaching and mentoring are still terms that are used 'lightly' and frequently (and in my opinion, often inappropriately) with many assuming they are unidirectional relationships. This publication provides the reader with the tools to adopt and/or implement some exemplary practice coaching and mentoring to aid students to be self-efficacious learners which not only helps them achieve but also will improve the outcomes for HEIs in which we work.

The one 'take-away' I have for readers wishing to introduce this worthwhile and powerful intervention is to ensure they fully invest in terms of time, resources and training for participants as the authors have clearly done. I hope they will recognise from this book what essential ingredients are required for quality coaching to enhance performance and improve wellbeing to effectively use them in their own institutions.

Introduction

Coaching and mentoring students in higher education

Enya-Marie Clay, Jennifer Hillman and Dave Lochtie

Coaching and mentoring for independent learning

> We as people are all unique individuals with specific dreams and potential, so we should not be afraid to pursue our purpose.
>
> (Student A)

There are many punchy definitions, inspirational quotations and exciting metaphors that we could have selected to open this volume on coaching and mentoring. Instead, we begin with a simple observation shared by a student evaluating the coaching and mentoring support they had received at university. Student A's awareness of themselves as unique, capable and determined captures the simple power of a person-centred helping relationship. Coaching and mentoring, as we seek to show in this volume, can be effective foundations for the creation of successful, independent learners (Grant, 2003; Bellman, Burgstahler, and Hinke, 2015; Fried and Irwin, 2016; Andreanoff, 2016c).

Helping students to develop as 'independent' learners is an objective many of us share in higher education (HE). Independent learning skills are part of the quality assurance of degree courses, a 'graduate attribute' and something which most tutors and student support practitioners seek to instil in students (Hockings *et al.*, 2018, p. 146). At campus-based

DOI: 10.4324/9781003486015-1

universities, independent learning generally refers to the time that students spend outside of timetabled contact hours with a tutor. In the context of distance-learning courses, students will spend the majority of their study hours engaging in independent study, with only occasional synchronous contact time. A hybrid model, which we know many universities are moving towards in the UK and internationally (Platonova *et al.*, 2022) would offer a combination of in-person and online teaching, with independent tasks. In all of these scenarios, the evidence tells us that the students who are able to engage in self-directed learning are more likely to achieve their goals (Henderson and Nathenson, 1984; Paul, 1990; Gurbutt and Gurbett, 2015; Thomas *et al.*, 2015; Grey, McIntosh and Stylianoudaki, 2017).

In foregrounding 'independence' here, there is a danger of inferring that we accept uncritically the view that students should be self-reliant in a way which pathologises the need for support at university (Leathwood, 2006, p. 615). In this volume, we take a more nuanced view of independence which recognises help-seeking behaviours and timely engagement with resources and support as positive skills which can be honed. As Student A went on to celebrate in their feedback, 'there are people who will listen and understand our stories, just like my tutor and my PLA [Personal Learning Adviser] did' (Student A, 2023). For this student, the self-determination to pursue their purpose was not at odds with needing to feel heard and understood. We share their view. In this volume, we regard independent learners as students who are empowered in the pursuit of their personal and study-related goals. Each chapter contributes to a growing body of evidence which shows that coaching and mentoring are important mechanisms to develop liberatory and often transformative 'independence' in student learning.

In this chapter, we offer an introduction to the volume in three parts. The first section charts the history of coaching and mentoring. It explores the interrelationship between coaching and mentoring as person-centred 'helping' relationships, how they differ from other forms of support such as counselling and therapy and how they have been translated to HE. The second part of this chapter sets the scene for the eight chapters in this book by outlining a culture of coaching and mentoring at one HE institution: The Open University (OU) (UK). It shows the evidence for the impact coaching and mentoring can have and considerations for other institutions developing coaching and mentoring cultures. The third and final section of this introductory chapter synthesises the eight chapters of this volume and offers a thematic discussion of the main threads running throughout them.

Coaching, mentoring and higher education

The relationship between coaching and mentoring

Beginning with the semantics of coaching and mentoring tells us a lot about why they have translated so well to HE. The usage of the word 'coach' in contexts other than transport is first evident in the nineteenth century. At this time, there were parallels between its usage and what we now understand as mentoring. A 'coach' was primarily 'university slang' for a tutor who 'prepares a student for an examination' (1836) (Oxford English Dictionary [OED], 2024). The origins of the term 'mentor' are said to be drawn from Homer's *Odyssey*, where 'Mentor' used his wisdom and experience to guide Odysseus' son Telemachus during his absence. Whilst they have distinct – and sometimes contested (Colley, 2002) – etymologies, both 'coach' and 'mentor' were related to the support given during journeys – whether towards academic achievement or towards personal growth and maturity.

There are several accounts which chart the history of coaching in detail which we will not seek to repeat here (Wildflower, 2013; Passmore, 2021a). However, it is worth noting the influence of the so-called 'counter-cultural (Passmore, 2021a, p. 4) Human Potential Movement of the 1960s on thinkers such as Sir John Whitmore – whose name has become synonymous with coaching. The Human Potential Movement pivoted on values such as 'tolerance, a basic optimism about human nature, the necessity of honest interpersonal communication, the importance of living life to the fullest in the 'here and now,' and a spirit of experimentation and openness to new experiences' (Human Potential Movement, 2016). These ideas were also linked to the psychology of Carl Rogers (1902–1987) and Abraham Maslow (1908–1970). Influenced by these ideas, Whitmore and other early contributors to the definitions of coaching, saw it as a way of supporting an individual to self-actualise. We can see this reflected in Whitmore's familiar and often-cited definition of 'unlocking people's potential to maximise their own performance' (Whitmore, 2017, pp. 12–13).

Currently, there is a movement that coaching is to be non-directive and client-led and thus, no longer necessitates the coach being a more experienced or knowledgeable partner in the coaching relationship. Instead, accredited coaching training courses, such as the government-sponsored Coaching Professional Apprenticeship (IfATE, 2020), instruct coaching as a malleable set of skills, knowledges and behaviours that are applicable to a wide variety of environments and sectors and are rooted in evidence-based approaches drawing from fields such as psychology, education and leadership. More generally, there has been an expansion of the fields in which coaching is translating to. As Neenan and Palmer show, coaching is no longer limited to corporate or executive coaching context but used in education, healthcare and stress management, domestic life and wellbeing (Neenan and Palmer, 2022, p. 1). Later in this introductory chapter, we address how this has manifested in HE specifically.

'Mentoring' was not in popular usage until the mid-twentieth century where it became prominent in US business literature (Irby and Boswell, 2016). The history of mentoring can be viewed through the evolution of its theoretical foundations (Dominguez and Hager, 2013). For example, developmental mentoring grew out of mentoring in the professional workforce during the 1980s, based on theories of career development (Levinson, 1978; cited in Dominguez and Hager, 2013, pp. 172–175). By the 1990s, the mentor was often regarded as critical to workplace learning and success (Caldwell and Carter, 1993). Many workplaces use different types of developmental and learning mentoring for staff – including reciprocal mentoring between staff where there is a significant power differential. The EMCC offers the following definition:

> Mentoring is a learning relationship, involving the sharing of skills, knowledge and expertise between a mentor and mentee through developmental conversations, experience sharing and role modelling. The relationship that values differences may cover a wide variety of contexts and is an inclusive two-way partnership for mutual learning.
>
> (EMCC, 2024)

Importantly, coaching and mentoring are both supportive relationships which aim, in different ways, to 'encourage reflective thinking and decision making' […] and support someone to 'achieve their aims and objectives in a way that is suitable for them' (Andreanoff, 2016a, p. 2). For clarity, we use 'helping' relationships to describe practice in professional contexts such as education, health and social care where practitioners have a specialist role requiring them to 'walk alongside rather than lead, to enable rather than to control, to assist rather than fix' those they support (Westergaard, 2016, p. 4). Coaching, mentoring, counselling, advising might all therefore be considered as helping relationships but with vital differences. We distinguish coaching and mentoring from therapeutic relationships such as counselling – for example – by acknowledging the non-clinical role of the practitioner, whose focus is to help a student explore the present and future, rather than delve into the past as a counsellor might do (Passmore, 2021a, p. 5). Like counselling, nevertheless, coaching and mentoring are 'person-centred' relationships heavily influenced by the work of Rogers

(1951) on 'client-centred therapy' (Mearns, 1998). Person-centredness is, in essence, an approach to helping relationships which rests on a belief in the 'actualising tendency' of a person (Rogers, 1986 cited in Bryant-Jefferies, 2021, p. 190) – or, in other words, their ability to grow, solve problems and achieve their potential.

In this volume, then, we explore coaching and mentoring together because we recognise their interconnections as facilitative, helping relationships which enable people to fulfil their potential. They are, as others have put it, both fundamentally based on 'open ended conversations with a purpose' (Megginson and Clutterbuck, 2009, p. 237). This is reflected in literature, where scholars use 'coach' to signify helping roles that cut across coaching and mentoring (Jones and Smith, 2022; Lancer, Clutterbuck and Megginson, 2016, p. 3). However, it is also vital that we do not gloss over the distinctions between the two – simplified in Table 0.1).

We acknowledge from the outset that a distinct identity for coaching remains to be defined, particularly as coaching moves closer to becoming a regulated profession. In this space, coaching tends to be identified by its purpose, its audience and its process, as well as by looking at its close neighbours – mentoring, counselling and consulting – to define what coaching is not (Bachkirova, Cox and Clutterbuck, 2014, p. 3). With this context in mind, we have invited contributing authors in this volume to share their own definitions of coaching and mentoring and how distinctions between the two might play out at different stages of a helping relationship. Like other scholars have done, we have also tried to show how practitioners working across the fields of coaching and mentoring can make selections about the techniques they use based on the needs of their coachee/mentees (Lancer, Clutterbuck, and Megginson, 2016; Megginson and Clutterbuck, 2009, pp. 237–240).

More broadly, at a time when HEIs are increasingly recognising their responsibilities for the provision of support, often necessitating multi-agency work across the student journey, we want to suggest that thinking

Table 0.1 Key differences between coaching and mentoring

Coaching	Mentoring
Formal	Informal
Short term	Long term
Coach is non-expert	Mentor is expert
Qualified	Experienced

Source: Adapted from Passmore (2021a, p. 6).

more holistically about the interconnectedness of 'helping' in HE might be instructive. Clearly, there is a need for well-defined roles where staff can contract clearly, maintain boundaries and help students access the right support. Yet that does not mean that practitioners in a range of roles in HE might not usefully be able to draw upon coaching and mentoring practice to meet the needs of students. Just as coaching and mentoring are at once distinct but overlapping, so too are coaching and mentoring with areas of student support such as guidance, academic advising and tutoring. In Chapter 2 of this volume, coaching and mentoring are positioned as part of a continuum of support and this is itself situated in the wider context of student support in Chapter 7. For now, let us turn to consider the distinct histories of coaching and mentoring as they evolved and how they have been adapted in HE.

Coaching and mentoring in HE

There is something paradoxical about editing a volume on coaching and mentoring in HE in 2024. In many ways, coaching and mentoring are so inherent in aspects of university culture that it feels banal to call this out. For example, coaching is deeply (if implicitly) connected to teaching and learning – perhaps best exemplified in social constructivist pedagogies, where dialogue is used to develop critical thinking, belonging and self-reflection in students. These foundations were laid by Socrates and Plato who used dialogue (questions and answers) as a form of instruction. Coaching is sometimes described as a 'Socratic dialogue' for this very reason (Passmore and Fillery-Travis, 2011, p. 74). Similarly, certain forms of mentoring are well established as support mechanisms for students and developmental tools for staff in many institutions.

Yet, in the period in between the conception and writing of this book, we have seen colleagues across different areas of the sector calling for ways to make these (implicit) practices, explicit. For example, the SEDA (Staff and Educational Development Association – UK) Jiscmail was recently used to establish a network of Educational Developers and other practitioners to explore how coaching might enhance student experience (SEDA, 2024). A very recent volume of work from the UK and Singapore has also made a very compelling case for coaching in HE (Lim and Patel, 2024, pp. 9–11). In a challenging financial climate for many universities, there is arguably an ongoing need to evidence the 'impact' and value of coaching and mentoring initiatives for HE providers which might inform future investment in staff skills training and development, and the funding of 'core' coaching and mentoring for students – either through tuition or student support.

A range of UK HEI websites indicates a coaching offer for undergraduates, postgraduates, apprentices and learners on CPD courses – including (but not limited to): St Andrews, Imperial College London, Birmingham City, Loughborough, Arden University, University of South Wales, York St John and The OU. This is also true internationally, most notably in the United States (NACADA, 2019). In addition to the hybrid learning model, this is, in part, a response to the regulatory (and commercial) interests that universities have in retaining students and ensuring equality, with a commitment towards equity of outcomes. The assessment on many programmes in HE now includes assessing student self-awareness and reflective practice; even its critics have noted the pervasiveness of 'reflective practice' in assessment (Tight, 2023). We hope that this book will speak to these currents, both in the UK and internationally, as practitioners coach students to successfully navigate the demands of hybrid study and become independent and effective learners.

It is important to make the point, then, that coaching and mentoring are not 'new' things in HE. What is more current, however, is the momentum gathering around these areas of practice and the evidence base they are generating. The difference that coaching can make to the student experience is increasingly clear from the literature cited across the eight chapters of this volume. Some key contributions to this body of evidence include the literature on coaching and 'academic coaching' from the United States (Alzen *et al.*, 2021, p. 542). The doctoral work of Alice Sepulveda (2020) and their collaborative research (Sepulveda *et al.*, 2020) has made significant contributions to our understanding of the impact coaching can have and, moreover, of the complexities of capturing statistically significant causal evidence (2020). One mixed-methods study of life coaching 94 undergraduate students over three academic years found, for example, evidence of impact on self-confidence, self-awareness, goal setting and attainment (Lefdahl-Davis *et al.*, 2018). Other studies have shown demonstrable causal evidence using randomised control trials. For example, Wang and Lu (2020) found that students receiving coaching showed improvements in learning, motivation and self-efficacy. Other relevant causal evidence from the international context comes from Israel where 88 students taught via lectures and coaching experienced higher levels of mental wellbeing, solution-focused thinking and goal attainment than 90 students taught by traditional lectures only (Atad and Grant, 2021).

In the UK, the work of Natalie Lancer and Virginia Eatough has advanced our understanding of the benefits coaching can bring to students (2018). Though smaller in scale than the US-based studies, and based solely on qualitative measures, Lancer and Eatough's work has also helped to reveal some of the challenges and barriers experienced by UK undergraduates and the ways in which coaching might support them to overcome these (2021). A study by Dionne Spencer is especially important for what it tells us about the role coaching can play in support for students from marginalised backgrounds (2021) and something which Dave and Jennifer sought to expand upon in research published elsewhere (Hillman, Lochtie and Purcell, 2024).

It is acknowledged here that coaching and mentoring is grounded in Eurocentrism and Western approaches which practitioners are often unaware of or uncertain of how to acknowledge and address (Roche, 2022). While this volume aims to contribute modes of coaching and mentoring for supporting students in HE that are anti-oppressive, decolonised and equitable in nature; we recognise that this is a movement to which we come to imperfectly and that there is much work to be done in developing globalised coaching and mentoring practices. A commonality we all share is the belief that coaching and mentoring can be tools for enacting social change. These can be well-employed within HE environments to make use of their existence as platforms for connecting across locations and populations to reach governments, professions, industry and the arts while purporting knowledge exchange, research, development, as well as rich cultural, scientific and societal growth and communities (Marginson, 2024). It is with this view that we hope readers are inspired and energised by the discussions presented in this volume to participate in a growing movement that seeks to continually develop and embed coaching and mentoring practices across HE institutions to create more equitable outcomes and experiences for our students.

Cultures of coaching and mentoring

Institutional culture

At the time of writing this volume, all our contributing authors are involved with projects linked to coaching, mentoring (or both) at The OU. Coaching and mentoring as mechanisms for the development of both staff and students is a welcome addition to the university's large eco-system, where colleagues support over 200,000 students studying across four faculties (The Open University, 2024a). The OU was established by Royal Charter in 1969 and, since then, over 2.3 million distance-learning students have graduated with The OU qualification (The Open University, 2024b).

The OU is one of the largest providers of HE in Europe delivered through a model of tuition known as 'supported open learning' (Bell and Lane,

1998, p. 635; Ison, 2000). In this model, tuition takes place variously in synchronous online group tutorials, in 1:1 individual support sessions and/or in the workplace – supplemented by correspondence tuition. Students study on a module-by-module basis, at a distance and in a self-directed way, with personalised support and assessment feedback. Supported open learning has also embraced significant pedagogical changes in the last decade – such as the use of learning analytics to inform differentiated support (Marr, 2018; Farrell *et al.*, 2024). The impact that tuition can have to support distance learners has been recognised in recent Advance HE National Teaching Fellowships (Advance HE, 2024). There is also a rich body of scholarship showing the value of this model for widening and equitable access to HE (The Open University, 2024c).

Coaching and mentoring are both person-centred 'helping' relationships which begin with the philosophy that each and every person has the capacity to achieve their goals and fulfil their potential. It is fitting, then, that a non-selective institution such as The OU, with a mission connected to the role of learning in social justice (The Open University 2024c), should be driving innovations in the application of coaching and mentoring to HE. There are many ways in which coaching and/or mentoring is becoming embedded within institutional culture for both professional services and academic staff – in both formalised and informalised ways. However, the genesis of this volume was initially concentrated within a specific coaching and mentoring pilot project in the institution which we will now turn to chart in detail.

The Personal Learning Advice Service: coaching and mentoring students

The Personal Learning Advice (PLA) Service was a centralised coaching and mentoring service for students which operated as a four-year pilot project at The OU. The PLA Service was established in 2020, a team of 21 practitioners was recruited in early 2021, and the service was operational between February 2021 and December 2024. During the project, 66,777 individual offers of remote telephone, video and email support were made to distance-learning students and, during that period, there were 4,610 occasions where individual students took up support for the first time, with many returning for subsequent support. The title Personal Learning 'Adviser' is, in many ways, a misnomer since the vision for the service was, from the outset, solutions-focused coaching and mentoring support. However, it is not unusual for the term 'adviser' to be used in UK HE to describe a host of student-facing roles where coaching might be employed, as we have noted above.

It its design, the PLA Service had equitable outcomes for students at the centre; it was launched as one of the initiatives in the institutional access and participation plan (APP) – a document which is a regulatory requirement for universities in England under the Office for Students (OfS, 2024). Funded for the 2021–2025 APP cycle, the service was offered to students across the university's four nations (The Open University, 2022). APPs are designed to help institutions identify interventions which will be used to address any inequalities that may exist for student access, participation and success (OfS, 2024). These are strategic but publicly available documents which help institutions to plan interventions for student equity and also require them to monitor, evaluate and be accountable for reducing inequalities. The PLA Service was part of The OU's strategic aims in the APP to address pass rate awarding gaps that exist between: Black and White students, Disabled students and those with no known disabilities, Students within the most and least deprived socio-economic areas, Students with mental health difficulties and those with no known disabilities, and students from other racially minoritised groups and White students (The Open University, 2022). There were also ambitions to test the impact of coaching and mentoring on the 'good' module pass gaps that exist between these groups. In 2022, regulatory changes were made to the APP cycle by the OfS and new APPs are being written across the sector for a new cycle from 2025 to 2029 (Figure 0.1).

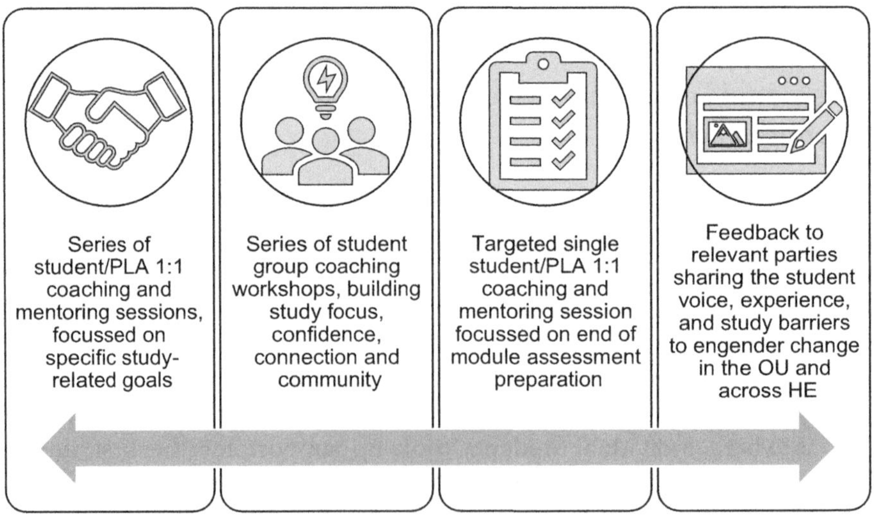

Figure 0.1 Overview of the Personal Learning Advice Service coaching and mentoring activities.

From the outset, the objective for the PLA coaching and mentoring service was to work exclusively with students from backgrounds which we know are disadvantaged by systemic barriers across all phases of the UK education system and compounded by wider societal issues. The service necessarily operated as a 'targeted' support model in order to provide differentiated support to students from backgrounds which we know are affected by institutional awarding gaps. Interventions which identify student groups who might be at risk because of systemic or structural issues are featured in several institutional APPs in HE in England and are considered as one route to removing awarding gaps. We know that being 'targeted' for support can be experienced in different ways by students, however, and it is not always welcome (Stevenson *et al.*, 2019). With this in mind, in the PLA Service, support was offered to students with an explicit acknowledgement of the wider systemic issues contributing to awarding gaps. This was articulated using a positioning statement that was developed in response to student feedback and in collaboration with Equality, Diversity and Inclusion subject matter experts. This was provided in all communications with students and placed on the PLA Service project website. Offers of coaching and mentoring support were also only made to students where the data showed that they might be 'at risk' of poorer outcomes. In other words, where learning analytics showed that they had a module pass probability prediction of 70 percent or less, assessed by a pass probability model, built upon at least 70 factors including previous studies and qualifications, engagement levels and demographic data (Calvert, 2014). This is a widely used institutional tool which is used to identify students who may need proactive support and is based on an algorithm which included previous module performance.

Several chapters in this volume offer further opportunities to reflect on some of the fundamental ethical issues with 'targeted' interventions. Until recently, we might have referred to students in the cohorts which the PLA Service worked with as 'non-traditional.' In this volume, contributors have deliberately adopted language which we suggest better captures the systemic (sector-wide) issues that are the root causes of inequitable outcomes and experiences for students. We do not refer to 'non-traditional' or disadvantaged students, but acknowledge that the students of the PLA Service were designed to support are variously underrepresented, marginalised and minoritised.

In delivering the coaching and mentoring support which the PLA Service was established to provide, 21 practitioners were recruited from a range of professional backgrounds – including 'Third Space' roles in further and HE, counselling and mental health services and professional coaching

(Whitchurch, 2003). In addition to professional qualifications and experience, the diversity of the team was enhanced via anonymised recruitment which was designed to recognise relevant lived experiences including ethnic diversity, neurodiversity and experiences of HE as mature, first-generation or distance-learning students. This helped to ensure that students would see themselves reflected in the staff coaching and mentoring them, which we know is often not in the case in HE (Bhopal and Pitkin, 2020; Thomas and Arday, 2021; Bhopal, 2023).

The diversity of the team and range of lived experience meant that the service was well-positioned for supporting students across APP cohorts. Once the service became operational, coaching and mentoring support was offered in the first six months on a pilot project basis where faculties could essentially 'bid' for PLA support for cohorts of students. In this phase of the service, coaching and mentoring was offered as part of discrete projects – including one focused on supporting care-experienced students and care leavers studying in Scotland, and another centred on access students with mental health needs. From June 2021 onwards, the service was redirected towards a centralised approach which prioritised coaching and mentoring for students identifying as Black, with a pass probability prediction of 70 percent or less studying across the nations and across all four faculties.

The launch of a coaching and mentoring service which was responsive to wider strategic aims required an iterative approach to developing the offer, which was rooted in our practitioners' learning about student experiences. This is reflected in the way in which PLA support grew and evolved over the four-year pilot period. Initially, for example, the offer was for a time-bound period of one-to-one coaching and mentoring which took place entirely by telephone or email as a reasonable adjustment (discussed further in Chapter 3). This was via the established, secure telephony system used to support students in recruitment contact centres and student support services at the university. Virtual video appointments were introduced by the PLA Service in late 2021 and, in 2022, group workshops were also launched leading to a multi-faceted offer of support for eligible students. Workshops are discussed in greater detail in Chapter 5 of this volume.

Coaching and mentoring support offers were made to eligible students proactively at the beginning of the two major module 'presentations' (or start dates) in the academic year – October and February. The PLA Service sent proactive communications by email and text to eligible students, and they could choose whether or not to 'opt' into coaching and mentoring, with the option to withdraw at any time. Students were also given the opportunity to indicate a preference with regard to the gender of their coach-mentor. Once students opted in, they were given access to a coaching and mentoring virtual learning environment website and allocated to a PLA who liaised with them directly to organise one-to-one appointments at a mutually convenient time. Each practitioner in the team was supported to work flexibly so that we could accommodate appointments outside of traditional working hours and meet the needs of distance-learning students managing employment, family life and study.

Coaching and mentoring racially minoritised (and particularly) Black distance-learning students via telephone, email and video call became a major focus for the PLA Service pilot. In working with Black students, one of the key aims of the service and its practitioners has been to add value within the complex eco-system of a large HE provider and ensure that learning from the service informs and engenders positive change, in the university's core activities. Chapters 2–5 of this volume demonstrate how – in different ways – practitioners in the service have driven innovations, challenged established ways of working and acted as a critical 'friends' to share (where appropriate) the experiences of racially minoritised students at university. Authors in this volume, and across the wider team of practitioners, have also helped to develop awareness of intersectionality and challenge assumptions about a single, homogenous 'Black student' experience.

Figure 0.2 shows the iterative development of the PLA Service project and key points at which new interventions were launched as part of the service's offer. The conclusion of the PLA Service pilot in December 2024 and the aspiration to share the insights of its practitioner played a significant

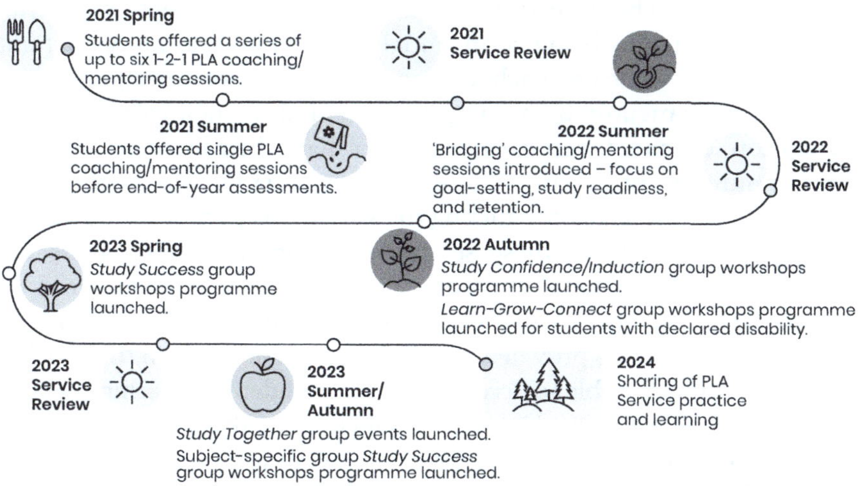

Figure 0.2 Timeline of the Personal Learning Advice Service pilot project.

part in the conception of this book. However, as we have noted, a legacy of learning from the PLA Service continues to inform the development of a broader culture at the university based on the evidence for coaching and mentoring and its potential impact. This, and the evaluation of the service, is discussed in greater detail below. Critically, many of our coach-mentors are themselves from underrepresented backgrounds and share aspects of lived experience with the students we support. In authoring several chapters of this volume, our contributors have used insights from their work with students to develop good practice which helps students to tap into different aspects of their lived experience and unlock their learning potential.

Coaching and mentoring initiatives

There are also local initiatives which have identified the potential benefits of coaching – specifically – for academic staff development. One example of this is a project collaboration between the PLA Service and The OU's School of Engineering and Innovation. This collaboration involved a small group of Personal Learning Advisors who were undertaking a Coaching Professional Higher-Level Apprenticeship, and academic staff (including lecturers and academic leadership). It was led by Enya-Marie Clay with Daphne Chang (senior lecturer and staff tutor). As part of this initiative, academic (teaching) staff were offered coaching sessions with PLAs. To maintain confidentiality and to keep the coaching a fluid, person-centred space, the coachees were offered six coaching sessions and a seventh, reflective session. This reflective session was more aligned with mentoring, was not contracted as being confidential and was used as an opportunity for coachees to either be coached on a specific area of their professional practice or to be mentored on using coaching skills in their role. In this seventh session, coachees were encouraged to share their learning with their own communities of practice. Moreover, this initiative also furthered the development of the PLAs conducting the sessions as part of the agreement was that they could use these sessions developmentally to assist with their Coaching Professional Apprenticeship and as a more structured way to experiment with alternative coaching styles and techniques with the coachees' consent. This provided a reciprocal benefit wherein the coachees (academic staff) were able to access up to six confidential coaching sessions and a seventh, reflective session which could then be shared with colleagues and was focused on developing professional practice. Additionally, the coaches (PLAs) were able to experiment with different coaching techniques with coachees who had given informed consent and who themselves were interested in learning more.

In feedback gathered as the project came to a close, participant coaches shared the value of being able to work with academic colleagues. This gave them an opportunity to gain a more rounded understanding of their own role and the roles of different types of academic staff within The OU. The themes within the participant coachees' feedback were around how this opportunity had given them an opportunity to build confidence, reflect on routines, energise work practices and consider the extent to which they could apply the coaching approach to enhance their teaching and support of students.

Speaking about the project as a co-lead, Daphne Chang found that the collaboration had made her realise how important it is to create a space and opportunity for colleagues who work remotely to connect and reflect on how their work articulates with their life in general. Unlike the brick universities, The OU teaching staff do not interact with each other in person on a daily basis; therefore, it is very easy to have a very one-dimensional view of each other. Coaching creates a space and mechanism to counteract that. All the participants are positive towards this experience, would recommend it to others and like to see it being made available to more colleagues. Daphne Chang also suggested that Coaching Professional Apprenticeship should be made available to appropriate student-facing staff as it enhances their professional capabilities. Furthermore, providing opportunities for members of staff to be volunteer coachees not only creates a space/mechanism to enhance coachees' wellbeing/practices, but also it is an excellent way to cascade the benefits of coaching.

Several other examples of practices shaping a wider culture of coaching and mentoring at the institution are discussed in this volume – such as student-led peer mentoring (Chapter 6), staff training and development (Chapter 7) and staff coaching and supervision (Chapter 8). Beginning with a wider view of the cultures of coaching and mentoring within our own organisation helps us to set the scene for this book, but what we have captured is not an exhaustive view. After all, we know that some of the most impactful coaching and mentoring happens organically between line manager and colleague, within teams, and even among student peer groups. As editors, we are also aware of projects in their genesis which we have not featured in this volume. The foundation of a coaching academy at The OU, for example, led within Organisational Learning and in partnership with faculties, is currently in its inception and perhaps the clearest testament to this nascent culture.

Evidencing the impact of coaching and mentoring

Colleagues from across the institution have begun to make significant contributions to the wider evidence base for the impact coaching and/or mentoring can have on academic leadership, teaching and learning and staff and student wellbeing (Lynden, Callaghan, and van Nieuwerburgh, 2024; Comfort, 2024; Callaghan, 2022). The evidence for student perceptions of coaching and mentoring and its impact on their study experience is something which has been collated through qualitative evaluation of the PLA Service. In the first full year of the service, this included a student experience survey for Black students who received support. This used a combination of the Likert scale and free text questions. In vivo analysis of the 102 student responses found that students who self-selected to receive one-to-one support reported behavioural changes including increased proactive help-seeking behaviour, greater recognition of achievements and strengths as well as improved self-efficacy and self-confidence. We have published the evidence gleaned from this qualitative evaluation elsewhere (Hillman, Lochtie and Purcell, 2024). Several authors in this volume, in collaboration with others, have also evaluated and shared findings about the impact of group interventions – such as coach-led online synchronous study spaces and other workshops (Lavery, Kinch and Hillman, 2023; Samuels-Hylton and Wilton, 2023; Lindley and Wilton, 2024).

In subsequent campaigns, the student experience survey was developed and used to evaluate the impact of one-to-one coaching and mentoring on students' sense of belonging and mattering, and additional questions were introduced to gauge student perceptions of group interventions delivered by the service (see Appendix A). 161 students opted-in to complete the survey – including students with mental health needs and disabilities, students from minoritised ethnic backgrounds and students living in low socio-economic areas of the UK. The results are shown in Table 0.2.

Several chapters in this volume draw upon the findings of this evaluation. The purpose of sharing these here is to strengthen what the literature is telling us about coaching and mentoring and the impact it can have on students. We also aim to show how student feedback helped practitioners design and shape different elements of the PLA Service's coaching and mentoring offer to meet student needs. The strength of the student feedback and perceived impact has helped the PLA Service achieve recognition for the innovative ways coaching and mentoring have been delivered by practitioners. The service was a part of The OU's successful 2023 Matrix Quality Standard Assessment (Department for Education, 2024) which noted the successful use of coaching as a vehicle across the institution

Table 0.2 Student experience survey responses 2023–2024

	Before receiving coaching and mentoring	**After** receiving coaching and mentoring
I feel confident I can cope with my studies	25% strongly agree or agree	90% strongly agree or agree
I feel I belong at The Open University	38% strongly agree or agree	85% strongly agree or agree
I feel like I matter to The Open University	37% strongly agree or agree	86% strongly agree or agree
I am more confident about asking for help when I need it as a result of PLA support	94% strongly agree or agree	
I have already done or intend to do things differently as a result of PLA support	96% strongly agree or agree	
Individualised/personalised support helped me complete my modules	90% strongly agree or agree	
It was important for me to see and hear students with similar lived experiences AND/OR shared challenges to me at PLA Service group sessions	86% strongly agree or agree	
Thinking about any study-related achievements, please say how much you think these are a result of working with your PLA.	96% strongly agree or agree	
Thinking about any achievements or positive changes in your personal life, please say how much you think these are a result of working with your PLA.	93% strongly agree or agree	
I achieved the goals set with my PLA	95% strongly agree or agree	
I felt comfortable sharing barriers with my PLA	93% strongly agree or agree	

for personal development and sharing effective practice. The service was awarded 'Team of the Year' by the Association for Learning Development in Higher Education (ALDinHE, 2023) and was shortlisted and commended in the 2024 National Education Opportunities Network, Widening Access Initiative (Retention and Progression) Award (NEON, 2024).

Whilst quantitative evaluation of the impact of coaching and mentoring on student outcomes is not the primary focus of this volume, in increasingly metric-driven times (Bamber, 2020) causal evaluation often has greater currency. It is worth noting that the institutional approach to evaluating the PLA Service was to consider the full complexity of the intervention (Sanders *et al.*, 2023), and to adhere to Office for Students standards of evidence (2019) by introducing 'test' and 'control' groups. This causal evaluation was carried out externally to the service and sought to measure outcomes for Black students. In 2021–2022, 327 students in a control group were not contacted by the service, whilst 2,414 students in an intervention group were proactively targeted, from which 414 students (17.1 percent) engaged with support. This evaluation did not find statistically significant causal indicators of impact on completion or pass rates. However, in one subset of the control and test group populations, where students had an overall pass rate probability of less than 50 percent, the evaluation reported a 6.9 percentage points higher completion rate and 7.1 percentage points higher pass rate in the test group (St-Hilaire *et al.*, 2023). Whilst neither difference was large enough to be statistically significant, as measured to the normal standard of 95 percent confidence, there is some indication that, when directed to 'at risk' students, coaching and mentoring may well improve outcomes.

The evaluation of the PLA Service has generated other correlative (not causal) evidence for an impact on student outcomes. For example, in 2022–2023, 926 of 2,758 eligible Black students engaged with support (34 percent) and analysis showed a 12.6 percentage points difference in completion rates and a 14.6 percentage points difference in pass rates comparing those who took up support and those who were eligible but did not. In order to overcome the issue of self-selection bias (i.e. the risk that the students who 'engage' are more likely to be successful), the paired evaluation tool was used to 'match' students who were eligible with students on the same module and presentation with similar pass probability, calculated at module start. This found students who took up the service were statistically significantly (10.9 pp) more likely to complete their module, significantly (9.3 pp) more likely to pass and significantly (14.9 pp) more likely to return for future studies when compared to 'matched' students who had not been offered the service. When students who did not engage with the service were similarly matched, with counterparts who had not received an offer, they were significantly (2.5 pp) less likely to complete their module and significantly (3.7 pp) less likely to pass but (not significantly, 0.4 pp) more likely to return. This suggests opt-in self-selection bias is a factor, but it is unclear how influential it is and therefore if/how much of any uplift in results can be attributed to coaching and mentoring.

There is, increasingly, in UK HE a drive to measure the impact of interventions like the PLA Service using the causal evaluation recommended by the OfS. There are, of course, significant ethical questions about intentionally withholding support for students in an RTC (Transforming Access and Student Outcomes in Higher Education [TASO], 2022, pp. 29–30; Sabri, 2023). Jill Andreanoff articulated the enduring question as to whether it is even possible to achieve a close enough match of 'test' and 'control' groups when evaluating the impact of coaching on students because of the range of extraneous variables that impact on academic attainment (Andreanoff, 2016b, pp. 203–204). There is also, perhaps, a wider discussion differentiating between 'value' and 'impact' for student support services such as the PLA Service, as raised at a recent conference (Hillman and Lochtie, 2024). However, as providers find ways to minimise harm, the approach will undoubtedly help to extend and refine the evidence we have for the ways in which students benefit from coaching and mentoring.

Chapter synthesis

This volume is comprised of eight chapters which are designed to be read together, and in order, but which will also serve as stand-alone examples of practice. All eight are based upon experiences in a distance-learning organisation but written with attentiveness to the ways they might be adapted for hybrid and in-person modes of delivery. Five of the eight chapters describe practice within the student-facing PLA Service; the remaining three chapters are authored by colleagues leading coaching and mentoring work across the wider institution. What we present is not exclusively for coaching or mentoring specialists, but instead a wider readership of practitioners who are interested in discovering more about the ways their own practices might be strengthened and diversified by coaching and mentoring techniques. Our intention is that this will speak to 'Third Space' (Whitchurch, 2003) advisor roles in professional services, as well as academic members of staff (for example, those that perform the role of Personal Academic Tutor or Advisor). It is also expected that the volume offers insights to help with strategic planning for organisational leaders and senior managers looking to support student success.

Coaching and mentoring offer techniques which we suggest can be utilised to positive effect in multiple roles in HE but, as Jill Andreanoff cautions in the foreword to this volume, they require a considered approach. In collating a volume which seeks to celebrate the value and impact of coaching and mentoring, we deliberately structured the first part of the text with the foundational elements of coaching and mentoring support for students: ethics, equity and contracting. Chapter 1 is an intentional challenge for both specialist and non-specialists to consider the ethicality of their work. In this, Jenny Lynden argues for the centrality of 'ethical maturity' to support effective practice and highlights the utility of the APPEAR framework to support practitioner reflexivity with 'ethical moments.' In Chapter 2, the power dynamics of helping relationships are probed more deeply as Jo Blissett and Enya-Marie Clay offer the 'equity lens' as a tool which can be used to centre anti-oppressive and antiracist practice in student support. In the third chapter, Chrissie Farley, Josh Samuels-Hylton and Emma Vance consider approaches to contracting with students from minoritised backgrounds. They outline how attentiveness to three different 'levels' of contracting (professional, procedural and psychological) helps to establish person-centred coaching relationships which support students to flourish.

The middle section of the book exemplifies how coaching and mentoring might work in practice to enhance three core elements of the student experience: wellbeing and mental health, learning and academic skills and peer support. In Chapter 4, Fareeha Karim and Leanne Lindsey outline the evidence for the role that coaching and mentoring might have in supporting mental health and wellbeing, with a particular focus on the experiences of students from racially minoritised backgrounds. Drawing upon their own experiences as a British born, Pakistani, Muslim woman and a British Black Caribbean woman, they also offer some constructive challenge regarding the commitment to long-term, meaningful change in HE. In Chapter 5, Mary-Jayne Wilton and Jennifer Hillman consider how coaching and mentoring techniques have begun to be adopted by Learning Developers to support widening participation and guard against dated 'deficit' approaches to 'study skills' support. They share ideas about how coaching and mentoring might be embedded in one-to-one and group settings. Student-led mentoring is the focus of Chapter 6, where Catherine Comfort and Chris Kubiak share lessons learned and best practice from the literature, on the creation of student peer mentoring programmes.

In calling attention to the ways that coaching and mentoring might enhance existing practitioner 'toolkits' or be operationalised as a discrete student service, we recognise the importance of considering staff development, facilitating communities of practice and planning appropriate support. In the final third of the book, authors provide perspectives from just some of the roles which are required to sustain a coaching and mentoring culture in an organisation – including learning and development and organisational learning, leadership and line management, as well as student-facing practitioners. In Chapter 7, Jane Dudeney and Georgina Durley relay their experiences of designing and implementing coaching skills training for staff in Student Support Services. Coaching skills training, they find, is a positive enhancement to help staff deliver the holistic support that universities are increasingly needing to provide. In the concluding chapter of the volume, Richard Peat, Julie Stock and Helen Williams focus on supervision as a way of providing reflective spaces for practitioners. They consider a range of approaches to implementing supervision in an organisation and highlight its place in the management of ethical practice. Finally, in the postscript, concluding reflections from Martin Ousley extends the central narratives of the book, whilst looking ahead to consider how AI might variously diversify, threaten and enhance the person-centred practice advocated for in this volume. Ousley also considers the critical role evaluation will play to secure investment in the future of coaching and mentoring in HE.

In bringing together this collection of authors, several of whom are publishing for the first time, we have prioritised practitioner insights without compromising on rigour. Each chapter is grounded in evidence from relevant programme and service evaluation and best practice from the wider literature, yet offer learning that is practical for readers looking to implement coaching and mentoring as a mode of support. Scenarios are used across all of the chapters to do so. Whilst these scenarios are based on practitioner experiences, to protect the anonymity of staff and students they have been adapted and should be treated as illustrative. We have already referred to the diversity of lived experience in the team that comprised the PLA Service and, learning from this, we have consciously adapted our approach as editors to ensure that distinctive authorial voices based on these lived experiences are discernible. Within each chapter, contributing authors have also curated questions and/or activities to help readers to engage with ideas in the text and explore what it may mean for their practice. We hope that this volume creates opportunities to be part of a dialogue on the value of coaching cultures at university, and the continued relevance of coaching and mentoring in the sector.

Note on sensitive content

By its nature, supporting students often involves the discussion of sensitive content including content which may be triggering. This volume also has themes discussing various protected characteristics and intersectionalities that practitioners often encounter in student-facing work as well as bringing their own lived experience to; authors have made efforts to explore these in an equitable, ethical and appropriate manner. It is with this understanding, and the acknowledgement that practitioners need adequate support in order to effectively support others in these spaces, that an appendix (Appendix C) has been included in this volume which shares principal networks for support as well as selected resources for issues directly discussed within the volume. Practitioner wellbeing is more directly discussed in Chapter 1, which broaches its implications on ethical practice; in Chapter 4, which explores how contracting can be a protective factor in practitioner wellbeing; and in Chapter 8, where the value of supervision is explored in its use in practitioner wellbeing.

Selected scenarios have been included in this volume which contain content that may be triggering for some readers:

- Chapter 1, scenario 1: Historical self-harm.
- Chapter 4, scenario 3: Alcohol dependency.
- Chapter 4, suicide (in the context of suicide prevention training).
- Chapter 5, scenario – Parts 1 and 2: Racism affecting maternal healthcare and infant mortality.

We have curated a list of resources to support with these issues in Appendix C.

Bibliography

Advance HE. (2024) *National teaching fellows 2024*. Available at: Dr Cora Beth Fraser | Advance HE (advance-he.ac.uk) (Accessed: 10 October 2024).

Ali, D. (2017) *Safe spaces and brave spaces. Historical context and recommendations for student affairs professionals, NASPA policy and practice series*. Available at: https://www.naspa.org/files/dmfile/Policy_and_Practice_No_2_Safe_Brave_Spaces.pdf (Accessed: 5 December 2024).

Alzen, J.L., Burkhardt, A., Diaz-Bilello, E., Elder, E., Sepulveda, A., Blankenheim, A. and Board, L. (2021) 'Academic coaching and its relationship to student performance, retention, and credit completion', *Innovative Higher Education*, 46, pp. 539–563. doi: 10.1007/s10755-021-09554-w

Andreanoff, J. (2016a) *Coaching and mentoring in higher education: a step-by-step guide to exemplary practice*. 1st edn. London: Bloomsbury Publishing Plc.

Andreanoff, J. (2016b) 'Issues in conducting quantitative studies on the impact of coaching and mentoring in Higher Education', *International Journal of Evidence Based Coaching and Mentoring*, 10, pp. 202–216.

Andreanoff, J.A. (2016c) 'The impact of a peer coaching programme on the academic performance of undergraduate students: a mixed methods study', *Journal of Learning Development in Higher Education*. doi: 10.47408/jldhe.v0i0.358

Arday, J. (2018) *Dismantling race in higher education: racism, whiteness and decolonising the academy*. Cham: Springer International Publishing. doi: 10.1007/978-3-319-60261-5

Arday, J., Branchu, C. and Boliver, V. (2022) 'What do we know about Black and minority ethnic (BAME) participation in UK higher education?', *Social Policy and Society: A Journal of the Social Policy Association*, 21(1), pp. 12–25. doi: 10.1017/S1474746421000579

Association for Learning Development in Higher Education (ALDinHE) (2023) *Team of the year award, 2023*. Available at: https://aldinhe.ac.uk/accreditation/aldinhe-awards/aldinhe-annual-team-award-2023/ (Accessed: 6 October 2024).

Atad, O.I. and Grant, A.M. (2021) 'Evidence-based coaching as a supplement to traditional lectures: impact on undergraduates' goal attainment and measures of mental well-being', *International Journal of Mentoring and Coaching in Education*, 10(3), pp. 249–266. doi: 10.1108/IJMCE-05-2020-0024

Bachkirova, T., Cox, E. and Clutterbuck, D. (2014) 'Introduction', in E. Cox, T. Bachkirova and D. Clutterbuck (eds.) *The complete handbook of coaching*. 2nd edn. London: Sage, pp. 1–18.

Bamber, R. (2020) 'Our days are numbered – how metrics are changing academic development'. Available at: https://wonkhe.com/blogs/our-days-are-numbered-how-metrics-are-changing-academic-development/ (Accessed: 6 October 2024).

Bell, S. and Lane, A. (1998) 'From teaching to learning: technological potential and sustainable, supported open learning', *Systems Practice and Action Research*, 11(6), pp. 629–650.

Bellman, S., Burgstahler, S. and Hinke, P. (2015) 'Academic coaching outcomes for students with disabilities pursuing science, technology, engineering, and mathematics', *Journal of Postsecondary Education and Disability*, 28(1), pp. 101–106.

Bhopal, K. (2023) '"We can talk the talk, but we're not allowed to walk the walk': the role of equality and diversity staff in higher education institutions in England', *Higher Education*, 85(2), pp. 325–339. doi: 10.1007/s10734-022-00835-7

Bhopal, K. and Pitkin, C. (2020) '"Same old story, just a different policy': race and policy making in higher education in the UK', *Race, Ethnicity and Education*, 23(4), pp. 530–547. doi: 10.1080/13613324.2020.1718082

Bradley, J.A., Tuck, M.E., Reynolds, M.A. and Bradley, L.H. (2024) 'Creating an integrated coaching culture in higher education', *Journal of Appreciative Education*, 11(1), pp. 15–24. Available at: https://janeway.uncpress.org/jae/article/id/1342/ (Accessed: 5 December 2024).

British Psychological Society. (2021) *British Psychological Society code of ethics and conduct*. Available at: https://www.bps.org.uk/guideline/code-ethics-and-conduct (Accessed: 5 December 2024).

Bryant-Jefferies, R. (2021) 'Person-centred coaching', in J. Passmore (ed.) *The coaches' handbook*. 1st edn. Abingdon: Oxford, pp. 187–196.

Caldwell, B. and Carter, E.M.A. (1993) *The return of the mentor: strategies for workplace learning*. 1st edn. London: Falmer Press.

Callaghan, G. (2022) 'Introducing a coaching culture within an academic faculty', *International Journal of Evidence Based Coaching and Mentoring*, 20(1), pp. 83–92. doi: 10.24384/2jqz-yp44 (Accessed: 6 October 2024).

Calvert, C. (2014) 'Developing a model and applications for probabilities of student success: a case study of predictive analytics', *Open Learning: The Journal of Open, Distance and e-Learning*, 29(2), pp. 160–173. doi: 10.1080/02680513.2014.931805

Campbell, J. (no date) *Cognitive dissonance, scaling and the coaching conversation, growth coaching international*. Available at: https://www.growthcoaching.com.au/resource/cognitive-dissonance-scaling-and-the-coaching-conversation/ (Accessed: 17 July 2024).

Clutterbuck, D. (2023) *Coaching and mentoring: a journey through the models, theories, frameworks and narratives of David Clutterbuck*. Abingdon: Routledge.

Colley, H. (2002) 'A "Rough Guide" to the history of mentoring from a Marxist Feminist perspective', *Journal of Education for Teaching: JET*, 28(3), pp. 257–273. doi: 10.1080/0260747022000021403

Comfort, C. (2024) 'Mentoring, social capital and young people', *International Journal of Evidence Based Coaching and Mentoring*, 22(2), pp. 38–52. doi: 10.24384/1ttg-gt35

Crenshaw, K.W. (1989) 'Demarginalizing the intersection of race and sex: a black feminist critique of antidiscrimination doctrine, feminist theory, and antiracist politics', *University of Chicago Legal Forum*, 14, pp. 538–554. Available at: https://chicagounbound.uchicago.edu/uclf/vol1989/iss1/8 (Accessed: 1 June 2024).

Crenshaw, K.W. (1991) 'Mapping the margins: intersectionality, identity politics, and violence against women of color', *Stanford Law Review*, 43(6), pp. 1241–1299. Available at: https://blogs.law.columbia.edu/critique1313/files/2020/02/1229039.pdf (Accessed: 1 June 2024).

Delderfield, R. and McHattie, H. (2018) 'The person-centred approach in maths skills development: examining a case of good practice', *Journal of Learning Development in Higher Education*, 13. doi: 10.47408/jldhe.v0i13.447

Department for Education. (2024) *Matrix standard*. Available at: https://matrixstandard.com/ (Accessed: 1 July 2024).

Dominguez, N. and Hager, M. (2013) 'Mentoring frameworks: synthesis and critique', *International Journal of Mentoring and Coaching in Education*, 2(3), pp. 171–188. doi: 10.1108/IJMCE-03-2013-0014

EMCC. (2024) *Mentoring*. Available at: https://www.emccglobal.org/leadership-development/leadership-development-mentoring/ (Accessed: 31 October 2024).

Farrell, T., Alani, H. and Mikroyannidis, A. (2024) 'Mediating learning with learning analytics technology: guidelines for practice', *Teaching in Higher Education*, 29(6), pp. 1500–1520. doi: 10.1080/13562517.2022.2067745

Foy, K. (2021) 'Contracting in coaching', in J. Passmore (ed.) *The coaches' handbook: the complete practitioner guide for professional coaches*. Abingdon: Routledge, pp. 345–353.

Fried, R. and Irwin, J. (2016) 'Calmly coping: a Motivational Interviewing Via Co-Active Life Coaching (MI-VIA-CALC) pilot intervention for university students with perceived levels of high stress', *International Journal of Evidence Based Coaching and Mentoring*, 14(1), pp. 16–33. Available at: https://radar.brookes.ac.uk/radar/items/6e73b6c5-29f6-49bb-9503-dc4e3f483bbf/1/ (Accessed: 12 June 2024).

Geraghty, T. (2022) *Psychological safety vs a 'safe space'*. Available at: https://psychsafety.co.uk/psychological-safety-vs-a-safe-space/ (Accessed: 20 October 2024).

Gibson, S., Baskerville, D., Berry, A., Black, A., Norris, K. and Symeonidou, S. (2016) ''Diversity' 'widening participation' and 'inclusion' in higher education: an international study', *Widening Participation and Lifelong Learning*, 18(3), pp. 7–33. doi:10.5456/wpll.18.3.7

Grant, A. (2003) 'The impact of life coaching on goal attainment, metacognition and mental health', *Social Behaviour and Personality: An International Journal*, 31(3), pp. 253–263. doi: 10.2224/sbp.2003.31.3.253

Grey, D., McIntosh, E. and Stylianoudaki, P. (2017) 'Student dashboards - the case for building communities of practice'. Presentation at the 2nd UKAT National Conference, Leeds: Leeds Trinity University.

Gurbutt, D.J. and Gurbutt, R. (2015) 'Empowering students to promote independent learning: a project utilising coaching approaches to support learning and personal development', *Journal of Learning Development in Higher Education*, 8, pp. 1–17. doi: 10.47408/jldhe.v0i8.225

Henderson, E.S. and Nathenson, M.B. (1984) *Independent learning in higher education*. Englewood Cliffs, NJ: Educational Technology Publications, Inc.

Hillman, J. and Lochtie, D. (2024) 'Evaluating our 'impact': reflections from the personal learning advice service', *Journal of Learning Development in Higher Education*, 32. doi: 10.47408/jldhe.vi32.1447

Hillman, J., Lochtie, D. and Purcell, O. (2024) 'Black students' experiences of coaching and mentoring in higher education: a case study', *International Journal of Mentoring and Coaching in Education*, 13(2), pp. 246–257. doi: 10.1108/IJMCE-01-2023-0011

Hockings, C., Thomas, L., Ottaway, J. and Jones, R. (2018) 'Independent learning – what we do when you're not there', *Teaching in Higher Education*, 23(2), pp. 145–161. doi: 10.1080/13562517.2017.1332031

Howlett, M. A., McWilliams, M. A., Rademacher, K., Maitland, T. L., O'Neill, J. C., Abels, K. and Panter, A. (2020). 'An academic coaching training program for university professionals: a mixed methods examination', *Journal of Student Affairs Research and Practice*, 58(3), pp. 335–349. doi: 10.1080/19496591.2020.1784750

'Human Potential Movement, Gale Encyclopedia of Psychology'. (2016) Available at: https://search.credoreference.com/articles/Qm9va0FydGljbGU6NDc3MTQ2MA== (Accessed: 12 June 2024).

IfATE. (2020) *Coaching professional.* Available at: https://www.instituteforapprenticeships.org/apprenticeship-standards/st0809-v1-0 (Accessed: 31 October 2024).

Irby, B.J. and Boswell, J. (2016) 'Historical print context of the term, "mentoring"', *Mentoring and Tutoring*, 24(1), pp. 1–7. doi: 10.1080/13611267.2016.1170556

Ison, R. (2000) 'Supported open learning and the emergence of learning communities. The case of The Open University UK', in R. Miller (ed.) *Creating learning communities. Models, resources, and new ways of thinking about teaching and learning.* Brandon, VT: Foundation for Educational Renewal, Inc., pp. 90–96.

Jones, J. and Smith, H.A. (2022) 'A comparative study of formal coaching and mentoring programmes in higher education', *International Journal of Mentoring and Coaching in Education*, 11(2), pp. 213–231. doi: 10.1108/IJMCE-03-2021-0054

Joseph, S. and Bryant-Jefferies, R. (2018) 'Person-centred coaching psychology', in S. Palmer and A. Whybrow (eds.) *Handbook of coaching psychology: a guide for practitioners*. 2nd edn. London: Routledge,pp.211–228.

Knowles, S. (2021) *Positive psychology coaching*. 1st edn. New York:Springer International.

Lancer, N., Clutterbuck, D. and Megginson, D. (2016) *Techniques for coaching and mentoring*. 2nd edn. London: Routledge.

Lancer, N. and Eatough, V. (2018) 'One-to-one coaching as a catalyst for personal development: an Interpretative Phenomenological Analysis of coaching undergraduates at a UK university', *International Coaching Psychology Review*, 13(1), pp. 72–88. doi: 10.53841/bpsicpr.2018.13.1.72

Lancer, N. and Eatough, V. (2021) 'The Eight Tensions Framework: a road map for coaches working with undergraduates', *Coaching Psychologist*, 17(2), pp. 64–74. doi: 10.53841/bpstcp.2021.17.2.64

Lavery, H., Kinch, D.P. and Hillman, J. (2023) 'Do live writing/study sessions for at risk students, in an online, distance learning environment, demonstrate the same benefits documented for face-to-face shared writing events?' *Ubiquity Proceedings*, 3(1), pp. 83–90. doi: 10.5334/uproc.72

Leathwood, C. (2006) 'Gender, equity and the discourse of the independent learner in higher education', *Higher Education*, 52, pp. 611–633. doi: 10.1007/s10734-005-2414-3

Lefdahl-Davis, E. M., Huffman, L., Stancil, J. and Alayan, A. J. (2018) 'The impact of life coaching on undergraduate students: a multiyear analysis of coaching outcomes', *International Journal of Evidence Based Coaching and Mentoring*, 16(2), pp. 69–83. doi: 10.24384/000560

Levinson, D.J. (1978) *The seasons of a man's life*. New York, NY: Knopf.

Lim, M.S.M. and Patel, N.S. (2024) 'Coaching in higher education: creating impact', in M.S.M. Lim and R. Shahdadpuri (eds.) *Coaching students in higher education: a solution-focused approach to retention, performance and wellbeing*. 1st edn. Abingdon: Routledge, pp. 3–17.

Lindley, J. and Wilton, M.-J. (2024) 'Creating online, inclusive spaces for learning: 'study together' with the personal learning advice service', *Journal of Learning Development in Higher Education*, 32. doi: 10.47408/jldhe.vi32.1406

Lynden, J., Callaghan, G. and van Nieuwerburgh, C.J. (2024) 'Bringing joy back into higher education: the potential contribution of coaching', *International Journal of Mentoring and Coaching in Education*, 13(3), pp. 378–393. doi: 10.1108/IJMCE-05-2023-0043

Marginson, S. (2024) 'Higher education and public and common good', Centre for Global Higher Education Working Paper 114. Available at: https://www.researchcghe.org/wp-content/uploads/migrate/wp114-1.pdf (Accessed: 5 December 2024).

Marr, E. (2018) 'Adult learning, social mobility and social justice: a view from the UK', *Making Room for Adults*, 5, pp. 61–79.

Mearns, D. (1998) *Person-centred counselling training*. London: SAGE.

Megginson, D. and Clutterbuck, D. (2004) *Techniques for coaching and mentoring*. London: Routledge.

Megginson, D. and Clutterbuck, D. (2009) *Further techniques for coaching and mentoring*. Amsterdam: Butterworth-Heinemann.

Morgan, J. (2024) *Fostering belonging in higher education: implications for student retention and wellbeing*. Available at: https://www.advance-he.ac.uk/news-and-views/fostering-belonging-higher-education-implications-student-retention-and-wellbeing#:~:text=In%20the%20Higher%20Education%20(HE,has%20become%20a%20strategic%20necessity (Accessed: 22 July 2024).

NACADA. (2019) *Academic coaching*. Available at: Academic Coaching Available at: https://nacada.ksu.edu/Resources/Clearinghouse/Academic-Coaching.aspx (Accessed: 5 December 2024).

National Education Opportunities Network (NEON). (2024) *Awards*. Available at: https://www.educationopportunities.co.uk/neon-awards-2024/ (Accessed: 6 October 2024).

Neenan, M. and Palmer, S. (2022) 'Introduction', in M. Neenan and S. Palmer (eds.) *Cognitive behavioural coaching in practice: an evidence based approach*. 2nd edn. Abingdon: Routledge, pp. 1–9.

Office for Students (OfS). (2019a) *Standards of evidence and evaluating impact of outreach*. Available at: https://www.officeforstudents.org.uk/publications/standards-of-evidence-and-evaluating-impact-of-outreach/ (Accessed: 6 October 2024).

Office for Students (OfS). (2019b) *Beyond the bare minimum insight are universities and colleges doing enough for disabled students? Insight 4*. Available at: https://www.officeforstudents.org.uk/media/3828/beyond-the-bare-minimum-are-universities-and-colleges-doing-enough-for-disabled-students.pdf (Accessed: 28 May 2024).

Office for Students (OfS). (2024) *Access and participations plans*. Available at: https://www.officeforstudents.org.uk/for-providers/equality-of-opportunity/access-and-participation-plans/ (Accessed: 15 October 2024).

Oxford English Dictionary (OED). (2024) *Coach*. Available at: https://www.oed.com/dictionary/coach_n?tab=meaning_and_use#9212316- (Accessed: 5 December 2024).

Passmore, J. (2021a) 'Coaching defined and explored', in J. Passmore (ed.) *The coaches' handbook: the complete practitioner guide for professional coaches*. Abingdon: Routledge, pp. 3–12.

Passmore, J. (ed.) (2021b) *Excellence in coaching: theory, tools and techniques to achieve outstanding coaching performance*. 4th edn. London, New York: Kogan Page.

Passmore, J. and Fillery-Travis, A. (2011) 'A critical review of executive coaching research: a decade of progress and what's to come', *Coaching: An International Journal of Theory, Research and Practice*, 4(2), pp. 70–88. doi: 10.1080/17521882.2011.596484

Paul, R. (1990) 'Towards a new measure of success: developing independent learners', *Open Learning: The Journal of Open, Distance and e-Learning*, 5(1), pp. 31–38. doi: 10.1080/0268051900050106

Platonova, R.I., Orekhovskaya, N.A., Dautova, S.D., Martynenko, E.V.,Kryukova, N.I. and Demir, S. (2022) 'Blended learning in higher education: diversifying models and practical recommendations for researchers', *Frontiers in Education*, 7, pp. 1–11. doi: 10.3389/feduc.2022.957199

Roche, C. (2022) 'Decolonising reflective practice and supervision', *Philosophy of Coaching: An International Journal*, 7(1), pp. 30–49. doi: 10.22316/poc/07.1.03

Rogers, C. (1951) *Client-centered therapy*. Boston, MA: Houghton-Mifflin.

Rogers, C.R. (1986) 'A client-centered/person-centered approach to therapy', in I. Kutash and A. Wolfe (eds.) *Psychotherapists' casebook*. San Francisco, CA: Jossey Bass, pp. 197– 208.

Sabri, D. (2023) 'Rethinking causality and inequality in students' degree outcomes', *British Journal of Sociology of Education*, 44(3), pp. 520–538. doi: 10.1080/01425692.2023.2179017

Samuels-Hylton, J. and Wilton, M.-J. (2023) 'Sharing stories of resilience: open university partnership work with Shelayna Oskan-Clarke', *Learning Development Magazine* (July), pp. 12–13. Available at: https://online.fliphtml5.com/lwhvl/xgpp/#p=12 (Accessed: 6 October 2024).

Sanders, M., Ellingwood, J. and Kozman, E. (2023) *Evaluating complex interventions using randomised controlled trials*. Available at: https://taso.org.uk/news-blog/evaluating-complex-interventions-using-randomised-controlled-trials/ (Accessed: 6 October 2024).

SEDA. (2024) SEDA Jiscmail. Available at: https://www.jiscmail.ac.uk/cgi-bin/webadmin?A0=seda (Accessed: 5 December 2024).

Sepulveda, A. (2020) *Coaching college students to thrive: exploring coaching practices in higher education*. PhD thesis. University of Northern Colorado. Available at: https://digscholarship.unco.edu/cgi/viewcontent.cgi?article=1690and context=dissertations (Accessed 31 January 2024).

Sepulveda, A., Birnbaum, M., Finley, J. B. and Frye, S. (2020) 'Coaching college students who have expressed an interest in leaving: a pilot study', *Coaching: An International Journal of Theory, Research and Practice*, 13(1), pp. 8–15. doi: 10.1080/17521882.2019.1574847

Spencer, D. (2021) 'Understanding the coaching experiences of non-traditional students in higher education in the UK', *International Journal of Evidence Based Coaching and Mentoring*, 15, pp. 84–95. doi: 10.24384/00v3-nm61

Stevenson, J., O'Mahony, J., Khan, O., Ghaffar, F. and Stiell, B. (2019). *Understanding and overcoming the challenges of targeting students from under-represented and disadvantaged ethnic backgrounds, Report to the Office for Students*. Available at: https://www.officeforstudents.org.uk/media/d21cb263-526d-401c-bc74-299c748e9ecd/ethnicity-targeting-research-report.pdf (Accessed: 5 October 2024).

St-Hilaire, E., Hillman, J. and Lochtie, D. (2023) *Closing the awarding gap: the role of the Personal Learning Advisor (PLA) Service at The Open University*. Available at: https://www.ukat.ac.uk/media/u2fn0mj0/ukat-equity-inclusion-sig-case-study-2.pdf (Accessed: 6 October 2024).

Student A. (2023) *22J personal learning advice service student experience survey* (unpublished), The Open University, UK.

The Open University (OU). (2022) *Access and participation plan*. Available at: https://www5.open.ac.uk/widening-participation/aps-england-access-and-participation-plan (Accessed: 9 October 2024).

The Open University (OU). (2024a) 'Facts and figures'. Available at: https://about.open.ac.uk/strategy-and-policies/facts-and-figures (Accessed: 09 October 2024).

The Open University (OU). (2024b) 'History of The OU.' Available at: https://about.open.ac.uk/strategy-and-policies/history-ou (Accessed: 09 October 2024).

The Open University (OU). (2024c). 'OU mission'. Available at: https://about.open.ac.uk/policies-and-reports/mission (Accessed: 09 October 2024).

Thomas, D.S.P. and Arday, J. (eds). (2021) *Doing equity and diversity for success in higher education: redressing structural inequalities in the academy*. Cham: Palgrave Macmillan.

Thomas, L., Hockings, C., Ottaway, J. and Jones, R. (2015) *Independent learning: student perspectives and experiences, Higher Education Academy*. Available at: https://s3.eu-west-2.amazonaws.com/assets.creode.advancehe-document-manager/documents/hea/private/independent_learning_final_1568037336.pdf (Accessed: 9 November 2024).

Tight, M. (2023) 'Ten years of editing Assessment and Evaluation in Higher Education', *Assessment and Evaluation in Higher Education*, 48(3), pp. 259–261. doi: 10.1080/02602938.2023.2181601

Transforming Access and Student Outcomes in Higher Education (TASO). (2022). 'Research ethics guidance'. Available at: https://cdn.taso.org.uk/wp-content/uploads/TASO_-Report_Research-Ethics-Guidance_AW-Secured.pdf (Accessed: 6 October 2024).

Wang, Q. and Lu, Y. (2020) 'Coaching college students in the development of positive learning dispositions: a randomized control trial embedded mixed-methods study', *Psychology in the Schools*, 57(9), pp. 1417–1438. doi: 10.1002/pits.22421

Westergaard, J. (2016) *An introduction to helping skills: counselling, coaching and mentoring*. London: Sage.

Whitchurch, C. (2003) *Reconstructing identities in higher education: the rise of Third Space professionals*. 1st edn. Abingdon: Routledge. doi: 10.4324/9780203098301

Whitmore, J. (2017) *Coaching for performance: the principles and practice of coaching and leadership*. 5th edn. London: Hodder and Stoughton Ltd.

Wildflower, L. (2013) *The hidden history of coaching*. Maidenhead: Open University Press.

Zawada, C. (2024) 'Student drop out and feelings of belonging and mattering in UK undergraduate allied health students', *Journal of Learning Development in Higher Education*, 31. doi: 10.47408/jldhe.vi31.1172

Confidentiality and the ethics of coaching and mentoring students

1

Jenny Lynden

Introduction

Coaching and mentoring have been demonstrated as effective for enabling students in higher education (HE) globally to flourish by fostering wellbeing and enhancing student performance (Atad and Grant, 2021; Robinson and Gahagan, 2010; Lefdahl-Davis *et al.*, 2018; Corti and Gelati, 2020; Jones and Smith, 2022; Wang and Lu, 2020). Studies have also identified significant benefits for postgraduate students in terms of fostering goal setting and goal striving, particularly in the areas of enhancing self-efficacy, resilience and problem solving (Grant and O'Connor, 2010; Kearns *et al.*, 2007) and for stress management (Dias, Foster and Zunszain, 2019; Grant, 2008). Research is demonstrating how coaching and mentoring is particularly useful in promoting widening participation, increasing retention and supporting diversity within HE (Alzen *et al.*, 2021; Capstick *et al.*, 2019; Hillman, Lochtie and Purcell, 2024). To be successful, a coaching or mentoring alliance relies on enhanced trust between the coach/mentor and student, established through a professional practice which, at its core, demonstrates integrity, benevolence and competency, each of which is practiced through ethical decision-making and ethical behaviour (Terblanche and Heyns, 2020). However, exactly because coaching and mentoring are effective in addressing the complex issues which diverse students manage, the ethical considerations faced by practitioners can be challenging to navigate. 'Practitioner' in this chapter refers to coaches and mentors, as well as those with other roles, such as lecturers and tutors, who integrate coaching and mentoring

DOI: 10.4324/9781003486015-2

approaches into their work in supporting students, as well as student peer mentors or coaches.

Embracing complexity requires practitioners to enhance their ethical maturity (Carroll and Shaw, 2013) when coaching and mentoring students in HE. Ethical maturity is a way of being which, by cultivating a sensitivity and self-awareness of the motivations for behaviour and its consequences, seeks to facilitate positive outcomes and avoid harm (Smith *et al.*, 2023). Ethical maturity relies on a practitioner's extensive knowledge and skilful practice to be effective, safe and legal when contracting and re-contracting for individual and group working, using different modalities, including online digital platforms and resources (McMahon *et al.*, 2005). Contracting, at the very least, involves a mutual agreement regarding confidentiality and limits to confidentiality, the focus of the coaching/mentoring work, ways of working together and boundaries to that work and the way it will be evaluated (Grant, 2013). Effective contracting enhances collaboration and trust, which supports psychological safety. Psychological safety is pivotal for coaching/mentoring as it is characterised by the student's preparedness to experience vulnerability, to take risks, to be open to and learn from new experiences and the emotional responses associated with them (Edmondson, 2018). Contracting is covered more comprehensively in Chapter 3.

Ethical maturity also requires practitioners to critically review and adapt their practice by recognising particular opportunities and risks when working with students who, for example, disclose challenging mental health experiences, neurodiversity, marginalisation and discrimination. Readers are invited to consider their practice and the ethical choices available to them using the reflective questions at the end of this chapter and by conducting a review of their practice through an equity lens as explored in Chapter 2 of this volume.

Working ethically and safely necessitates practitioners to engage with research, including an evidence base, to support joint decision-making with students about appropriate coaching and/or mentoring interventions, as well as recognising the boundaries to practice, for example, when supporting students with mental health concerns. It relies on the ability of the practitioner to recognise cultural biases, both within themselves and within the complex organisational systems within which they and the student inhabit, and how these may intersect to impact positively or negatively on the coaching/mentoring alliance and the student's opportunity to engage with the coaching/mentoring process. As importantly, ethical maturity relies on the coach/mentor having an enhanced self-awareness to attend to their own wellbeing, accessing resources for promoting self-care and recognising the risks associated with emotional work and burnout.

This chapter will explore a wide range of topics which bring to life ethical decision-making for both specialist and non-specialist practitioners supporting students in HE contexts. This chapter will begin by critically *defining* 'ethics' and *reviewing* professional ethical codes of practice and frameworks which support ethical decision-making. The next section will *explore* a wide range of ethical considerations when coaching and mentoring students in HE, particularly focusing on diversity and how ethical decision-making can promote opportunity and equality and inclusion for students and practitioners, in part, by challenging institutional and societal marginalisation and discrimination. We avoid the term 'ethical dilemma' as this often has more negative connotations. As De Jong (2006) and Van Nieuwerburgh (2020) suggest, practitioners are regularly presented with 'ethical moments of choice' each of which holds opportunities for increasing 'critical consciousness' by enhancing curiosity, courage and a commitment to learning. This chapter, therefore, focuses on 'ethical choices' and 'ethical decision making.' The fourth section of this chapter will *explore* ethical maturity and the APPEAR model as one framework for enhancing ethical decision-making and practice and *illustrate* how it can be applied to considering ethical choices when working across a range of coaching and mentoring contexts. Finally, the concluding section of this chapter will *offer* reflective questions and resources. It will also *propose* how we might work together as a community to learn from each other as we build a network of practitioners working effectively, safely and legally to support students to flourish in HE.

What is ethics and why is it important in coaching and mentoring?

Definition of ethics

Ethics is defined broadly as 'a system of moral principles that affect the way in which people make decisions and lead their lives' (Townsend, 2011, p. 142). Historically, the word 'ethics' has its roots in the Greek word 'ethikos' which translates to 'habitual or customary conduct' and the Latin word 'ethice,' which is 'the science of right or wrong' (Townsend, 2011, p. 142). The development of moral philosophy in the eighteenth and nineteenth centuries focused on three main ethical perspectives:

I. Deontological ethics, also known as 'the ethics of principles,' emphasises 'reasoning,' 'duty' and 'obligation' as a basis for universal moral 'laws' to guide ethical decision-making.

II. Utilitarian ethics emphasises ethically neutrality in decision-making to guide behaviour and decision-making which results in the greatest benefit to the majority.
III. Virtue ethics which emphasises individual characteristics and virtues (such as honesty, courage, integrity, fairness) in guiding ethical behaviour (Iordanou and Hawley, 2020).

Philosophical ethical perspectives underpin professional ethics, a discipline which also integrates social sciences and legal frameworks to develop ethical codes of practice. While historically developed in the practice of medicine and law, and later psychotherapy and counselling, ethical codes have, more recently, been extended to other helping professions such as coaching and mentoring (Iordanou and Hawley, 2020).

A practitioner is likely to reconcile different perspectives, balancing moral and ethical codes with legal, institutional and policy frameworks when considering their ethical choices. Ethical decision-making will generally be a consideration of multiple stakeholder perspectives and lead to outcomes which are least harmful. This chapter argues that, when coaching and mentoring students in HE contexts, ethical practice does not involve identifying one right answer to a particular ethical consideration by following an ethical 'code of practice.' Ethicality involves developing cycles of reflexive practice which engage the practitioner in the interpretation and application of ethical codes of practice, by taking into consideration different ideologies and cultural differences situated across contexts (Karin Askeland, 2009). From this perspective, and often using an ethical framework to facilitate a reflective dialogue, a practitioner will recognise how ways of practicing are socially constructed based on the values and interests which reflect socio-political contexts and involve relations of power and use this understanding to consider how they may influence their decision-making (Fatien and Clutterbuck, 2023). This process is often facilitated through individual, group or peer supervision. The importance of the reflective space provided by supervision for ethics is discussed in full in Chapter 8 of this volume.

Importantly, a practitioner will seek to work respectfully and in collaboration with the student or students and, when relevant, with other stakeholders to practice effectively, safely and legally. A partnership approach, which recognises and contracts for mutual rights and obligations, within the coaching/mentoring alliance is needed to facilitate ethical decision-making to explore and resolve ethical choices. The next section will review a range of ethical codes of conduct for coaching and mentoring to identify key ethical principles which serve to guide practitioner reflection and ethical choices.

Ethical codes of conduct

In HE in the UK, most of us will align our work in teaching and learning with codes such as the Professional Standards Framework (Advance HE, 2023). However, it is the ethical codes for coaching and mentoring which should directly inform coaching and mentoring work. There are many of these, reflecting different professional bodies operating within different national legal frameworks and cultural contexts. Some are internationally recognised as setting benchmarks to uphold professional standards and guide ethical professional practice. This chapter will briefly review three of these:

i. The Association for Coaching (AC) and European Mentoring and Coaching Council (EMCC) Global Code of Ethics.
ii. The International Coaching Federation (ICF) Code of Ethics.
iii. The British Psychological Society (BPS) Code of Ethics and Conduct.

AC and EMCC Global Code of Ethics

Originally developed in February 2016, the Global Code of Ethics has over ten signatories and sets out a professional code of conduct for members practising coaching and mentoring across a range of contexts. The code has three key sections, 'Working with Clients,' 'Professional Conduct' and 'Excellent Practice' (European Mentoring and Coaching Council [EMCC], 2021). When working with clients, members are expected to engage in a process of contracting which is client-centred and transparent in agreeing the focus and duration of the work to be undertaken, confidentiality, boundaries to practice and the ethical code to which the practitioner will adhere. Members are expected to act with integrity at all times, effectively manage conflicts of interest, avoiding inappropriate relationships and respecting the client's rights throughout the coaching/mentoring process. This includes ending the working relationship effectively and recognising ongoing professional responsibilities to the client. The code requires that members conduct themselves professionally by maintaining the reputation of the profession, acting responsibly, adhering to legal and statutory obligations and duties (including those relevant to the practice context and legal frameworks) and adhering to a complaint procedure. The code identifies excellent practice as the ability to perform competently and engage in ongoing supervision and continuous professional development.

ICF Code of Ethics

The stated purpose of the ICF Code of Ethics is 'to promote professional and ethical coaching practices, and to raise the awareness of people outside of the coaching profession about the integrity, commitment and ethical conduct of ICF members and ICF credentialed coaches' (Townsend, 2011). The code is based on the core values of 'professionalism,' 'collaboration,' 'humanity' and 'equity' (International Coaching Federation [ICF], 2021), each of which are expected to guide members' interpretation of the ethical standards. These include, 'Responsibility to clients,' 'Responsibility to practice and perform,' 'Responsibility to professionalism' and 'Responsibility to society' (ICF, 2021, pp. 4–7). Responsibility to clients focuses on contracting, maintaining confidentiality appropriately, recognising boundaries to practice, managing conflicts of interest, protecting client data and recognising multiple relationships and managing appropriate endings and ongoing responsibilities with the client. Practising and performing responsibly focuses on adhering to the Code of Ethics across all interactions, seeking to resolve conflicts of interest and being committed to excellence through continuing professional development. Responsibility to professionalism concerns practising with integrity, including working within the boundaries of competency and setting 'clear and appropriate culturally sensitive boundaries to govern interactions,' and avoiding inappropriate relationships. Societal responsibilities include practising fairly and equitably, respecting cultural practices and avoiding discrimination on the basis of 'age, race, gender expression, ethnicity, sexual orientation, religion, national origin, disability or military status' (ICF, 2021, p. 6). Additionally, this standard extends to acting with integrity when working with intellectual property and also adhering to the philosophy of 'doing good' rather than 'avoiding bad' (ICF, 2021, p. 7).

BPS Code of Ethics and Conduct

The BPS sets out and upholds the professional standards for Chartered Psychologists, including Chartered Coaching Psychologists, working in the UK and elsewhere. The Society maintains a Code of Ethics and Conduct which is regularly reviewed and updated in light of societal changes and the changing expectations on professional practitioners (British Psychological Society [BPS], 2021). The code identifies four ethical principles:

i. respect;
ii. competence;
iii. responsibility; and
iv. integrity.

'Respect' is a core value in recognising the dignity of all clients as having 'inherent worth' irrespective of ethnic origin, gender, social status, capabilities or any other 'group-based characteristic.' This principle emphasises the importance of working with compassion, empathy and generosity as well as with courage in preserving privacy and confidentiality, and recognising and managing issues of power, consent and self-determination. 'Competence' requires BPS members to have the requisite knowledge, skills and abilities to offer professional services to a professional standard, and to recognise the limits to their practice and engage in appropriate referral. BPS members, under this principle, are required to engage in supervision and continuing professional development, with a particular focus on working with the evidence base for their practice. 'Responsibility' emphasises the accountability incumbent upon chartered psychologists working with a high level of professional autonomy in terms of their practice and in respecting 'the welfare of humans, non-humans and the living world,' as well as 'competing duties.' 'Integrity' requires members to set aside 'self-interest' and practice with honesty, openness, non-bias and fairness in avoiding exploitation and conflicts of interest as well as managing personal and professional boundaries and addressing misconduct (BPS, 2021).

While each ethical code has a different emphasis, Lowman (2013) argues that there are eight generic ethical principles in coaching and mentoring. These are:

i. competence;
ii. avoiding harm;
iii. integrity;
iv. informed consent;
v. avoiding or effectively managing multiple relationships;
vi. confidentiality;
vii. managing conflicts of interest; and
viii. being multiculturally and internationally competent.

The next section will explore each of these to consider a number of pertinent ethical considerations when coaching and mentoring students in HE.

Ethical principles and unique challenges for coaching and mentoring in HE

As identified at the start of this chapter, and indeed in the introduction to this volume, coaching and mentoring have been demonstrated as being effective by enabling diverse students in HE to flourish (Hillman, Lochtie and Purcell, 2024; Capstick *et al.*, 2019; Alzen *et al.*, 2021). Practitioners, including the student peer mentors and coaches discussed in Chapter 6 of this volume, will integrate a wide range of interventions and activities across diverse contexts and different modalities. This provides many opportunities and strengths in coaching and mentoring, but this also presents challenges. This is the 'space' in which ethical choices are made.

This section will explore the eight generic ethical principles identified by Lowman (2013) in turn by considering the unique issues for each principle when coaching and mentoring students in HE. The section will explore different aspects of diversity and consider how the ethical principles 'spotlight' practical issues. Importantly, this section takes an eclectic approach to model the integration of a wide range of concepts and theories for developing *ethical awareness* and highlights the importance of effective contracting, re-contracting and evaluation of the coaching or mentoring work.

1. **Competence**

   Competent practice relies on practitioners critically reflecting on their knowledge and skills, which are informed by a scientific and professional evidence base. However, the evidence base for coaching and mentoring students in HE is still very much in development. It still reflects cultural biases which do not yet recognise the diversity of experiences and which types of interventions are likely to have efficacy, and which may lead to harm (Maltbia and Prior, 2023). Practising competently will involve practitioners engaging in regular supervision to evaluate practice and identify areas where professional development is needed. Engaging in supervision is likely to include a focus on areas of 'unconscious incompetence' (Curtiss and Warren, 1973), where the coach or mentor has not yet recognised or valued necessary competences for their current practice. Competences for contracting and re-contracting for appropriate interventions and activities and their evaluation, as well as the skills needed for managing endings and dependencies within coaching and mentoring will be particularly important (Van Nieuwerburgh, 2020). An in-depth knowledge and sensitivity to barriers for participation, such as masking behaviours to avoid stigmatisation of differences, including those associated with disability, learning styles and neurodiversity, could be argued as a key competency for practitioners working in HE.

   Competency also extends to professionalism for managing self-care and wellbeing, particularly in the context of coaching and mentoring in HE where workloads can be intense alongside the emotional labour required when supporting students effectively.
2. **Avoiding harm**

   Practitioners working with students in HE need to take reasonable steps to avoid harm or to minimise harm where it may be unavoidable.

While any ethical challenge, which is not effectively managed, has the potential to do harm to students, this section focuses on avoiding or minimising harm by recognising and managing boundaries when contracting and re-contracting. It is important for practitioners to recognise the boundaries for coaching/mentoring students who are experiencing mental health issues, and whether interventions are effective and safe. In some situations, coaching may be harmful, and in others, it may be helpful when clearly bounded and in conjunction with other mental health interventions, such as counselling or psychotherapy. As Buckley and Buckley (2012) comment, a sports person who has a musculoskeletal problem and struggling to perform will not benefit from sports coaching, and indeed it could lead to permanent physical damage. To avoid harm when coaching/mentoring students who may have temporary or more permanent mental health issues, a practitioner will need the ability to recognise the signs and reflect on the ethical, legal and practical circumstances, working in partnership with the student, before deciding on whether coaching/mentoring is appropriate.

Of course, a student may or may not be aware of their own mental health issues, and may choose not to disclose these if they are. Where a student is not aware or chooses not to disclose a concern, it is important for the practitioner to be alert to a number of signs. Buckley and Buckley (2012) suggest looking for patterns by focusing on appearance, behaviour, mood, thoughts, perception and cognition to consider whether suffering is present, and therefore whether coaching/mentoring is appropriate. Of course, suffering is a normal part of life which we all experience at times, whether it is a bereavement, redundancy, a conflict at work or at home or a relationship breakdown. While generally we learn to cope with these types of stressors, they can act as 'Tiny T traumas,' where multiple negative experiences can lead to feelings of uncertainty and anxiety (Arroll, 2023). Students accessing coaching/mentoring may show signs of high-functioning anxiety, maladaptive perfectionism, imposterism and sleep disturbance, for example, which indicate higher levels of stress. Suffering may also be as a result of trauma associated with, for example, bullying, harassment or physical or psychological abuse which has occurred either in the past or more recently. These experiences can lead to post-traumatic stress or complex post-traumatic stress. Signs of post-traumatic stress can include depression and irritability, intense anxiety, flashbacks of the traumatising event, social withdrawal and difficulty with relationships. Suffering may be present if students are experiencing generalised anxiety, phobias, drug addiction and dependency, eating disorders, psychosis or personality disorders such as narcissism or sociopathy (Buckley and Buckley, 2012).

Sensitivity when making ethical choices will involve the practitioner working with the student to explore whether coaching/mentoring is appropriate, potentially alongside medical and/or therapeutic interventions. Contracting for activities which might be helpful (e.g. strategies for enhancing wellbeing or goal striving using a solution-focused approach) and contracting to avoid those which might be harmful (e.g. ruminating on traumatic events, which can be triggered when using problem-focused approaches) will be necessary, as will regular feedback and evaluation, and re-contracting when needed.

3. **Integrity**

   Practising with integrity requires practitioners to place a high value on honesty, accuracy, clarity and fairness across all their interactions with students and, where appropriate, other stakeholders which avoids deceit or exploitation. In its most basic form, integrity requires practitioners, particularly at the contracting stage, to be transparent about their coaching or mentoring experience, training and accreditations and how these are appropriate for the student's specific requirements of the coaching or mentoring support. Additionally, practitioners working with a high level of integrity are likely to critically reflect on all aspects of their practice to ensure that they best meet the needs of the student.

   Practising with integrity will, at times, involve bravery and courage. For example, recognising, and acting on, implicit bias, that is unconscious negative attitudes towards social groups which are likely to result in behaviour that is discriminatory towards those groups (Nosek *et al.*, 2002) is critical to avoid unintended consequences with serve to reinforce inequality, marginalisation, discrimination and exclusion. This can operate at an individual or organisational level and, therefore, presents a number of ethical choices. These biases can also operate within the coaching and mentoring context. For example, Bernstein (2023) undertook research in the United States which compared coaching conversations between 105 White executive coaches and their Black and White coachees. The findings identified that the coaches engaged in less challenging and more supportive discussions with Black coachees compared to White coaches. Additionally, Black coaches received less constructive feedback. Practising with integrity will require practitioners to regularly review their practice to consider where implicit bias may influence their decision-making with diverse students studying in HE.

4. **Avoiding or effectively managing multiple relationships**

   Avoiding or effectively managing multiple relationships is a particular ethical consideration when coaching and mentoring students in HE. Many practitioners are likely to have other relationships with students, such as personal tutor, or educational, careers or wellbeing advisors.

Additionally, even if these relationships are not present during the coaching/mentoring work, it may be that they become salient are after the coaching/mentoring work has completed. This could result in both unintended and potentially harmful consequences. For example, a tutor could provide mentoring or coaching support where at the time there are no conflicts of interest. The student could disclose sensitive information, such as mental health concerns or barriers to their performance. Subsequently, if the student were to enrol on a programme of study which involved the tutor assessing the student's performance, the student could feel empowered or vulnerable knowing they disclosed information that they might otherwise not have done in the assessment context.

Given the complexity of practitioner roles in HE institutions, practitioners are likely to consider the appropriateness of engaging in coaching and mentoring support for students given their other, current or future, professional relationships with the student. Where coaching and mentoring support are offered, practitioners will need to identify the obligations and expectations of each party. This would include explicitly recognising power imbalances, and the steps that will be taken to act in the best interests of the student, avoiding 'bias, lack of objectivity and any risks of exploitation' (Lowman, 2013, p. 79).

5. **Informed consent**

Informed consent requires that the practitioner ensures students are fully aware and consent to the coaching/mentoring processes involved. This includes contracting for the roles and responsibilities of the practitioner and student, which types of behaviours are expected of each, the anticipated outcomes of the work, which interventions and activities are likely to be involved, and a consideration of the benefits, limitations and risks of the coaching/mentoring process (Lowman, 2013).

Working in a HE context, a particular challenge might involve whether consent is truly voluntary. A practitioner would need to consider whether organisational cultural or contextual expectations, perhaps articulated by institutional stakeholders, may serve to 'coerce' students into participating, or participating with a process that they have not had the opportunity to explore in terms of how it might be adapted to best reflect their values, cultural differences to meet their requirements. Additionally, if other stakeholders or sponsors are involved, or if there are likely to be requests to share evaluation or research data, this would require further contracting, and the informed consent on the part of the students before their participation.

6. **Confidentiality and data protection**

Confidentiality is a key ethical obligation which extends to any communication between the coach/mentor and the student, and data that is shared by the student or generated from the process. Mentors and coaches are required to contract with students as to what and how information will be stored and protected, and when and how it will be destroyed. This includes student contact details, such as an email address, as well as any records of the sessions and reports on progress or outcomes. It is also imperative that any exceptions to confidentiality, such as student disclosure of risks to self or others, are identified, and what procedures will be followed by the practitioner in these circumstances. Practitioners will need to consider their responsibilities under data protection laws, including familiarisation with data protection laws in other countries, if working with students internationally. As a minimum, practitioners will need to consider how they collect, store and destroy the data in a way that is lawful, fair and transparent, and that their practice protects client data at all times. This can be additionally challenging when third-party platforms, such as those used for video-conferencing or AI-assisted coaching or mentoring tools are used (Diller, 2024; Köbis and Mehner, 2021). Chapter 3 in this volume discusses some of the ways confidentiality when coaching in HE might be affected by institutional policy and legal duties towards students.

7. **Managing conflicts of interest**

   Conflicts of interest involve any context in which the practitioner has a 'vested interest' in the coaching or mentoring work or its outcomes which may be incompatible with the client's best interests. It also involves a situation where there are risks that the practitioners' judgement may be impaired (Lowman, 2013). A conflict of interest may lead to the exploitation or harm of the student, in either intended or unintended ways. In a HE context, there are particular risks given the multiple roles and/or relationships a practitioner may have with the student, and the expectations multiple stakeholders or sponsors, including those funding and evaluating coaching/mentoring services, may have. It is important, therefore, to identify existing or potential conflicts of interest and take action to mitigate any risk of harm or exploitation to the student. This includes transparency, honesty, accuracy and openness when contracting about the practitioner's training and competency, as well as other roles and responsibilities.

8. **Multicultural and international competence**

   As identified earlier, coaching and mentoring support in HE can enable students from very diverse and non-traditional academic backgrounds to be successful and to flourish. However, if coaching and mentoring is to be effective and avoid harm, practitioners need to ensure they are competent to work with students from different ethnic and religious backgrounds, who have different sexual orientations, genders, sexualities and who are neurodivergent. This requires practitioners to engage in CPD and reflection, particularly working with an emerging evidence base, to identify the most effective interventions to support diversity in coaching and mentoring, and to develop their 'multicultural competence' (Lowman, 2013, p. 84). In particular, recognising Western values embedded in coaching which privilege individualism, and which may represent a barrier to participation for students whose values reflect collectivism, is important particularly at the contracting stage. Sensitivity to how different social identities, associated with different cultural backgrounds may intersect or combine to intensify discrimination or privilege is important when working with students in HE if barriers to participation and success are to be effectively navigated (Schlosser and Foley, 2008). Additionally, recognition of the diversity of practice-based locations and contexts, particularly in different international legal and political jurisdictions, is important in recognising both legal frameworks for practice, such as Data Protection laws, but also the challenges of working safely and securely online. Developing policies and frameworks for managing emergencies across country locations when coaching and mentoring students at a distance, would be a further ethical consideration in demonstrating competence to work internationally.

In summary, coaching and mentoring diverse students in HE is complex and requires practitioners to be competent across a number of domains to increase their awareness and sensitivity in recognising ethical moments and in resolving them. The ethical principles, which are embedded within professional and ethical codes of conduct can act as a guide but are not sufficient in themselves for developing ethical decision-making and ethical practice. The next section will argue that practitioners need to develop and enhance ethical maturity, particularly by participating in regular supervision, to provide effective and safe support for students.

Ethical maturity for coaching and mentoring students in higher education contexts

As noted in the previous section, ethical choices and decisions when coaching and mentoring students in HE can be complex, uncertain and often involve balancing different benefits and risks. This reflects research into the experiences of coaches and mentors working in educational and other contexts. For example, a study involving experienced coaching psychologists identified particular ethical issues when working with coachees and/or other stakeholders where there were emotional, personality or behavioural issues, and which were considered risks to coachee wellbeing or the wellbeing of those around them (Duffy and Passmore, 2010). Managing boundaries, as well as dual or multiple relationships, especially in organisational settings were cited as important and challenging areas for ethical decision-making (Duffy and Passmore, 2010). Similarly, in a study involving 60 mentors working in an Israeli education system managing confidentiality and disclosure, when mentees were perceived to be at risk, and balancing duties of care to different stakeholders were cited as involving particularly challenging ethical decision-making (Shapira-Lishchinsky, 2012).

There is research which suggests that practitioners value opportunities to raise ethical awareness, reflect on ethical codes and personal values, critically review situations and context, engage in supervision and keep a reflective journal to record key strategies to inform decision-making and evaluate the process and outcomes (Turner and Passmore, 2018).

There is also research that suggests these opportunities for reflection are not available to practitioners. In a study involving coach supervisors, nearly a fifth surveyed stated that they never discussed their supervisee's values when considering ethical choices (Turner and Passmore, 2018). In another study, involving 260 coaches, ten believed their ethical training was not useful, ten reported not receiving any ethical training and 76 believed it was for 'foundational purposes' (Heitz and Leach, 2022). In particular, some participants stated that they found ethical training was too brief and only involved a 'shallow knowledge and awareness' (Heitz and Leach, 2022).

In contrast, enhancing practitioner ethical maturity involves a developmental approach which goes beyond simplistic applications of codes of conduct and behaviour, and its regulation (Carroll and Shaw, 2013). In their model, Carroll and Shaw (2013, p. 133) identify ethical maturity as involving a 'relativist stance' avoiding absolute claims to truth by recognising multiple perspectives gained through in-depth critical reflection. Carroll and Shaw (2013) identify 'six components' which are associated with ethical maturity. Each will be considered in turn.

Ethical sensitivity

The first focuses on developing a watchfulness and sensitivity to ethical issues. Ethical sensitivity involves heightened awareness of the self, of others and the intended and unintended consequences of behaviour. It not only reflects a practitioner's knowledge of their professional and ethical code of conduct and the legal framework in which they work but also in awareness of their values and principles, important to them personally and within their community of practice and organisations. These will reflect personal characteristics such as empathy, integrity, humility, wisdom and courage. Enhancing ethical sensitivity also involves becoming aware of motivation, relations of power, active listening skills and proactively enhancing self-care, attending to emotional responses, and critically reflecting on practice (Carroll and Shaw, 2013).

Ethical discernment

The second component concerns 'ethical discernment' which involves the practitioner in considering ethical choices to inform decision-making. Importantly, decision-making is informed by many intrinsic (e.g. personal values, personality characteristics, emotional responses) as well as extrinsic (e.g. socio-cultural contexts) factors. Decision-making is vulnerable to becoming 'automated' and processes such as confirmation bias where there is a tendency to favour preferred beliefs (Klayman, 1995) and cognitive dissonance where important information may be disregarded to reduce uncertainty and associated stress responses (Festinger, 1959). Lewis (1990) proposed that it can be helpful to explore personal values when considering ethical choices as it can offer a critical framework to inform decision-making. From this perspective, considering what value is placed on our lived experience, logic and reason, emotional responses, intuition, authority or a scientific evidence base can make visible bias and assumptions. Embracing the complexity and chaos of lived experienced serves to enhance ethical awareness and decision-making.

Ethical implementation

The third component focuses on 'ethical implementation' and enhancing awareness of any barriers to action on ethical decision-making. There is evidence of a gap between ethical decision-making, knowing what to do, and implementing the actions needed across a number of different professional contexts, including coaching and mentoring (Carroll and Shaw, 2013). There can be significant barriers to behaving ethically including personal cost, particularly perceived or real conflict with others, conflicting values including misalignment between personal and professional values, collusion, competing commitments, neurological factors and personality characteristics. Recognising and overcoming these barriers can involve courage, commitment and the avoidance of procrastination (Carroll and Shaw, 2013).

Ethical conversation and accountability

The fourth component involves an 'ethical conversation' in which the practitioner is confident in justifying their decision-making to others and in light of their professional ethical code of conduct. Narration of the decision-making, action implementation and evaluation can enhance critical reflection, not least by recognising the language or discourses being mobilised to construct different versions and accounts. Constructing these narrations for audiences, such as supervisors or peers, can make visible current limitations in awareness, enhance scrutiny and accountability. Group supervision, in particular, can offer significant insights from a range of different perspectives to deepen practitioner reflection and reflexivity. Of course, groups can also be influenced by biases, such as groupthink, often linked to cultural and organisational values. Valuing diversity within supervision groups can make such biases more visible (Shaukat, 2024).

Ethical sustainability and peace

The fifth component focuses on 'ethical sustainability and peace,' where the decision-making and subsequent actions are accepted, including learning from the outcomes. It can be difficult if, in the light of unanticipated outcomes, an ethical decision was wrong, in part or in whole. Many cultures privilege being right and there can be significant social and, potentially, legal sanctions for making wrong ethical decisions (Carroll and Shaw, 2013). Experiences of guilt and shame, often involving excessive rumination, are not uncommon in this situation. Shame, in particular, can diminish a sense of 'self,' and lead to feeling powerless, anxious and possibly depressed (Dryden, 1997). Ethical maturity involves developing skills and thinking processes which enable reconciliation, self-compassion and forgiveness which can support living with discomfort, uncertainty and learning (Dryden, 1997). Self-compassion, in particular, is important as it is linked to self-esteem, self-efficacy and wellbeing (Neff, 2003). It is from a place of wellbeing that we are more likely to search for meaning from our experience, learning from that experience and then integrating that learning into practice (Carroll and Shaw, 2013).

Ethical growth and development of moral character

The sixth component of learning from experience and integrating that experience into our personal and professional identities requires us to feel safe. Psychological safety is associated with higher levels of agency and empowerment in risk management, and surfacing concerns when things go wrong without fear of being ridiculed or shamed or experiencing reprisals (Wanless, 2016). For this reason, it is important that practitioners can access supervision which involves psychological contracting which is characterised by a strong empathic connection and working alliance, and one which fosters trust, agency, empowerment and healing (McLean, 2023). This form of supervision is associated with deeper levels of reflection and learning which support an integration of self-awareness and self-knowledge into personal and social identity, as well as behaviour to enhance ethical sensitivity and reduce the gap between intention and behaviour.

The development of ethical maturity is not considered to involve the linear development of skills readily transferred from one context to another but involves the creation of safe spaces which serve to support practitioners to explore their ethical choices and make ethical decisions, particularly at times when they may feel challenged or disorientated by the ethical challenges they face (Carroll and Shaw, 2013). The next section will outline the APPEAR framework, which was developed from research, undertaken by Duffy and Passmore (2010), involving semi-structured interviews with experienced coaches to understand the key processes involved in ethical decision-making.

The APPEAR framework and its application for ethical decision-making in HE

The APPEAR ethical decision-making model involves practitioners working across six stages, which are unlikely to be considered in a linear way, and usually involves reflection and action which integrates an in-depth knowledge of professional and ethical codes of conduct, legal considerations, personal and moral values and sociopolitical and systemic contexts. The six stages are: (1) awareness; (2) practice; (3) possibilities; (4) extending the field; (5) acting on reflections; and (6) reflecting on learning. Each will be considered in turn (Passmore and Turner, 2018).

(1) Awareness

Ethical maturity involves enhancing awareness through strengthening the capability of noticing 'ethical moments' and the preparedness to explore these moments by enhancing self-awareness. Becoming aware of the complexities of ethical issues includes the skills for considering multiple stakeholder perspectives, as well as a preparedness to explore practitioner emotional responses, values and ideologies which may influence their decision-making.

(2) **Practice**

Enhancing ethical maturity usually involves engaging in regular supervision, including group, peer and one-to-one supervision and participating in training and continuous professional development. This supports the enhancement of professional knowledge and expertise, particularly in terms of keeping up-to-date with new developments and the advances in the evidence base which underpin practice. Importantly, the integration of knowledge and the development of skills can be facilitated by creating reflective spaces, including undertaking regular journalling and record-keeping.

(3) **Possibilities**

When ethical issues arise, there are likely to be a number of ethical choices, each one having strengths and limitations. Enhancing the capacity to reflect critically and creatively in identifying a wide range of ethical choices and assessing their potential to lead to the most effective, and least harmful outcomes is the cornerstone of working with ethical maturity. Exploring the complexities of multiple stakeholder perspectives, as well as the application of ethical principles embedded in ethical and professional codes of conduct, institutional policies and legal frameworks usually requires collaboration with others, such as a supervisor or experienced peers. In particular, this is the dimension in which, as much as possible, unexpected and unanticipated consequences can be imagined. Opportunities for extending reflection with others, who have diverse experience and expertise, is likely to ensure greater visibility is given to the consequences of ethical decision-making and subsequent practitioner actions.

(4) **Extending the field**

In considering options for ethical decision-making, a practitioner will necessarily extend their knowledge, particularly integrating new insights and awareness into their practice, but also considering how enhancements to practice fit or develop professional and institutional codes of conduct, and legal frameworks. Additionally, at this stage Hawkins and Turner (2019) suggest that practitioners develop 'systematic ethical maturity' (Hawkins and Turner, 2019, p. 178). This, they argue, can be achieved by practitioners enhancing their cultural awareness, considering multiple stakeholder perspectives and being empathetic to them, and having a future focus in mind when considering ethical choices. As importantly, extending the field also involves practitioners actively sharing their experiences and reflection on their practice with other practitioners to support the co-construction of ethical maturity within the profession and across institutional contexts.

(5) **Acting on reflections**

This stage involves the commitment to the ethical decisions made, and the development of a detailed action plan, taking into consideration all actions and interventions which are to be enacted. At this stage, supervision can be useful to consider logistical and practical issues, as well as contingency actions which aim to address possible responses from different stakeholders. Sources of support for the practitioner can also be usefully identified at this stage. These may include attending to the practitioner's strategies for protecting their wellbeing and attending to their emotional responses to the situation.

(6) **Reflecting on learning**

The final stage is an opportunity to reflect on the ethical moment and the ethical choices made, their outcomes and how this will inform future practice, both for the practitioner and, where appropriate, where this new understanding can be shared with the wider practice community. In particular, it can be useful for the practitioner to consider any new approaches which were helpful in informing their ethical decision-making and action, and whether there were any unexpected or unanticipated consequences. It can also be useful for the practitioner to consider how their personal values and beliefs may have influenced the decision-making and to what extent that influence was positive, or if they had any unintended or negative consequences. These insights can support the practitioner in identifying what they might do differently, both for managing similar scenarios or in considering approaches for ethical decision-making more generally. As importantly, recognition of the emotional impact of the experience, and which sources of support were available, and if they were sufficient, can enhance practitioner resilience.

The next section will explore how the APPEAR model for ethical decision-making can be applied to three fictitious case study scenarios. Each one highlights different ethical complexities and choices for practitioners and how they respond.

Applying the APPEAR model to ethical decision-making when working with students in HE

Scenario one

Ieman is a senior careers adviser providing support to undergraduate and postgraduate students in a large campus-based university. Ieman is also an EMCC practitioner coach and contracts with students to integrate coaching into her work with them. Ieman has contracted with Jackie, a second-year undergraduate engineering student, for careers coaching for five sessions. Jackie requested support in planning her career development, uncertain of whether engineering was the right career pathway. Jackie also wanted to work on confidence issues associated with her studies and professional development. Despite getting good grades and feedback for her assessment, Jackie feels underconfident and worries that her academic and professional skills are not good enough.

Jackie has engaged with two coaching sessions which have explored her motivations, interests, skills and strengths, as well as the practicalities of working as an engineer, and has decided that the professional role is a good match and will give her the opportunities she wants. Jackie says she feels excited about her future, she knows engineering is a great profession for her, but still has concerns that she is not going to be good enough and will fail. Ieman has supported Jackie to explore her beliefs about not being good *enough*. Jackie has stated that she often feels worried, anxious, inadequate, overwhelmed and scared. Ieman has encouraged Jackie to reflect on her beliefs, and they have talked about imposterism and perfectionism, as well as wider cultural issues such as gender bias in the engineering profession. Ieman has encouraged Jackie to challenge her beliefs about not being good enough and suggested using some online self-compassion resources. Some goal focussed work has been successfully undertaken and Jackie has said that she is eating and sleeping better, making more time to be with friends and doing sports.

Although Jackie has said she has found this helpful Ieman senses something is impacting on Jackie's wellbeing. Ieman asks Jackie if something else has been happening recently. At this point, Jackie becomes upset and tells Ieman that she has experienced depression at difference times since she was 14 years and has, in the past, self-harmed. Jackie says she has received counselling when she was younger, and that helped her to feel better and to complete her A levels, but she is now worried that the depression is returning and that although she doesn't think she is currently depressed and is not self-harming, she can see the signs that she might be on a downward spiral. Jackie says she has kept this a secret, she really doesn't want her university lecturers to know about her past experiences of depression and self-harm. She says she is worried about being stigmatised and losing her credibility as an engineering student, and that she won't be able to complete her degree or develop her career.

Ieman knows that she does not have the skills to assess Jackie's mental health concerns and that she will have to take action to ensure that Jackie has appropriate support, but wants to respect Jackie's right to confidentiality and autonomy, as much as possible, in the decision-making about what happens next. Ieman holds a space for Jackie, using active and empathic listening skills, to hear Jackie's concerns about her mental health and fears about the consequences for making these known to her Faculty. Ieman reassures Jackie that many other students have similar experiences, that there is a wide range of support at the University and that she does not have to feel alone. Ieman asks Jackie about how she feels, and whether she currently has thoughts about self-harming. Satisfied that there are no immediate risks of self-harm, Ieman explains that she would like to reflect with her supervisor on what additional support is available to Jackie and how best to access it. Ieman reassures Jackie that she will not share any personal or identifying details with her supervisor. At this stage, Ieman does not want to talk about 'disclosure' with Jackie or the possible requirement to inform Jackie's personal tutor of her mental health concerns. She would like to consider the ethical choices available to her to inform her decision-making. Ieman agrees to a time to meet with Jackie later in the week and offers Jackie some information about the University's Counselling Services and the 24/7 student helpline.

Ieman and her supervisor, Brian, agree to meet later that day. Ieman outlines the issues she is concerned about ensuring that she does not reveal Jackie's identity. Ieman is concerned that although the student has reassured her there is no immediate risk, she is not qualified to assess the student's mental health concerns. Ieman understands the student's reluctance to seek help and support, but Ieman knows she has a legal and professional duty of care, and that she believes the student may have disclosed a disability.

Brian acknowledges Ieman's concerns and asks if Ieman would like to explore her own responses to what has happened before considering the ethical choices available to her.

Ieman reflects on her empathy with the student and states that she can relate to feelings of vulnerability and experiences of feeling 'powerless.' In a previous job, managers made decisions about Ieman's work portfolio which she believed she was informed by their biases about her ability based on her ethnicity. It was that experience, Ieman explains, which led her into coaching as she particularly wanted to address issues of power and prejudice in educational and training settings. She highly values a client's right to autonomy and freedom of choice, supporting their empowerment.

Brian invites Ieman to pause for a moment, he can see Ieman's body language has changed, and acknowledges that the student's experience resonates deeply for Ieman. Ieman explores her emotional responses and takes time to recognise the importance of these in exploring her ethical choices. Ieman also recognises the importance of understanding the emotional work involved in supporting the student, in this moment, and identifies strategies to attend to her own wellbeing.

Brian then asks Ieman to consider what ethical choices would be congruent with her values. Ieman says that her preference would be to explore, with the student, different types of support, including options for counselling support with a qualified professional. Ieman believes that, given the student had found the coaching work useful, as long as it was clearly bounded, they could continue for the planned sessions, but would need to evaluate how helpful they were for the student, and whether there were mental health concerns not being addressed. Ieman would prefer for the student to self-access counselling or medical support and avoid the need for formal disclosure. Brian invites Ieman to consider the benefits and risks associated with this strategy.

Ieman recognises that because the student has disclosed information about mental health risks, Ieman has a responsibility to comply with the University's Disability Equality Scheme and the Disability Discrimination Act, to ensure the student accesses the support she needs. Brian invites Ieman to consider whether there are other choices available to her, which would support the student to feel empowered, and retain as much autonomy as possible, while fulfilling Ieman's duty of care to her. Ieman notes she is scheduled to meet with the student later that week and wonders if she could explain the situation, honestly and transparently, and ask if they could explore together a way forward that would work for the student to ensure that she can access the support she needs. Ieman knows she has contracted with the student for limits to confidentiality and so feels more comfortable in having this conversation.

As a minimum intervention, Ieman notes she will have to notify one of the teaching staff that the student has disclosed a possible health concern in her coaching sessions, but the student could choose who this would be. Ieman will convey the student's right to confidentiality and that she does not need to share details of the health concern. Ieman is comfortable with this approach as she believes there is no immediate risk of self-harm. Ieman is keen for the student to feel supported and cared for, and she wants to offer continued coaching for the remaining sessions planned. Ieman wants to reflect with the student what coaching support would be helpful, how this is different from counselling support, and how they will evaluate their work together to ensure the student is getting the support and care they need to succeed. Brian also wants Ieman to feel supported and invites Ieman to contact him after the session to debrief.

Ieman meets with Jackie and checks how she is feeling, and if she has had some further thoughts about getting more support since they last met. Jackie says she would like some more support, she's been struggling since she started her degree, but since talking with Ieman earlier that week feels like a weight has been lifted off her. Ieman talks with Jackie about the support that the University can offer, in particular the Counselling Service. Ieman also talks about her duty of care to Jackie, and that she will need to be in touch with a member of the teaching staff, and proceeds to discuss the options as she had planned. Jackie takes some time to think about who she would feel most comfortable with Ieman contacting and decides she would be happy for her personal tutor to be contacted. Jackie understands that Ieman will not disclose any personal information, only noting there may be a health concern. They agree a plan of action for the remaining three coaching sessions to focus on wellbeing and self-care strategies. Ieman meets with Jackie for a coaching session the following week. Jackie has spoken with her personal tutor and has had a counselling session which she found helpful, with more sessions planned. Jackie tells Ieman how she feels cared for, respected and safe. In reflecting on the student's feedback with her supervisor, Ieman states how she also felt cared for, respected and safe in her supervision sessions too. They reflect together on how Ieman can use her learning to influence future ethical decision-making. Ieman particularly wants to share the importance of reflecting on personal values and how these influence ethical decision-making, as well as review approaches to contracting for confidentiality and disclosure in her next peer group supervision session.

Scenario two

Peter is a senior lecturer in social sciences and an ICF-accredited coach. Alongside an intensive teaching and research portfolio, Peter is also participating in a coaching project which aims to provide coaching support to students and colleagues across the University. Peter enjoys his coaching work and has supported over 50 under- and postgraduate students, in the last two years, to strive towards study and professional development goals. Peter also coaches professional and academic colleagues working in other Faculties in the University. Peter has noticed over the last few months that he has been feeling quite tired, and on occasions quite irritable, which is unusual for him. On reflection, he knows is working very long hours, often missing lunch and has very little time with his family. He has started to resent working in the evenings and at weekends. Additionally, Peter has given up playing cricket and never seems to have a chance to catch up with his friends.

Peter participates in bi-monthly group supervision and has signed up for a session which is focused on practitioner wellbeing. Peter's first thought is that he doesn't have time for this, there are more important priorities, but given his tiredness decides to make time to participate. The group supervisor asks the group of six coaches to contract for their session and the group agrees, in particular, to contract for honesty, empathy, openness and kindness in the session, as well as confidentiality. Each group member has the opportunity to share their strategies for supporting their own well-being. Peter begins to feel uncomfortable as his colleagues share their strategies and their concerns about their wellbeing. Peter has not experienced a group discussion where colleagues are very open and honest about their mental health and is aware of their and his vulnerability. Peter knows he would feel more confident in a group discussion focused on work priorities and planning for these and wonders if attending this group was a mistake. Peter recognises that he is experiencing an unexpected emotional response and realises that the group discussion has become triggering for him. Peter decides to share this with the group and is open about how he has compromised so many of the things that he values in his life in order to prioritise his teaching, research and coaching practice. Peter notes that he feels guilty, even taking time out of the working day to talk about this. On reflection, Peter realises that his mental health has been compromised and that if he doesn't make some changes he could be at risk of 'burnout.' Peter expects the group to be judgemental and finds his colleagues' warmth and empathy towards him surprising; he says how 'nurtured' he feels. One colleague asks what practical things Peter could do to promote his own wellbeing and his level of preparedness to make those changes in the next month, which Peter explores. As part of the debrief at the end of the session, the group supervisor reminds the group that individual group supervision is available if anyone would like to follow-up on the topics raised in the group session and that the employee assistance programme and counselling support are also accessible to all staff.

Peter recognises that the group session has surfaced some important issues for him and decides to follow these up in a one-to-one session with his supervisor, Francesca. Peter begins the session by apologising to Francesca for bringing something more 'trivial' to discuss and notes that he feels a sense of guilt for not focusing the session on a coachee issue. Francesca invites Peter to explore his beliefs about his own health and wellbeing as a focus for supervision. Peter recognises he is devaluing his wellbeing and prioritising work tasks over his health. He notes how he has always prioritised service to others and links this to the value he places in personal achievement and thinks this reflects his 'conscientious' personality. He has a very strong work ethic and cares deeply about the students and colleagues he works with, identifying benevolence and care of others as core values. Francesca first asks Peter to consider the strengths and risks of working in this way and then whether there is an ethical concern in terms of avoiding harm to his health and wellbeing. Peter is taken aback by these questions and at first can't see any ethical concerns in terms of risks to himself. Peter says this is how everybody works in universities, he is no different and achieving high standards in the service of others is what is expected. Francesca acknowledges that many HE cultures reflect the values that are important to Peter and that caring for others and working in their service are important values, but challenges Peter on whether this has to be to the detriment of health and wellbeing. She notes that Peter has said he works very long hours and asks him what activities he is not doing when he is working in the evenings and at the weekends. At this point, Peter becomes aware of his sadness, he reflects on how little time he has with his partner and children, even time spent with his children is rushed, and tends to be focused on 'tasks' such as mealtimes and school runs, rather than just 'hanging out' with them. Peter is sad that he no longer sees his friends or plays cricket, is aware that he is getting about five hours of sleep a night, at most, and is often missing lunch. Peter says he feels stressed and exhausted all the time and is struggling with some of his emotional responses, often feeling irritable at the very times he knows he wants to show compassion. Trying to hide his feelings of irritability is adding to his fatigue. Peter senses that, in particular, the coachees he is working with are probably picking up on his tiredness and he feels frustrated that they probably know he sometimes 'acts out empathy and compassion,' as he often struggles to genuinely feel it.

Francesca thanks Peter for being open and honest about his experiences and for sharing his feelings about how difficult things are for him at the moment. Francesca recognises the importance of Peter's values, his work ethic and his care of colleagues and students and asks Peter how hopeful he feels about being able to make changes to the way he is working. Peter says he does feel like changes are possible, he's just got into a rut and would like to explore options to find some compromises which would enable him to work with his values and to protect his health and wellbeing.

Peter knows he wants to have a conversation, in light of this reflection, with his line manager to explore his work portfolio, identifying projects that could be adapted or deprioritised. In particular, Peter wants to return to 'normal' working hours as the norm within two to three months, with only occasional evening and weekend working. When Francesca asks Peter how he would spend the reclaimed time, Peter's body language and facial expressions change. Francesca invites Peter to reflect on his somatic responses when planning for more time with his family and friends. Francesca invites Peter to consider other strategies for enhancing his well-being, such as improving sleep hygiene and eating and exercise habits. Peter develops an action plan to improve his mental and physical health and wellbeing and asks if he can check in with Francesca in a month to reflect on how it is going. Francesca is aware, one month later, how differently Peter looks and how much more optimistic he is about his work. Peter describes how he is made some changes, now working two *to* three nights a week, and only one morning at the weekends, which he will cut back on in the next month or so. He loves spending time with his family and enjoys meeting up with friends, and playing sports. He's lost a bit of weight and is starting to feel physically fitter, enjoying more sleep and just generally feeling happier. He is using guided meditations and mindfulness exercises to manage stress and to feel more relaxed. Francesca shares with Peter how happy she is to see these changes and wonders how he is now feeling at work. Peter notes that he has more energy, is less irritable and is beginning to 'bring more of himself' into his teaching and coaching practice, including genuine empathetic responses which were becoming difficult for him before. Peter pauses and says he would like to acknowledge how important it was to raise his awareness about how personal, professional and institutional values influenced his priorities and led him to ignore important signs about risks to his health and wellbeing. He is now much more aware of this process, both in terms of maintaining the changes he has made, but integrates this awareness into his own coaching practice. He is keen to enhance his coaching practice by supporting coachees to explore their health and wellbeing, alongside performance-based goals. Peter states that he now considers risks to his own health and wellbeing, as well as others, as an important ethical issue and uses this awareness to inform his practice when working with students and colleagues.

Scenario three

Abdul is a Personal Learning Adviser working in a Student Services Department in a large distance-learning university. Abdul is an EMCC-accredited practitioner coach and offers one-to-one support to students who have been identified as at risk of not completing their studies. Abdul is working with Hussein, a first-year economics student who has no formal qualifications, but has successfully completed an access course for HE. Hussein was assessed as dyslexic during his access course studies and has shared with Abdul how this was a relief for him as prior to this he didn't think he was capable of studying at university. Hussein has shared his worries about failing his university modules and programme of study, as he believes he has a history of failing at school and is probably not 'academic.' Being assessed as dyslexic, and knowing that there is support, has helped Hussein feel more optimistic. Hussein has aspirations for becoming a researcher specialising in research to promote equality and opportunity for everyone, and wants, in the longer term, to progress to a research degree, if he can succeed with his undergraduate studies.

Hussein now has support in place, including a specialist mentor, who is helping him to develop strategies to work with his dyslexia to successfully complete his assignments. Abdul and Hussein have contracted to work together for eight sessions across a nine-month period coinciding with his first year studies. Abdul has contracted with Hussein for confidentiality, but also agreed limits to confidentiality, and has been transparent that he engages in regular supervision where he reflects on his coaching practiced, explaining that details about clients are anonymised. Hussein has said he is comfortable with this.

In their first and second sessions together, Hussein identified study and professional goals, as well as goals to improve his well-being. Hussein is developing study strategies and beginning to feel more confident about his studies. He enjoys working with his tutor and specialist mentor and feels well supported. Hussein has made some changes in his personal life by making time for social activities, catching up with friends and joining a local sports club. Abdul has supported Hussein in challenging beliefs around 'not being good enough' and encouraged Hussein to consider building his professional network. Hussein has attended some events with the New Economics Foundation and is in touch with university alumni who are working in his field of interest. He is enjoying making new friends and says he is already talking with researchers about their work and routes into the profession.

Abdul meets with Hussein for their third session and is immediately struck by how anxious and upset Hussein is. Hussein says that he is going to give up his studies, he's not good enough, it was all a mistake, university study isn't for people like him. Abdul listens carefully to Hussein giving him time and space to share what he is feeling. Abdul empathises with Hussein and compassionately asks if something specific has happened that has led him to the decision to give up his studies. Initially reluctant, Hussein shares an incident on a student online forum the day before. Hussein has been very reluctant to post to online forums, worrying that his spelling and grammar will not be good enough and that he will 'make a fool of himself.' However, he was feeling so positive about his studies that he decided to engage with an activity and wrote a piece about a new economic and social settlement in society. While feeling a bit anxious about it, he was looking forward to other students' responses and a discussion about the topic. When he logged on to his computer later that day, he read a post from another student who had said they couldn't understand what he had written, it didn't make sense and the writing was 'strange.' Hussein said he felt so ashamed and foolish, and he immediately deleted his post. It had brought back memories of being at school and being mocked by other students, and of teachers being critical of his work. Hussein said this had convinced him that university study was not for him, it was all a mistake, and he knew this would happen.

Abdul said how sorry he was that Hussein had had this experience and asked Hussein if it would be okay to discuss what had happened in more detail. Using reflective and active listening skills, Abdul encouraged Hussein to challenge his beliefs about not being good enough, and whether this event could be considered a 'setback' from which he could recover, rather than the end of his studies. Abdul encouraged Hussein to consider the evidence of what he was achieving in his studies, and more broadly, his motivation for studying and his aspirations for professional development. Abdul also encouraged Hussein to review what had happened with the forum post and noted that critical messages about student's posts were likely to be of concern to other students, especially if they were feeling less confident. Abdul encouraged Hussein to explore options for the action he could take to address the issue. Hussein said he would reconsider giving up his studies, he needed more time to think but had found the conversation helpful. He agreed he would talk to his tutor about the incident. Abdul asked if he could catch up with Hussein at the end of the week, just to see how things were going for him, and Hussein said he would be happy to do this.

Although the coaching session had concluded reasonably positively, Abdul was unsettled by what Hussein had shared. Abdul had a supervision session the following day and used that time to reflect on his approach in supporting Hussein and to consider ethical issues. In particular, he wanted to explore whether he needed to take further action. After outlining his session with Hussein, Abdul was asked by his supervisor, Aisha, how he felt about what had happened. Abdul expressed anger and frustration. Abdul knew how hard Hussein had worked to overcome many obstacles to studying and was just beginning to gain confidence and optimism about his future. How could one student be so insensitive in posting such a message? Abdul also wondered if racism might have been involved, reflecting on his own experiences as a student and professional, when he sometimes felt he was being judged negatively by others on the basis of his ethnicity. And why hadn't the teaching staff seen it and intervened?

Aisha asked if there was evidence that Hussein might believe racism was involved in the incident. Abdul said there wasn't any evidence, and he didn't want to suggest it in case it wasn't relevant for Hussein at this time, but that he would keep it in mind in future sessions, if Hussein continued to experience such behaviour from the other student. Aisha asked Abdul to reflect on the support he had offered Hussein and if, on reflection, other approaches could have been useful. Abdul was happy, overall, that the session had been successful, and he believed Hussein would continue with his studies. He was also pleased to be able to see him at the end of the week.

Abdul did wonder, though, whether he should report the incident to one of the teaching staff in the Economics Department. Aisha asked Abdul what his options would be to do that and what ethical issues could arise. Abdul said he could *just* check with Hussein that he had spoken with his tutor. Alternatively, he could ask Hussein if he could speak to one of the teaching staff about the incident on the basis of having broader concerns about student conduct within the online forums. A further option would be to speak with teaching staff about online forum communication, and not identify Hussein. Aisha and Abdul quickly agreed that the third option would probably identify Hussein anyway as the teaching staff would check the forum and, as forum moderators, be able to see his deleted message. Aisha asked Abdul if he had any evidence that the other student's post had breached the University policy for student conduct when communicating online. Abdul reflected that he had not seen the post, so it was difficult to make this assessment, or indeed whether other incidents had occurred which might constitute bullying or harassing behaviour towards other students.

On reflection, Abdul believed he had a responsibility to discuss the matter with a member of the teaching staff, reflected on different approaches for raising this with Hussein. Abdul knew Hussein felt shame and embarrassment for what had happened and was worried that he might not be aware that his deleted post could still be viewed by the teaching staff. He knew he needed to approach this carefully and sensitively. Abdul agreed a plan of action with Aisha for his discussion with Hussein later in the week. He would be honest with Hussein about why he needed to raise the matter with the teaching staff, and that any message criticising student posts not only impacted on the recipient negatively but other students too. He would explain why he could not raise the concern anonymously, but would reassure Hussein that the purpose of his actions would be to ensure that the forums were a safe space for all students to work together and share ideas. He would ask the teaching staff to ensure that any interventions on their part did not explicitly identify Hussein or this particular incident but instead focus more generally on netiquette when using forums.

Abdul met with Hussein later that week and he was pleased to see Hussein looking much more relaxed and happier. Abdul asked Hussein how he was feeling and whether he had had a chance to discuss the forum message with one of the teaching staff. Hussein smiled and said that actually one of the teaching staff, Rosie, had been in touch with him and said how sorry she was to see that he had deleted his message. Rosie said she had deleted the other student's message and was now in touch with them about appropriate communication in online forums. Hussein said Rosie was really interested in his arguments and was keen to respond to them if he reinstated his post. Rosie had also reassured Hussein that she was going to run a message thread about netiquette and closely monitor the forum. Since he last met with Abdul, Hussein said he had posted a few more messages in response to other students' posts and was enjoying the discussion. Hussein had also asked his mentor if she would work with him on strategies for spelling and grammar checking his posts. Hussein was back on track and feeling good about his studies and his future plans.

Updating his supervisor, Abdul decided not to take further action in contacting the teaching staff. He considered carefully his duty of care to report a potential bullying incident but believed that Hussein had managed the situation in partnership with his tutor, and any further action on his part may serve to disempower Hussein. Abdul did additionally contract with Hussein to contact him outside of scheduled sessions if anything like that happened again, or if Hussein felt he couldn't continue with his studies. Additionally, Abdul reflected on the challenges in making ethical decisions and how important it was to reflect on his emotional responses to the situation. He also noted the importance of considering the wider institutional culture and boundaries when other staff may need to become involved. Abdul asked Aisha if it would be possible to run a group supervision session with the personal learning adviser team to reflect on how to work with these types of issues, and how to effectively work in partnership with students to support their agency and autonomy whilst complying with legal and institutional duties of care.

These case study scenarios have explored how the APPEAR decision-making model can support in-depth reflection and complex ethical decision-making. In particular, it has focused on the importance of raising awareness, including awareness of practitioner emotional responses, as well as values and biases, and how this may inadvertently influence ethical decision-making. The scenarios have shown that with sensitive and supportive supervision, practitioners can be encouraged to critically reflect on a range of ethical choices and consider how these attend to different stakeholder perspectives and needs, as well as possible unexpected and unintended consequences. The case studies have identified how this reflection can enhance decision-making which is likely to lead to more effective and less harmful outcomes. Additionally, the scenarios have highlighted the importance of supporting practitioners when they are working with complex ethical decisions and their implementations, ensuring that they have the support they need.

Summary

This chapter has explored the complex ethical choices that practitioners work with when coaching and mentoring students in HE. This chapter began by exploring a wide range of philosophical, ideological, professional, institutional and cultural influences which guide practitioner ethical decision-making. Particular emphasis has been placed on practitioners working reflectively and reflexively to explore multiple stakeholder perspectives, and relations of power to raise awareness of ethical moments, to review ethical choices and to influence ethical decision-making. This is particularly important in a university context where practitioners, offering coaching and mentoring, are likely to have multiple roles where conflicts of interest may not be immediately visible and unintended consequences could result in harmful outcomes.

This chapter has argued that embracing this level of complexity requires practitioners to enhance their ethical maturity by developing a way of being characterised by a high level of sensitivity and awareness of others' perspectives. As importantly, this chapter has argued that practitioners need to cultivate a high level of self-awareness of how their values, biases and emotional responses could influence ethical decision-making, positively or negatively. The APPEAR framework has been offered as one reflective tool which can enhance ethical decision-making. Three scenarios have been presented to illustrate how the APPEAR framework, in the context of supervision, can support practitioners to enhance their reflection in considering their ethical choices, working in partnership with their clients, to achieve the most effective outcomes. Of course, there will be other equally valid perspectives not considered in the scenarios offered here which might lead to different ethical decisions and actions. This is perhaps where a community of practice could be usefully established for mentors and coaches working to support students in HE, to extend the field of ethical decision-making in this context. This might also help attend to practitioner wellbeing and ensuring that adequate support and resource are made available, particularly when managing challenging ethical issues.

Reflective questions

- Which ethical codes inform your practice as a coach/mentor working with HE students? Do they adequately address the ethical issues you work with?
- How do you enhance your ethical maturity when coaching and mentoring students in HE?
- What key values influence your coaching and/or mentoring practice?
- How do you keep up-to-date with developments in the evidence base for coaching and mentoring to extend your field of practice?
- Which ethical issues do you find most challenging and what resources could you use to support you in addressing them?
- How do you contract for confidentiality when coaching and mentoring students in HE?

What indicators do you use to assess mental health concerns when working with students? How do you contract for boundaries to coaching or mentoring when working with vulnerable students?

How do you recognise implicit bias in your practice when working with diverse students in HE? What strategies do you use to address this bias?

Which data protection laws guide your practice, and do these reflect different legal frameworks across countries if you are working with students internationally?

On the basis of reading this chapter and reflecting on your ethical practice:

- What should you start doing?
- What should you stop doing?
- What should you continue doing?

Bibliography

Advance HE. (2023) *Professional standards framework*. Available at: https://www.advance-he.ac.uk/teaching-and-learning/psf (Accessed: 5 December 2024).

Alzen, J.L., Burkhardt, A., Diaz-Bilello, E., Elder, E., Sepulveda, A., Blankenheim, A. and Board, L. (2021) 'Academic coaching and its relationship to student performance, retention, and credit completion', *Innovative Higher Education*, 46, pp. 539–563. doi: 10.1007/s10755-021-09554-w

Anderson, S.K. and Handelsman, M.M. (2021) *Positive ethics for mental health professionals: a proactive approach*. Hoboken, NJ: John Wiley and Sons.

Arroll, M. (2023) *Tiny traumas: how to stop feeling stuck, anxious, low, unmotivated and unhappy, take back control of your life, and heal for good*. London: Thorsons.

Association for Coaching (AC). (2021) *Global code of ethics*. Available at: https://www.associationforcoaching.com/page/AboutCodeEthics?andhhsearchterms=%22professional+and+ethics%22 (Accessed: 9 December 2024).

Atad, O.I. and Grant, A.M. (2021) 'Evidence-based coaching as a supplement to traditional lectures: impact on undergraduates' goal attainment and measures of mental well-being', *International Journal of Mentoring and Coaching in Education*, 10(3), pp. 249–266. doi: 10.1108/IJMCE-05-2020-0024

Bazerman, M.H. and Tenbrunsel, A.E. (2011) *Blind spots: why we fail to do what's right and what to do about it*. Princeton: Princeton University Press.

Bernstein, A.F. (2023) 'Race matters in coaching: an empirical study of coaches' willingness to have difficult conversations with leaders of color', *Consulting Psychology Journal*, 75(1), pp. 32–50. doi: 10.1037/cpb0000241

Brann, A. (2017) *Neuroscience for coaches: how to use the latest insights for the benefit of your clients*. London: Kogan Page Publishers.

British Psychological Society (BPS). (2021). *Code of ethics and conduct*. Available at: https://www.bps.org.uk/guideline/code-ethics-and-conduct (Accessed: 9 December 2024).

Buckley, A. and Buckley, C. (2012) *A guide to coaching and mental health: the recognition and management of psychological issues*. Abingdon: Routledge.

Capstick, M.K., Harrell-Williams, L.M., Cockrum, C.D. and West, S.L. (2019) 'Exploring the effectiveness of academic coaching for academically at-risk college students', *Innovative Higher Education*, 44, pp. 219–231. doi: 10.1007/s10755-019-9459-1

Carroll, M. and Shaw, E. (2013) *Ethical maturity in the helping professions: making difficult life and work decisions*. London: Jessica Kingsley Publishers.

Corti, L. and Gelati, C. (2020) 'Mindfulness and coaching to improve learning abilities in university students: a pilot study', *International Journal of Environmental Research and Public Health*, 17(6). doi: 10.3390/ijerph17061935

Curtiss, P.R. and Warren, P.W. (1973) *The dynamics of life skills coaching*. Prince Albert: Saskatchewan New Start Incorporated.

De Jong, A. (2006) 'Coaching ethics: integrity in the moment of choice', in J. Passmore (ed.) *Excellence in coaching: the industry guide*. London: Kogan Page, pp. 191–202.

Dias, G.P., Foster, J. and Zunszain, P.A. (2019) 'Time to flourish: designing a coaching psychology programme to promote resilience and wellbeing in postgraduate students', *European Journal of Applied Positive Psychology*, 3(7), pp. 1–12.

Diller, S.J. (2024) 'Ethics in digital and AI coaching', *Human Resource Development International*, 27(4), pp. 584–596. doi: 10.1080/13678868.2024.2315928

Dryden, W. (1997) *Overcoming shame*. London: Sheldon Press.

Duffy, M. and Passmore, J. (2010) 'Ethics in coaching: an ethical decision making framework for coaching psychologists', *International Coaching Psychology Review*, 5(2), pp. 140–151.

Edmondson, A.C. (2018) *The fearless organization: creating psychological safety in the workplace for learning, innovation, and growth*. Hoboken, NJ: John Wiley and Sons.

European Mentoring and Coaching Council (EMCC). (2021). *The global code of ethics*. Available at: https://www.emccglobal.org/leadership-development/ethics/ (Accessed 16 December 2024).

Fatien, P. and Clutterbuck, D. (2023) 'What is ethics, and how does it apply to coaching?' In W.-A. Smith, J.E. Turner, Y.-L. Lai and D. Clutterbuck (eds.) *The ethical coaches' handbook*. Abingdon: Routledge, pp. 22–35.

Festinger, L. (1959) *Cognitive dissonance*. New York: Row, Peterson and Company.

Grant, A.M. (2008) 'Personal life coaching for coaches-in-training enhances goal attainment, insight and learning', *Coaching: An International Journal of Theory, Research and Practice*, 1(1), pp. 54–70. doi: 10.1080/17521880701878141

Grant, A.M. (2013) 'The efficacy of coaching', in J. Passmore, D. Peterson and T. Freire (eds.) *Handbook of the psychology of coaching and mentoring*. Chichester: Wiley Blackwell, pp. 15–39.

Grant, A.M. and O'Connor, S.A. (2010) 'The differential effects of solution-focused and problem-focused coaching questions: a pilot study with implications for practice', *Industrial and Commercial Training*, 42(2), pp. 102–111. doi: 10.1108/00197851011026090

Hawkins, P. and Turner, E. (2019) *Systemic coaching: delivering value beyond the individual*. Abingdon: Routledge.

Heitz, H.K. and Leach, M.M. (2022) 'Ethical knowledge, dilemmas and resolutions in professional coaching', *Coaching: An International Journal of Theory, Research and Practice*, 15(2), pp. 264–277.

Hillman, J., Lochtie, D. and Purcell, O. (2024) 'Black students' experiences of coaching and mentoring in higher education: a case study', *International Journal of Mentoring and Coaching in Education*, 13(2), pp. 246–257. doi: 10.1108/IJMCE-01-2023-0011

International Coaching Federation (ICF). (2021) *Global code of ethics*. Available at: https://coachingfederation.org/app/uploads/2021/01/ICF-Code-of-Ethics-1.pdf (Accessed: 9 December 2024).

International Coaching Federation Ethics Resources. (2024) Available at: https://coachingfederation.org/ethics/ethics-resources (Accessed: 9 December 2024).

Iordanou, I. and Hawley, R. (2020) 'Ethics in coaching', in J. Passmore (ed.) *The coaches' handbook: the complete practitioner guide for professional coaches*. Abingdon: Routledge, pp. 333–343.

Iordanou, I., Hawley, R. and Iordanou, C. (2016) *Values and ethics in coaching*. London: Sage.

Jones, J. and Smith, H.A. (2022) 'A comparative study of formal coaching and mentoring programmes in higher education', *International Journal of Mentoring and Coaching in Education*, 11(2), pp. 213–231. doi: 10.1108/IJMCE-03-2021-0054

Karin Askeland, M. (2009) 'A reflexive inquiry into the ideologies and theoretical assumptions of coaching', *Coaching: An International Journal of Theory, Research and Practice*, 2(1), pp. 65–75. doi: 10.1080/17521880902783132

Kearns, H., Forbes, A. and Gardiner, M. (2007) 'A cognitive behavioural coaching intervention for the treatment of perfectionism and self-handicapping in a nonclinical population', *Behaviour Change*, 24(3), pp. 157–172. doi: 10.1375/bech.24.3.157

Klayman, J. (1995) 'Varieties of confirmation bias', in J. Busemeyer, R. Hastie and D.L. Medin (eds.) *Psychology of learning and motivation*. London: Academic Press, pp. 385–418. doi: 10.1016/S0079-7421(08)60315-1

Köbis, L. and Mehner, C. (2021) 'Ethical questions raised by AI-supported mentoring in higher education', *Frontiers in Artificial Intelligence*. doi: 10.3389/frai.2021.624050

Lefdahl-Davis, E.M., Huffman, L., Stancil, J. and Alayan, A.J. (2018) 'The impact of life coaching on undergraduate students: a multiyear analysis of coaching outcomes', *International Journal of Evidence Based Coaching and Mentoring*, 16(2), pp. 69–83. doi: 10.24384/000560

Lewis, H. (1990) *A question of values*. San Francisco: Harper and Row.

Lowman, R.L. (2013) 'Coaching ethics', in J. Passmore, D. Peterson and T. Freire (eds.) *The Wiley-Blackwell handbook of the psychology of coaching and mentoring*. Chichester: Wiley-Blackwell, pp. 68–88.

Maltbia, T.E. and Prior, D.M. (2023) 'Race: ethical perspectives on equity-based coaching', in W.-A. Smith, J. Passmore, E. Turner, Y.L. Lai and D. Clutterbuck (eds.) *The ethical coaches' handbook: a guide to developing ethical maturity in practice*. Abingdon: Routledge, pp. 282–299.

Mcdowall, A. and Doyle, N. (2023) *Neurodiversity coaching: a psychological approach to supporting neurodivergent talent and career potential*. Abingdon: Routledge.

McLean, P. (2023) 'The psychological contract in coaching', in W.-A. Smith, J. Passmore, E. Turner, Y.L. Lai and D. Clutterbuck (eds.) *The ethical coaches' handbook: a guide to developing ethical maturity in practice*. Abingdon: Routledge, pp. 114–127.

McMahon, G., Palmer, S. and Wilding, C. (2005) *Achieving excellence in your coaching practice: how to run a highly successful coaching business*. Abingdon: Routledge.

Neff, K. (2003) 'Self-compassion: an alternative conceptualization of a healthy attitude toward oneself', *Self and Identity*, 2(2), pp. 85–101.

Nosek, B.A., Banaji, M.R. and Greenwald, A.G. (2002) 'Harvesting implicit group attitudes and beliefs from a demonstration web site', *Group Dynamics: Theory, Research, and Practice*, 6(1), pp. 101–115. doi: 10.1037/1089-2699.6.1.101

Passmore, J., Peterson, D. and Freire, T. (2013) 'The psychology of coaching and mentoring', in J. Passmore, D. Peterson and T. Freire (eds.) *The Wiley-Blackwell handbook of the psychology of coaching and mentoring*. Malden, MA: Wiley-Blackwell, pp. 3–11.

Passmore, J. and Turner, E. (2018) *Reflections on integrity – the APPEAR model. Coaching at Work*. Available at: https://www.coaching-at-work.com/2018/02/23/reflections-on-integrity-the-appear-model/ (Accessed: 18 December 2024).

Project Implicit. (no date) *Implicit association tests*. Available at: https://www.projectimplicit.net/ (Accessed: 9 December 2024).

Riordan, B.G. (2020) *Feedback fundamentals and evidence-based best practices: give it, ask for it, use it*. Abingdon: Routledge.

Robinson, C. and Gahagan, J. (2010) 'Coaching students to academic success and engagement on campus', *About Campus*, 15(4), pp. 26–29.

Rosinski, P. (2010) *Coaching across cultures: new tools for leveraging national, corporate and professional differences*. London: Nicholas Brealey Publishing.

Ryde, J. (2009) *Being white in the helping professions: developing effective intercultural awareness*. London: Jessica Kingsley Publishers.

Schlosser, L.Z. and Foley, P.F. (2008) 'Ethical issues in multicultural student–faculty mentoring relationships in higher education', *Mentoring and Tutoring: Partnership in Learning*, 16(1), pp. 63–75.

Shapira-Lishchinsky, O. (2012) 'Mentors' ethical perceptions: implications for practice', *Journal of Educational Administration*, 50(4), pp. 437–462.

Shaukat, R. (2024) 'Impact of group think in decision making process across different professional groups', *International Research Journal of Management and Social Sciences*, 5(2), pp. 410–432.

Smith, W.-A., Passmore, J., Turner, E., Lai, Y.-L. and Clutterbuck, D. (2023) *The ethical coaches' handbook: a guide to developing ethical maturity in practice*. Abingdon: Routledge.

Taylor, C. (2015) 'A guide to ethics and student engagement through partnership'. Available at: https://www.heacademy.ac.uk/sites/default/files/guide_to_ethics.pdf (Accessed: 20 November 2024).

Terblanche, N.H. and Heyns, M. (2020) 'The impact of coachee personality traits, propensity to trust and perceived trustworthiness of a coach, on a coachee's trust behaviour in a coaching relationship', *SA Journal of Industrial Psychology*, 46(1), pp. 1–11.

Townsend, C. (2011) 'Ethical frameworks in coaching', in J. Passmore (ed.) *Supervision in coaching: supervision, ethics and continuous professional development.* London: Kogan Page, pp. 141–149.

Turner, E. and Passmore, J. (2018) 'Ethical dilemmas and tricky decisions: a global perspective of coaching supervisors' practices in coach ethical decision-making', *International Journal of Evidence Based Coaching and Mentoring*, 16(1), pp. 126–142.

UK General Data Protection Regulation Guidance. (2024) Available at: https://uk-gdpr.org/ (Accessed: 9 December 2024).

Van Nieuwerburgh, C. (2020). *An introduction to coaching skills: a practical guide.* London: Sage.

Wang, Q. and Lu, Y. (2020) 'Coaching college students in the development of positive learning dispositions: a randomized control trial embedded mixed-methods study', *Psychology in the Schools*, 57(9), pp. 1417–1438. doi: 10.1002/pits.22421

Wanless, S.B. (2016) 'The role of psychological safety in human development', *Research in Human Development*, 13(1), pp. 6–14.

2 Coaching and mentoring through an equity lens

Jo Blissett and Enya-Marie Clay

The equity lens is a tool with roots in anti-oppressive practice and universal design (UD) which can be widely applied across higher education (HE) student support services and to individual practice. By taking this approach, professionals can enhance equity in both their own practice and within the systems and processes in which they work. In doing so, equity can be further embedded into student support in HE which in turn, contributes to greater outcomes and opportunities for all to thrive in the manner that is most important to them as an individual.

Authors Jo Blissett and Enya-Marie Clay invite readers to consider how equity can be embedded within the heart of both practice and service design using a person-centred, equity-minded and reflexive approach. This chapter discusses the benefits of treating students differently to treat them fairly using the Personal Learning Advice (PLA) Service's Coaching and Mentoring Professional Framework as an example of how this can be applied in practice. It also invites readers to view their own practice and student support mechanisms through an equity lens by providing an overview of the approach alongside a series of reflective exercises. This is situated within wider contexts of anti-oppressive practice, UD and decolonisation in student support services. It is hoped that in doing this, a ripple effect is created wherein transformative change in professional practice and systems benefits students and staff, as well as the institutional spaces we inhabit, to create improved equity in teaching and learning.

DOI: 10.4324/9781003486015-3

Introduction

This chapter invites practitioners to use an equity lens approach to review and develop their own professional practice as well as the systems and processes within which their practice sits for the purpose of enhancing equity within HE through person-centred approaches, informed reflexivity and creativity. It does this by introducing a practitioner framework that was developed to meet the needs of a specific coaching and mentoring service, The Open University's (OU) PLA Service, as a mechanism to demonstrate how an equity lens approach may be practically applied in a specific context (Clay *et al.*, 2023). The learning gained from developing this framework is then shared so that it may be widely applied in student-facing contexts across HE. This chapter then discusses the literature and rationale underpinning this approach and offers practical and reflective exercises for practitioners to apply to their own professional practice for the purposes of working towards equitable access to and experiences of education for all. In doing this, key concepts from UD, intersectionality and anti-oppressive practice are explored with the application of the equity lens being a practical method for bringing these elements together and applying them to both practice and service design. Considerations for future applicability and expansion of the equity lens approach bring this chapter to a close, inviting practitioners to critically engage with the development and functionality of the approach including its applicability across student support services, for instance, in decolonisation work and co-production among staff and students.

PLA Service coaching and mentoring framework: background and context

The PLA Service was established in 2021, employing a team of professional coaches and mentors to deliver tailored one-to-one and small group support to undergraduate students as part of a wider institutional aim to achieve equity in student experiences and outcomes. As noted in the introduction to this volume, this approach was one of many identified by the institution's 2020–2025 Access and Participation Plan (APP, Open University, 2020) and was designed to complement and not replace the existing Information, Advice and Guidance (IAG) support already available to students (described further in Chapter 7). It became evident during the iterative development of the service and of the team that clear practitioner guidelines were required to:

a. Foster shared understanding of core practices involved in the role.
b. Support reflective practice of the PLA team.
c. Provide a framework to inform quality assurance (QA).
d. Allow flexibility for all practitioners.

It was in this context a working group was set up to create a Coaching and Mentoring Framework. Our working group consisted of five Personal Learning Advisors (PLAs, all coach/mentors, including this chapter's authors). Our approach involved desk activity reviewing existing coaching and mentoring literature and frameworks, exploring anti-oppressive practice and more broadly, equitable practice; and examining our institution's Equality, Diversity and Inclusion (EDI) work. Based on the findings of this interdisciplinary literature review, practitioner experience and feedback, we identified a suitable approach to create the PLA Coaching and Mentoring Framework which consisted of (Figure 2.1).

As a result of this, as a working group we further identified several additional important factors that were elemental in the consideration of our approach and the development of our Coaching and Mentoring Framework (Clay *et al.*, 2023). Specifically, we also aimed to:

a. Establish coaching and mentoring for equity in HE for practitioners from a range of professional backgrounds.
b. Identify coaching and mentoring core competencies and key skills to support student equity.

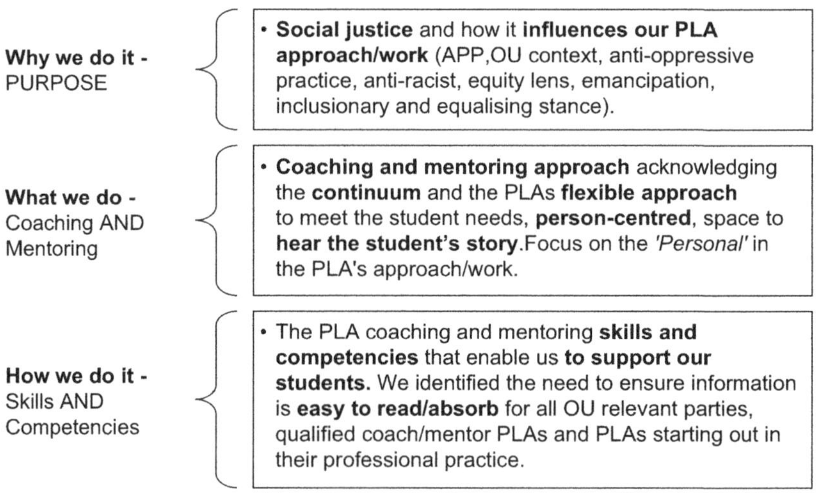

Figure 2.1 Overview of the PLA framework.

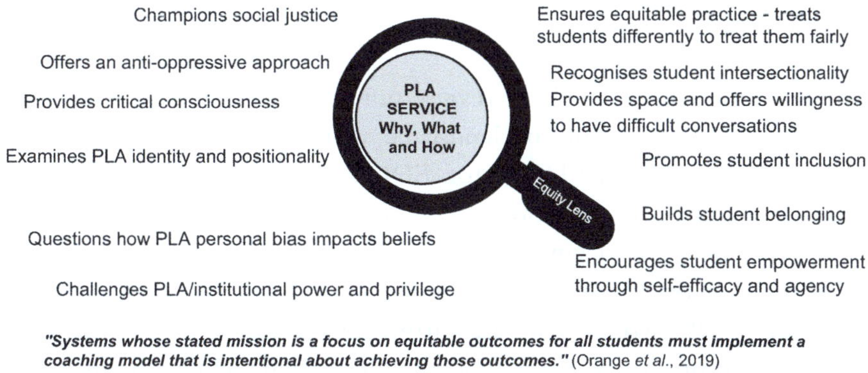

Figure 2.2 PLA coaching and mentoring through an equity lens.

c. Recognise societal context and the impact of coaching and mentoring interventions beyond study.
d. Centre our learning from students and ensure our practice is 'anti-oppressive,' accessible and inclusive.

Taking these previously identified needs and additional elemental factors into consideration our working group identified and developed the 'equity lens'; this became fundamental to our approach, as well as to the Framework in its entirety. Taking an equity lens approach is essentially using a mechanism to look at a service or at professional practice that recognises student intersectionality and incorporates UD principles of embedded accessibility for all (Center for Applied Special Technology [CAST], 2018), as well as anti-oppressive approaches (Figure 2.2).

In summary, introducing an equity lens to our Coaching and Mentoring Framework helped us:

- Ensure equitable practice;
- Recognise student intersectionality;
- Provide space and willingness to have difficult conversations;
- Promote student inclusion;
- Build student belonging;
- Encourage student empowerment through self-efficacy and agency;
- Champion social justice;
- Offer an anti-oppressive approach;
- Examine practitioner identity and positionality;
- Provide critical consciousness;
- Question how practitioner personal bias impact beliefs; and
- Challenge practitioner/institutional power and privilege.

Development

Through conducting a literature review, our working group gained a more nuanced understanding of the landscape within which the PLA Service sits – within The OU, the HE sector, EDI and social justice work and the fields of coaching and mentoring. This research identified both the need and value of applying an 'equity lens' to the PLA Service, at a Service design level as well as a practitioner level, in addition to the process of creating the Framework itself. To do this, we drew from various sources in our reading to identify key components of equitable practice which included but were not limited to: the value of a person-centred approach (Joseph, 2006); avoiding a potential 'deficit' approach (Campbell and McKendrick, 2017); flexibility and adaptiveness to individual needs (Clutterbuck, 2014; Megginson and Clutterbuck, 2015); recognising that coaching is not neutral (Shoukry and Cox, 2018); acknowledging practitioner privilege (Terry, 2021; Chiu, 2022); and practitioner bias (Orange *et al.*, 2019). From our discussions and critical reflections around these areas, we also drew from practitioner experiences and observations, and student qualitative feedback.

These findings include:

- Holding space for deep storytelling;
- Co-creating a trusting relationship;
- Validating student lived experiences;
- Being comfortable with uncertainty;
- Normalising seeking support and challenging;
- Delivering support along the coaching-mentoring continuum;
- Advocating for students;
- Building connection and community in student and staff contexts;
- Reflecting upon our own biases and privileges;
- Valuing the breadth and depth of practitioner experience with the team; and
- Proactively communicating challenges and feedback to the institution and existing systems to affect change.

Using these points as well as our findings from the contexts explored above (Clay *et al.*, 2023), we created a framework that is intended to be both functional and research informed and that has equity at its heart.

Higher education context

To familiarise ourselves with approaches to equity in education, we explored critical race theory (Reid, 2020, 2021), Bourdieu's theory of practice (Bourdieu, 1977) and anti-oppressive pedagogies (hooks, cited in: Valcarlos *et al.*, 2020). We also explored ongoing work in racial inequalities within the HE sector, accessibility of language and awarding gaps from both an institutional and student standpoint (for instance, using a National Union of Student report, Universities UK, 2019 as well as student blogs and publications).

A key finding from this exploration was the entrenched nature of inequality across levels of education within the UK and the impact this has on degree awarding gaps, both in regard to degree outcomes but also in student experiences and student satisfaction. A further finding was the identification of a need for institutional commitment to change, and how centralising student narratives and placing further value on experiential knowledge could support the effectiveness of this change. While decolonisation has been an area of focus for universities in recent years, the focus of this work primarily concerns broader institutional changes and curriculum development (Omodan, 2024). It is hoped that by looking at student support service provision and practice through an equity lens, practical ideas for creating transformative change are brought to the fore.

Coaching and mentoring contexts

We used Shoukry's 'Coaching for Emancipation' as a starting point for examining the potential limitations of coaching in supporting individuals in oppressive environments (Shoukry, 2016, p. 17). Shoukry demonstrates the importance for the individualistic nature of coaching practice not to detract from societal and structural oppression. Instead, an anti-oppressive approach is a vehicle for creating change through 'framing, challenging, and questioning' current system(s) (Shoukry, 2016, p. 17).

We explored various texts and resources on coaching and mentoring as approaches for social justice and equity work, as well as their application in a HE context. Findings from this reading were extensive as coaching and mentoring both encompass a broad and diverse range of activities (Ives, 2008) and are relatively new areas of formalised practice. These diverse approaches are underpinned by different assumptions and understanding regarding the roles involved (e.g. coach/mentor, coachee/mentee), as well as the focus of the coaching and mentoring, and the mediums through which they are deployed. A key finding was using traditional goal- or performance-based coaching/mentoring in an educational context can risk placing undue emphasis and pressure on students to adapt to an unequal system, rather than addressing and alleviating the structural inequalities they experience. Our exploration into using an equity lens approach for coaching and mentoring sought to address this by ensuring equitable practice was at the core of the PLA Service's Framework approach.

Meeting the needs of the PLA Service

PLA coaching and mentoring approach

When creating our PLA Coaching and Mentoring Framework, our working group identified the need to build on 'why' (our purpose), to explore the 'what' – or specifically what coaching and mentoring in our service looked like, and to outline the 'how' – which involved developing core competencies, skills and development areas. Looking at the two propositions of coaching and mentoring, it is useful to note that there are far more similarities than differences in approaches, with the two areas often being described as 'intertwined and mixed' (Passmore, 2021, p. 8). Both have at their heart the intention of using the learning conversation co-actively to help the individual to elicit and develop their own capacity to find solutions, to see new perspectives and to move in new directions.

Coaching and mentoring combine to create an applied form of practice that has intellectual roots in a range of disciplines. There is a wealth of learning materials in the coaching and mentoring literature and with the support of peer-led continuing professional development (CPD), such as monthly 'spotlight sessions' that explore specific techniques, models or areas of best practice; PLA practitioners are enabled to understand the theories and psychological models behind their work. This allows them to apply these effectively and appropriately in a student support context using the Framework as an underpinning structure.

In the PLA team, we are student-led using active listening throughout to enable 'useful conversations.' We are open to knowledge of simple models and processes such as GROW, OSKAR and CLEAR (Passmore, 2021). GROW and OSKAR are both outlined in detail in Chapters 4 and 7 of this volume; and CLEAR is set out in Chapter 8. We use these models when we feel they are appropriate but are not bound by one specific model or resource base. Megginson and Clutterbuck (2015) reason that both coaching and mentoring are primarily open-ended conversations with a purpose. They go on to argue that there is a negative impact of using a prescriptive toolkit (model, process or theoretical framework) to drive the learning conversation, rather than the conversation driving the selection and use of tools and techniques. In an approach Clutterbuck calls 'managed eclecticism,' it is argued these techniques, models and processes ought to be understood within the origins of their own philosophy. This, in turn, enables a coach to develop their own, continually expanding, adapting and evolving philosophy based on experimentation and reflective learning. Clutterbuck argues that this liberates the practitioner, and the development of their own philosophy is a measure of their relative maturity as a professional coach (Clutterbuck, 2010).

Cox, Bachkirova and Clutterbuck (2014) offers investment in more in-depth models of coaching ranging from Wellbeing Coaching to Existential Coaching to evoke new awareness in students of what can be. It is often considered that no one model will work for all. Providing flexibility and an individualised, person-centred approach is core to the PLA Service, with 90 percent of students agreeing or strongly agreeing this personalised support helped them complete their module(s), and our working group identified this as being a valuable component to equitable practice.

Overview of the PLA coaching and mentoring continuum

Coaching/mentoring sessions give time and space to a student. They enable a coaching/mentoring approach to take place and skills to be used from the PLA coaching/mentoring continuum. This allows appropriate provision for each individual student and how they are presenting that day.

The Venn diagram in Figure 2.3 encapsulates the space PLAs offer to students. A PLA session will not often follow a linear journey, there is movement between coaching and mentoring. There is no assumption that one approach is superior to the other; we meet the student where they are and navigate the journey with them. Central to this approach, is creating a holistic and collaborative learning conversation between student and practitioner which is supported by a range of coaching and mentoring skills applied in mutuality. The centre of the Venn diagram highlights the 'five pillars' of our Coaching and Mentoring Framework:

- Establishing the approach;
- Co-creating the relationship (contracting);
- Communicating effectively;
- Empowering action; and
- Reviewing results.

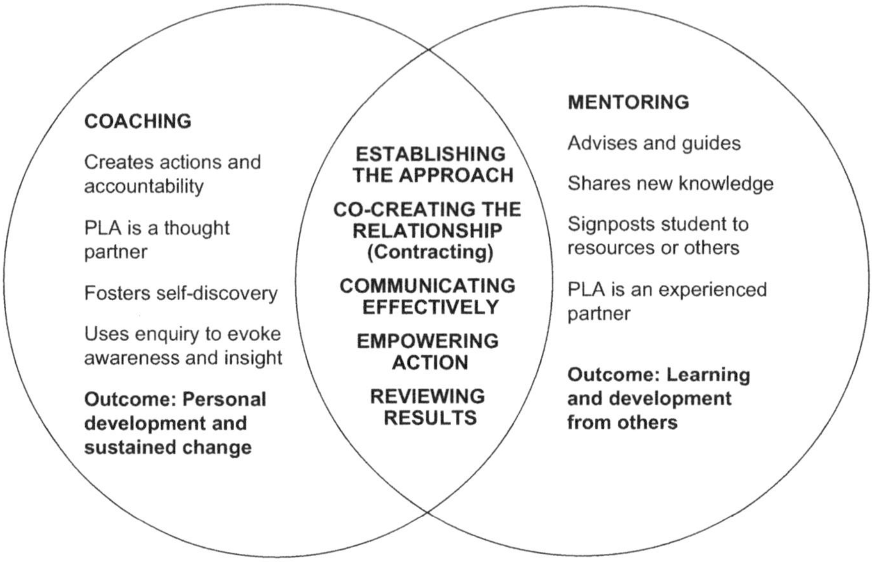

Figure 2.3 Overview of PLA coaching and mentoring practice.

These five pillars form the foundation of our core competencies and they underpin our coaching and mentoring practice as well as the key skills we employ.

In demonstrating the 'five pillars,' a PLA (coach/mentor) will be using skills that are chosen to best serve the student in front of them at that moment in time. This person-centred approach allows a unique experience to take place based on the context, lived experience and individual set of circumstances. It recognises student narratives with unconditional positive regard, as originally developed by Carl Rogers (1957; Yates, 2022), openness and curiosity.

Building on the *'PLA Why'* (our purpose) and the *'PLA What'* (our coaching and mentoring continuum), in our working group we turned our attention to the core competencies and key skills that inform 'how' we work as coaches. There were several key factors that our working group took into consideration when identifying core competencies and key skills that would support student groups traditionally underrepresented in HE. These factors included:

- Using a person-centred approach which considers a person holistically, an individual and not as part of a homogenous group;

- Flexibility in working with students in a way that allows them to access PLA coaching/mentoring support to ensure a differentiated approach and recognition of the value of difference;
- Recognising intersectionality and respecting students' decisions whether to share aspects of their identity;
- Encouraging students to move away from limiting beliefs;
- Empowering students to take action;
- Committing to change PLA (coach/mentor) self-awareness, recognition of privileges and recognition of biases; and
- Sharing feedback about learning in the PLA Service to engender meaningful, long-term change to challenge structural inequities in The OU and across HE.

Combining our 'PLA Why and What' approaches with these factors, in our working group we identified a set of PLA coaching and mentoring core competencies and key skills, adapted from the International Coaching Federation (ICF) Core Competencies (International Coaching Federation [ICF], 2019).

The example in Figure 2.4 demonstrates a selection of the skills that could be used in a session by a PLA (coach/mentor) drawing from a comprehensive list in the Framework (Appendix D – *How we do it – PLA core competencies and key skills*). They are examples on either end of the Coaching and Mentoring continuum. The skills on the left-hand side of

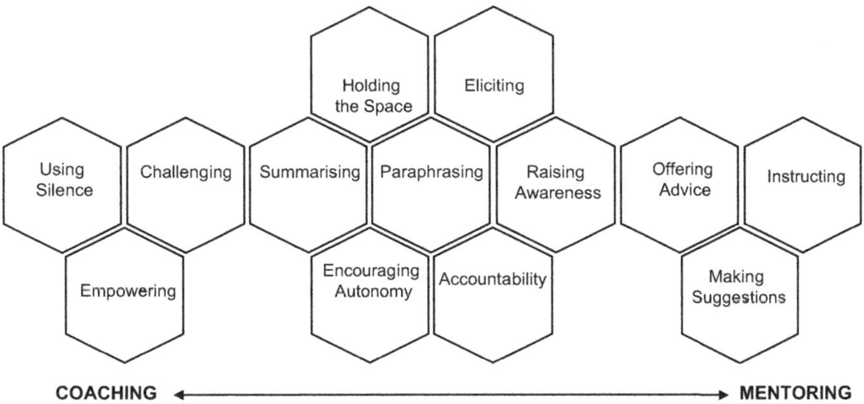

Figure 2.4 Example core competencies/key skills used within the PLA coaching and mentoring continuum – adapted from the International Coaching Federation (2022).

the image place more of an emphasis on coaching while the skills on the right-hand side place more of an emphasis on mentoring. Our work covers the whole spectrum and many of our sessions will sit as a hybrid mix, often covering a multitude of identified skills from across the continuum, in order to adapt to and provide flexibility for individual student needs.

The specific details of the competencies and skills use in our service are detailed in Appendix D – *How we do it – PLA core competencies and key skills.* This explicit list covers the whole spectrum of Coaching and Mentoring and ensures we keep the equity lens at the heart of our work.

In summary, the PLA Service's coaching/mentoring work has been developed through an equity lens. This involves exploring the individual needs of a student to provide the right support at the right time. PLA coaching/mentoring seeks to remove barriers to student opportunity, advancing anti-oppressive practice and promoting diverse and inclusive practice – *treating students differently to treat them fairly.* We invite readers to reflect on the following questions to consider the core competencies and key skills necessary to effectively support all students in their own professional practice or service:

1. How do you identify the essential core competencies and key skills that are needed to effectively support your students?
2. How, when and where do you demonstrate these core competencies and key skills?
3. How do you ensure that these core competencies and key skills meet the needs of all your students?
4. What training, support or professional qualification might you/others need to further develop your core competencies or key skills?
5. How frequently will you review your core competencies and key skills, and what time and resources can you commit to their development?

Equity lens: beyond protected characteristics

In developing the equity lens, two other concepts became a key part of our working group discussions: *intersectionality* (Crenshaw, 1989, 1991) and, at a service level, *universal design* (CAST, 2018). An in-depth exploration of both is beyond the scope of this chapter. Instead, however, we aim to share our experiences of how both concepts can be applied to coaching and mentoring and wider areas of student support to underpin student equity and inclusion.

Considering student intersectionality

Within the HE landscape, it is important to acknowledge the current legal and ethical responsibilities to provide a non-discriminatory and supportive educational environment. As universities, we are obligated to uphold anti-discrimination laws and promote equity, diversity and inclusion in all aspects of learning and university life (UK Equality Act, 2010). In our research, we observed that most HE interventions select a particular student cohort or demographic group based on characteristics or identity markers that are often tied to the specific 'protected characteristics' outlined in the Equality Act 2010 and detailed in individual Access and Participation Plans – a regulatory requirement for HE institutions (HEIs) in England (Office for Students [OfS], 2024). Although this approach represents an initial step in acknowledging the various levels at which students experience discrimination and inequalities occur, it often forms a fragmented understanding of these characteristics. It overlooks the systemic foundations and interconnected nature of these discriminations, which together create systems of disadvantage and exclusion that can impact on student participation, experience, achievement and outcome.

Intersectionality offers an alternative to this approach. It stems from CRT and is most often associated with scholar Kimberlé Crenshaw (1989, 1991) who introduced the term to explain how individual aspects of identity (gender, ethnicity, class, etc.) interact with race. Crenshaw identified three key concepts; first, that social inequalities are not experienced as isolated, separate phenomenon of race, class, age, gender, sexuality, ability, socio-economic status and other identity markers, but as mutually constitutive (having equal and interconnected influence on each other), or reciprocally constructed phenomena. Second, rejecting the notion of defining an individual's experience based on a single identity or category of difference and assuming the primary importance of any one category. Third, and most crucially, intersectionality focuses on how gender, race and other identity markers interact, along with the situational context of when, where and how these identities emerge and shape an individual's experiences across various forms of societal oppression. Overall, intersectionality acknowledges the differences between individual identities while also considering the influence of social power structures and the resulting social inequalities.

In the context of HE in the UK, intersectionality has increasingly become a focus for addressing inequalities and ensuring that institutions support and celebrate diverse student populations in more inclusive and equitable ways. This focus is further emphasised by the regulatory measures that universities need to address such as gaps in access, retention, attainment and progression among traditionally underrepresented groups (OfS, 2024).

The Office for Students identifies student intersectionality as being critical to successfully addressing these measures as it encourages universities to move beyond one-dimensional approaches to tackling inequality, taking into account the overlapping disadvantages experienced by students with intersecting identities or characteristics. There is also the increasing recognition that traditional university approaches to teaching and learning, student wellbeing and the provision of student support services may not adequately serve students with complex identities, particularly where multiple aspects of these intersectional identities may risk the student to experiencing various systemic inequalities. However, as coaching/mentoring practitioners we acknowledge the critique surrounding the concept of intersectionality.

Firstly, while intersectionality has gained widespread recognition in academia, activism and policymaking; Christofferson (2021) and Nash (2019), among others, argue that as the concept becomes more mainstream and commodified to encompass a wide range of identities, its original focus on race and ethnicity, particularly Black women's experiences, has been diluted or downplayed. Secondly, intersectionality's institutional acceptance can result in its use as a 'buzzword' – stripped of the radical critique of power that underpins it. This can lead to intersectionality being employed in ways that serve institutional measures or goals, sector evaluation and reporting, or as a catch-all for institutional EDI initiatives, while failing to engage with the deeper issues of racial and social justice. This position is also supported by Ahmed (2012) who argues that diversity initiatives in universities often tokenise intersectionality without fully addressing the structural inequalities it aims to confront. Furthermore, Ahmed contends that universities may adopt intersectionality as part of their institutional language yet fail to tackle deeply rooted racial and ethnic disparities. This 'surface-level' engagement with intersectionality may serve to maintain institutional power structures while giving the appearance of inclusivity.

Notwithstanding these criticisms and the competing understandings of intersectionality, at a service level, it was important that we ensured our approach to providing coaching and mentoring through an equity lens incorporated student intersectionality that demonstrated cultural competency and was sensitive to various student identities. We approached this in three ways. Firstly, by recognising and valuing the diverse identities of our students and by giving priority to listening to their individual voice and lived experience in order to better understand how the intersections of their identities shaped their lives, and in turn their study experience. Secondly, by recognising the significance that students possess multiple, overlapping identities and that they do not experience discrimination or privilege in a singular or isolated manner. Students from intersecting marginalised groups often face unique barriers that are not experienced by those with singular or less marginalised identities. For instance, a Black, disabled, neurodivergent student may experience racism and ableism simultaneously, which can affect and influence their university experiences, challenges and outcomes. Thirdly, we identified the importance of deepening our knowledge and understanding of the broader key elements of intersectionality, such as how power dynamics shape the interaction of different identities, influencing students' access to resources and opportunities and ultimately affecting their overall university experience. Furthermore, when focussing on student intersectionality as a working group we considered it vital to build our equity lens approach around the knowledge that students are not just members of a particular demographic 'group' and to look beyond the often oversimplified, institutional data driven view of students. However, we acknowledge that this 'grouping' or 'labelling' is often connected to wider HEI regulatory reporting and sector funding. Two students from the same 'group' might have very different experiences, so in our coaching and mentoring activities we continually check that we are not falling back on assumptions about homogeneity or stereotypes. We also maintain that a focus on student intersectionality is not employed to replace specific focus on racial justice within institutions and the wider HE sector. Understanding student intersections has helped us in addressing individuals specific study challenges more holistically and built on our 'person-centred' approach to ensure that we are not delivering coaching and mentoring in a vacuum.

The effect of our focus on student intersectionality combined with an equity lens approach in our work became apparent when reviewing student feedback (Hillman, Lochtie and Purcell, 2024; Blissett *et al.*, 2023). When students received coaching and mentoring from the PLA Service that acknowledged their intersectional identities it reduced feelings of isolation and marginalisation, leading to an increased sense of belonging and mattering, combined with developing self-confidence and self-advocacy:

> I felt listened too and understood all the time [sic]. I felt safe and welcome. Being able to say that things weren't all that great, at particular times, was a relief beyond words. Being heard is different to being listened to. Being allowed to speak and being respected for having a voice was such an incredible experience.
>
> At the group workshops it was encouraging to note that there were others who had the same fears that you had. Others who sometimes felt they could give up but persevered. It was good to know that you are not alone.
>
> They helped me to see the skills that I have and helped me realise that being Neurodivergent is not a flaw, but actually, something, that

> brings out lots of positive strengths. The coaching sessions made me find purpose through challenging times, also made me realise that I am the one who can unlock all these great powers because I have the skills and I am determined.
>
> Having [a coach/mentor] has helped to steady me at times when I have felt overwhelmed. It has been very helpful having someone to talk to about study that is involved with the [university].
>
> My [coach/mentor] challenged my some of my patterns/blocks of thinking (with permission), enabled slight paradigm shifts and support and encouraged me consistently. This alone improved my TMA [tutor marked assessment] grades by about ten percent and created new ways of how I approached some of my personal challenges within work and home. It enabled more time balance within my life structures and was a great source of information and guidance.

As professional practitioners we create and hold space for our students, using an equity lens to see, hear and acknowledge the intersectional challenges and inequalities they face; and together we explore possible study solutions. In turn, on behalf of our students we can also use our own 'voice and power' to continue to draw attention to and inform our institutions and the wider sector of these entrenched inequalities. Nevertheless, we acknowledge the numerous challenges and barriers that staff within HEIs can face when looking at their own approaches and work in supporting students. These are often, but not limited to time and money constraints; sector reporting demands; institutional processes and procedures; a lack of knowledge and resources; limited staff awareness; and access to training. In our work we hope to highlight the benefits of applying an equity lens to student practice and we argue that this approach has a more holistic, wider service applicability ensuing that students are better supported. In turn, more staff and services can use their own voice or power to draw attention to entrenched inequalities, undertaking this labour on behalf of students.

For the PLA Service, incorporating intersectionality within our equity lens coaching and mentoring approach was not just beneficial but crucial for developing effective strategies to recognise the diverse needs of all our students, promoting social justice, equity and inclusion. By incorporating this complexity in our framework, we have been able to create a more tailored, inclusive coaching and mentoring approach that seeks to ensure that students' lived experiences are not overlooked or misunderstood and that students feel seen, heard, understood and valued in their full identities. Consequently, we invite readers to consider the following questions when considering student intersectionality and their own professional practice or service.

Reflective questions: intersectionality

- How does your race, gender, class and other social positions enable your actions in some instances and constrain them in others?
- What assumptions might you be making about the students you work with?
- How do you seek to understand your students' or colleagues' lived experiences?
- How/where can you engage in wider conversations to develop your knowledge and understanding around intersectionality?
- How frequently will you review your understanding around intersectionality, and what time and resources can you commit to developing this?

Universal design – accessibility and inclusion

Looking more widely at the PLA Service, the UD principles of embedded accessibility, ease of use and inclusion (CAST, 2018) are key elements within our equity lens approach.

> By building inclusive practices into an institution's structure and operations, fewer reasonable adjustments will be needed over time. Where such adjustments are needed, the institution can be much more responsive to individual needs.
>
> (OfS, 2019, p. 2)

UD originated in the field of architecture from the work of Ron Mace. The premise behind UD was to create spaces that could be accessible to all individuals, regardless of age, ability or other factors. This is with the goal being to design environments that did not require subsequent adaptations or specialised designs, promoting inclusivity from the outset. Further work by the Center for Universal Design at North Carolina State University developed the seven foundation principles of UD to help guide the design of any product, service or environment to ensure they are accessible, usable and inclusive. These seven foundation principles identify the importance of equitable use, flexibility in use, simple and intuitive design, perceptible information, tolerance for error, low physical effort and size and space appropriate for approach and use – aiming to eliminate barriers before they arise (Centre for Excellence in Universal Design [CEUD], no date).

Although UD has its roots in the design field of architecture, further work by CAST (Center for Applied Special Technology) adapted its principles for application within education, leading to the development of universal design for learning (UDL) (CAST, 2018). UDL is founded on the principle of inclusion and aligns with the UK Professional Standards Framework for teaching and supporting learning in HE (Advance HE, 2023). It is a teaching and learning framework designed to ensure learning is accessible to a wide range of students by incorporating multiple methods of representation, engagement and expression. This approach emphasises flexibility in how information is presented, how students interact with it and the ways in which they demonstrate their knowledge and skills (Martin *et al.*, 2019). The goal of UDL is to proactively design instructional materials and methods that support all needs of learners, rather than retrofitting existing systems, processes or procedures to accommodate those with disabilities (Maguire and Hall, 2018). Moreover, this highlights the concern that providing students with an 'adjustment approach' to learning and support is frequently untimely and costly and requires an intense amount of resources from students and staff, including emotional labour and administrative burden.

Firstly, this 'adjustment approach' often requires the student to know in advance what adjustments or support they might need and have the skills, confidence and resources to self-advocate. Secondly, it can also force the student to identify as 'different' or accept a 'label,' in some instances requiring a formal medical diagnosis, and then to disclose this. Finally, when applying for or accessing adjustments, students often need to navigate complex systems and bureaucratic procedures, resulting in delays in decision-making and support provision (Policy Connect, 2020). These processes deepen inequalities as students depend on a series of steps that demand significant understanding and effort, for example, applying for Disabled Students' Allowance. As a result, it can be argued that an 'adjustment approach' focusses on student 'deficits' and is aligned to the medical model of disability that requires the individual to change. Instead, incorporating UD principles into service offerings focuses on the eradication of barriers, accessibility and participation and in turn, it aligns with the social model of disability and the view that an individual is not disabled by their impairment but from society and the environment (Oliver, 2009).

Looking wider afield, in considering the principles of UD, we acknowledge that universities and education regulatory bodies have previously identified that UDL can be viewed as a broader concept to incorporate both university physical spaces, social demands and processes and procedures.

As an extension to our work on the equity framework, we maintain that the concept of UD can be further extended to wider student support services (Burgstahler and Moore, 2009; Maguire and Hall, 2018; Policy Connect, 2020). Applying the same UD principles to student coaching and mentoring, information advice and guidance services, wellbeing and mental health support, careers and employability services, and learning development support can help ensure that these services are accessible and inclusive for all students, including those with disabilities, first-generation students and those from underrepresented backgrounds (DO-IT, no date). It is important to note that the principles of UD can be applied to all aspects of a student's study journey and their educational experience to underpin student equity.

When looking at the principles of UD and the work we have carried out in constructing our equity lens approach, we maintain that UD offers a number of wider benefits to practitioner practice, whole-service approaches and the wider institution concerns and measures; these include:

- **Promotion of equity and inclusion**: UD helps ensure that all students have access to the same resources and opportunities, regardless of their individual needs.
- **Improvement in student engagement and success**: By accommodating diverse needs, UD helps students engage more fully in their education.
- **Reduction in barriers**: UD addresses potential obstacles before they become issues, reducing the need for individual accommodations and retrofitting.
- **Support during the student journey:** A universally designed service is welcoming and functional for all students, contributing to a positive educational experience.
- **Increase efficiency:** UD can save time, effort and energy (both physical and mental) for both students and practitioners, alongside reducing the need for wider service or institutional adjustment cost (DO-IT, no date).

For example, the PLA Service offers coaching and mentoring through a range of mediums including phone calls, video calls via MS Teams and email in order to meet the diverse needs of students and how they want to engage. We are also able to offer 'flexible scheduling' to accommodate students juggling other commitments and/or life circumstances, such as employment, caring responsibilities or those managing their wellbeing while studying – working together to identify what works best for the individual student. Similarly, we offer a range of ways students can engage with our coaching and mentoring support (e.g. series of one-to-one sessions, group workshops, a single 'action-focused session, online resources) to help ensure that students with different needs, learning approaches or communication preferences can access support.

UD principles are intended to be a wide framework to inform rather than a rigid approach or specific procedures (CUDE, no date). Therefore, as an initial starting point, we invite readers to consider their individual practice or service approach to applying UD principles by completing the review activity in Table 2.1. We have also used this space to provide an example in Table 2.1 based on our activity in the PLA Service.

As previously indicated, we highlighted several benefits of incorporating UD principles to promote an inclusive and equitable approach, however,

Table 2.1 Mapping UD principles to service/practitioner activity

UD principles mapped to service/practitioner activity
Equitable use: *Useful to and accessible by people with diverse abilities. Provide the same means of use for all students; identical whenever possible, equivalent when not.*
• Offering coaching sessions via a variety of delivery methods – telephone, video/MS Teams, email, small group coaching. • Offering group workshops with materials sent in advance. • Offering 1:1 session to support workshop content. • Signposting to other support services – mental health team, disability support team, careers and employability service. • Working with students to access student support by normalising help-seeking behaviours and self-advocacy thereby encouraging independent learning.
Flexibility in use: *Accommodates a wide range of individual preferences and abilities. Provides choice.*
• Offering students a coaching space to *'come as you are.'* • Actively offering session adjustments to provide students with a choice of when and how to engage depending on how they feel in any given session thereby encouraging student 'ownership' and a balance of coachee/coach power. • Actively offering shorter sessions and flexible rescheduling to students with dynamic disabilities. • Providing a strengths-based reflective session on assessment feedback, developing student reflection. • Ensuring coaching sessions are undertaken at an adjustable pace to allow time for the student to process and engage in the coaching conversation.

(Continued)

Table 2.1 (Continued)

UD principles mapped to service/practitioner activity
Simple and intuitive design: *Easy to understand, regardless of the user's experience, knowledge, language skills or concentration level.*
• Using clean language throughout coaching sessions and in all communications. • Providing guidelines and instructions to inform students of what coaching is, how our coaching sessions and workshops are delivered. • Providing clear contracting that is boundary driven. • Identifying an adaptive approach to help fully explore students' individual needs and preferences. • Using/offering a range of coaching models or tools to ensure inclusivity and individualised support to encourage student growth mind-set.
Perceptible information: *Communicates necessary information effectively to the user, regardless of conditions or the user's sensory abilities.*
• Encouraging use of uncomplicated language. • Offering to explain 'academic language' and 'hidden curriculum,' which can increase feelings of belonging and improve accessibility among groups such as first-generation students and students who have been educated outside of the UK. • Identifying how students want to receive information – 'bite sized,' bullet-pointed, summarised, visual recordings or audio. • Providing students with a space to explore and experiment with their learning preferences. • Supporting students in exploring what works best for them as an independent learner and in self-advocacy when discussing specific learning needs across their learning journey.
Tolerance for error: *Minimises hazards and the adverse consequences of accidental or unintended actions.*
• Offering identified opportunities for regular student review and feedback. • Providing students with a confidential, safe space with a high level of psychological safety and trust. • Providing an automatic email reminder to the student ahead of a session or workshop. • Offering follow-up email after a session to recap/identify key actions.

(Continued)

Table 2.1 (Continued)

UD principles mapped to service/practitioner activity
• Checking/reviewing use of practitioner language, bias, power. • Inviting students to co-create the space and explore what works for them thereby individualising the space and working in partnership with learners. • Using feedback from students to ensure the student voice is captured and used as part of a continual improvement model to inform future service offers (in line with the theory of change methodology, Drucker, 1954).
Mindful of students' physical, mental and emotional energy and capacity levels: *Can be used efficiently and comfortably with minimal fatigue; student is in control of the level of challenge given.*
• Providing options of how to access coaching support – shorter sessions, ability to reschedule, coaching via video, phone or email. • Offer of providing notetaking/follow-up action plans with level of detail to be agreed with student. • Option of involving a student advocate and/or carer in coaching sessions. • Working with the student to support them in identifying and managing their own energy levels and capabilities in order to encourage healthy and sustainable learning practices.
Size and space appropriate for approach and use: *Appropriate size and space are provided for approach, reach, manipulation and use for all.*
• Offering a choice of length and frequency of coaching session(s) to accommodate range of student needs. • Offering both 1:1 and small group coaching sessions. • Offering coaching-based group workshops wherein students have full agency over their preferred level of interaction. • Ensuring software and hardware requirements kept to a minimum – a phone capable of receiving phone calls or a device connected to the internet that can use MS Teams (available on browser or via an app) or Skype; or can send and receive emails.

we also acknowledge certain limitations. UD may overgeneralise solutions, potentially neglecting the specific needs of some student groups. In some cases, tailoring services to unique individual needs might be more effective. Implementing UD can be resource-intensive, requiring significant time, effort and financial investment. Smaller institutions or services with limited budgets may struggle to fully adopt UD principles. Integrating UD into existing structures can also be complex and challenging, necessitating substantial changes to policies, curricula and infrastructure, which can pose difficulties for already stretched institutions. Additionally, there is often insufficient awareness and training about UD among faculty and staff. Without proper education and understanding, the effectiveness of UD implementation can be compromised. Lastly, some universal solutions might dilute specialised services crucial for certain groups, favouring broader solutions that do not fully meet their needs (Maguire and Hall, 2018; Martin *et al.*, 2019).

Notwithstanding, we argue that UD plays an important role in ensuring an equitable approach to student coaching and mentoring, as well as playing a crucial role in enhancing wider student services in HE. By employing its principles, we can help ensure that all students, regardless of their abilities, backgrounds or circumstances; have equal access to resources, support and opportunities for success. The overall goal here is that every student who needs to use a service should be able to do so comfortably and efficiently. By integrating UD principles into student services, HEIs can help create inclusive environments that cater to the diverse needs of their whole student population. Furthermore, when considering our own professional practice or service we can apply the UD principles to elements of our own work as a development and self-reflection tool to review how well we are considering student diversity and meeting the needs of all students. Accordingly, we invite readers to consider the following questions when thinking about their own professional practice or service.

Reflective questions: applying universal design principles

- What are the diverse characteristics of potential students who use your service? Who, if anyone, are you not considering/ignoring?
- What do you already do that ensures accessibility, useability and inclusion for all students, especially those in marginalised groups?
- What areas/elements of best practice from others/other services can you identify?
- How do you ensure student feedback on accessibility, useability and inclusion helps shape your professional practice/service?
- What training or support might you/others need to further develop your understanding?

Equity lens: an anti-oppressive approach

Alongside being underpinned by principles of intersectionality and UD, using the equity lens asks practitioners to adopt an anti-oppressive approach in their professional practice which this chapter will now explore. It is vital to emphasise here that exploring, learning about and discussing anti-oppression and inclusion will always be a dynamic, ongoing process. This is due to the pace at which the conversation and practice is evolving, but also due to the necessary nuance in understanding complex issues that affect both groups and individuals in a myriad of ways, particularly when in response to shifting societal, political and economic climates.

In recognising this, it is also valuable to acknowledge that this is a learning journey which we will all come to imperfectly and that can bring both vulnerability and discomfort. Sitting with that discomfort and vulnerability is part of the process. In the following section, the key concepts involved in this will be discussed in relation to an equity lens approach and readers will be invited to undertake a range of activities to prompt reflection, learning and engagement with that approach. Finally, we will share an example of how practitioners in our own service have engaged with this via the creation of staff development workshops.

With roots in social work, the term 'anti-oppressive' has derived from disciplines of sociology, psychology, history, philosophy and politics (Burke and Harrison, 2002). In taking an anti-oppressive approach, one is going beyond inclusion and is, instead, *actively* seeking for ways to challenge oppressive structures. When discussing the concept of oppression in this context, we are discussing institutionalised power that is historically formed and perpetuated over time in addition to the prejudicial thoughts and actions of individuals (*Research Guides: Anti-Oppression and Equity Resources,* no date). Anti-oppressive practice also involves being reflexive and asks that practitioners continually reflect on how their own identities, intersectionality, power and privilege impacts on their practice. This reflexivity lends itself well to coaching and mentoring practice where reflection is embedded within the main coaching bodies' codes of ethics and is a core component to practitioner development as well as the coaching and mentoring processes themselves (Abrahamsson *et al.*, 2015).

In HE, the terms 'belonging,' 'inclusion' and 'widening participation' are often used when discussing equality and diversity (Gibson *et al.*, 2016; Cureton and Gravestock, 2019). While these terms are widely accepted and yet, not uncontested in their appropriateness, they are suggestive of student assimilation rather than institutional change. These terms refer to the acknowledgement, valuing, celebration and empowerment of difference whereas anti-oppression challenges the systems and systemic biases that devalue and marginalise difference. The use of the term 'anti-oppressive' brings up stronger associations of active challenge and looks beyond the view of the legal obligations required towards protected characteristics (Berila, 2023, p. 5). By incorporating all of these terms into our values and our individual practices as well as our processes and systems, practitioners can commit to and actively work on how they can be part of positive change in the promotion of educational opportunity, social justice and equity.

Anti-oppressive and inclusive practice workshops

One of the ways in which we shared our learning and best practice in the PLA Service around anti-oppressive and inclusive practice using the aforementioned concepts was by creating a workshop for staff development purposes. Developed with volume co-authors Enya-Marie Clay, Mary-Jayne Wilton and Helen William; the workshops sought to create a safe and reflective environment for attendees to share learning and discuss what the concepts meant to them and how it impacted upon their role as a professional. Initially created with student-facing staff in mind, this workshop was then extended to other professional services colleagues within the university. These workshops used coaching and mentoring approaches, as well as some of the activities used in the next section of this chapter, to offer challenge and a reflective space to the attendees in a collaborative thinking environment.

It was found that attendees wanted to use the workshops as a discussion space to reflect on their own experiences, to respond to the concepts introduced and to process their learning from the session. Feedback from attendees was positive with attendees talking about the impact it had made on their practice and on the benefits of having a held space to discuss professional practice through this lens.

Key learning from creating and facilitating these workshops include:

- Contracting at the beginning of the session around topics like psychological safety (Advance HE, no date), bringing curiosity rather than judgement, confidentiality and the logistics of the session and referring back to these throughout the session (explored further in Chapter 3). For example, referring to the post-session support available before discussing a challenging area of the workshop such as reflecting on one's own privilege and lived experiences (explored further later in this chapter).

- Allowing a generous amount of time for discussion and being prepared to facilitate the discussion with personal reflections and/or provide example scenarios.
- Holding time at the end of the workshop to pick up discussion on any earlier points and allow attendees to ask questions – this also supported facilitators with moving the session on sensitively and to use the time effectively.
- Being mindful of the power dynamics in the space and how this may impact on the level of professional vulnerability and openness of discussion attendees are comfortable with.
- The workshop facilitators positioning themselves as fellow learners, with the understanding that equitable practice is a dynamic, ongoing process; and modelling professional vulnerability by being open about their own learning journeys.

These workshops were successful in opening conversations on anti-oppressive and inclusive practice and contributed to wider discussions on EDI initiatives within the university. Moreover, as facilitators of the workshop, these sessions were a valuable space to continually reflect on our practice as well as the processes and practice of the PLA Service and our reflections often informed our contributions to the development of the PLA Service and our equity lens approach.

Identity, privilege and power

When considering our work and the use of an equity lens approach, the concept of the practitioner's own identity, including their privilege and power (Terry, 2021; Chiu, 2022), became key. With this in mind, we invite the reader to consider their own identity in the following activities. You can be as creative with this as you like – the learning is in the process, not necessarily the outcome. There are no wrong answers, and we ask that you pay attention to what thoughts and feelings come up for you instinctively without attaching judgement. These activities can be adapted for facilitation in a group setting and expanded upon, for instance, by asking participants to draw or select an object that resonates with them when reflecting upon these questions. If doing this in a group setting, it is suggested that the facilitator emphasises the private nature of the reflection so that there is no pressure for attendees to share, this can support the attendees with engaging with the exercise authentically which requires vulnerability and reflection while also promoting a psychologically safe space.

Activity: reflecting on identity

The first step is to consider these questions:

- How might you describe yourself?
- How might others describe you?
- How does context affect this (e.g. at work, among friends, in a public space)?
- How do different parts of your identity interact with each other?

The second part of this exercise is to go beyond your own individual identity and to consider:

- How does our understanding of identities inform our thoughts, judgements and expectations of others?
- What can we learn about ourselves through deepening our understanding of how we perceive identities?
- How can we address conscious and unconscious biases when considering identities and identity markers?

The purpose of this exercise is to invite practitioners to consider their own identity and the complexities within this by considering intersectionality, how identities are perceived (and how we perceive them as being perceived) and how context impacts upon this. It then uses this self-reflection as a foundation for thinking beyond the self and more generally on one's understanding of identities. Another consideration of this exercise is to reflect on what identity markers you associated yourself with and how these changed depending on context.

You may want to consider:

- How many, if any, of these identity markers related to protected characteristics?
- Were any identity markers relating to protected characteristics less or more present when thinking about how your identity is being perceived?
- You may also find it insightful to reflect on what feelings came up for you as you responded these questions and where and how you felt these emotions in your body.

In placing this activity in the context of the wider question regarding our understanding of identities, it reinforces the value of recognising intersectionality as discussed earlier in this chapter. It also highlights the challenges in recognising the nuances of intersectionality when working in systems which often group individuals by characteristics.

Activity: insider/outsider reflection

In this exercise, a range of identity markers are put forward and the reader is asked to identify whether they feel they are an insider (i.e. feel a sense of belonging with that identity marker) or outsider (as though they are on the outside looking in). Intentionally, no context is provided so that the reader can make their own meaning and follow what response instinctively comes up for them. However, it is recognised that this lack of context can diminish the accessibility of this exercise. To support with this, some suggested contextual scenarios are given beneath the table. This exercise has been adapted from brap's 'In Group/Out Group' resource and has been used here with written permission from brap who retain the copyright; brap is a registered UK-based charity specialising in supporting organisations, communities and cities in engaging with meaningful work on equality (brap, no date).

Step one

We invite the reader to take a few moments to consider the following identity markers and reflect on whether they experience feelings of inclusion or exclusion. Note, this exercise is by no means an exhaustive list of identity markers and no weight should be given to the ordering of identity markers (Table 2.2).

Supporting contextual scenarios

For those who find it helpful to have contextual scenarios to support with this exercise, we have included several suggestions:

- In a work team meeting or in your regular work environment;
- In a place of worship or community space;
- Among your friends and/or family groups;
- Visiting a public museum, library or park;
- When on vacation;
- When viewing/reading/listening to national or local news; and
- When on a university campus.

Step two

Next, take a few moments to think about a time in your life where you have felt like an 'insider' – notice what feelings come up for you here and allow yourself space to sit with these. When you are ready, move your focus

Table 2.2 Activity: insider/outsider reflection table

	Insider	Outsider
Gender		
Ability		
Ethnicity		
Profession		
Skin Colour		
Education		
Accent		
Social class		
Age		
Sexuality		
Religious beliefs		
Disposable income		
Experience		
Family status		
Personality type		
Political views		
Body image		
Language		
Culture		
Nationality		

to thinking about a time or a situation where you have felt like an 'outsider' – again, notice what feelings are coming up for you and allow yourself space to reflect on these feelings.

Step three

Finally, using your reflections from Step Two, consider your responses to the questions in Table 2.3. You may want to draw symbols that represent these responses, consider specific scenarios that come to mind or list adjectives that feel authentic to what came up for you in Step Two.

Taking these concepts of identity and belonging in a HE context, research shows that enhancing feelings of student belonging contributes

Table 2.3 Insider/outsider, responses and perceptions

'In' group	'Out' group
When you are in 'Insider' mode, what do you feel about yourself?	When you are on the outside, what do you feel about yourself?
How do insiders perceive others/outsiders?	How do outsiders perceive others/insiders?

Source: Adapted from brap (no date).

to students' academic success and wellbeing (Morgan, 2024). While the ways in which universities can successfully enhance students' feelings of belonging is debated, as is the extent to which this is an institutional responsibility, there is certainly merit in building connections with students to show that they are valued and that they matter (Humphrey and Lowe, 2017). The coaching and mentoring relationship lends itself well to this as its student-centred, holistic approach gives students time and space to explore their own narrative, challenges and opportunities. By having an awareness of their own feelings when in an 'In' group or an 'Out' group, practitioners can mobilise their own experiences of these feelings and be more conscious and intentional in their work to enhance student belonging and promote student connection.

A further advantage of undertaking this activity as a practitioner is that this self-reflective work can set the foundations for recognising and acknowledging our own privilege and how that shapes our worldview and lived experience.

Privilege

Privilege refers to an advantage that a person or a group of people have due to societal or systemic structures and processes (Holiday and Gable, 2022). With one's privilege being embedded within their own lived experience, it is challenging to identify what privilege(s) you have, what advantages privilege has afforded to you, and how different an experience may be for a person or person(s) without that privilege. Though often presented in a binary fashion (you either experience a certain privilege or you do not), incorporating intersectionality is a more nuanced approach to considering privilege which requires personal reflection on how one's privilege impacts on their own experience of the world (Coston and Kimmel, 2012).

It is acknowledged that exploring one's own privilege is challenging and uncomfortable. With this in mind, we would like to draw readers' attention back to the beginning of the section – the value of sitting with that vulnerability and discomfort as part of the process. It is also pertinent to consider reframing the action of acknowledging one's privilege as an act of community, allyship and empathy that is reflective of systemic oppression rather than an act that undermines one's sense of self and achievement (Pancost, 2022).

Reflecting on one's own privilege is essential to equitable practice. It is useful to note here that, while we are discussing this in the context of the individual, that privilege ought to also be considered beyond our own individuality when working collaboratively. For example, when you are in working in a group to deliver a project or service, it is beneficial to consider privileges you may share collectively as a group, what impact this could have and what actions you can take to address this impact. There is immense value in seeking to learn about lived experiences different from your own and that of your closest communities and social groups. Where it is not possible to work or engage with representative diversity, it is imperative that seeking feedback from diverse populations is undertaken and that this feedback is then valued and acted upon appropriately to promote equitable outcomes.

That being said, we also acknowledge that asking for feedback from students and students with certain lived experience carries the weight of both emotional and physical labour. When seeking feedback from marginalised voices, this can compound, particularly where the same individuals are being asked for feedback repeatedly or when they may not necessarily be seeing change as a result of their feedback. Similarly, where students are sharing their own lived experiences of oppression or inequity and this touches upon the lived experiences of practitioners it can increase emotional resonance to a challenging degree and impact upon practitioner wellbeing. One way in which our service managed this was to engage with group supervision where coach practitioners were invited to share their experiences and seek support in a safe space under the facilitation of a qualified supervisor, more information about this can be found in Chapter 8 of this volume.

Activity: reflecting on unearned advantage and disadvantage

Taking a similar approach to the 'insider/outsider reflection' activity, we invite the reader to use this activity on unearned advantage and disadvantage as a practical way to reflect on their own privilege.

Step one

Think and reflect on:

- What are one or more ways in which you have had unearned disadvantage in your life and what impact has this had?
- What are one or more ways in which you have had unearned advantage in your life and what impact has this had?

Step two

Think and reflect:

- What is it like for you to reflect on these experiences of unearned disadvantage and advantage?

You may want to consider what emotions are coming up for you here, how you feel those emotions in your body and what thought process you went through as you considered the questions in step one.

Power

The topic of power dynamics is an emerging space in coaching research and is often explored in an organisational context (Dima and Diochon, 2018). In the ICF Core Values, there are notions that allude to the acknowledgement of power such as sections on 'Humanity' and 'Equity' which outlines that practitioners should bring 'awareness to systemic patterns of conscious and unconscious biases in my own self and others,' and explore 'to understand and bring awareness to social diversity, systemic equality and systemic oppression and how they show up in the coaching profession' (*ICF Core Values*, no date, pp. 3–4).

In the HE context, the power dynamics suggested by Hawkins concerning three types of power: role power, cultural power and individual power; can be a useful foundation for considering how power dynamics impact upon the professional student support space in HE (Hawkins and McMahon, 2020). While these power dynamics are based on cross-cultural supervision, they lend themselves well to thinking about the coaching and mentoring space in HE when using an equity lens.

To expand on these types of power further adapting Hawkins' definitions:

Role Power is the power inherited in the role of the practitioner – for students this may well be the status of the practitioner in the university or the impact that practitioner can possibly have on their studies. For example, when discussing this type of power in our anti-oppressive and inclusive practice workshops, attendees shared how it could be a challenging space to navigate and connect with a student when the student has full awareness that the practitioner holds the decision over whether the student is able to continue with their studies.

Cultural Power derives from being from the dominant social and ethnic group. It can also derive from certain professions as well. For example, in coaching and mentoring sessions with students, students often express that they feel there are barriers to talking to their lecturer because their lecturer's title of 'Dr' can evoke feelings of uncertainty and vulnerability when the student wants to ask questions that they feel are too simple or basic.

Personal Power is the particular power of the individual that can be over and above the power given to that person through role or culture. This can come from the authority of their expertise as well as the presence and impact of their personality. Hawkins identifies that this also includes French and Raven's term 'referent power,' that in a supervisor context, derives from the supervisee wishing to identify with or be like their supervisor (Hawkins and McMahon, 2020). Within the PLA Service, the benefits and considerations around modelling vulnerability and openness with students have been discussed at length. For example, with practitioners sharing when they have found their own studies challenging or have had difficulty in meeting a deadline. Students have also shared finding it reassuring when lecturers have apologised for not being able to meet a marking deadline or respond to an email in an agreed timeframe as this humanises the lecturer, particularly in a distance-learning context, and models a culture of honesty and openness. However, this must also be balanced with consideration to professionalism, credibility and maintaining a student-centred space.

Equity lens: further development and applicability

Our aim in this chapter has been to share our experiences in researching, creating and developing a coaching and mentoring equity lens approach. Now, let us turn to consider its potential wider applicability and the benefits it may bring.

Firstly, and most importantly, to continue to help remove the inequalities that under-represented and marginalised students face throughout their HE

Reflective questions: student voice

- How can we responsibly ask for students' time and recognise the emotional labour involved of discussing issues related to equity? How do we also manage this for staff?
- How can we seek to achieve representational diversity among respondents when seeking student feedback?
- What commitment can you make to use the feedback offered by students and how can the impact of their feedback be demonstrated practicably?
- In what ways can applying an equity lens to an area of practice be co-created with students?
- What opportunities are there in staff/student partnerships and collaboration when using the feedback given by students?

journey, we acknowledge the benefit and importance of championing the student voice in the equity lens and Framework's development. In addition, working with our students to co-develop our approach will undoubtedly advance our own professional practice and in turn, increase equity awareness in the coaching and mentoring field in HE. Consequently, we invite readers to consider how they may involve the student voice in applying an equity lens to their own practice and services.

In addition to this, it is recognised that an area for development of the equity lens concerns decolonisation. While decolonisation is prevalent in curricula and teaching practices, there is considerably less research and movement in decolonising student support in HE. Though this was not within the scope of the equity lens in its iterative development, it is an area which we would encourage readers to embed within their own practice and services with the mindfulness that there is a hazard that the term 'decolonisation' can become tokenistic rather than to denote a transformative change (Smith, 2021). One way in which decolonisation could be further explored is by considering the language and models used within coaching and mentoring to bring in perspectives and voices that are outside of Western-dominant approaches into practice. Like other forms of decolonisation, this is about challenging hegemonic systems and voices but also – as bel hooks described – interrogating our own perspectives so that we do not recreate 'the imperial gaze—the look that seeks to dominate, subjugate, and colonize' (hooks, 2015, p. 7). Another suggestion is to include cultural competency, including the impacts of colonisation and its legacies, within practitioner training. A further suggestion is the involvement of the student voice in shaping decolonised student support services which could be gained through co-creation and student consultation. In a case study by Takhar, it is argued that the student voice is central to decolonising curricula at British universities as they can provide input at the point of accessing the curriculum and be co-producers in decolonising universities (Takhar, 2023). There are also examples of good practice highlighted by Omodan (2024) wherein indigenous knowledge and concepts have been used as an approach to conflict management in student support services.

A coaching and mentoring approach that supports wider decolonisation in curriculum could also be an avenue of exploration, whereby practitioners use coaching and mentoring skills to support the critiquing of the curriculum and of pedagogical practice as part of the decolonisation process. For instance, by providing the student with a neutral, confidential space to challenge and critique pedagogy and curriculum with the view that students are then encouraged to voice this in learning development spaces or that practitioners may seek student consent to disseminate this learning to relevant parties who may then affect change as part of wider decolonisation work.

Secondly, looking at our own coaching and mentoring practice to evaluate how we are working and striving for continual improvement requires a means to assess our own performance. This can be achieved through being

Reflective questions: decolonising student support

Concerning decolonisation in student support practice, practitioners may want to consider the following reflective questions:

- How is our practice culturally responsive?
- In what ways are we creating decolonised spaces in which colonised narratives and practices can be safely challenged?
- How can we globalise our approach to practitioner skills, knowledge and behaviours, going beyond Euro-centric and Western-dominant practices and discourses?
- How can our approaches in student services create synergy with and support decolonisation efforts across HE, including the decolonisation of curricula and pedagogy?

a reflective practitioner (Schön, 1983) by undertaking paired or triad practitioner mentoring; participating in group supervision and via ongoing CPD training. To evaluate our practice effectively we need to know what we are looking for and to understand what good coaching and mentoring looks like. We can then assess our practitioner work against core competencies and key skills. Using the equity lens and the five coaching and mentoring pillars from the coaching and mentoring continuum as criterion for evaluation can help support practitioners to both reflect on and evaluate their work and the development of their core competencies and key skills. An example of how this can look in practice is shown in Table 2.4.

This self-reflection approach emphasises what went well alongside the identification of what could be better, in other words, areas for further development. It is based on the premise that good coaching and mentoring is an ongoing cycle of improvement based on continual reflection (Starr, 2021). This practitioner self-reflection can be further used and developed in management reviews and collaborative staff development discussions.

In addition, when seeking professional accreditation practitioners may find it advantageous to adopt an equity lens as a tool for showcasing their personal practice and professional approach. For instance, all three levels of ICF professional coaching certification emphasise continuous professional development, requiring practitioners to use reflection to demonstrate their mastery of core coaching competencies (ICF, no date). Similarly, the Advance HE Fellowship is granted to practitioners who provide evidence of their professional practice in line with the Professional Standards Framework 2023. This framework mandates the evaluation and demonstration of key

Table 2.4 Example practitioner reflection, focused on empowering action

Empowering action (reflection/evaluation focus)	
What went well – skills present in the session	**Missed opportunities – skills to work on**
Worked with the student to create options, possibilities and solve challenges.	Invite the student to share how to move forward, including resources, support and potential barriers.
Partnered with the student to design goals, actions and accountability measures.	Invite the student to explore barriers to their accountability.
Partnered with the student to summarise learning and insight within or between the sessions.	Understand how *Powerful* questions could elicit this.

Reflective questions: using the equity lens in professional reflection

- How much time and energy can you allocate for regular, uninterrupted reflection and how can you protect this time?
- What do you hope to achieve or understand better through your reflection?
- Where can you gain different perspectives and insights to add to your own reflection? For example, consider seeking feedback from your students, trusted colleagues, coaching supervisors, mentors or managers.
- How will you ensure that your reflection is honest? Personal reflection is most beneficial when you are open and truthful about your experiences, feelings and behaviours.
- How will you ensure your reflection leads to you taking action?

professional values, core knowledge and areas of activity that promote inclusive approaches, ensuring all learners are respected and valued, and have equitable opportunities for success (Advance HE, no date).

For these reasons, we invite readers to consider how they can use the equity lens in their own reflective practice or service review.

Thirdly, the work undertaken by the working group identified a number of possible wider service benefits to using an equity lens approach. These include but are not limited to, the completion of Equality Impact Assessments (part of the Public Sector equality duty), which is an evidence-based approach to help organisations ensure that their policies, practices, events and decision-making processes are fair and do not create barriers or disadvantages for any protected groups. In addition, the use of an equity lens review may help identify areas of practice or services that can be changed to address student inequalities and better meet the needs of all students. By systematically evaluating existing policies, procedures and practices through an equity lens, institutions can uncover underlying biases and structural barriers that contribute to disparities in educational outcomes. As a result of implementing an equity lens review, institutions can proactively work towards creating a more inclusive environment that promotes opportunities for all students, regardless of their background or circumstances. Looking externally, using an equity lens approach can help underpin key QA processes and procedures such as the matrix Standard (Department for Education, 2024) to ensure the delivery of high-quality

IAG (explored in further detail in Chapter 7) services to enable individuals to reach their full potential.

Conclusion

Developing the equity lens within our Coaching and Mentoring Framework has provided the working group and the PLA Service with a deeper and more nuanced understanding of the broader context in which the service operates – encompassing University approaches, HE sector demands and measures, institution-led EDI plans and social justice initiatives, and the areas of coaching and mentoring (Clay *et al.*, 2023). It has given us as practitioners the opportunity to connect our values, practice and purpose, and to unite them under an approach that places student equity at its heart. The working group is proud that the equity lens and our coaching and mentoring framework are functional, exploratory, inclusive and anti-oppressive and that it seeks to meet the needs of our students, practitioners and relevant parties. However, importantly, we acknowledge that the equity lens approach is not a 'quick fix' or panacea to eliminating student inequity. The work in this area is dynamic and ongoing, it often necessitates having difficult conversations exploring challenging language and individual's biases, involves complex practitioner reflexivity and requires wider institutional support and investment. It is also situated within wider contexts of anti-oppressive practice, UD and decolonisation across HE, as well as within student support services more specifically.

Overall, we strongly believe that adopting an equity lens approach to coaching and mentoring within HE not only strengthens our ability to positively impact student equity within the institution, but it also aligns with broader educational movements like UDL and curriculum decolonisation. These efforts reflect a growing recognition of the need to dismantle systemic barriers in education, ensuring inclusivity and representation in teaching and learning practices. However, while significant strides are being made in transforming pedagogy and curriculum design, related areas such as student support (information, advice and guidance; therapeutic interventions and academic study skills) have not advanced at the same pace. Practice in these areas can often lag behind, with limited integration of equity-focused frameworks or critical reflection on entrenched norms that may inadvertently disadvantage certain groups of students.

Through this chapter, we aim to spark a 'ripple effect,' inviting and encouraging readers to critically evaluate their own practices through an equity lens. This involves questioning whether current approaches genuinely address the diverse needs of students, identifying gaps and

Table 2.5 Stop, start, continue plan

Stop	Start	Continue
Actions you are going to stop or do less	Actions you are going to introduce to your practice or do more	Actions of equitable practice you are already doing that you would like to recognise and continue doing

embracing the challenge of change where necessary. By sharing these insights and experiences with their wider communities of practice, educators and support professionals can collectively work towards a more equitable and inclusive educational ecosystem – one where every student has the opportunity to thrive, both academically and personally.

As this chapter comes to a close, we invite readers to reflect on what they are taking away. A suggested way of doing this is using a 'stop, start, continue plan.' This activity was used as a closing section in the anti-oppressive and inclusive staff development workshops and it was found that setting realistic, manageable actions – as well as recognising what actions are already being taken – towards more equitable practice gave an individualised, practicable takeaway from the concepts introduced. Incidentally, there is also merit in using this model as a way of collecting student feedback (Hoon *et al.*, 2014). To do this, we invite you to identify two to three action points for the following (Table 2.5).

Recommended resources that can support this activity and that have especially influenced our work include

Blake, S., Capper, G. and Jackson, A. (2022) *Building belonging in higher education.* Publication. Pearson and WonkHE. Available at: https://wonkhe.com/wp-content/wonkhe-uploads/2022/10/Building-Belonging-October-2022.pdf (Accessed: 5 December 2024).

Holiday, T. and Gable, T. (2022) *Equity review tool: a process guide for equity centered instructional materials*. Every Learner Everywhere. Available at: https://www.everylearnereverywhere.org/resources/ (Accessed: December 2024).

ICF Coaching Education (2022) *A resource guide on diversity and inclusion for coaching education providers*. Available at: https://coachingfederation.org/app/uploads/2021/07/ICF-Coach-Training_DEIJB-Resource-Guide.pdf (Accessed: 5 December 2024).

Lamont, A. (2016) *Guide to allyship*. Available at: https://guidetoallyship.com/ (Accessed: 5 December 2024).

Bibliography

Abrahamsson, G., Hemmer, N., Margareti, M., Moral, M., Oliveira Pinto, A., Skelton, N. and van Vlerken, A. (2015) *EMCC coaching and mentoring competence framework, EMCCGlobal*. Available at: https://emccdrive.emccglobal.org/api/file/download/0gzGExIyhoRpVFnq5DB7ucXeu1FpQ6pJZk35YbTh (Accessed: 22 July 2024).

Advance HE. (no date) 'Education for mental health toolkit – psychologically safe learning environment'. Available at: https://www.advance-he.ac.uk/teaching-and-learning/curricula-development/education-mental-health-toolkit/social-belonging/psychologically-safe-learning-environment (Accessed: 06 September 2024).

Advance HE. (no date) 'Fellowship'. Available at: https://www.advance-he.ac.uk/fellowship#overview (Accessed: 01 September 2024).

Advance HE. (2023) 'Professional standards framework for teaching and supporting learning in higher education'. Available at: https://advance-he.ac.uk/knowledge-hub/professional-standards-framework-teaching-and-supporting-learning-higher-education-0?_ga=2.104401860.552448274.1713129177-10091247.1713129177 (Accessed: 07 July 2024).

Ahmed, S. (2012) *On being included: racism and diversity in institutional life*. Durham, NC: Duke University Press.

Berila, B. (2023) *Integrating mindfulness into anti-oppression pedagogy*. Abingdon: Routledge, pp. 1–46.

Blake, S., Capper, G. and Jackson, A. (2022) *Building belonging in higher education*. Pearson and WonkHE. Available at: https://wonkhe.com/wp-content/wonkhe-uploads/2022/10/Building-Belonging-October-2022.pdf (Accessed: July 2024).

Blissett, J., Clay, E.-M. and Williams, H. (2023) 'Who "belongs" anyway?: Looking at APP students' own words to explore the accuracy and purpose of the term "belonging"'. *Access, Participation and Success Seminar: Words Matter*. 21 November, 2023. Available at: https://www5.open.ac.uk/widening-participation/sites/www.open.ac.uk.widening-participation/files/files/Enya-Marie%20Clay%20et%20al.pptx (Accessed: 29 June 2024).

Bourdieu, P. (1977) *Outline of a theory of practice Richard nice*. Translated by R. Nice. Cambridge: Cambridge University Press (Cambridge Studies in Social and Cultural Anthropology).

brap (no date) 'About us'. Available at: https://www.brap.org.uk/about (Accessed: 09 September 2024).

Burgstahler, S. and Moore, E. (2009) 'Making student services welcoming and accessible through accommodations and universal design', *Journal of Postsecondary Education and Disability*, 21(3), 151–174. Available at: https://files.eric.ed.gov/fulltext/EJ831433.pdf (Accessed: 14 August 2024).

Burke, B. and Harrison, P. (2002) 'Anti-oppressive practice', in R. Adams, L. Dominelli and M. Payne (eds.) *Anti-oppressive practice*. Basingstoke: Palgrave MacMillan Ltd, pp. 227–236.

Campbell, L.A. and McKendrick, J.H. (2017) 'Beyond aspirations: deploying the capability approach to tackle the under-representation in higher education of young people from deprived communities', *Studies in Continuing Education*, 39(2), pp. 120–137. doi: 10.1080/0158037X.2017.1293630

Center for Applied Special Technology (CAST). (2018) Available at: https://www.cast.org/impact/timeline-innovation (Accessed: 19 July 2024).

Centre for Excellence in Universal Design (CEUD). (no date) *The 7 principles*. Available at: https://universaldesign.ie/about-universal-design/the-7-principles (Accessed: 24 July 2024)

Center for Universal Design in Education (CUDE). (no date) Available at: https://www.washington.edu/doit/programs/center-universal-design-education/overview (Accessed: 24 July 2024).

Chiu, L. (2022) 'Conceptualising allyship for coaching to promote social change', *International Journal of Evidence Based Coaching and Mentoring*, (S16), pp. 40–54. doi: 10.24384/AJWW-CE78

Christofferson, A. (2021) 'The politics of intersectional practice: competing concepts of intersectionality', *Policy and Politics*, 49(4), pp. 573–593. doi: 10.1332/030557321X16194316141034

Clay, E.-M., Blissett, J., Williams, H., Lindley, J. and O'Neil, L. (2023) 'Developing an equity lens: the experience of creating a professional framework for coaches and mentors', *Journal of Learning Development in Higher Education*, 26. doi: 10.47408/jldhe.vi26.932.

Clutterbuck, D. (2010) 'Coaching reflection: the liberated coach', *Coaching: An International Journal of Theory, Research and Practice*, 3(1). doi: 10.1080/17521880903102308.

Clutterbuck, D. (2014) *Everyone needs a mentor*. 5th edn. London: CIPD.

Coston, B.M. and Kimmel, M. (2012) 'Seeing privilege where it isn't: marginalized masculinities and the intersectionality of privilege', *Journal of Social Issues*, 68(1), pp. 97–111. doi: 10.1111/j.1540-4560.2011.01738.x

Cox, E., Bachkirova, T. and Clutterbuck, D. (2014) *The complete handbook of coaching*. 2nd edn. London: Sage Publications Ltd.

Crenshaw, K.W. (1989) 'Demarginalizing the intersection of race and sex: a black feminist critique of antidiscrimination doctrine, feminist theory, and antiracist politics', *University of Chicago Legal Forum*, 14, pp. 538–554. Available at: https://chicagounbound.uchicago.edu/uclf/vol1989/iss1/8 (Accessed 1 June 2024).

Crenshaw, K.W. (1991) 'Mapping the margins: intersectionality, identity politics, and violence against women of color', *Stanford Law Review*, 43(6), pp. 1241–1299. Available at: https://blogs.law.columbia.edu/critique1313/files/2020/02/1229039.pdf (Accessed 1 June 2024).

Cureton, D. and Gravestock, P. (2019) ''We belong': differential sense of belonging and its meaning for different ethnicity groups in Higher Education', *Compass: Journal of Learning and Teaching*, 12(1). doi: 10.21100/compass.v12i1.942

Department for Education. (2024) *Matrix standard*. Available at: https://matrixstandard.com/ (Accessed: 1 July 2024).

Dima, L. and Diochon, P.F. (2018) 'The coaching space: a production of power relationships in organizational settings', *Organization*, 25(6), pp. 710–731. doi: 10.1177/1350508418779653

DO-IT. (no date) *Equal access: universal design of advising*. Available at: https://www.washington.edu/doit/sites/default/files/atoms/files/Equal_Access_Advising.pdf (Accessed: 24 July 2024).

DO-IT. (no date) *Universal design: process, principles, and applications*. Available at: https://www.washington.edu/doit/sites/default/files/atoms/files/Universal_Design_04_12_21.pdf (Accessed: 24 July 2024).

Drucker, P.F. (1954) *The practice of management*. New York: Harper Business.

Gibson, S., Baskerville, D., Berry, A.,Black, A.,Norris, K. and Symeonidou, S. (2016) ''Diversity' 'widening participation' and 'inclusion' in higher education: an international study', *Widening Participation and Lifelong Learning*, 18(3), pp. 7–33. doi: 10.5456/wpll.18.3.7

Hawkins, P. and McMahon, A. (2020) *Supervision in the helping professions*. 5th edn. Maidenhead: Open University Press.

Hillman, J., Lochtie, D. and Purcell, O. (2024) 'Black students' experiences of coaching and mentoring in higher education: a case study', *International Journal of Mentoring and Coaching in Education*, 13(1). doi: 10.1108/IJMCE-01-2023-0011

Holiday, T. and Gable, T. (2022 April) *Equity review tool: a process guide for equity-centered instructional materials*. Every Learner Everywhere. Available at: https://www.everylearnereverywhere.org/resources/ (Accessed: 24 July 2024).

hooks, B. (1994) *Teaching to transgress: education as the practice of freedom*. Routledge. Cited in: Valcarlos, M.M., Wolgemuth, J.R, Haraf, S. and Fisk, N. (2020) 'Anti-oppressive pedagogies in online learning: a critical review', *Distance Education*, 41(3). New York: Routledge, pp. 345–360. doi: 10.1080/01587919.2020.1763783

hooks, B. (2015) *Black looks: race and representation*. 2nd edn. Abingdon: Routledge.

Hoon, A., Oliver, E., Szpakowska, K. and Newton, P. (2014) 'Use of the "stop, start, continue" method is associated with the production of constructive qualitative feedback by students in Higher Education', *Assessment and Evaluation in Higher Education*, 40(5), pp. 755–767. doi: 10.1080/02602938.2014.956282

Humphrey, O. and Lowe, T. (2017) 'Exploring how a "sense of belonging" is facilitated at different stages of the student journey in Higher Education', *The Journal of Educational Innovation, Partnership and Change*, 3(1). doi: 10.21100/jeipc.v3i1.583

International Coaching Federation (ICF). (2019) *Current ICF core competencies.* Available at: https://coachingfederation.org/credentials-and-standards/core-competencies (Accessed: 1 June 2024).

International Coaching Federation (ICF). (2022) *A resource guide on diversity and inclusion for coaching education providers.* rep. ICF Coaching Education. Available at: https://coachingfederation.org/app/uploads/2021/07/ICF-Coach-Training_DEIJB-Resource-Guide.pdf (Accessed: 22 July 2024).

International Coaching Federation (ICF). (no date) *ICF core values.* Available at: https://coachingfederation.org/app/uploads/2022/01/ICF-Core-Values.pdf (Accessed: 22 July 2024).

Ives, Y. (2008) 'What is "coaching"? An exploration of conflicting paradigms', *International Journal of Evidence Based Coaching and Mentoring*, 6(2), pp. 100–113. Available at: https://radar.brookes.ac.uk/radar/items/ed490c36-e4c1-4263-ad7b-24cc99b97b04/1/ (Accessed: 20 June 2024).

Joseph, S. (2006) 'Person-centred coaching psychology: a meta-theoretical perspective', *International Coaching Psychology Review*, 1, pp. 47–54. Available at: https://www.researchgate.net/publication/242684265_Person-centred_coaching_psychology_A_meta-theoretical_perspective/link/5d27311492851cf44079a466/download (Accessed: 20 June 2024).

Maguire, F. and Hall, R. (2018) *A literature review of universal design for learning.* Available at: https://dora.dmu.ac.uk/server/api/core/bitstreams/74caef5a-b16c-4d90-ac35-129320d49585/content (Accessed: 01 August 2024).

Martin, N., Wray, M., James, A., Draffan, E.A., Krupa, J. and Turner, P. (2019) 'Implementing inclusive teaching and learning in UK Higher Education – utilising Universal Design for Learning (UDL) as a route to excellence', *Society for Research into Higher Education.* Available at: https://openresearch.lsbu.ac.uk/download/97cc3ce39fb4b9c06d631188fac19ac43c3fe317915210dad4d54e5f7d1a5309/817348/Nicola-Martin-SRHE-Research-Report.pdf (Accessed: 30 August 2024).

Megginson, D. and Clutterbuck, D. (2015) *Further techniques for coaching and mentoring.* Abingdon: Routledge.

Morgan, J. (2024) 'Fostering belonging in higher education: implications for student retention and wellbeing', Advance HE. Available at: https://www.advance-he.ac.uk/news-and-views/fostering-belonging-higher-education-implications-student-retention-and-wellbeing#:~:text=In%20the%20Higher%20Education%20(HE,has%20become%20a%20strategic%20necessity (Accessed: 22 July 2024).

Nash, J.C. (2019) *Black feminism reimagined: after intersectionality.* Durham, NC: Duke University Press.

Office for Students (OfS). (2019) 'Beyond the bare minimum: are universities and colleges doing enough for disabled students?', *Insight 4.* Available at: https://www.officeforstudents.org.uk/media/3828/beyond-the-bare-minimum-are-universities-and-colleges-doing-enough-for-disabled-students.pdf (Accessed 28 May 2024).

Office for Students (OfS). (2024) *Access and participation plans.* Available at: https://www.officeforstudents.org.uk/for-providers/equality-of-opportunity/access-and-participation-plans/ (Accessed: 24 June 2024).

Oliver, M. (2009) *Understanding disability, from theory to practice.* 2nd edn. Basingstoke: Palgrave Macmillan.

Omodan, B.I. (2024) 'Decolonising student services: implications for conflict management in higher education', *Routledge Open Research*, 3. doi: 10.12688/routledgeopenres.18311.1

Open University. (2020) *Access and participation plan 2020/21–2024/25.* Available at: https://www5.open.ac.uk/widening-participation/sites/www.open.ac.uk.widening-participation/files/files/OU%20Access%20and%20Participation%20Plan%202020-2025.pdf (Accessed: 24 June 2024).

Orange, T., Isken, J., Green, A., Paranchini, N. and Francois, A. (2019) 'Coaching for equity', *The Learning Professional*, 40(6), pp. 45–49. Available at: https://learningforward.org/wp-content/uploads/2019/12/coaching-for-equity.pdf (Accessed: 20 July 2024).

Pancost, R. (2022) 'Acknowledging your privilege is an act of community', *The Uncertain World*. University of Bristol Blogs. Available at: https://richpancost.blogs.bristol.ac.uk/2022/09/24/acknowledging-your-privilege-is-an-act-of-community-and-love/ (Accessed: 06 September 2024).

Passmore, J. (ed.). (2021) *Excellence in coaching: theory, tools and techniques to achieve outstanding coaching performance.* 4th edn. London, New York: Kogan Page.

Policy Connect. (2020) *Arriving at thriving: learning from disabled students to ensure access for all.* Available at: https://www.policyconnect.org.uk/research/arriving-thriving-learning-disabled-students-ensure-access-all (Accessed: 07 April 2024).

Reid, D.C. (2020) 'Are we ready for cultural sensitivity coaching?', *Psychology Today*, Available at: https://www.psychologytoday.com/us/blog/coaching-corner/202006/are-we-ready-cultural-sensitivity-coaching (Accessed: 01 July 2024).

Reid, D.C. (2021) 'Critical race theory and coaching', *ICF Philadelphia*. Available at: https://www.icfphiladelphia.org/Blog/10727491 (Accessed 1 July 2024).

Research Guides: Anti-Oppression and Equity Resources: Anti-Oppression. (no date) *Anti-oppression – anti-oppression and equity resources – research guides atModesto Junior College Library.* Available at: https://libguides.mjc.edu/equity#:~:text=Oppression%20%3D%20prejudice%20%2B%20powerandtext=This%20means%20oppression%20is%20built,%2C%20and%20raising%2Fadopting%20children (Accessed: 22 July 2024).

Rogers, C.R. (1957) 'The necessary and sufficient conditions of therapeutic personality change', *Journal of Consulting Psychology*, 21, pp. 95–103.

Schön, D.A. (1983) *The reflective practitioner: how professionals think in action.* London: Temple Smith.

Shoukry, H. (2016) 'Coaching for emancipation: a framework for coaching in oppressive environments', *International Journal of Evidence Based Coaching and Mentoring*, 14(2), pp. 15–30. Available at: https://radar.brookes.ac.uk/radar/items/5d592ac5-2f54-4b23-bde2-8e279137f19f/1/

Shoukry, H. and Cox, E. (2018) 'Coaching as a social process', *Management Learning*, 49(4), pp. 413–428. doi: 10.1177/1350507618762600

Smith, L.T. (2021) *Decolonizing methodologies: research and indigenous peoples*. London: Zed Books.

Starr, J. (2021) *The coaching manual – your step by step guide to becoming a great coach*. London: Pearson Education.

Takhar, S. (2023) 'The student voice: decolonising the curriculum', *Equity in Education and Society*, 3(2), pp. 114–129. doi: 10.1177/27526461231192671

Terry, P.E. (2021) 'Crossing the empathy chasm: unpacking a knapsack full of unearned advantage', *American Journal of Health Promotion*, 35(5), pp. 604–608. doi: 10.1177/08901171211011266

UK Government: The Equality Act. (2010) Available at: https://www.legislation.gov.uk/ukpga/2010/15/contents (Accessed: 15 May 2024).

Universities UK, National Union of Students. (2019) *Black, Asian and minority ethnic student attainment at UK Universities: #ClosingTheGap*. Available at: https://www.universitiesuk.ac.uk/sites/default/files/field/downloads/2021-07/bame-student-attainment.pdf?mc_cid=0263df3146andmc_eid=a074c3256a (Accessed: 22 July 2024).

Yates, J. (2022) *The career coaching handbook*. 2nd ed. Abingdon: Routledge.

Working with students 3

Contracting and chemistry

Chrissie Farley, Joshua Samuels-Hylton and Emma Vance

Introduction

At the time of writing, the three authors of this chapter are qualified professional coaches working as coach-mentors in the Personal Learning Advice (PLA) Service. As outlined in the Introduction to this volume and expanded in Chapter 2, the PLA Service was established to provide non-academic coaching and mentoring to distance learners. For the purposes of this chapter, we have viewed contracting through three different lenses: the 'professional,' the 'procedural' and 'psychological' (Hay, 2011). We selected Hay's approach (2011) – which is rooted in transactional analysis – to invite readers to reflect upon the potential for an imbalance of ego states. We suggest that this helps ensure both coach and student enter the helping relationship as equals.

As practitioners, we acknowledge that our approaches to contracting with students are necessarily individualised and inflected by our own varied positionalities. The role that our subjectivities might play is something which is increasingly recognised within qualitative research and might usefully be extended to practitioner work with students in higher education (HE) (Jacobson and Mustafa, 2019). The first section of this chapter which introduces contracting and its purpose in establishing and maintaining a structured coaching and mentoring relationship, is authored by Chrissie. Chrissie's perspective is shaped by her professional experience in widening participation (WP) management, advocacy and facilitation across London and Sussex, as well as her coaching qualification. Chrissie's personal lived

DOI: 10.4324/9781003486015-4

experiences also shape her positionality. As a first-generation graduate from a low socio-economic area, Chrissie has reflected on having 'lost' a year of study due to a severe lack of confidence at university and how this shapes her approach to careful contracting with students. The second section of this chapter is authored by Emma, a Scottish educator and qualified coach with experience in WP, employability, outreach and student support. Emma's focus here is on the procedural aspects of contracting and how these are shaped by the structure of the coaching offer and/or service, the profile of students and the individual approaches and experiences of practitioners. In the third section of this chapter, Josh addresses the role chemistry plays within contracting. Josh is a qualified coach and teacher, with an academic background as a Social Sciences lecturer. Josh is motivated by his belief in empowering students who might feel they are held at the peripheries of HE, by centring their voices and actively listening to their individual journeys. Josh's focus in this chapter, is how the chemistry in contracting can help to establish helping relationships conducive to this.

Our collective aims for this chapter are to describe the meaning and purpose of contracting in the context of coaching and mentoring work with students. We address how to contract with students when working across a coaching and mentoring continuum and ways to navigate scenarios which require advice and guidance. We also seek to:

- Demonstrate how a contracting conversation might be used to support the student to determine whether coaching is a suitable intervention for them.
- Facilitate practitioner reflection on how to conduct chemistry and contracting sessions for coaching students.
- Provide guidance for practitioners in student-facing roles on how to develop an appropriate contract.

Before moving to consider three levels of contracting in depth, we will first consider the importance of establishing ways of working with other relevant parties and stakeholders who have an interest in a coaching relationship in the context of HE.

Coaching and mentoring students in higher education

Coaching and mentoring students in HE involves a member of staff (coach/mentor), a student (coachee) and their shared organisation (the university). Generally, additional parties will affect the helping relationship.

Working with students in this (and other similar) contexts requires practitioners to be able to contract carefully and effectively with students, so that the support offered is suitably positioned. In our experience, this has been a non-academic personal development opportunity within the parameters of the coachee's identity as a student. Contracting ensures a student has the agency to bring whatever they choose to a session. This could be a clear study goal, but it might be a personal development goal, or a thought or belief affecting their ability to learn.

Whilst the coaching and mentoring relationship is primarily a bilateral partnership between practitioner and student, the institution is also invested in the outcomes of coaching. Key parties in the wider coaching relationship are – namely – the tutor, relevant student support services where applicable, the institution and by extension, the associated funding or regulatory body. To explore this and consider implications for our own practice, we conducted a mapping exercise to outline the different points in the coaching and mentoring relationship where the interests of other relevant parties might shape the offer. Table 3.1 offers a simplified view of this.

Conducting this exercise supports us as practitioners to develop our understanding of all parties' interests, build trust and credibility with the student and work with the tutor, other specialist services and the organisation. The tripartite relationship between the coach-mentor (ourselves), the coachee (student) and our shared organisation (the university) is represented in Figure 3.1.

This visual representation of the interplay between relevant parties enables the coach to maintain professional boundaries by clearly delineating where the interests and expectations of the different parties might intersect or conflict. Having established these interrelationships, we will now consider the first of our three levels of contracting.

Contracting at the 'professional' level

In coaching, contracting usually begins with an initial conversation that takes place between coach and coachee prior to the commencement of the helping relationship. It acts as a framework to underpin the practical, personal and dialogic conditions in which the coaching takes place. The contracting conversation sets the scene; it usually begins with the coach clarifying what coaching is. A coach may offer something comparable to the following statement: 'coaching is a person-centred dialogue that provides space for the individual to reflect, think, explore and grow.' There are other useful alternatives in the literature – such as:

Table 3.1 Nine stages of the contracting process and the parties involved

What/when	Organisation	Coach/ mentor	Student	Tutor and/ or other student support
Determining coaching project objectives	Yes	Yes		
One-to-one coaching offer made to student	Yes	Yes	Yes	
Student opts in and books initial chemistry appointment		Yes	Yes	
Contracting conversation and (with student consent) liaison with tutor and others in support network		Yes	Yes	Yes/no
Sessions one and two (of six) take place		Yes	Yes	
Session three mid-point review (with student consent this may involve reviewing progress with tutor and/or referral to other support services)		Yes	Yes	Yes
Session four and five take place		Yes	Yes	
Session six conclusion of coaching: Reflection and next steps		Yes	Yes	
Coaching evaluation	Yes		Yes	

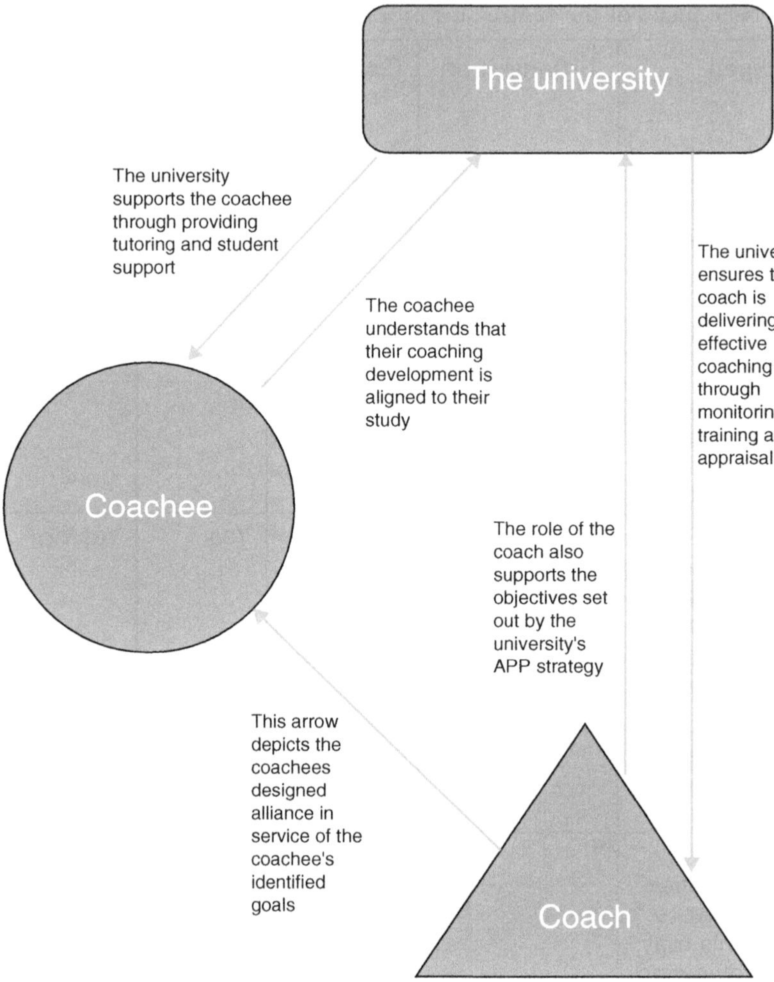

Figure 3.1 The tripartite relationship between coach, coachee and university.

> A collaborative coach believes in the ability of the individual to create ideas, decide for themselves and move their situation forward [using] [...] advanced skills of listening, questioning and reflection.
>
> (Starr, 2021, p. 8)

However it is defined, the agreed contract is the thread which runs throughout the duration of the relationship. The Association for Coaching (Association for Coaching [AfC], 2012), European Mentoring and Coaching Council (European Mentoring and Coaching Council [EMCC], 2015) and the International Coaching Federation (International Coaching Federation [ICF], 2019) all cite contracting – also referred to as 'the coaching agreement' – as a core common coaching competency. The Global Code of Ethics (2021, p. 4) encourages coaches to consider the following approach to contracting:

> Before starting work with a client, members will explain and strive to ensure that the client and sponsor know and fully understand the nature, terms, and conditions of the coaching, mentoring or supervision contract, including financial, logistical, and confidentiality arrangements.

When working with students, contracting is the commitment made between staff and student to work *in partnership*. Ideally, it is a co-designed framework that provides both parties with a working boundary within which they can safely begin to explore and return to if at any point the helping relationship begins to deviate from its initial aim(s). The contracting conversation is the process of clarifying what coaching is and equally as important, what it *isn't*. It is where a mutual understanding and agreement of the approach and the process is established.

Clarifying what coaching isn't

In HE, it is rare to have 'pure' coaching conversations without occasionally drawing on our 'expert power' (French and Raven, 1959) when we recognise that something is hindering the student from making progress towards their goals. As authors in Chapter 2 of this volume have already set out, our 'expert power' in HE is why, in practice, our work as coaches in the PLA Service cuts across a coaching and mentoring continuum. Chapter 7 also shows the ways in which coaching might usefully be seen as an extension of the Information, Advice and Guidance continuum. Also important, is the HE context: as members of staff, we have an obligation to fulfil a duty of care to students which necessitates a relationship which goes beyond a 'pure' coaching relationship. Figures 3.2 and 3.3 illustrate the relationship between coaching, expert power and individual agency in

Figure 3.2 A spectrum illustrating the flow between expert power and individual agency in helping relationships – adapted from (Webster, no date).

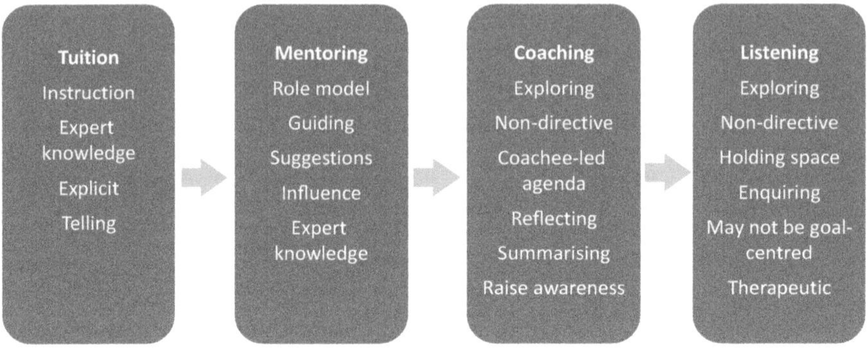

Figure 3.3 The four typical roles involved in supporting a student in higher education.

this setting. This image might also serve as a useful tool for reflecting on the scenarios when practitioners may offer their expert power. Perhaps, for example, when a student feels they have thoroughly explored their options without success.

Counselling (or 'listening') and the importance of boundaries

Definitions of coaching very often involve many of the same verbs used in definitions of counselling: 'converse,' 'reflect,' 'explore,' 'reframe,' 'commit to' and so on. Without careful contracting it would be easy, therefore, for a student to assume that, like counselling, coaching is primarily therapeutic (Bachkirova and Baker, 2018). In Chapter 1 of this volume, Jenny Lynden outlines some of the ethical considerations when using coaching approaches in one-to-one interactions with students: differentiating these from clinical or therapeutic interventions is one of these.

Experienced coaches often take an integrative approach to their practice by making appropriate use of theories of psychology, such as person-centred, cognitive behaviour therapy and/or solution-focused (British Association for Counselling and Psychotherapy, 2024). A solution-focused coaching approach works well for experienced and novice coaches as well as specialist coaches who support students in HE, as it provides a safe structure to empower the student to draw upon their own resources in developing solutions to problems (Devine, Meyers and Houssemand, 2013), explored further in Chapters 4 and 7. It is imperative that the contracting conversation clarifies the key differences between counselling and coaching and establishes the boundary beyond which coaching would not be the most appropriate intervention. It might be usefully summarised as follows:

- Counselling: Looking back to understand the present.
- Coaching: The present as a catalyst for looking forward

This is not to say there will not be overlapping themes, nor that coach-mentors should steer a student away from exploring past experiences. Yet to honour the ethos of coaching, practitioners will ideally use this to support the student in clarifying their desired objectives and, in doing so, developing a forward momentum. A clearly understood and agreed coaching contract is one in which the student gives permission to staff to re-align them with their desired future self and direction, and where they (the coach-mentor) observe when the student may be getting 'stuck' in regression.

Effective contracting means that practitioners can confidently highlight areas that may be more appropriately addressed outside the parameters of the helping relationship. This serves not just as a clarification for the student, but also as a reminder and a safeguard for the coach that they must ethically consider their remit and the limits of the coaching space to minimise the risk of harm – as discussed in Chapter 1. When contracting takes place, it may therefore be useful to invite a student to consider who or what else could be identified as an appropriate source of support where the discussion and/or identified need clearly sits beyond the boundary of the relationship with the coach-mentor.

What about mentoring?

We have already acknowledged that, as practitioners within the PLA Service pilot project, we have comfortably drawn upon techniques from across a coaching and mentoring continuum. For example, there may be times when a student requires, or explicitly requests, the expertise of their coach-mentor to support them in developing their own thinking. They may need practical information, advice or guidance, for example. In such instances, the practitioner is not coaching, but mentoring. In the scenario below, we offer an example of how this might transpire in a helping relationship and how to manage this through contracting, and re-contracting.

Scenario one: 'Coach' as a mentor

A student who is new to HE identified 'building academic confidence' as the overall goal they wanted to work towards with a coach-mentor. The student has been asked to write a reflective statement as part of an assessment and requests help. Their coach-mentor has enquired as to where they may be able to source information on how to do this and has asked them what they have tried so far. The student advises that they have read the resource supplied by their tutor, but still require help. They have spoken to their tutor but remain unsure of how to express themselves in writing. It becomes apparent to the coach-mentor that as the student is describing this 'block,' that their energy is changing. They begin to appear tense and emotional.

In this scenario, the student's support need requires the practitioner to adapt. When moving towards the mentoring end of the continuum in this way, it can be helpful to acknowledge this with the student and highlight the temporary nature of the potential shift in power dynamic. This is because during this shift, the staff member becomes expert. This caveat can be articulated by referring the student back to the contracting agreement and asking their permission to give information or advice. Where the student takes up this offer, the practitioner may offer to recontract temporarily to continue a role further towards the mentoring end of the continuum until they agree with the student otherwise.

Tutoring: a special mention

Mentoring and tutoring share many elements – not least of all in the demonstration and application of expert knowledge, and coaching is often used in personal tutoring, outside of subject-specific tuition (Lochtie et al., 2018). However, in the context of contracting, we have identified tuition separately to highlight the nature of expert academic knowledge. The reticence that students can feel when approaching a lecturer or tutor on their module for support is well known in the literature on help seeking in HE (Morosanu, Handley and O'Donovan, 2010, p. 673). This can be the case even when students are academic high achievers (Wong and Chiu, 2019, pp. 875–876). Through the lens of transactional analysis (Berne, 1958), we might consider the student as operating from their child ego state and the tutor in the critical parent role. This power dynamic can lead to an emotional reaction from the student, and as empathetic practitioners, we might feel inclined to intervene and 'fix' the situation to alleviate the student's distress. To explore this further, let us consider a scenario.

Scenario two: how much 'helping' to do in coaching

A student tells their coach-mentor that they do not know how to create a PowerPoint Presentation for an assignment, and they feel stuck. They are reluctant to ask their tutor, as their tutor has already delivered a 'how to' tutorial. What could the practitioner do? Here, it is important to remember that working on the coaching side of the continuum, a practitioner would seek to help the student identify the barriers and explore possible solutions. It is critical that coaching does not remove the barrier for the student where options for developing self-efficacy exist (Harris, 1969). For the coach to assume the role of 'fixer' they may remove agency from the student to find their own way forward. Furthermore, in the above example, a practitioner may recognise that there is a barrier *behind* the barrier that also needs to be addressed: the student's apparent reluctant to ask for help.

In such scenarios, contracting can play a crucial role in addressing assumed power dynamics (French and Raven, 1959). For example: Does the student view the coach as another 'expert' or 'tutor'? To help to clarify this, practitioners might usefully define their role at the outset, emphasising that they are generally acting as a facilitator rather than an expert, thereby helping the student understand that the relationship is collaborative rather than hierarchical. How does the coach-mentor explain the difference and seek to foster an adult-adult relationship? They might explain that, unlike a tutor who imparts knowledge, their role is often to support the student to discover their own solutions. This explanation can help to encourage mutual respect and positions both parties on an equal footing, fostering an 'adult-adult' relationship (Berne, 1958).

PLA Service evaluation has found that help seeking can be enhanced by coaching (94 percent of respondents stated they more confident about asking for help when needed as a result of PLA support; see Figure 1.4) – which further highlights the importance of contracting. For example, in the student experience survey between 2023 and 2024, a significant number of students who had identifying help seeking as a barrier went on to say how coaching enabled them to seek support from their tutors (and how impactful that was subsequently for their studies). Some students talked explicitly about the way coaching reframed their view of help seeking as a positive behaviour:

> I feel more confident about admitting I'm struggling and need help. [My PLA] has made me see that asking for help is not a weakness but a strength, as it shows I am willing to work at improving to make things better […] It sounds daft to say that the ability to ask for help, to reach out, was such a difficult thing for me to do, but knowing someone was there, for me was so alien.
>
> (Student Experience Survey, 2023–2024)

Others identified help seeking as a change they made after PLA support – sharing that coaching helped them to develop 'a more open approach in contacting [my] tutor for help/guidance,' approach tutors 'directly for assistance.' In these and many other student cases, effective contracting underpinned a relationship in which coach-mentors did not 'fix' issues but helped students to identify the support they needed and seek it.

Recommendations for inclusive contracting in HE

Contracting with students will, of course, depend on the needs of the student, the forum in which contracting takes place (such as in-person, over the telephone or video call, or even by correspondence), and the personal style of the coach-mentor. Van Nieuwerburgh (2017, pp. 43–46) recommends that the following are important tenets of co-creating an effective coaching contract:

1. **Operational issues**: Number, duration, location and frequency of sessions.
2. **Shared understanding of coaching**: That coach and coachee expect the same kind of interaction and that the coachee understands the difference between coaching, counselling and mentoring.

3. **Cancellations and endings**: Agreement about how to cancel a session or withdrawing from the coaching relationship altogether.
4. **Ethical conduct**: The coach explains which code of ethics they are adhering to.
5. **Confidentiality**: The coach outlines how they will ensure confidentiality of the coaching conversations, as well as clarifying where confidentiality may need to be broken (such as where a safeguarding concern arises). The coach should also mention the context in which supervision may be used to aid their own professional reflections.
6. **Competence**: The coach is clear about the boundaries of their role and is explicit about their level of experience.
7. **Permissions**: The coach should seek permission for taking notes and enquire as to the level of challenge a coachee is comfortable with.
8. **Personal style**: The coach shares their coaching style with the coachee (for example, being non-directive).

By including 'personal style,' Van Nieuwerburgh highlights the importance of how the coach communicates their coaching approach to the student. As practitioners, it can be helpful to consider our coaching style, both in the context of rapport building and boundary maintenance. Is it jovial, cautious, challenging, neutral, non-directive? It is important to describe that approach to a student and invite them to share what approach they would value. Consider the student with ADHD, who may like to get up and walk around and/or stim (a self-stimulatory behaviour) whilst they do their thinking. Or the student recovering from a stroke who needs shorter sessions because they tire after 20 minutes. Or perhaps a student who is hearing impaired and needs sessions via video call so that live captions and transcripts can be available.

Adapting our approach to contracting should go beyond the requirement to offer adjustments to students with disabilities, however. As outlined in Chapter 2, being inclusive by design is a central tenet of the PLA Service's equity-centred approach. A simple principle is to ask students if they would like to make you aware of any needs or preferences, or anything you could do more generally to align your approach with theirs. If they are unsure, seeking their permission to offer suggestions can be valuable. Not all students will know what adjustments they can access. Therefore, an open discussion at the contracting stage that invites them to revisit their needs *at any stage* of the coaching partnership will help to build trust and psychological safety.

Confidentiality

Exploring confidentiality is a key part of any helping relationship. The ethics of confidentiality in coaching are introduced in Chapter 1 of this volume. In HE, there are additional considerations which will determine confidentiality in coaching and mentoring relationships. For instance, institutional safeguarding policies might determine occasions where confidentiality would need to be breached, where there was a safeguarding concern for a child and/or vulnerable adults, and/or welfare concerns (such as if they are at risk of harm or pose a risk to others). Transparency regarding record keeping is another important foundation and may depend on institutional systems. In most cases, only minimal, relevant information will need to be recorded and in a manner that protects student confidentiality. For example, if notes are digital, they would be stored in an encrypted, password-protected system. If they are physical notes, they would be kept in a locked drawer or cabinet that only the practitioner has access to. In our own practice, we have found that it can be helpful to reassure students that records are for practitioner use, aimed at enhancing the quality of coaching, and that they are stored in compliance with UK GDPR. Depending on the practitioner's role, it may be necessary to acknowledge any instances where consultation with other professionals in reflective practice or supervision may take place. However, it can reassure students to know what whilst this may necessitate giving examples, identifiable information is not disclosed. What is critical is that students are involved in co-creating the confidentiality agreement in a helping relationship. Inviting students to ask questions about confidentiality also helps to ensure they feel comfortable and secure.

What are the pitfalls of poor contracting?

In cases where practitioners have not clearly contracted with students, the helping relationship may be adversely impacted. Below is an example of poor contracting and how this may impact on the coaching relationship.

Scenario three: open-ended support

A coach-mentor and student agree on a programme of six coaching sessions over a duration of six months. As the six-month period draws to a close, the student asks for continued support.

The practitioner feels invested in their progress and wishes to support the student until the end of their programme. They therefore agree to continuing to offer them open-ended sessions for as long as they find them useful.

The potential impact here is that the professional boundaries of the coaching and mentoring relationship are blurred. This could lead to a dependency, where the student might rely on the support for longer than necessary, hindering their ability to develop self-sufficiency. The absence of a clear end point may also create possible ambiguity around goals and outcomes. The student might not have a specific objective in mind, which can lead to less effective sessions. There is also a risk that practitioners become overextended, especially if they feel obliged to continue offering open-ended support, and a potential impact on the quality of the coaching and mentoring.

In this discussion of the professional' underpinnings of contracting, we have seen how this helps establish a coaching and mentoring relationship. Contracting helps to establish the mechanism for collaboration, not only between the coach-mentor and student but also with other invested parties such as the university. In the next part of this chapter, Emma considers the logistical elements of contracting with students – or contracting at the 'procedural' level (Hay, 2011).

Contracting at the 'procedural' level

The procedural aspects of contracting in coaching refer to the formal processes and agreements that outline the 'where' and 'when' of coaching. As discussed by Wheatley and Hawkins (2022), it is imperative that we get the *procedural* elements of contracting correctly from the beginning, as doing this helps with establishing trust, helps ensure psychological safety and helps manage expectations. If we do not contract effectively, we risk damaging rapport, trust and confidence in the relationship.

Formality in contracting

Establishing whether to adopt a formal or informal approach to contracting with students is perhaps the first consideration for practitioners. In their comparative study of coaching and mentoring programmes in HE, Jones and Smith observe that a critical requirement of these programmes is to enable the students to take ownership of their learning, improve skills and progress towards their career goals; they cite examples in the literature which show the benefits of a formal approach to doing so (2022, p. 215). In their research on coaching non-traditional students within university, Spencer (2024) noted that many of the coaches working with students chose to adopt a relaxed/informal approach with the aim of encouraging students to commit to and engage with, coaching support.

When working with students in HE, contracting may well take a blended approach. As practitioners in the PLA Service, for example, we initiate a student's coaching and mentoring journey with an introductory interaction (sometimes known as a 'chemistry call'). Here, we adopt formal and informal elements. A contracting template provides structure but – like Spencer (2024) – we aim for an approach which creates a sense of psychological safety needed for curiosity, openness and challenge. Table 3.2 is an example of a contracting template, building on recommendations in Van Nieuwerburgh (2017). It could also be used to cover elements of contracting at the 'professional' level such as confidentiality and ethics, before exploring the logistics of one-to-one sessions.

Contracting templates can be valuable tools for ensuring consistency and professionalism across teams (as well as covering legal protection and compliance). They can also help aid accountability and help practitioners adhere to ethical practice. Deciding whether to use coaching templates, or informal approaches, are key considerations for the procedural elements of contracting. Below, are some further reflective questions to support this decision-making and design.

Table 3.2 Template to support contracting when coaching and mentoring students

Topics to cover with student	Content (examples of points to discuss within contracting)
Permission	• Seek permission for taking notes (now and in sessions)
What contracting is	• Purpose of the contract is to establish a transparent, mutual agreement as the basis on which to build the relationship – what you can expect from me and what I can expect from you. • Contracting is a partnership, and both coach and coachee may bring questions.

(Continued)

Table 3.2 (Continued)

Topics to cover with student	Content (examples of points to discuss within contracting)
Shared understanding of coaching and mentoring	• Boundaries and what coaching isn't. • Practitioner approach (for example: non-directive, non-judgemental, challenging). • Coaching and mentoring continuum • Explain which Code of Ethics will be applied (for example the EMCC, 2021 or ICF, 2021).
Confidentiality	• Confidentiality assurance • Occasions when confidentiality may be broken (for example safeguarding or welfare concerns).
Contract details and information sheet Roles and responsibilities	My commitment is to: • Be available to you at agreed times. • Provide providing a trusting, confidential relationship for you to explore issues and difficulties and move towards change. • Endeavour to support you in this process. Your commitment is to: • Be open and honest. • Be committed to optimising the use of the coaching time. • Have a serious intent and desire to change. • Be willing to try new ways of learning. • Keep to your commitments and inform me ASAP if things are not working for you. • Be willing to explore, challenge and change thoughts, feelings and actions if you feel it will be beneficial for you. • Cancellations in writing as soon as possible and a minimum of three working days before the scheduled session. • Towards the end of these sessions, we can discuss progression and next steps. • Termination at end of coaching should be in writing and agreed before the final coaching session to allow time for closure.
Operational issues	• Number of sessions • Length of sessions • Location of sessions • Frequency of sessions
Date of first appointment.	• XX/XX/XXXX

Reflective questions: decision-making and design in contracting

- What is the purpose of the coaching engagement?
- What are the expectations of the student?
- What is the student's personality and learning style?
- How motivated and engaged is the student?
- What type of follow up or accountability is required?
- What cultural and social factors should be considered?
- How will feedback and evaluation be undertaken?

Communication preferences

Coaching and mentoring in the context of distance and hybrid learning means that establishing communication preferences is a vital part of contracting. In the PLA Service, we discovered that offering students the agency to select their preferred method of communication for coaching sessions – over the phone or through a video call – proved helpful for engagement and resulted in a broadly even split. For example, from September 2023 to July 2024, 54 percent of students who registered for coaching with the PLA Service, opted to undertake the coaching via the phone, with approximately 46 percent choosing to undertake coaching via Video call (using Microsoft Teams). Anecdotally, students shared that 'FaceTime' sessions with their PLA were valuable.

Support by correspondence can also offer an additional mechanism where students require a reasonable adjustment or are otherwise unable to engage with telephone and video calls. This might be because of a mental health need, or hearing impairment. Within the PLA Service, we created a procedure and accompanying guidelines that allowed the team to provide email coaching to students (Clay and Peat, 2023). There are examples elsewhere in the literature of enhancing communications in coaching via text-based (SMS) communications or social media (Miller, 2020). Accessing services in this way can take down barriers to receiving support. Isaacson (2021) has found that artificial intelligence (AI) will further transform coaching by adapting to diverse communication preferences. There is, of course, a much wider conversation about AI coaching and its place in HE (Diller, 2024). This is revisited in the postscript to this volume.

Timing and pacing of sessions

Contracting will also involve reaching an agreement on the timing and pacing of coaching and mentoring appointments. As outlined in the introduction to this volume, coaching is generally time bound but long term. This requires practitioners to work with their students to consider how to use the support and when. It could be, for instance, that students are encouraged to consider when these meetings might be most effective in relation to assignment due dates, or tutor feedback. They might also be supported to consider when it would be most beneficial for them to receive coaching. In our experience, it can be constructive to approach this through questions such as:

- How will you make the best use of your coaching sessions?
- How quickly do you want to achieve your goals?
- How would you prefer to pace your sessions?
- How much time do you need to reflect and act on insights between sessions?
- Would it be helpful to arrange coaching sessions around assignment due dates, tutor feedback dates, etc?
- What will you do if you need to access support in between those sessions?

Using prompts such as these during contracting, it is critical to keep in mind that a significant portion of coaching and mentoring work takes place outside of sessions. This allows for steps to be taken towards goals, as well as developmental space and time for learning. Giving the student time and space to think is imperative if coaching and mentoring is to be impactful. As Kline noted in her seminal work, 'thinking for yourself is the thing on which everything else depends' (1999, p. 24).

Where coaching is taking place in a one-to-many (or group) setting, there may be less flexibility to accommodate individual student preferences with regard to precise timing or pacing, but contracting will nevertheless take place. The contract will be drawn up and agreed between the group members and the coach and it is important to contract from the off to ensure that all parties have clarity, an understanding of the objectives of the session and expectations of each member of the group are met. It is also an opportunity to consider how to work together, what might be achieved and to agree confidentiality and boundaries. In Chapter 5 of this volume, an example of group contracting is provided in the PLA Service's 'ways of working' template.

Re-contracting – why, when and its purpose

We have seen some of the critical elements of procedural contracting which create positive foundations with students, but it is the role of the practitioner to listen for opportunities within all coaching sessions to 're-contract.' Re-contracting refers to the ongoing process of revisiting and updating the agreements made at the beginning of the coaching and mentoring relationship. The maxim, 'Always Be Contracting,' has been shaped by thought leaders, such as Block (2011) to emphasise the importance of clarity, alignment and continuous re-evaluation in professional relationships.

When working with students, re-contracting could be required if the student's goals or situation change. For example, a student may originally ask to use their coaching and mentoring sessions to improve their motivation, but later realise they need more help with time management. In this case, the practitioner and student could discuss the new priority and adjust the coaching plan to address time management techniques. Another common occurrence which might necessitate re-contracting is where students feel that they are not making the expected progress in achieving their goals. In this case, the practitioner and student could evaluate the current approach, identify any barriers and potentially set new goals or methods to overcome the stagnation. Re-contracting can also help when students are regularly missing appointments. In this case, the practitioner could usefully revisit the cancellation policy and methods of communicating with them as coach-mentor. Re-contracting here can present the opportunity to discuss why the student is missing sessions and whether there are any obstacles or barriers stopping them from attending sessions. Table 3.3 provides an example of steps involved in the re-contracting process and questions that might be used in these, and other, common scenarios.

Creative contracting in coaching

Creative contracting in coaching is useful when a standard, formal approach may not fully address the unique needs or dynamics of a coaching relationship. It can allow for a more personal and adaptability in the coaching journey. The two scenarios below offer examples of situations where creative contracting can help planning work with students.

Table 3.3 Re-contracting in action

Re-contracting in action	
Coach initiates the conversation	Initially, when you opted into coaching, you set out your main goal as X Y Z. However, over the last two sessions, I'm noticing you have moved towards ABC.
Reflect and review current goals and progress.	*Suggested questions* What progress have you made towards your initial goals? What challenges have you encountered? Which goals feel completed or no longer relevant? How have your goals changed? What is currently the most important thing for you to focus on – academically or personally? Have any new priorities or changes come up that we should consider? Is there anything you would like to explore that we haven't discussed yet?
Clarify new objectives.	*Suggested questions* What feels most important to you right now? Are your priorities different now compared to when we first set your goals? What areas do you feel most excited or concerned about? What specific goals do you want to focus on going forward? What is important to you about achieving these new goals? What difference will it make if you achieve this goal?
Adjust the coaching plan.	*Suggested questions* What exactly would you like to achieve, and by when? How will you know when you've achieved this goal? What steps can we break this down into to make it more manageable?

(*Continued*)

Table 3.3 (Continued)

Re-contracting in action	
Summarise goals, document and agree.	Once the new goals are clarified, document these, timelines and any agreed-upon accountability measures.
Confirm understanding.	Ensure the student feels confident about the new goals and is clear on the next steps. *Suggested question* Are we clear on the next steps and how we'll measure progress?

Scenario four: contracting for inclusion

A student opts in to receive coaching and mentoring via online, video meetings. On beginning their coaching relationship, the practitioner acknowledges that the student has a physical disability and suggests using creative contracting to explore alternative ways of working together which may enhance the accessibility and the effectiveness of the for the student's individual needs. After discussing the impact of the student's disability and how this might manifest in the coaching space, the student and the practitioner agree to include the following points as part of their contracting:

- Shorter, more frequent sessions to minimise prolonged sitting, along with incorporating breaks for stretching and movement.
- Option of 'walk and talk' sessions conducted over the telephone, which allows the student to stay active.
- Option to experiment with different ways of working at any point in the coaching relationship should the student wish to try out an idea for a new adjustment.

By regularly revisiting the student's preferences, the coach-mentor is able to ensure that the environment was conducive to growth and learning.

Scenario five: students with dependents

A student is a single-parent family with two young children and limited access to childcare. Typically, it would be part of coaching contract that sessions must be confidential and uninterrupted. However, together, the student and practitioner agree to:

- Use audio (not video) calls, so that children were not being recorded for safeguarding reasons.
- Prioritise children's safety and wellbeing and allow for sudden interruptions, breaks and sudden endings.
- Acknowledge that coaching may be less effective due to divided attention and interruptions.
- Accept noise and distraction and discuss what is the most effective way for this to be managed during the session.

In this case, the coach was also mindful of safeguarding policies and their duty of care towards children's wellbeing. They were also mindful that the same approach may not be possible in other contexts and to manage the student's expectations with this.

Tools to aid contracting

There are a range of tools which support coaches and mentors to identify goals, strengths and areas of development in their coachees. These are often referred to as 'diagnostic' tools because they help both parties understand each other better; they can also help pinpoint and prioritise areas on which the coaching relationship can usefully focus (Clutterbuck, no date). The word 'diagnostic' is problematic because it can infer a deficit in the coachee which the coach-mentor is there to 'diagnose.' These tools are perhaps better thought of as self-reflective or self-assessment exercises which coach-mentors can use to raise self-awareness in students and support the monitoring of 'distance travelled' (or progress against goals). Strengths assessments might be used, for example, to help students identify their core strengths and talents, allowing them to focus on areas where they naturally excel. The VIA Strengths Survey (no date) is designed to surface strengths and provide strategies to leverage them. Related to this are motivational and value assessments.

Another example of a tool which can enhance contracting with students and could be employed in a range of helping relationships, is the Wheel of Life exercise (Coactive Coaching, no date; Whitworth et al., 2010). The Wheel of Life is a widely used and readily available diagram which helps coachees to assess and reflect on their own needs, in a holistic way. This is designed for self-assessment, where individuals can rate their satisfaction in each area by shading or marking sections of the wheel (explored further in Chapter 4). When supported to use the Wheel of Life at the contracting stage of a relationship, students can evaluate their current situation, set priorities for their actions and create goals to focus on within their coaching journey. This might include:

- Wellbeing – considering factors such as self-care, physical health, mental health, relaxation, recreation, hobbies, time management and home environment.
- Studying and academic skills – considering planning, focus, organisation, essay writing skills, motivation, confidence, self-esteem and time management.
- Holistic – considering wider issues such as finances, relationships, studying, work, friends, family and career.

Clearly, the needs of the person being coached, the context and the aims of the coaching or mentoring relationship all play a role in a coach choosing and adapting the right tool based upon experimentation and reflective learning (Clutterbuck, 2010). Indeed, a focus on the needs of a student will also inform many of the decisions made about contracting at the 'procedural' level. In the final section of this chapter, Josh takes us through some of the 'psychological' dimensions of contracting which can help to strengthen a support relationship with a student (Hay, 2011).

Contracting at the 'psychological' level: understanding 'chemistry'

In executive and career coaching, practitioners will often use 'chemistry' meetings to establish the foundations of a relationship; for coachees, they are an opportunity to consider the compatibility between themselves and a coach and select who they choose to work with (Pedrick, 2020, p. 106). Coaching and mentoring in HE generally does not afford these opportunities, yet establishing 'chemistry' at the contracting stage of a helping relationship remains important.

In our practice in the PLA Service, to help form relationships with the distance-learning students we support, an initial 'chemistry' conversation forms part of the contracting process. Like Chrissie and Emma, I use contracting to ensure a student has a secure understanding of the service, negotiate ways of working and outline the parameters of support. Moreover, goal clarification, shared expectations and desired outcomes may also be agreed at this juncture. As practitioners, we can often determine quite quickly whether coaching and mentoring is an appropriate intervention for the student; this interaction also gives a student the opportunity to establish if they would like to commit to coaching. As discussed in Chapter 1 of this volume, there is an ethical imperative for coach-mentors in HE to make appropriate and timely onward referrals when coaching is not appropriate.

Here, we use 'chemistry' to refer to the positive connection between coach-mentor and student. Moreover, chemistry is commonly used in conjunction, and sometimes interchangeably, with the word 'rapport,' to denote a degree of affinity, understanding and the comfort to be one's true self (Thiers, 2019; Foy, 2021). The evidence shows that building chemistry from the outset creates firmer grounds for effective work to take place in subsequent sessions. As fluently summarised by Koh (2020, no pagination), chemistry is fundamental to the coaching relationship:

> Chemistry calls are conversations that matter, and it's not just about closing the client, but it's also about the conversation of the heart. It's about the realness and authenticity of the call. It's about two people coming together in a masterful coaching conversational process to create change. And the coaching process becomes the great catalyst for the clients to experience the breakthroughs in their lives.

Incompatibility

There are occasions where it becomes apparent at an early stage of the coaching relationship that the pairing is incompatible. Incompatibility can be defined as the inability for coaching goals to be efficiently met (Starr, 2021). Incompatibility can present itself in a myriad of ways based on factors relating to that of the coach, the coachee or a combination of the two. Differences in gender, culture, religion, class, sexual orientation and even availability can, consciously or unconsciously, create barriers to building the chemistry needed for effective coaching sessions to take place and the relationship to develop over time (Bennett, 2008; Foy, 2021). If such factors have the capacity to cause bias, negative impact or influence the trajectory and effectiveness of the intervention, it would be best to make alternative arrangements at the earliest point possible. This will allow the coach to adopt a 'no-fault divorce' approach in which they constructively re-align the student by promptly recommending another coach they envision would best fit the student's expectations and coaching requirements (Megginson and Clutterbuck, 2004; Tulpa, 2015). In some cases, this may result in an internal referral to another coach. However, on other occasions, it may be that the student requires an alternative form of support, in which case they can be referred or signposted accordingly.

In some cases, it becomes clear over time that even if a helping relationship has the correct focus yet lacks chemistry, it will most likely have an unproductive outcome (Megginson and Clutterbuck, 2004). The importance of the chemistry between student and practitioner has been a clear theme in the evaluation of the PLA Service. Students have expressed that they feel a greater sense of belonging, empowerment to overcome challenges and increased confidence about their capabilities because of the coaching received (Hillman, Lochtie and Purcell, 2024). The safety of the helping relationship is often at the centre of this, as the following examples attest to:

> I felt listened too [sic] and understood all the time. I felt safe and welcome. Being able to say that things weren't all that great, at particular times, was a relief beyond words. Being heard is different to being listened to. Being allowed to speak and being respected for having a voice was such an incredible experience.
>
> Having a PLA really helped me as it felt like I had someone who understood the challenges I was facing, helped to keep me accountable when I felt like giving up, as well as providing a 'safe space' to talk openly without any judgement.
>
> My PLA was extremely supportive, and I looked forward to every session with them. They made me feel like I am human and that they cared. They became a major part of my support network who took time to understand the way I work.

The literature also highlights this interplay of experience, relatability and credibility in creating an environment that feels safe and supportive (Burgoon and Hoobler, 2002; Van Coller-Peter and Manzini, 2020; Starr, 2021).

Most importantly, regardless of the presence or absence of common lived experiences between practitioner and student, chemistry emerges organically when both parties make an intentional effort to comprehend the other, understanding their perspective and experience of the world (Starr, 2021). Also, as Van Coller-Peter and Manzini (2020, p. 6) assert, it is most beneficial when both coach and student show up as their true selves: as authentic as possible. The work a coach does, whether overtly or covertly, to close the gap of difference, is welcomed as Thiers (2019) suggests that human nature predisposes people to innately like that which is like them. In executive coaching, it has been observed that resemblance can help coachees to feel comfortable (Dembkowski, Eldridge and Hunter, 2012) which allows for meaningful and effective repeated engagement. Having the 'best fit' allows a student to play an active role to 'own the space' and lead the journey of their own self-discovery (Tulpa, 2015, p. 45). Additionally, when a coach and student share authentic chemistry, it makes for a deeper working rapport. The questions below are examples of prompts which can be used in an initial meeting between a coach-mentor and student to explore their computability and begin to establish chemistry.

- How has your experience of coaching been so far?
- If you could define the type of coach that would be best suited to help you achieve your goals, how you would describe them?
- What deeper level of knowledge and understanding might a coach need to have to best support you?
- If I said the word 'compatibility,' what comes up for you?
- How will you know that I am compatible for you as a coach?
- What would indicate we were incompatible?
- What might cause us to become incompatible?
- How might a coach who has a different lived experience to you impact how effectively you use this coaching space?
- How might a coach who has a similar lived experience to you impact how effectively you use this coaching space?

Boundaries

In any helping relationship, there is a delicate balance between pleasantness and approachability, and being a friend. For the coaching relationship to be ethically sound and in line with contemporary coaching codes of ethics, the correct boundaries must be firmly outlined and adhered to throughout. In a professional relationship, practitioners will be able to offer constructive challenge without hesitation and any disharmony (Megginson and Clutterbuck, 2004). Ideally, they remain in a position of neutrality. This helps to prevent any sense of competition or 'parent–child' dynamics (Bennett, 2008; Starr, 2021). Certainly, some commentators have noted that coaching relationships that feature an element of tension due to the presence of accountability and challenge can lead to favourable outcomes for coachees (Dembkowski, Eldridge and Hunter, 2012). Striking a balance between 'chemistry' and a boundaried relationship is, then, a key part of contracting. This can also help to guard against dependency. In the PLA Service, as a pilot project commissioned to help improve access, participation and equitable outcomes in HE, it has always been our vision to equip students with a toolkit they could draw upon even after completing their final session with the service.

In the previous section of this chapter, Emma explored the value of re-contracting. This is one way to help manage boundaries with students, reinforcing interactions as time-bound conversations with purpose and direction attached to SMART goals (Foy, 2021). A skilled coach will always be contracting, thus staying vigilant of the signs and cues of where the dynamic shifts, needs are unmet or goals change during the relationship. Megginson and Clutterbuck assert that:

> Relationships with low rapport but high clarity can still deliver results in terms of performance, learning or both together. Relationships with low clarity but high rapport can be enjoyable but are likely to deliver less personal change. Relationships high in both can be argued to be the most rewarding and successful, in terms of measurable outcomes. Where both rapport and goal clarity are low, little can reasonably be expected.
>
> (2004, p. 17)

Regular re-contracting with regards to expectations and agreed ways of working is pivotal. It sets the tone for the atmosphere and manner in which the interactants work together and also prevents dependency (Foy, 2021).

Power dynamics

The power dynamic between staff and students is a limitation to the 'chemistry' that can be established in coaching and mentoring. In our own practice, this issue has been at the centre of our professional reflections because of our own positionality coaching in a service which was commissioned to reduce awarding gaps for Black students, and students from other racially minoritised groups (Hillman, Lochtie and Purcell, 2024). Due to the UK socio-political climate at the time, our unique positionality as a service and the premise behind its very creation, there were active discussions surrounding identity, belonging and power politics. We suggest that these themes are worthy of close consideration and especially when 'targeting' students for support. As a team, we have engaged in an active, reflective and reflexive process on this.

In my own practice, what has become clear is the importance of students being able to 'show up,' be recognised and be respectfully acknowledged in their truth. Upon discovering that coaching could provide them with an empowering 'safe space' which they could cultivate howsoever they chose, I found that students increased their trust in coaching (Hillman, Lochtie and Purcell, 2024; Fanon, 2012). For us as professionals, this safe space provided the flexibility to be creative, employing a series of innovative strategies and approaches to centring equity in our practice (Clay *et al.*, 2023; Hillman, Lochtie and Purcell, 2024). We have found that having a broad awareness and curiosity equips us as coach-mentors with enough knowledge to celebrate the diversity of our students if the opportunity arises and it is appropriate to do so. Consider the scenario below as an example of how the cultural competency of a coach-mentor might help to establish chemistry.

Scenario six: creating chemistry

Chemistry ensures helping relationships are more than transactional. It widens the parameters of the discourse into a relational space which many students might not have journeyed with a member of staff before.

Student A is several weeks into the holy month of Ramadan. As a working parent, they have selected to use their appointment to discuss the complexities of managing the demands of their studies, targets at work and domestic commitments during such a pivotal, spiritual time in their personal life. The practitioner begins by asking the student the following questions:

- If you were to create a study schedule around your prayers, what might that look like?
- Outside of your studies, what might your small daily wins be?
- What would your ideal weekly routine look like post-Eid?

Other questions that could be used to expand this include:

- What do your studies currently require of you?
- What does work currently require of you?
- Where are the complexities found?
- How might you simplify things?
- What seems most important?
- What needs to happen?
- When seems right to do that?
- Who might be able to assist you with your responsibilities during this period?

The coach uses their cultural competency to ask questions which are relevant to the lived experience of this student.

Verbal and non-verbal techniques for creating chemistry

Establishing chemistry in contracting requires us as practitioners to observe the kinesics of the student, meets them where they are at and communicates with them as such (Burgoon and Hoobler, 2002). A member of staff's presence, the energy that they exude and the mannerisms they display, have a profound impact on how the chemistry will feel, how the student will experience the space and how rewarding the session will be (Chamberlin, 2000). Therefore, it is of the utmost importance that as coach-mentors, we are mindful of our demeanour and/or body language.

'Matching' and 'mirroring' are key examples of techniques we can use. When a coach-mentor seeks to match the student, they will slowly and subtly present in the same fashion. For example, if a student enters the session in a distinctively upbeat manner, the coach will progressively project an upbeat manner back. In other cases, matching can be used to change the tone or pace of a conversation. For example, if a student was becoming angry about something, a coach might be deliberately slower with their own behaviours to promote a sense of calm. When a coach-mentor 'mirrors' a student, they will use the exact wording that a student uses in order to reflect back what has been said, to gain clarity and understanding (Burgoon and Hoobler, 2002; Starr, 2021). This can be vital at the contracting stage. For example, 'What I am hearing you say is…,' 'You mentioned…what does that mean to you?' and 'It sounds as if…how accurate is that?,' this allows the student to know that their coach is actively listening and giving validation to how they are feeling without agreeing with their point of view or what they are saying – we let them know it is okay to feel how they feel. This ultimately increases their confidence, trust and the chemistry shared. Moving beyond the performative, these are techniques which can create resonance. Mirroring language can also help students struggling with the language (and jargon?) used in HE.

The work of Hunter et al (2006), gave a word of admonition by highlighting that coaches should veer on the side of caution when trying to attach or decipher meaning from the behaviours or gestures of a student. It was argued that a myriad of social, cultural and spiritual factors can influence the reason behind such things. Moreover, actions can be done involuntarily and unconsciously. Therefore, it can be valuable to spend time observing the changes and considering the impact they may be having on the student (Feldman, 2002; Burgoon and Hoobler, 2002). For example, in moments where there are noticeable energy shifts, a coach might alter their tonality, timbre or pitch to meet the needs of the student accordingly. However, it must be stressed, it is important not to overdo matching or mirroring as this can paradoxically have the opposite effect and create distance (Chamberlin, 2000; Starr, 2021).

In the context of our work with distance learners in the PLA Service, non-verbal cues are more difficult to discern when working over the telephone. In these situations, it can be helpful to intentionally bring to the student's awareness what is being heard, sensed or experienced in the moment. This could be to reframe, to identify the use of an operative word or highlight the emergence of a pattern of thinking. This is to ensure clarity and understanding but also to allow the student to be cognisant of what the coach is picking up within the space. This is exemplified in the work of Van Coller-Peter and Manzini (2020, p. 7) as a participant ('Client B') of their virtual coaching research affirmed that:

> When the coach says, 'What I am actually hearing you say, is …' Or, 'what I hear you say is this …' And, 'What I am getting from you that you are not saying is the following …' So, those kinds of conversations, then I know that although the coach is miles away, they are present to who I am.

This serves as a reminder that whilst chemistry is built from the outset, it is also part of a continuous, collaborative effort between coach and coachee (Feldman, 2002; Tulpa, 2015, pp. 35–45).

Below, we share some reflective questions to support other practitioners to consider how they might establish chemistry with students at the contracting stage and throughout a helping relationship.

Reflective questions

- How can chemistry be established in your context?
- How might it benefit coaching interactions?
- What might you need to consider regarding boundaries?
- How might you handle incompatibility?
- How might your own positionality affect chemistry in your work with a student?

Summary

In this chapter, we have offered a view of contracting with students and how this might work at three different levels: the professional, the procedural and the psychological. In the first part of this chapter, Chrissie outlined the ways in which contracting serves as the foundation for any successful coaching (or mentoring or helping) relationship and offered strategies and approaches for translating this to work with students in HE. In the second part of this chapter, Emma shared insights about navigating the procedural aspects of contracting with students. In the part of this chapter, Josh explored the value, as well as risks, of creating chemistry.

Our aspiration is that, together, we might have offered some insights about the kinds of approaches that could usefully underpin the work of practitioners coaching and mentoring students from marginalised groups in HE. What we have provided is not exhaustive. In many ways, we envisage this as an invitation for others to reflect on and share more about, the foundations we set when we work with students – whether as coaches, mentors, tutors or others in 'helping' relationships. What we would find useful, and anticipate that others may too, is a more comprehensive toolkit for contracting with students. Contracting plays a pivotal role in our interface with students in HE and likely impacts their future access to support and readiness to seek help. Investing time to reflect on our individual approaches to the professional, procedural and psychological levels of contracting has been a valuable exercise for us as practitioners, and we encourage others to engage in this reflexivity.

Bibliography

Association for Coaching (AfC). (2012) *Coaching competencies*. Available at: https://cdn.ymaws.com/www.associationforcoaching.com/resource/resmgr/Accreditation/Accred_General/Coaching_Competency_Framewor.pdf (Accessed: 24 September 2024).

Bachkirova, T. and Baker, S. (2018) 'Revisiting the issue of boundaries between coaching and counselling', in S. Palmer and A. Whybrow (eds.) *Handbook of coaching psychology: a guide for practitioners*. 2nd edn. Abingdon: Routledge, pp. 487–499.

Bennett, J.L. (2008) 'Contracting for success', *The International Journal of Coaching Organisations*, 6(8), pp. 7–14.

Berne, E. (1958) 'Transactional analysis: a new and effective method of group therapy', *American Journal of Psychotherapy*, 12(4), pp. 735–743.

Block, P. (2011) *Flawless consulting: a guide to getting your expertise used*. 3rd edn. San Francisco, CA: Jossey-Bass.

British Association for Counselling and Psychotherapy. (2024) *What is coaching?* Available at: https://www.bacp.co.uk/about-therapy/types-of-therapy/coaching/ (Accessed: 24 September 2024).

Burgoon, J.K. and Hoobler, G.D. (2002) 'Nonverbal signals', in M.L. Knapp and J. Daly (eds.) *Handbook of interpersonal communication*. 3rd edn. Thousand Oaks, CA: Sage Publishing, pp. 240–299.

Carsch, M., Tiknaz, Y., Cooper, P. and Sage, R. (2006) *The handbook of social, emotional and behavioural difficulties*. London: Continuum International Publishing Group Ltd.

Chamberlin, C.R. (2000) 'Nonverbal behaviors and initial impressions of trustworthiness in teacher-supervisor relationships', *Communication Education*, 49(4), pp. 352–364. doi: 10.1080/03634520009379223

Clay, E.M., Blissett, J., Williams, H., Lindley, J. and O'Neil, L. (2023) 'Developing an equity lens: the experience of creating a professional framework for coaches and mentors', *Journal of Learning Development in Higher Education*, 26. doi: 10.47408/jldhe.vi26.932

Clay, E.M. and Peat, R. (2023) *Creating flexible accessibility*. Available at: Creating flexible accessibility for distance-learning students while developing a remote coaching and mentoring service | Widening Access and Success at The Open University. Available at: https://university.open.ac.uk/widening-participation/external-events-and-publications/biennial-aps-conference/2023-abstracts-creating-flexible-accessibility (Accessed: 12 December 2024).

Clutterbuck, D. (2010) 'Coaching reflection: the liberated coach', *Coaching: An International Journal of Theory, Research and Practice*, 3(1), pp. 73–81. doi: 10.1080/17521880903102308

Clutterbuck, D. (2013) *Powerful questions for coaches and mentors*. Liverpool: Wordscape.

Clutterbuck, D. (2023) *Coaching and mentoring: a journey through the models, theories, frameworks and narratives of David Clutterbuck*. Abingdon: Routledge.

Clutterbuck, D. (no date) *Using diagnostic tools*. Clutterbuck Coaching and Mentoring International. Available at: https://clutterbuck-cmi.com/briefings/using-diagnostic-tools/ (Accessed 19 November 2024).

Clutterbuck, D. and Hussain, Z. (2010) *Virtual coach, virtual mentor*. Charlotte, NC: Information Age Publishing.

Coactive Coaching. (no date) *Wheel of life toolkit*. Available at: https://coactive.com/toolkit/ (Accessed: 13 December 2024).

Diller, S.J. (2024) 'Ethics in digital and AI coaching', *Human Resource Development International,* 1–13. Available at: https://coachingfederation.org/blog/navigating-bias in-the-age-of-ai (Accessed: 1 December 2024).

Dembkowski, S., Eldridge, F. and Hunter, I. (2012) *The seven steps of effective executive coaching*. London: Thorogood Publishing.

Devine, M., Meyers, R. and Houssemand, C. (2013) 'How can coaching make a positive impact within educational settings?' *Procedia – Social and Behavioral Sciences*, (93), pp. 1382–1389. doi: 10.1016/j.sbspro.2013.10.048

Dotlich, D.L. and Cairo, P.C. (1999) *Action coaching: how to leverage individual performance for company success*. Hoboken, NJ: Wiley.

European Mentoring and Coaching Council (EMCC). (2015) *EMCC global competence framework*. Available at: https://www.emccglobal.org/leadership-development/competences/ (Accessed: 13 December 2024).

Fanon, F. (2012) *Black skin, white masks*. New York: Grove Press.

Feldman, D.A. (2002) 'Distance coaching', *Training and Development*, 56(9), pp. 54–56.

Foy, K. (2021) 'Contracting in coaching', in J. Passmore (ed.) *The coaches' handbook: the complete practitioner guide for professional coaches*. Abingdon: Routledge, pp. 345–353.

French, J.R.P., Jr. and Raven, B. (1959) 'The bases of social power', in D. Cartwright (ed.) *Studies in social power*. Michigan: University of Michigan, pp. 150–167.

Global Code of Ethics. (2021) *Global code of ethics*. Available at: https://www.globalcodeofethics.org/ (Accessed: 24 September 2024).

Grant, A.M., Franklin, J. and Langford, P. (2002) 'The self-reflection and insight scale: a new measure of private self-consciousness', *Social Behavior and Personality: An International Journal*, 30(8), pp. 821–835.

Harris, T.A. (1969) *I'm OK you're OK: a practical guide to transactional analysis*. New York: Harper and Row.

Hay, J. (2011) 'Setting up the coaching contract', *Transactional Analysis for Coaches and Mentors, IDTA Newsletter*, 6(2), pp. 5–6.

Hillman, J. and Lochtie, D. (2023) 'Coaching and mentoring as "targeted" learning development provision', *Learning Development Magazine*, (April), pp. 20–21. Available at: #LoveLD magazine issue 2 (fliphtml5.com) (Accessed: 20 May 2024).

Hillman, J., Lochtie, D. and Purcell, O. (2024) 'Black students' experiences of coaching and mentoring in higher education: a case study', *International Journal of Mentoring and Coaching in Education*, 13(2), pp. 246–257. doi: 10.1108/IJMCE-01-2023-0011

International Coach Federation (ICF). (2019) *Core competencies*. Available at: https://coachingfederation.org/credentials-and-standards/core-competencies (Accessed: 24 May 2024).

Isaacson, S. (2021) *How to thrive as a coach in a digital world*. London: Open University Press.

Jacobson, D. and Mustafa, N. (2019) 'Social identity map: a reflexivity tool for practicing explicit positionality in critical qualitative research', *International Journal of Qualitative Methods*, 18, pp. 1–1. doi: 10.1177/1609406919870075

Jones, J. and Smith, H.A. (2022) 'A comparative study of formal coaching and mentoring programmes in higher education', *International Journal of Mentoring and Coaching in Education*, 11(2), pp. 213–231. doi: 10.1108/IJMCE-03-2021-0054

Kline, N. (1999) *Time to think: listening to ignite the human mind*. London: Cassell.

Kimsey-House, H., Kimsey-House, K., Sandahl, P. and Whitworth, L. (2010) *Co-active coaching*. 3rd edn. Yarmouth: Nicholas Brealey Publishing.

Koh, J.A. (2020) *How to create powerful chemistry coaching calls*. Available at: https://coachingfederation.org/blog/create-powerful-chemistry-calls (Accessed: 13 December 2024).

Lochtie, D., McIntosh, E., Stork, A. and Walker, B. (2018) *Becoming an effective personal tutor: supporting learners through personal tutoring and coaching*. 2nd edn. Norwich: Critical Publishing.

Martin, A.J. and Marsh, H.W. (2006) 'Academic resilience and its psychological and educational correlates: a construct validity approach', *Psychology in the Schools*, 43(3), pp. 267–281.

Megginson, D. and Clutterbuck, D. (2004) *Techniques for coaching and mentoring*. Abingdon: Taylor and Francis Group.

Megginson, D. and Clutterbuck, D. (2005) *Techniques for coaching and mentoring*. London: Routledge.

Megginson, D. and Clutterbuck, D. (2009) *Further techniques for coaching and mentoring*. Amsterdam: Butterworth-Heinemann.

Miller, S. (2020) *Coaching: Time to talk or time to text?*. Available at: https://www.linkedin.com/pulse/coaching-time-talk-text-simon-miller/ (Accessed: 10 October 2024).

Morosanu, L., Handley, K. and O'Donovan, B. (2010) 'Seeking support: researching first-year students' experiences of coping with academic life', *Higher Education Research and Development*, 29(6), pp. 665–678. doi: 10.1080/07294360.2010.487200

Nagy, A. and Ajit (2024) *A coach's guide to 3 essential holistic coaching strategies for unleashing breakthroughs*. Available at: https://blog.mindvalley.com/holistic-coaching/ (Accessed: 10 October 2024).

Passmore, J., Diller, S.J., Isaacson, S. and Brantl, M. (eds.). (2024) *The digital and AI coaches' handbook: the complete guide to the use of digital technologies in coaching*. Abingdon: Routledge.

Passmore, J., Schlosser, M., Stokes, J. and Grindle, A. (2024) *Trends in digital and AI coaching: executive report 2024*. EMCC Global. Available at: https://www.jonathanpassmore.com/technical-reports/future-trends-in-digital-ai-coaching-executive-report (Accessed: 10 October 2024).

Pedrick, C. (2020) *Simplifying coaching: how to have more transformational conversations*. Maidenhead: McGraw Hill Education.

Spencer, D. (2024) 'The challenges of coaching non-traditional students in higher education: applying a coaching intervention at a UK University', *International Journal of Evidence Based Coaching and Mentoring*, 22(1), pp. 199–213. doi: 10.24384/14c4-yj08

Starr, J. (2021) *The coaching manual: the definitive guide to the process, principles and skills of personal coaching*. 5th edn. Harlow: Pearson Education.

Thiers, N. (2019) 'Seen on the screen: coaching in action: developing rapport', *Educational Leadership*, 77(3), pp. 11–59.

Tulpa, K. (2015) 'Coaching within organizations', J. Passmore (ed.) *Excellence in coaching: The industry guide*. London: Kogan Page, pp. 33–51.

Van Coller-Peter, S. and Manzini, L. (2020) 'Strategies to establish rapport during online management coaching', *SA Journal of Human Resource Management*, 18(2), pp. 1–9. doi: 10.4102/sajhrm.v18i0.1298

Van Nieuwerburgh, C. (2017) *An introduction to coaching skills: a practical guide*. 2nd edn. London: Sage.

VIA Strengths Survey. (no date) *Strengths survey*. Available at: https://www.viacharacter.org/ (Accessed: 10 October 2024).

Webster, H. (no date) *One to one training – rattus scholasticus*. Available at: https://rattusscholasticus.wordpress.com/training-resources/one-to-one-training/ (Accessed: 29 October 2024).

Wheatley, J. and Hawkins, Z. (2022) 'Contracting for a coaching conversation', *The Coaching Crowd* [podcast]. Available at: https://www.igcompany.co.uk/blog/episode025 (Accessed: 10 October 2024).

Wong, B. and Chiu, Y.-L.T. (2019) '"Swallow your pride and fear": the educational strategies of high-achieving non-traditional university students', *British Journal of Sociology of Education*, 40(7), pp. 868–882. doi: 10.1080/01425692.2019.1604209

Coaching and mentoring for wellbeing

4

Fareeha Karim and Leanne Lindsey

Introduction

Our intention in this chapter is to provoke thought, to stimulate reflection and to positively challenge how student wellbeing and mental health can be addressed by coaching and mentoring practitioners. It has been suggested that we are in the midst of a mental health 'crisis' in higher education (HE) and there is a growing body of scholarship and commentary on how to address it (Advance HE, 2024). Our discussions are rooted in evidence-based best practice, derived from this literature as well as learning and evaluation from our own experiences delivering coaching and mentoring in the Personal Learning Advisor (PLA) Service at The Open University (UK). We seek to explore existing coaching and mentoring approaches and how they can be part of a more holistic approach to supporting student wellbeing at university. As discussed in the Introduction to this volume, and further in Chapter 2, coaching and mentoring as part of a continuum of 'helping' approaches and, in this chapter, we draw upon examples from across that continuum. We also seek to explore and address the challenges relating to supporting students from racially minoritised backgrounds as there is a growing body of evidence showing these students are disproportionately impacted by factors affecting wellbeing and study compared to their white counterparts (Arday, Branchu and Boliver, 2022).

As authors, we bring different perspectives to this. A fuller biography for each of us is provided in the contributor list to this volume but for the purposes of this chapter, we highlight Fareeha's identity as a British born, Pakistani, Muslim woman with experience of providing coaching and

DOI: 10.4324/9781003486015-5

mentoring to students from diverse backgrounds. These experiences have prompted further reflection on the ways we might have a positive and meaningful impact on students' wellbeing throughout their study journey by challenging HE policy, where relevant. Leanne is a British Black Caribbean woman with experience delivering careers advice, coaching and mentoring. Leanne's experiences have prompted reflection on ways we can make coaching accessible and inclusive, focusing on supporting communities strategically disadvantaged by institutional, social and economic barriers. Whilst neither of us describe ourselves as health or wellbeing coaches, we share a commitment to ensuring equitable opportunities for everyone to reach their full potential and maintain optimum wellbeing.

In this chapter, we use a broad definition of 'wellbeing' which encapsulates its mental, physical and social factors. Here, The Department of Health definition of wellbeing is simple but instructive: 'feeling good and functioning well and comprises an individual's experience of their life; and a comparison of life circumstances with social norms and values' (2014, p. 6). Often, mental and physical health are unhelpfully considered in isolation, when the reality is that both interact to contribute to overall wellbeing. As such, we feel it appropriate to consider the two as part of the whole, holistically, when it comes to understanding and supporting students' wellbeing. We address the close relationship between study and wellbeing and write about the interventions, tools and models our team of coach-mentors have used that have positively impacted student wellbeing. Additionally in this chapter, we make suggestions for managing boundaries and referrals, explore wellbeing factors that disproportionately impact students from a diverse background and offer recommendations for further research.

The relationship between wellbeing and study

The relationship between wellbeing and study success is symbiotic. One can very often positively or negatively impact on the other. Research has shown the correlation between sleep and enhanced cognitive performance or capacity for learning (Curcio, Ferrara and De Gennaro, 2006; Gillen-O'Neel, Huyng and Fuligni, 2013; Scullin, 2019). There is also evidence to show that those who have a good support network and have regular and positive interactions with others have a positive outlook and are more able to respond to external events in a beneficial way. Studies have revealed that those who are isolated or perceive themselves to be isolated had higher stress levels and face increased challenge when dealing with situations that arise (Tinto, 1975; Cacioppo *et al.*, 2000; Baumeister, Twenge and Nuss, 2002). There is a relevant body of work which has found a significant link between diet and mental health, particularly through the 'gut-brain axis' with the food and nutrients consumed having a positive or negative impact of neuroplasticity, mood, different mind states, memory and cognition (Florence, Asbridge and Veugelers, 2008; Craig and Zinkiewicz, 2010). Regular, sustained exercise has been shown to positively impact academic attainment, wellbeing and happiness (Rothenberg, 2006; Quinn *et al.*, 2009) and help to guard against depression and anxiety (Csikszentmihalyi, 1992). Some studies have even begun to find links between spiritual or religious faith and student wellbeing but only when their faith is accepted within the HE environment or the effect can be detrimental (Abdullah *et al.*, 2021; Watson, 2024).

Motivation for studying also has an impact on academic performance and student wellbeing. This can be intrinsic, for internal satisfaction, or extrinsic, for external reward or outcome. Intrinsic motivation has been shown to have a positive effect on academic performance and wellbeing with lower stress levels experienced by students on their study journey whilst extrinsic motivation is correlated with increased stress levels impacting their wellbeing and performance (Baker, 2004; Ayub, 2010; Goodman *et al.*, 2011).

Student wellbeing can also be negatively impacted by institutional barriers which can be hard to change. The challenge of navigating intranet platforms or virtual learning environments is one example of this. Knowing how to search for and access support is a skill itself that is rarely 'taught.' Furthermore, some support for students may be externally provided or government funded. For example, in the UK, access to Disabled Student Allowance support requires a level of bureaucracy and provision of supporting medical or diagnostic evidence which often precludes access to support before the commencement of study. This can pose a significant barrier with potential impact upon student wellbeing and is also influenced by a wide variety of factors such as language background, mental and physical health comorbidities, status as a 'first-generation' student in HE (Patfield, Gore and Fray, 2022), inequalities in tertiary education and time constraints. Related to this, there is evidence from across the sector that assessment practices in HE are damaging for student wellbeing (Jones *et al.*, 2020). Whilst we know that 'resilience' is a determinant in student success (Slack and Priestley, 2023), institutions must continue to review these damaging practices.

Institutional culture, student demographics and the profile of university staff also affect student wellbeing at university. Many HE institutions (HEIs) require prospective students to go through a registration process where there is little emphasis placed on wellbeing. In cases where the wellness of students impacts their ability to study, this may only manifest during 'fitness to study' or similar processes which apply when students reach crisis point.

Positive interventions and proactively addressing wellbeing can reduce the likelihood that students reach this crisis point in the first instance. Clearly, this might present in unexpected ways and will differ depending on the student's study intensity, age, background – such as racial and economic, additional commitments and life circumstances. Students from racially minoritised backgrounds face these same challenges, however, also face increased barriers, lack of understanding and meaningful support to overcome them (Arday, Branchu and Boliver, 2022). Through working with students with these lived experiences, as well as our own personal experiences, we know that the lack of genuine and sustained change in HE takes an emotional, mental and physical toll, often adding to traumatic past experiences.

Many of the students we work with are considered 'mature' (aged 21+ at the beginning of their undergraduate studies) and commonly manage their studies alongside work commitments, as well as caring responsibilities for children, an older person, or a disabled dependent. Issues such as procrastination, perfectionism and negative experiences within education are not uncommon. Coaching and mentoring often allows students the space to share how they have been impacted by prior experiences. In the context of our work in the PLA Service, where students do have a diagnosis or their mental health support needs have been discerned by staff, formal support is available from a specialist mental health casework team on a referral basis. Coaching and mentoring support exists outside of this specialist mental health provision but is part of a more holistic student support services offer.

In many cases, our experiences have been based on supporting students who do not have an official diagnosis and/or have not made a formal mental health 'declaration.' This is important as we found the level of understanding and support students had varied greatly whether they had a declaration or not. It is never the coach-mentor's role to 'diagnose' or be led by assumptions, but rather to be open to raising self-awareness around wellbeing. This is not without its challenges. Students themselves often underestimate the importance of their overall wellbeing and the impact it can have on their studies. It is important that we, as coach-mentors with a duty of care to our students, are mindful of various ways wellbeing issues may present within the many intersectionalities that exist and that we reflect on how we can best support students.

Supporting student wellbeing with coaching and mentoring

As noted in the introduction to this volume, there is now a wealth of evidence for the impact that coaching and mentoring can have on student success in HE. It has been argued that coaching can create an inclusive learning environment, support academic accommodations, nurture caring relationships, promote on-campus events and support and create a safety net system, all to support psycho-socio-emotional wellbeing among students (Woloshyn *et al.*, 2019; Cliff, 2024). There is also a growing body of work which has revealed its value for helping students to effectively manage a range of stressors during their academic journey (Bernard, 2023; Ciff, 2020; Dekker *et al.*, 2020; Cliff, 2024). In a review of the literature, Lefdahl-Davis *et al.* (2018, p. 71) cited Grant's study (2003) of 20 postgraduate students which discovered that, as well as goal attainment, stress, anxiety and depression also reduced considerably following coaching. Lefdahl-Davis *et al.*'s review (2018) also cited Short, Kinman and Baker (2010) and Fried and Irwin (2016), who found that coaching helped manage stress among undergraduate students, and Devine, Meyers and Houssemand (2013) who found that improving mental health overall, and better managing stress and anxiety can result in improved academic performance. From these findings, Lefdahl-Davis *et al.* (2018, p. 80) asserted that:

> Coaching can be a powerful intervention for students who are in a transitional, challenging season of life. It can also be helpful to those in the minority, those who may feel misunderstood or invisible, and those who face significant oppressive factors in their personal or professional lives.

Findings from the evaluation of coaching and mentoring in the PLA Service might further strengthen this body of evidence. The student experience survey which formed the basis for this evaluation is discussed in the introduction to this volume and is provided in Appendix A. 93 percent of students who received coaching and mentoring support and responded to a survey in 2023 stated their PLA had a positive impact, or significantly positive impact, on achievements or positive changes in their personal life (see Figure 1.4). In what follows, we offer a synthesis of some of the more specific ways in which coaching and mentoring can enhance student wellbeing, with further insights from the findings of our own evaluation work.

Reduced crisis intervention

The pressure on mental health services in HE and in the wider community across the UK continues to grow and many services are unable to meet the demands of those most in need (British Medical Association, 2024). Literature suggests that both undergraduate (Neves and Hillman, 2017) and postgraduate (Evans *et al.*, 2018) students might experience lower levels of wellbeing when compared to the wider population. An increasing demand for wellbeing, mental health and counselling support for students has been widely observed (British Association for Counselling and Psychotherapy, 2024) and there has also been a significant impact on the roles of professionals who support students who are not mental health professionals (Hughes *et al.*, 2018). More generally, the proportion of students disclosing mental health conditions to their university has also risen (Lewis and Stiebahl, 2024). Corresponding with this broader trend, mental health was frequently cited as a barrier to success in the PLA Service student survey, with statements such as 'my mental health is a barrier when it comes to my education, both anxiety and low mo[o]ds where [sic] obstacles I was able to discuss with my PLA.'

There are examples in the wider literature where coaching has been used to support wellbeing including Van Nieuwerburgh and Barr (2016) which focuses primarily on secondary and tertiary education, Atad and Grant (2021) which surveys Israeli undergraduates, and Breslin *et al.* (2023) concentrating on UK-based medical students' wellbeing. A study of a four-session online life coaching program for undergraduate students at a US university (Jackson, 2019) was built upon an online life coaching curriculum, developed by Steinhardt and Dolbier (2008), and suggested that over three decades of research has shown that a range of populations can learn coping skills that increase their ability to manage their lives and life's inevitable crises more effectively. Jackson (2019) concluded that the use of coaching models can improve undergraduate coping skills and decrease the number of mental health-related incidents occurring on campuses.

Supporting students through group and one-to-one coaching and mentoring interventions adds a valuable layer of support. Coaches are uniquely positioned to identify any concerns or support needs prior to a student reaching crisis point and can proactively make referrals or signpost as appropriate. One student shared in their survey responses, for example, that the PLA 'guided' them 'to get mental health help.' This is particularly helpful as students may not be aware of the support and resources available to them. Additionally, through the coaching and mentoring relationship, a coach can encourage and empower a student to engage with other relevant teams and interventions.

Improved coping skills

The results of a quasi-experimental study on the efficacy of coaching interventions for undergraduates to increase positive coping behaviour showed that all participants in the study experienced some level of positive change in their coping skills (Jackson, 2019). Even for those in the comparative group, the study acted as a catalyst to focus on their stress management skills. In the PLA Service evaluation, as shown in Figure 1.4 of the introductory chapter, only 25 percent of respondents felt confident in their ability to cope with study prior to receiving coaching and mentoring, whereas 90 percent agreed or strongly agreed after receiving the support.

As practitioners, we have witnessed how coaching can help students to recognise what is currently not working, as well as helping them to reflect and identify what has worked in the past to manage stress and/or maintain wellbeing. Coaching and mentoring also offer approaches to co-creating new strategies. As one student shared in their survey response: 'I have high anxiety which acts as a blockage for me, speaking to my PLA we came up with ideas on how to overcome my anxiety.' By working together to identify stressors, ineffective habits, past successful strategies and potential new approaches, a coach and student can develop a comprehensive plan to improve the student's mental health and wellbeing.

Coaching and mentoring can also help a student to identify and implement interim coping strategies while they await specialised support. We have seen the value in working with students to develop a crisis management plan that outlines steps to take if their situation worsens. This plan can include emergency contact numbers, a list of supportive activities and strategies for seeking immediate help. With enhanced coping skills, students are better prepared to manage stress, maintain or improve mental health and navigate the complexities of HE and their academic responsibilities. In turn, this contributes to a positive academic experience, improved overall satisfaction and better engagement with their studies.

Enhanced resilience

There are several compelling case studies which evidence how coaching and mentoring can help school and university students to build resilience by fostering a growth mindset, encouraging them to view challenges as opportunities for learning and development rather than impossible obstacles (Dias, Foster and Zunszain, 2019; Fried, Atkins and Irwin, 2019).

The results of a pilot study that examined the effectiveness of a four-week intervention to enhance resilience factors found that the experimental group had significantly higher resilience scores, more effective coping strategies (e.g. higher problem solving, lower avoidant behaviours), higher scores on protective factors (e.g. positive affect, self-esteem, self-leadership) and lower scores on symptomatology (e.g. depressive symptoms, negative affect, perceived stress) postintervention than did the wait-list control group (Steinhardt and Dolbier, 2008; Jackson, 2019). Factors covered during the four-week resilience intervention included problem-focused coping strategies (e.g. active coping, planning, positive reframing, acceptance), emotion-focused coping strategies (e.g. denial, behavioural disengagement, self-distraction, venting), taking responsibility for one's behaviour, changing their disempowering interpretations or thinking into empowering interpretations and increasing participants' awareness of the link between connecting with or withdrawing from friends and loved ones and the corresponding impact on thinking, behaviour and health.

Coaching and mentoring over a number of sessions lends itself to a similar approach with similar effects. For example, one student who worked with our service stated:

> before PLA I lack the support, resilience and tenacity, to set a goal and achieve it (sic) [...] when my confidence was low speaking and sharing my concerns with my advisor supported me. The service I found was vital for me.

Another student shared their experiences as the carer for their two children with autism. In this case, it was coaching and tutor support that contributed to their growing resilience and future focus as they shared that 'PLA support has helped me to gain confident (sic) [...] I am also grateful for [my] tutor who [has] been giving me support in general learning.' They felt that both of these together gave them the 'strength' to 'study' and 'look forward for [a] better future.'

Among the survey responses, there is a notable frequency of words we might associate with resilience such as 'overcome' and 'manage.' Through coaching and mentoring, students appear to develop a toolkit of skills and strategies that enable them to overcome setbacks, maintain a positive outlook and persist in the face of adversity. This resilience enhances their capacity to cope with the immediate pressures of academic life and supports long-term wellbeing.

Increased self-awareness

A student's mental health and wellbeing can greatly affect their ability to identify, pursue and achieve their goals. As demonstrated in a small study on the impact of life coaching on undergraduate students, coaching is an effective intervention for increasing awareness of individual values and strengths (Lefdahl *et al.*, 2018). With increased self-awareness, students are more able to recognise patterns of behaviour that may be detrimental to their progress as well as identify priorities, commitments and habits that are negatively impacting their mental health and wellbeing (Lim *et al.*, 2024).

In some cases, student respondents to the PLA Service survey in 2023–2024 explicitly referenced the impact of coaching and mentoring on their self-awareness, identifying 'paying more attention to self-awareness' as a changed behaviour, or recognising the support they need:

> We discussed issues that I had difficulties dealing with over the years and looking at the idea of completing my degree and realising that the issues I have were really holding a lot of my head space and not allowing me to achieve my goals. I believe that the way forward for me is to be able to talk to someone who will help to widen my thoughts and allow me to weigh up issues.

The feedback we received showed that, through reflective discussions and personalised guidance, students gain deeper insights into their thoughts, feelings and behaviours and are supported to achieve greater clarity about the outcomes they want to achieve for themselves. Increased self-awareness empowers students by giving them a clearer understanding of their strengths and areas for improvement, helping them to make informed decisions about their future.

Stronger sense of belonging and mattering

Developing a strong and trusted connection with a coach can make a student feel accepted, valued and included and provide an anchoring point of connection with the university (Hillman *et al.*, 2024). It can increase students' sense of belonging and mattering, within the coaching relationship and the HEI more broadly, which has been linked to students' intention to persist with their studies (Zawada, 2024).

In particular, the wellbeing of Black and Minority Ethnic students, academics and professional staff within universities is integral in terms of establishing a sense of belonging, which facilitates integration rather than marginalisation within spaces where ethnic minorities are often few in number (Arday, Branchu and Boliver, 2022). For students from marginalised and underrepresented groups, feeling seen, heard, represented and supported can strengthen their sense of belonging which often leads to enhanced confidence and increased engagement.

Moreover, through specific group coaching interventions, students can experience a deepened sense of belonging by connecting with their peers. Group sessions provide a platform for students to share their experiences, challenges and successes, encouraging a sense of community and mutual support. Interacting with peers who may be facing similar struggles or who have overcome comparable obstacles can be incredibly validating and encouraging. It helps students realise that they are not alone in their journey, reducing feelings of isolation and promoting a shared sense of purpose.

In one study looking at the experience of postgraduate students with online group coaching, students reported that the online group coaching was useful as it provided a supportive and safe environment for them to share and work through the challenges they were facing. Participants also noted that the emotional connection with the group allowed them to feel heard and able to express their individual (and sometimes difficult) experiences which they found beneficial (Nacif *et al.*, 2023). For students from marginalised backgrounds, these connections can be particularly empowering as they see their identities and experiences reflected in their peers, further reinforcing their sense of belonging and inclusion at university. This is something we saw reflected in the PLA Service evaluation where 86 percent of student survey respondents felt that it was important for them 'to see and hear students with similar lived experiences and/or shared challenges' in group sessions (see Figure 1.4).

Coaching approaches that facilitate coaching and mentoring as a positive intervention for supporting mental health and wellbeing

A fundamental principle of effective coaching and mentoring is to meet the students where they are. This means that sessions should be student-led, with the approach tailored to support the student's specific needs and desired outcomes. To ensure that the session is relevant, impactful, tailored to the student's unique situation and aligns with the student's goals, it is considered good practice to contract with the student, as detailed in Chapter 3. This is an opportunity to ensure the maintenance of boundaries and ethical responsibilities explained in Chapter 1.

Solution-focused coaching and the GROW coaching model (Whitmore, 2009; Devine, Meyers and Houssemand, 2013) are two approaches that have proven effective for wellbeing support due to their focus on goal setting, actionable steps and positive outcomes. There are differences between the two approaches, therefore integrating them can sometimes better meet the diverse needs of students; these three approaches are explored below.

Solution-focused coaching

A solution-focused approach to coaching in HE concentrates on guiding individuals towards their desired future by using their existing skills, strategies and ideas. This approach views the student as the expert, recognising that they are best placed to identify suitable solutions for themselves. Practitioner and student work together with a growth mindset, structuring each coaching session around a clearly defined, realistic and attainable goal. The student is responsible for clarifying and refining this goal, ensuring it aligns with their needs and aspirations. Additionally, there is an expectation that the student will make positive changes by undertaking agreed-upon actions after each session. OSKAR is a popular framework used to structure solution-focused coaching conversations with 'Outcome,' 'Scaling,' 'Know-how,' 'Affirm' and 'Action' and then 'Review' (McKergow and Jackson, 2002; Passmore, 2021), explored further in Chapter 7.

Criticisms of the solution-focused approach have included the suggestion that it seeks to over-simplify complex problems without addressing underlying problems (Devine, Meyers and Houssemand, 2013, p. 1383). Combining it with other approaches has been found to improve resilience, wellbeing, problem-solving, coping and study skills and ultimately achievement (Campbell and Gardner, 2005; Green, Grant and Rynsaardt, 2007). Furthermore, students navigating more complex circumstances or experiencing significant emotional distress will require a referral for specialist support. However, we have found that in scenarios where students are highly motivated, have a clear idea of what they want to achieve and are ready to seek practical solutions to their challenges, a solution-focused approach can be effective.

GROW

The GROW acronym will be familiar for many practitioners in coaching and mentoring and denotes 'Goals,' 'Reality,' 'Options' and 'Will' (Whitmore, 2009). This model is particularly effective when a student is finding it challenging to balance their immediate circumstances with future aspirations. This coaching model offers a structured framework similar to solution-focused coaching, but with an additional emphasis on understanding the current reality (R) of the student (Passmore, 2021). This allows the student to explore their present situation in detail. This includes examining existing challenges, resources and behaviours that might impact or influence their progress. By understanding their current reality, students can gain insights into what is and is not working. This awareness encourages creative problem solving, informed decision-making, realistic goal setting and intentional action taking (Whitmore, 2009).

An integrative approach

An effective practitioner will often use a blend of techniques to meet the needs of their students. As students often come to coaching and mentoring support unsure of what it is or how it can help them, it can be particularly effective to use an integrative approach in scenarios where a student is unclear about their goal or desired outcome. In a reflective paper on coaching, David Clutterbuck observed this, stating that 'in many cases, defining a clear goal may be the outcome of coaching - at which point the client has no further need of help, knowing in their own mind what they need to do and how they will do it' (2010, p. 73). The scenario below illustrates an integrated approach to a support session, combining the GROW model and solution-focused approaches (Campbell, no date).

Scenario one: An integrative approach

COACH: What would you like to focus on during our time together today?

STUDENT: I'm not doing as well as I know I can with my studies, and I can't seem to improve.

COACH: OK, I'd like to invite you try an exercise with me. Are you happy to give it a go?

STUDENT: Sure.

COACH: I'd like you to close your eyes if you feel comfortable doing so. Imagine we meet again one year from now, having done as well as you can with your studies. What would you be telling me?

STUDENT: I achieved distinctions for all my assignments following our coaching session and I graduated with a 2:1. I am so proud of my achievement, and I had a huge graduation party with my friends and family to celebrate. I am now working as a translator, and it truly is my dream job.

COACH: Thanks for sharing that with me. Now, can you tell me a bit more about your current situation?

STUDENT: I keep aiming for distinctions in all my assignments, but so far in my past three assignments, I have missed the required grade by a few marks, and I feel frustrated and disappointed. I want to achieve distinctions to increase my chances of being awarded a 2:1 classification for my degree.

COACH: What outcome would you like by the end of today's session in relation to this?

STUDENT: I would like to figure out what is stopping me from doing as well as I know I can in my assignments and have a plan for achieving a distinction in my upcoming assignment.

COACH: Can you tell me more about how you currently approach your assignments?

STUDENT: I usually start my assignment around 3–5 days ahead of the assignment deadline, mainly in the evening once my children are in bed.

COACH: Approximately how many hours do you spend on your study each night?

STUDENT: I try to aim for two hours each night during the week in the evening but realistically, it is closer to an hour.

COACH: How much study time do you think is required to meet your goal of achieving distinction grades?

STUDENT: Based on the course information, for a 60-credit module approximately 16–18 hours of study is recommended and it is probably more to achieve a distinction grade. I know I need to spend more time studying but I'm often too tired and overwhelmed that when I do finally sit down, I find it difficult to concentrate.

COACH: You mentioned weekday evenings, do you spend any time studying at the weekend?

STUDENT: I don't have time at the weekends as my children are involved in many activities and we spend time visiting and running errands for my parents.

COACH: It sounds like you are juggling a lot of commitments and responsibilities. Thinking about your current approach to assignments, what could you stop, start or continue doing that would move you closer to your goal of achieving distinction grades?

STUDENT: Well, it is obvious: spend more time studying! However, realistically, the only time I have available is during my commute. That said, currently I listen to music or scroll social media. By the end of the working day, I need to decompress but I could use my one-hour train commute in the morning to do some reading, make notes and plan my upcoming assignment.COACH: What else?STUDENT: Thinking about it now, I could bring my books and laptop with me to my parents and study for a few hours while they spend time with the kids. I could also ask their dad in advance to have them for the night or take them to their activities at the weekend when I know I have an upcoming assessment deadline to meet.

COACH: Anything else?

STUDENT: Well, I haven't read any of the feedback for my previous assignments. I feel so disappointed when I see the mark that I don't open the feedback. But it would probably be helpful, especially as I keep getting similar marks, just missing the distinction grade.

COACH: Great, it sounds like you have a few options. Which option do you think will have the biggest positive impact on your goal of achieving a distinction grade?

STUDENT: Having my parents or ex-partner take care of the children for a few hours would give me more time to work on my assignments.

COACH: What actions will you now take as a result of this conversation?

STUDENT: I will speak to my children, ex-partner and my parents about having more childcare support. I will also read the assignment feedback I have received so far.

COACH: On a scale of 0–10, how committed are you to having a conversation around childcare with everyone you mentioned, with ten being absolutely committed and zero being totally uncommitted?

STUDENT: 10! This conversation has shown me how much I am trying to fit in and the negative impact it is having not only on my studies but also my mental wellbeing. It has also highlighted my tendency to try to do everything on my own when there is no need because I have support available.

COACH: What about spending time reading your assignment feedback, how committed are you to doing that?

STUDENT: Again 10. It's such a simple thing that is likely to help me improve my grades. I've been too mentally exhausted to notice small things that could help.

In this scenario, the practitioner uses a number of tools that can be helpful for raising self-awareness around goal setting and wellbeing. They begin by asking the 'Miracle Question' (Imagine we meet again one year from now, having done as well as you can with your studies. What would you be telling me?). This is a technique that is often used in a solution-focused coaching approach and can be particularly useful for students who desire change but feel apprehensive when accessing additional, alternative or external support (de Shazer *et al.*, 2021). It is designed to help an individual envision a future where their current challenges or issues have been 'miraculously' solved. This approach can help an individual to clarify their goals and desired changes, visualise the benefits and possibilities of taking action and identify the small steps needed to achieve these changes.

The practitioner also uses reframing. ('It sounds like you are juggling a lot of commitments and responsibilities. Thinking about your current approach to assignments, what could you stop, start or continue doing that would move you closer to your goal of achieving distinction grades?') This is another example of a solution-focused technique that is particularly valuable in helping people challenge and change ingrained patterns of thought that may be detrimental to their personal development or wellbeing. Reframing (Lochtie *et al.*, 2018) can be used to help an individual shift their thinking from a negative or limiting viewpoint to one that is more empowering or hopeful.

This scenario offers – in a simplified way – an example of how a student can engage with coaching and mentoring support but without a clear goal in mind. In this case, the student is also unaware of how their mental well-being is impacting their ability to study and, as a result, their academic performance. The realities are that practitioners would probably need to spend time supporting the student to explore the impact of their many commitments and responsibilities on their wellbeing, before moving onto the solution-focused element of the conversation.

Further coaching tools and techniques

Within solution-focused coaching approaches and alongside the GROW coaching model, there are several coaching tools and techniques that have proven effective for coaching and mentoring in wellbeing.

The wheel of life

The Wheel of Life (Coactive Coaching, no date; Whitworth *et al.*, 2010), discussed in Chapter 3 is a visual tool, which can be used to support wellbeing, that allows a student to self-assess different aspects of their life, via facilitated conversation, to see where there are potential areas of imbalance and dissatisfaction. Using the results, a coach can facilitate a discussion about what a more balanced life might look like for the student should they wish to achieve this and explore specific, achievable steps to enhance satisfaction in the areas they identify as being important. It can be particularly useful at the start of a coaching relationship where a student is unclear about what they want to focus on within coaching. The scenario below demonstrates how the Wheel of Life might be used for coaching and mentoring with a student.

Scenario two: The wheel of life and wellbeing

Sandra, a distance learning student juggling two 60-credit modules and a full-time job, expressed unhappiness during a coaching session despite excelling academically with distinctions in her assignments. Using the Wheel of Life for Wellbeing, Sandra was able to see that while she scored eight out of ten for the personal growth category, she scored the spiritual wellbeing, fun and recreation and health categories four, three and three out of ten respectively. Through discussion with her coach-mentor, Sandra identifies that while she was doing well in her studies, she was sleeping an average of four to five hours each night and had stopped playing netball several times a week. She shared that at night she was using social media as a way to unwind but too often this resulted in very late nights. Sandra recalled how playing netball energised her and committed to reintroducing twice weekly training sessions into her schedule. Additionally, she committed to leaving her phone outside her bedroom to improve her sleep quality.

This scenario illustrates that through exploration using a tool such as the Wheel of Life we can begin to see how a student could be deprioritising areas of their life that could be negatively impacting their wellbeing and not actually supporting them to do well. There is never a 'magic' question that will help us to raise the student's self-awareness or ability to identify where they are getting stuck but approaching it with empathy, understanding and holding the space for the student to explore may help them to surface what is really going on for them

Core values exercise

Core values guide an individual's decision-making and actions (Brosch and Sander, 2014). Therefore, working with a student to identify and articulate their core values can be powerful as it helps them to recognise what is most important and reveal any areas of incongruence where their current life choices may not align with their identified values. Two simple core values exercises are:

1. Use open questions such as 'What is most important to you in life?' or 'Think about a time when you felt really good about a decision you made. What was driving that feeling?' to explore what matters most to the student.
2. Share a list of common values with the student and ask them to identify the values that resonate most with them (often limited to ten values). Then, ask the student to prioritise their chosen values. This helps the students to clarify which values are truly the most significant to them.

In the PLA Service, we also developed resources to help students to reflect on their values independently with guidance (Blissett and Williams, 2021a, 2021b).

- Group coaching and mentoring

  In the PLA Service, a significant tool for enhancing student wellbeing occurred in a group setting – supporting similar findings in the general literature (Berne, 1958; Style and Boniwell, 2012) and specifically in HE (Collings, Swanson and Watkins, 2014; Byrom, 2018; Bosmans, Young and McLoughlin, 2019; Nacif *et al.*, 2023). This included an induction programme designed to support students before their module officially began, enhancing (not duplicating) existing induction activities (Foley and Marr, 2019). Another group coaching and mentoring campaign (entitled 'Learn, Grow Connect' was designed as a collaboration between the PLA team and the Faculty of Arts and Social Sciences (FASS). These sessions were offered exclusively to students who had shared a diagnosis of a mental health condition (Farley and Kaur, 2023). The service also offered synchronous, online writing sessions (Lavery *et al.*, 2023; Lindley and Wilton, 2024), building upon good practice established in the literature (Kornhaber *et al.*, 2016; Eardley *et al.*, 2021; Morley and Aston, 2023). These programmes, and some of the student feedback on their impact, are discussed further in Chapter 5.

Recommendations for using coaching and mentoring to support wellbeing

Creating 'safe' spaces

University can be a period of significant stress and transition for students. Therefore, creating a safe space where students feel comfortable is important as it enables students to explore their challenges and opportunities openly and empowers them to seek any necessary support with confidence. We are aware that the term 'safe space' can be interpreted in different ways, including in relation to free speech (Whitten, 2018) and that other terms such as a brave space (Ali, 2017), or supporting psychological safety (Geraghty, 2022) have become common place. As authors and practitioners, we incorporate these into what we describe to students as a 'safe space': an environment where they can feel secure, respected and free to express their thoughts, feelings and concerns without fear of judgement or criticism. A safe space allows a student to feel comfortable enough to bring their whole self to coaching and mentoring sessions – as discussed in Chapter 3 in this volume.

When a coach-mentor recognises and incorporates an awareness of common issues relating to EDI (Advance HE, no date), it allows a student to feel respected and valued which then contributes to their sense of psychological safety within the coaching relationship. There is value in creating opportunities for meaningful dialogue, acknowledging and celebrating diversity, advocating for equitable opportunities and access to resources and providing tailored support that respects and values a student's unique experiences and identities. To be effective, it is also essential for practitioners to be aware of and continuously challenge their own preferences and biases, as well as those within the HEI.

Acknowledging student and organisational barriers

The PLA Service pilot project has worked exclusively with students from marginalised and underrepresented groups, raising awareness of the barriers that can have an impact on student mental health and wellbeing.

There are, for example, limitations in the way organisations identify students for additional support. Finding students 'at risk' and campaign parameters often, paradoxically, act as a barrier to accessing support. Many students may not meet the criteria to access support, despite the fact they have experienced disadvantage and would benefit from it (Universities UK, 2021b, 2024, also explored in greater detail later). Universities might also offer different support mechanisms by department or faculty, which might further complicate this. There are also significant barriers posed by demanding administrative processes for accessing support funded by the UK Disabled Students Allowance. Some issues are within the control of HEIs, such as organisational study funds and bursaries, and where possible amending eligibility criteria or including an element of accepted variance from the criteria. At an institutional level, insights from the coach-mentors in the team have been used to inform the university's approach to driving systemic change in the Access and Participation Plan 2025–2029.

Clear routes to multi-agency support

As we have already noted, when providing positive interventions across large organisations, the multiplicity of options might complicate and obscure where students can access relevant support. If a student is accessing multiple internal and external services, we need to consider the mental toll and emotional labour of recalling potentially distressing experiences repeatedly, as well as the time commitment. The student may also simultaneously experience this outside the institution to compound the issue. For example, a student might be awaiting a second round of NHS counselling, whilst in a wellbeing group provided by a third sector organisation, working with a DSA-funded mentor, whilst having social services involvement in their home and mental health medication reviews with their GP. In what follows, we offer some guidance on ensuring timely and effective referrals to help mitigate against these challenges.

At the outset of the coaching and mentoring relationship, it is possible that the student may not need additional support, or that neither the student nor the coach-mentor were aware of any such needs. However, deeper issues can surface during the coaching and mentoring journey, and it may become evident that the student requires specialised support. This often occurs when issues arise that fall outside the scope of coaching and mentoring. In the following fictional scenario, we see an example of where a student does not initially enter the coaching relationship for support with their wellbeing, but it later emerges that the student is experiencing several challenges that are impacting their mental health.

Scenario three: Referrals

Paul initially enrolled in university for personal interest and consistently achieved good grades in previous modules. More recently, there has been a significant decline in his academic performance. In the first session with his coach-mentor, Paul shares that he decided to engage in coaching due to his lack of motivation. This often results in frequent extension requests for assignments and lower grades than he is used to.

As the helping relationship develops, Paul begins to share more personal challenges. Paul reveals that he has recently been made redundant which has significantly impacted his sense of purpose and financial security. Additionally, he discloses a return to alcohol dependency, a problem he thought he had overcome. Most days, Paul experienced very low moods and struggled with basic self-care, including getting out of bed, showering and eating.

In this scenario, a practitioner has several options for offering support effectively. Firstly, addressing the student's immediate mental health needs, which includes managing the low moods and alcohol dependency, is critical. This should prioritise helping the student to identify any support services available, encouraging them to seek professional support and connecting them with mental health resources. Additionally, a coach-mentor might help by supporting Paul to rebuild their daily routine by establishing small, manageable goals that promote basic self-care and gradually reintroducing structure to their day. They could also assist the student in identifying new career paths or hobbies that align with their interests and signposting to the university careers team.

In Paul's case, referral to specialist services is key. Other indications that a student may benefit from working with an alternative or additional service or professional include:

- A student exhibiting signs of anxiety, depression or other emotional issues that go beyond the scope of coaching and mentoring (or the remit of your role).
- A student mentioning or displaying symptoms of mental health conditions such as panic attacks, obsessive-compulsive behaviours, eating disorders or severe stress.

- A student expressing thoughts of self-harm or suicide or revealing previous attempts.
- A student revealing or implying the misuse of alcohol or drugs.
- A student withdrawing from activities or exhibiting drastic changes in mood and/or behaviour.
- A student revealing experiences of trauma, abuse or other significant past events that impact their current functioning.
- A student mentioning or exhibiting signs of a disability – (diagnosed or undiagnosed, declared or undeclared).

If at any point during the coaching and mentoring relationship it becomes apparent that a referral may be necessary, it is crucial for the practitioner to clearly explain how the boundaries between coaching and mentoring and another service or profession have been crossed. When doing so, it is important to be mindful of the language we use, ensuring it does not make the student feel they have done something wrong or that there is something wrong with them. Instead, emphasise that seeking specialised support is a positive step towards addressing their needs effectively and promoting their overall wellbeing and success. Ideally, the referral process will have been covered during the contracting stage. However, it is still important that the process you will follow is clearly explained to the student at the point a referral needs to be made.

Referrals might be made by the coach-mentor on the student's behalf or, alternatively, the student might be 'signposted' to the relevant service or professional. This will demand on the nature of the referral and the student's readiness to engage with support. A coach-mentor ideally empowers students; therefore, it is important not to make assumptions about their ability to act independently. It is also vital that, where relevant (i.e. not a safeguarding or wellbeing referral where consent is not an absolute requirement), practitioners obtain explicit consent from the student to make the referral. Reaching an agreement about what information should be shared will help maintain trust.

Where practitioners instead 'signpost' students to further help, it is helpful to offer information about available resources, services or professionals who specialise in addressing the specific concerns identified. This may include counselling services within the university, the disability support team, community mental health services or other relevant resources (Lochtie *et al.*, 2018). Coaching can be used to assist and empower the student to access the recommended service or professional. As a coach you can work with the student to identify how confident and committed they feel about accessing and engaging with the recommended service or professional. Where a student's confidence or commitment level is low, you can use coaching to identify, challenge and overcome any obstacles, fears or concerns.

A process for managing referrals, and considerations along the way, is detailed in Figure 4.1.

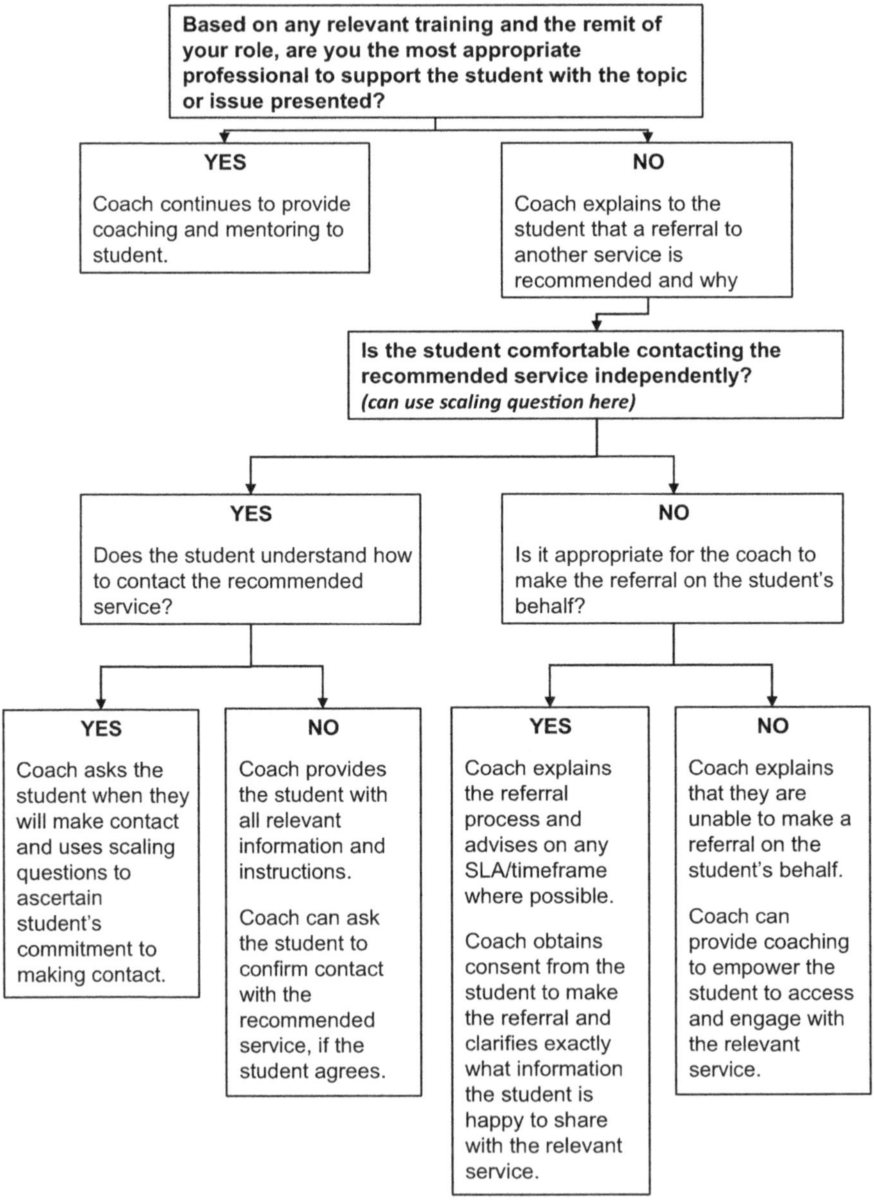

Figure 4.1 A flowchart for managing referrals.

It has been observed that coaches tend to be less confident in their ability to assist students with mental health challenges (Cliff, 2024) but, as mentioned above, they can play a key role in coaching a student around accessing and engaging with other support and resources when the student does not initially feel comfortable or confident enough to do so themselves.

Core, embedded (not 'add on') services for marginalised students

The positive interventions HE institutions can provide to students from racially minoritised groups rely on funding which is often temporary. Take a moment to consider and reflect on this excerpt:

> In the long struggle for racial equality throughout the sector, the pace of change remains slow, often lacking resource, sustainability and penetration. From fiscal and human resource perspectives, universities have historically been non-committal in this endeavour, resulting in the continued exclusion and marginalisation of ethnic minority staff and students.
>
> (Arday, Branchu and Boliver, 2022, p. 8)

Temporary projects linked to short-term outcomes lack this sustainability. Consider how your own institution might offer interventions that fall into this category. How could they have been altered to place ethnic minority student, and staff, voices at the centre to create a genuine and permanent intervention that will affect meaningful change?

There is a tendency within HE to target students on the basis of their 'risk' of poorer outcomes to deliver cost-effectiveness. This means that high-achieving students are often overlooked for support. Part of a core coaching and mentoring offer is acknowledging that a student achieving high marks on assignments is not always an indication that they have good mental health and wellbeing, thus their scores act as a barrier when support staff let their assumptions enter the session. Additionally, some students achieve this despite their struggles and that ensuring they receive the right support from their organisation can help them to unlock their full potential and achieve more. Our learning from the PLA Service pilot and recommendation for service design is to ensure coaching and mentoring is offered as a core, university support service. This requires a wider infrastructure and environment where mental health and wellbeing is measured, so this is not conducted solely to measure return on investment of interventions (Sontag-Padilla *et al.*, 2018).

Consideration of diversity and representation

A student's lived experience within learning environments and interactions with others can significantly impact how they interact with their learning material, support services and any disclosure(s) of important details about their physical or mental needs within their HE institution. There is evidence, for example, of significantly lower help-seeking and mental health declarations among students underrepresented in HE, specifically including Black students, linked to notions of stigma and lack of cultural understanding among predominantly White support practitioners (Butcher *et al.*, 2021; Winograd and Rust, 2014). One of our students stated that prior to PLA support:

> I would never ask for help before in any area of my life, I thought that this made me look weak' [then realising] 'there is absolutely no shame in seeking help if I am struggling, it is actually a strength. Now I make full use of any support that I am offered and do not feel ashamed about this.

Representation can help to create a sense of belonging and community within the student body (Blake *et al.*, 2022). When students feel they could be misunderstood, treated differently or cannot relate to those providing support it can be incredibly alienating and make it harder for students to request and access support. As well as stating it was important to see and hear peers with similar lived experiences, several students requested PLAs with similar lived experiences, and the importance of diverse representation among staff, particularly in terms of ethnicity, is highlighted extensively in the literature (Bhopal, 2018; Arday, 2018; Doharty *et al.*, 2021).

When creating project proposals for positive interventions the language used can also have a significant impact. The 'deficit' language of targeted support is a concern we have raised as practitioners. Thus, a well-intentioned intervention to support student success and wellbeing can become a barrier to engagement. Interventions should also be made with a commitment to taking ownership for creating supportive and inclusive learning environments that promote student success and wellbeing. Shifting responsibility from the institution to student is an example of poor practice. For example, research by Slack and Priestley (2023) suggested that resilience is an important factor in a student's ability to manage their wellbeing alongside challenges faced within HE. Whilst this is undoubtedly important, 'resilience' itself is a problematic and loaded term. Proposing wellbeing interventions around resilience situates the need for change within individual students and may disproportionately impact racially minoritised students. We suggest that the narrative needs to shift from discussing student resilience, to challenging HEI accountability.

As individuals, we all have a role in this and invite readers to consider how they might contribute to the development of inclusive, representative and culturally appropriate wellbeing support for students. Some suggestions we can offer:

- Take ownership of uncovering unconscious biases, prejudice, and privilege, to avoid making potentially harmful assumptions when providing diverse students with support. The limitations of diversity training for HE staff, supporting and challenging individuals in these areas, have been noted (Devine and Ash, 2022).
- Be willing to have conversations that challenge perceptions and experiences and be mindful of the emotional and mental toll this could have on students.
- Collaborate with diverse staff to challenge the status quo and think of sustainable solutions to wellbeing and study success together.
- Create time for intentional understanding and reflection on the difference in the impact on yourself vs your diverse counterparts in relation to current events.
- Work on recognising and encouraging dialogue with diverse students and staff around these issues and support change through allyship rather than saviour or indifferent stances (Anti-Racist Curriculum (ARC) Project, 2021).

As authors, we want to take a moment to note that whilst writing this chapter the UK saw an outbreak of violent riots in response to the murder of three children in Southport (Downs, 2024). The racist, Islamophobic and anti-immigrant natures/values expressed as part of these riots have impacted many students and staff from all over the country (Blake, 2024). The need for HE institutions to proactively address systemic issues and institutionalised racism has arguably never been greater.

Staff wellbeing

The emotional demands of coaching and mentoring can be significant as coaches often encounter students' complex personal and academic challenges as well as past experiences. To provide effective support, coaches must ensure their own wellbeing is prioritised, allowing them to remain resilient, empathetic and clear-headed (Lim, Patel and Shahdadpuri, 2024). The institutional responsibilities here are also key. As Chapters 1 and 8 in this volume show, staff in these roles should have access to both immediate and longer-term support where they can discuss and process their experiences. Debriefing and supervision can help a coach to alleviate stress and prevent the buildup of emotional strain. The appendix to this volume also offers a list of peer support networks which may be helpful for readers.

Staff development

Mental health and wellbeing conditions among students such as depression, post-traumatic stress disorder, anxiety, phobias and addiction should be treated by psychologists and/or psychiatrists but coaches should be trained to improve their preparedness and confidence in supporting student mental health and wellbeing (Green, Grant and Rynsaardt, 2020; Cliff, 2024). Mental Health First Aid (MHFA) training is an excellent starting point, providing coaches with essential skills and knowledge to provide initial support, encouragement and signposting to identify and access sources of further support (MHFA, 2023). It is also recommended that each HEI should have their own suicide safer strategy (Universities UK, 2021a) that provides a clear framework for practitioners to follow when dealing with students identified as being at risk of suicide. Students with intersecting protected characteristics often face additional barriers and challenges and EDI training should enable practitioners to provide tailored support to these students, addressing issues such as discrimination, microaggressions and systemic inequalities.

Further research

In this chapter, we have explored some of the ways in which racially minoritised students face additional challenges relating to their wellbeing within HE. Whilst coaching and mentoring has been shown to positively impact students' wellbeing, more research is needed on how to ensure this support is accessible, culturally sensitive and appropriate so that students from all backgrounds can benefit from these interventions. The interplay between 'resilience' and the demands placed on students from marginalised backgrounds needs research if we are to better understand how to support wellbeing. Finally, research exploring the relationship between lived experience and race is needed to better inform the design of support services.

Summary

In this chapter, we have explored how coaching and mentoring can play a crucial role in supporting and enhancing student wellbeing. We have highlighted findings from the evaluation of our own coaching and mentoring programme, as well as evidence from the literature, showing areas of impact. These include a reduced need for crisis intervention, improved coping skills, enhanced resilience, increased self-awareness and a sense of belonging. We have highlighted the need for tailored interventions, particularly for students from diverse backgrounds who may encounter additional barriers to accessing support.

Ultimately, we have argued that whilst coaching and mentoring is a positive intervention for supporting mental health and wellbeing, significant funding, support and training is needed alongside a commitment to further research excavating the link between race and lived experience if we are to design services that work. Finally, we have called for the integration of coaching and mentoring into university support services to ensure the provision of holistic wellbeing support for students.

Reflective questions

- How do wellbeing concerns present for students in my context?
- What alternative support mechanisms or provision exists in my context for supporting students with their wellbeing?
- How might I approach raising a student's self-awareness of the challenges in their lives and how they might be impacting their wellbeing?
- What does 'good' wellbeing look like in my institution's culture?
- How do I manage my own wellbeing?

Post-coaching session practitioner wellbeing

- How did this session impact on my wellbeing?
- What support, actions or resources do I need to process this experience?
- What support or resources are available to support my wellbeing?
- Who within my organisation, or externally, could I approach for support with my wellbeing?

- What's the kindest action I can take for myself next?
- What do I need in this moment?

Longer-term wellbeing toolkit

- How can I better prepare myself for conversations that potentially challenge my wellbeing or that are triggering?
- How effectively am I outlining and maintaining my personal and professional boundaries?
- What are my resources and strategies for managing compassion fatigue?
- What are my resources and strategies for managing work/life balance?
- How can I raise my own self-awareness of my wellbeing?
- How much time, energy and resources can I commit to regularly reviewing my wellbeing and what are the opportunities to do this?

Creating and maintaining a safe space

- How am I creating a space where this student feels comfortable bringing their whole self and to share openly and honestly?
- What judgements or biases are present for me?
- What impact, if any, do my own personal judgements and biases have on how I coach, view and interact with this student? How can I mitigate those?
- How am I ensuring that I treat this student equitably?Could another support or intervention be more appropriate for this student?How do I strive for impartiality as a practitioner in the context of working for/representing the HEI?

Defining, establishing and maintaining appropriate boundaries

- What is the remit of my role?
- Based on my own training, knowledge and expertise, what support am I comfortable and permitted to provide to a student?

- How much advocacy (if any) is involved in my role?
- How confident am I with understanding of and ability to apply my organisation's suicide prevention and safeguarding policies?
- What does a manageable caseload of students look like for me currently?
- How will I identify when a coaching relationship is ready to conclude?
- How will I avoid/minimise dependency and manage bringing longer-term coaching relationships to an end?
- What support and resources do I have available to me that will aid me in defining, establishing and maintaining appropriate boundaries in my work?

Diversity, representation and barriers to success

- What role can I take in ensuring the team I work with embodies the acceptance and understanding students need to feel valued and connected?
- Where can I contribute to and/or learn from diverse lived experiences?
- What actions can I take to ensure my team's diversity, or lack of, is not a barrier for students?
- What reasons can you think of that would make Black or other racially minoritised students specifically feel like they cannot or should not disclose their medical conditions?

Bibliography

Abdullah, Z., Banbury, S., Visick, A. and Mohiuddin, I. (2021) 'The role of religiosity in depression and anxiety among Muslim students in the UK: a whole-person approach to teaching and learning', *Journal of Islamic and Muslim Studies*, 6(1), pp. 84–101. doi: 10.2979/jims.6.1.04

Advance HE. (2024) *Beyond the student mental health crisis: a collaborative transatlantic symposium*. Available at: https://www.advance-he.ac.uk/programme-events/supporting-equality-diversity-inclusion-higher-education/beyond-student-mental-health-crisis (Accessed: 1 October 2024).

Advance HE. (no date) *Equality, diversity and inclusion*. Available at: https://www.advance-he.ac.uk/guidance/equality-diversity-and-inclusion (Accessed: 11 November 2024).

Ali, D. (2017) *Safe spaces and brave spaces. Historical context and recommendations for student affairs professionals, NASPA policy and practice series*. Available at: https://naspa.org/report/safe-spaces-and-brave-spaces-historical-context-and-recommendations-for-student-affairs-professionals (Accessed: 19 December 2024).

Ammentorp, J., Uhrenfeldt, L., Angel, F., Ehrensvärd, M., Carlsen, E.B. and Kofoed, P.E. (2013) 'Can life coaching improve health outcomes? A systematic review of intervention studies', *BMC Health Services Research*, 13(1), pp. 428–440. doi: 10.1186/1472-6963-13-428

Ann Craft Trust. (no date) *An introduction to safeguarding adults in higher education-eLearning*. Available at: https://www.anncrafttrust.org/an-introduction-to-safeguarding-adults-in-higher-education-e-learning/ (Accessed: 11 November 2024).

Anti-Racist Curriculum (ARC) Project. (2021) *Allyship in developing an anti-racist curriculum*. Available at: https://www.advance-he.ac.uk/sites/default/files/2021-10/Allyship%20in%20ARC.pdf (Accessed: 17 November 2024).

Arday, J. (2018) 'Understanding race and educational leadership in higher education: exploring the Black and ethnic minority (BME) experience', *Management in Education*, 32(4), pp. 192–200. doi: 10.1177/0892020618791002

Arday, J., Branchu, C. and Boliver, V. (2022) 'What do we know about Black and Minority Ethnic (BAME) participation in UK higher education?' *Social Policy and Society*, 21(1), pp. 12–25. doi: 10.1017/S1474746421000579

Atad, O.I. and Grant, A.M. (2021) 'Evidence-based coaching as a supplement to traditional lectures: impact on undergraduates' goal attainment and measures of mental well-being', *International Journal of Mentoring and Coaching in Education*, 10(3), pp. 249–266. doi: 10.1108/IJMCE-05-2020-0024

Ayub, N. (2010) 'Effect of intrinsic and extrinsic motivation on academic performance', *Pakistan Business Review*, 12, pp. 363–372.

Baker, S.R. (2004) 'Intrinsic, extrinsic, and amotivational orientations: their role in university adjustment, stress, well-being, and subsequent academic performance', *Current Psychology*, 23, pp. 189–202. doi: 10.1007/s12144-004-1019-9

Baumeister, R.F., Twenge, J.M. and Nuss, C.K. (2002) 'Effects of social exclusion on cognitive processes: anticipated aloneness reduces intelligent thought', *Journal of Personality and Social Psychology*, 83(4), pp. 817–827. doi: 10.1037/0022-3514.83.4.817

Bernard, M. (2023) *The successful mind in study, work and life mentoring program*. Available at: https://youcandoiteducation.com.au/ (Accessed: 18 November 2024).

Berne, E. (1958) 'Transactional analysis: a new and effective method of group therapy', *American Journal of Psychotherapy*, 12(4), pp. 735–743.

Bhopal, K. (2018) *Towards a post-racial society: how to make universities more inclusive*. Available at: https://www.theguardian.com/higher-education-network/2018/

apr/11/towards-a-post-racial-society-how-to-make-universities-more-inclusive (Accessed: 17 November 2024).

Blake, S. (2024) *How universities respond to the riots needs careful consideration.* Available at: https://wonkhe.com/blogs/how-universities-respond-to-the-riots-needs-careful-consideration/ (Accessed: 17 November 2024).

Blake, S., Capper, G. and Jackson, A. (2022) *Building belonging in higher education.* Available at: https://wonkhe.com/wp-content/wonkhe-uploads/2022/10/Building-Belonging-October-2022.pdf (Accessed: 19 December 2024).

Blissett, J. and Williams, H. (2021a) *Understanding yourself with self-coaching.* Available at: https://thehootstudents.com/door-8-understanding-yourself-with-self-coaching/ (Accessed: 10 November 2024).

Blissett, J. and Williams, H. (2021b) *Personal values.* Available at: https://thehootstudents.com/understanding-yourself-self-coaching-personal-values/ (Accessed: 10 November 2024).

Bosmans, D., Young, E. and McLoughlin, R. (2019) 'Does PAL work? An exploration of affect amongst first-year HE in FE students', *Athens Journal of Education*, 6(1), pp. 13–31.

Breslin, L., Dyrbye, L., Chelf, C. and West, C. (2023) 'Effects of coaching on medical student well-being and distress: a systematic review protocol', *BMJ Open*, 13(8). doi: 10.1136/bmjopen-2023-073214

British Association for Counselling and Psychotherapy. (2024) *University mental health day: 'counselling gives students the space to reflect and grow'.* Available at: https://www.bacp.co.uk/news/news-from-bacp/2024/14-march-university-mental-health-day-counselling-gives-students-the-space-to-reflect-and-grow/ (Accessed: 1 October 2024).

British Medical Association. (2024) *Mental health pressure in England.* Available at: https://www.bma.org.uk/advice-and-support/nhs-delivery-and-workforce/pressures/mental-health-pressures-data-analysis (Accessed: 6 December 2024).

Britton, J. (2010) *Effective group coaching: tried and tested tools and resources for optimum group coaching results*. Mississauga: John Wiley & Sons Canada.

Brosch, T. and Sander, D. (2014) 'Appraising value: the role of universal core values and emotions in decision-making', *Cortex: A Journal Devoted to the Study of the Nervous System and Behavior*, 59, pp. 203–205. doi: 10.1016/j.cortex.2014.03.012

Butcher, J., Awan, R. and Gray, D. (2021) 'How do we talk about race…and mental health? *Widening Participation and Lifelong Learning*, 23, pp. 147–162. doi: 10.5456/WPLL.23.3.147

Byrom, N. (2018) 'An evaluation of a peer support intervention for student mental health', *Journal of Mental Health*, 27(3), pp. 240–246. doi: 10.1080/09638237.2018.1437605

Cacioppo, J.T., Ernst, J.M., Burleson, M.H., McClintock, M.K., Malarkey, W.B., Hawkley, L.C., Kowalewski, R.B., Paulsen, A., Hobson, J.A., Hugdahl, K. and Spiegel, D. (2000) 'Lonely traits and concomitant physiological processes: the MacArthur social neuroscience studies', *International Journal of Psychophysiology*, 35(2–3), pp. 143–154. doi: 10.1016/S0167-8760(99)00049-5

Campbell, J. (no date) *Cognitive dissonance, scaling and the coaching conversation, growth coaching international*. Available at: https://www.growthcoaching.com.au/resource/cognitive-dissonance-scaling-and-the-coaching-conversation/ (Accessed: 17 July 2024).

Campbell, M.A. and Gardner, S. (2005) 'A pilot study to assess the effects of life coaching with year 12 students', in M. Cavanagh, A. Grant and T. Kemp (eds.) *Evidence-based coaching*. Brisbane: Australian Academic Press, pp. 159–169.

Ciff, T. (2020) *Coaching in secondary and tertiary education: the effects of two interventions on students' well-being and teachers' stress*. PhD thesis. University of Groningen. doi: 10.33612/diss.135802015

Cliff, T. (2024) 'Whether and how coaching for mental health and well-being should be offered in post-Covid-19 pandemic Dutch higher vocational education: coaches' perceptions', *International Journal of Mentoring and Coaching in Education*, 13(8), pp. 493–510. doi: 10.1108/IJMCE-07-2023-0057

Clutterbuck, D. (2010) 'Coaching reflection: the liberated coach', *Coaching: An International Journal of Theory. Research and Practice*, 3(1), pp. 73–81.

Collings, R., Swanson, V. and Watkins, R. (2014) 'The impact of peer mentoring on levels of student wellbeing, integration and retention: a controlled comparative evaluation of residential students in UK higher education', *Higher Education*, 68(6), pp. 927–942. doi: 10.1007/s10734-014-9752-y

Covey, S.R. (2013) *The 7 habits of highly effective people: powerful lessons in personal change*. London: Simon and Schuster.

Craig, N. and Zinkiewicz, L. (2010) *Inclusive practice within psychology higher education*. York: The Higher Education Academy Psychology Network. Available at: https://www.advance-he.ac.uk/knowledge-hub/inclusive-practice-within-psychology-higher-education (Accessed: 19 December 2024).

Csikszentmihalyi, M. (1992) *Flow: the psychology of happiness*. London: Rider and Co.

Curcio, G., Ferrara, M. and De Gennaro, L. (2006) 'Sleep loss, learning capacity and academic performance', *Sleep Medicine Reviews*, 10(5), pp. 323–337. doi: 10.1016/j.smrv.2005.11.001

de Shazer, S., Dolan, Y., Korman, H., Trepper, T., McCollum, E. and Berg, I.K. (2021) *More than miracles: the state of the art of solution-focused brief therapy*. 2nd edn. Abingdon: Routledge.

Deci, E.L. and Ryan, R.M. (1985) *Intrinsic motivation and self-determination in human behavior*. New York: Plenum.

Dekker, I., de Jong, E.M., Schippers, M.C., de Bruijn-Smolders, M., Alexiou, A. and Giesbers, B. (2020) 'Optimizing students' mental health and academic performance: AI-enhanced life crafting', *Frontiers in Psychology*, 11, pp. 1–15. doi: 10.3389/fpsyg.2020.01063

Department of Health. (2014) *Wellbeing: why it matters to health policy*. Available at: https://assets.publishing.service.gov.uk/media/5a7ba1d6ed915d4147621a24/Narrative__January_2014_.pdf (Accessed: 19 December 2024).

Devine, P.G, and Ash, T. L. (2022) *Diversity Training Goals, Limitations, and Promise: A Review of the Multidisciplinary Literature*, Annual Review of Psychology, 73, pp.403–429. Available at: https://doi.org/10.1146/annurev-psych-060221-122215

Devine, M., Meyers, R. and Houssemand, C. (2013) 'How can coaching make a positive impact within educational settings?' *Procedia – Social and Behavioral Sciences*, 93, pp. 1382–1389. doi: 10.1016/j.sbspro.2013.10.048

Dias, G.P., Foster, J. and Zunszain, P.A. (2019) 'Time to flourish: designing a coaching psychology programme to promote resilience and wellbeing in postgraduate students', *European Journal of Applied Positive Psychology*, 3(7), pp. 1–12.

Doharty, N., Madriaga, M. and Joseph-Salisbury, R. (2021) 'The university went to "decolonise" and all they brought back was lousy diversity double-speak! Critical race counter-stories from faculty of colour in "decolonial" times', *Educational Philosophy and Theory*, 53(3), pp. 233–244. doi: 10.1080/00131857.2020.1769601

Douwes, R., Metselaar, J., Pijnenborg, G.H.M. and Boonstra, N. (2023) 'Well-being of students in higher education: the importance of a student perspective', *Cogent Education*, 10(1). doi: 10.1080/2331186X.2023.2190697

Downs, W. (2024) *Policing response to the 2024 summer riots*. Available at: https://commonslibrary.parliament.uk/policing-response-to-the-2024-summer-riots/ (Accessed: 17 November 2024).

Eardley, A.F., Banister, E. and Fletcher, M. (2021) 'Can academic writing retreats function as wellbeing interventions?', *Journal of Further and Higher Education*, 45(2), pp. 183–196. doi: 10.1080/0309877X.2020.1744542

Evans, T.M., Bira, L., Gastelum, J.B., Weiss, L.T. and Vanderford, N.L. (2018) 'Evidence for a mental health crisis in graduate education', *Nature Biotechnology*, 36(3), 282.

Farley, C. and Kaur, H. (2023) Introducing 'Learn, grow, connect': a group intervention to support students with mental health needs. Available at: https://university.open.ac.uk/widening-participation/external-events-and-publications/biennial-aps-conference/2023-abstracts-introducing-learn-grow-connect (Accessed: 11 April 2025).

Florence, M.D., Asbridge, M. and Veugelers, P.J. (2008) 'Diet quality and academic performance', *Journal of School Health*, 78(4), pp. 209–215.

Foley, K. and Marr, L. (2019) 'Scaffolding extracurricular online events to support distance learning university students', *Journal of Interactive Media in Education*, 17, pp. 1–6. doi: 10.5334/jime.525

Fried, R., Atkins, M.-A. and Irwin, J. (2019) 'Breaking grad: building resilience among a sample of graduate students struggling with stress and anxiety via a peer coaching model - an 8-month pilot study', *International Journal of Evidence-Based Healthcare*, 17, pp. 3–19. doi: 10.24384/sa09-av91

Fried, R.R. and Irwin, J.D. (2016) 'Calmly coping: a motivational interviewing via co-active life coaching (MI-VIA-CLAC) pilot intervention for university students with perceived levels of high stress', *International Journal of Evidence Based Coaching and Mentoring*, 14(1), pp. 16–32. Available at: https://radar.brookes.ac.uk/radar/items/6e73b6c5-29f6-49bb-9503-dc4e3f483bbf/1/ (Accessed: 19 December 2024).

Geraghty, T. (2022) *Psychological safety vs a "safe space"*. Available at: https://psych-safety.co.uk/psychological-safety-vs-a-safe-space/ (Accessed: 20 October 2024).

Gibbs, G. (1988) *Learning by doing: a guide to teaching and learning methods.* Oxford: Further Education Unit.

Gillen-O'Neel, C., Huyng, V.W. and Fuligni, A.J. (2013) 'To study or to sleep? The academic costs of extra studying at the expense of sleep: genomics', *Child Development*, 84(1), pp. 133–142. doi: 10.1111/j.1467-8624.2012.01834.x

Goodman, S., Jaffer, T., Keresztesi, M., Mamdani, F., Mokgatle, D., Musariri, M., Pires, J. and Schlecter, A. (2011) 'An investigation of the relationship between students' motivation and academic performance as mediated by effort', *South African Journal of Psychology*, 41(3), pp. 373–385. doi: 10.1177/008124631104100311

Grant, A.M. (2003) 'The impact of life coaching on goal attainment, metacognition and mental health', *Social Behavior and Personality: An International Journal*, 31(3), pp. 253–263. doi: 10.2224/sbp.2003.31.3.253

Green, S., Grant, A. and Rynsaardt, J. (2007) 'Evidence-based life coaching for senior high school students: building hardiness and hope', *Coaching Researched: A coaching psychology reader*, eds. Jonathan Passmore and David Tee, pp. 257–268. Hoboken: John Wiley & Sons.

Hillman, J., Lochtie, D. and Purcell, O. (2024) 'Black students' experiences of coaching and mentoring in higher education: a case study', *International Journal of Mentoring and Coaching in Education*, 13(1). doi: 10.1108/IJMCE-01-2023-0011

Hobson, A.J. and Van Nieuwerburgh, C.J. (2022) 'Extending the research agenda on (ethical) coaching and mentoring in education: embracing mutuality and prioritising well-being', *International Journal of Mentoring and Coaching in Education*, 11(1), pp. 1–13. doi: 10.1108/IJMCE-11-2021-0099

Hughes, G., Panjwani, M., Tulcidas, P. and Byrom, N. (2018) *Student mental health: the role and experiences of an academic*. Available at: https://www.studentminds.org.uk/uploads/3/7/8/4/3784584/180129_student_mental_health__the_role_and_experience_of_academics__student_minds_pdf.pdf (Accessed: 1 October 2024).

Jackson, A.C. (2019) *The efficacy of coaching interventions for undergraduates to increase positive coping behavior: a quantitative quasi-experiment*. PhD thesis. Concordia University. Available at: https://www.proquest.com/docview/2198767812?sourcetype=Dissertations%20and%20Theses. (Accessed: 6 October 2024).

Jones, E., Priestley, M., Brewster, L., Wilbraham, S.J., Hughes, G. and Spanner, L. (2020) 'Student wellbeing and assessment in higher education: the balancing act', *Assessment and Evaluation in Higher Education*, 46(3), pp. 438–450. doi: 10.1080/02602938.2020.1782344

Kimsey-House, H., Kimsey-House, K., Sandahl, P. and Whitworth, L. (2010) *Co-active coaching*. 3rd edn. Yarmouth: Nicholas Brealey Publishing.

Kornhaber, R., Cross, M., Betihavas, V. and Bridgman, H. (2016) 'The benefits and challenges of academic writing retreats: an integrative review', *Higher Education Research and Development*, 35(6), pp. 1210–1227. doi: 10.1080/07294360.2016.1144572

Lavery, H., Kinch, D. and Hillman, J. (2023) 'Do live writing/study sessions for at-risk students, in an online, distance learning environment, demonstrate the same benefits documented for face-to-face shared writing events?' *Ubiquity Proceedings*, 3(1), pp. 83–90. doi: 10.5334/uproc.72

Lefdahl-Davis, E., Huffman, L., Alayan, A. and Stancil, J. (2018) 'The impact of life coaching on undergraduate students: a multiyear analysis of coaching outcomes', *International Journal of Evidence Based Coaching and Mentoring*, 16, pp. 69–83. doi: 10.24384/000560

Lewis, J. and Stiebahl, S. (2024) Student mental health in England: statistics, policy, and guidance. Available at: https://commonslibrary.parliament.uk/research-briefings/cbp-8593/#:~:text=Prevalence%20of%20mental%20health%20issues,chart%20below%20represents%20this%20trend (Accessed: 6 October 2024).

Lim, M.S.M., Patel, N.S. and Shahdadpuri, R. (2024) *Coaching students in higher education: a solution-focused approach to retention, performance and wellbeing*. 1st edn. Abingdon: Routledge.

Lindley, J. and Wilton, M.-J. (2024) 'Creating online, inclusive spaces for learning: 'study together' with the personal learning advice service', *Journal of Learning Development in Higher Education*, 32: Special Edition ALDinHE Conference Proceedings and Reflections. doi: 10.47408/jldhe.vi32.1406

Lister, K. and Riva, E. (2024) *Helping students means taking university staff wellbeing seriously*. Available at: https://wonkhe.com/blogs/helping-students-means-taking-university-staff-wellbeing-seriously/ (Accessed: 17 November 2024).

Lochtie, D., McIntosh, E., Stork, A. and Walker, B. (2018) *Becoming an effective personal tutor: supporting learners through personal tutoring and coaching*. 2nd edn. Norwich: Critical Publishing.

MacDonnell, J. and Bisel, A. (2021) 'Identifying and addressing differential Black, Asian and Minority Ethnic student experiences at a post 1992 institution', *Widening Participation and Lifelong Learning*, 23(3), pp. 9–36. Available at: https://university.open.ac.uk/widening-participation/sites/www.open.ac.uk.widening-participation/files/files/6th-conference/S2%20-%20MacDonnell%20and%20Bisel.pdf (Accessed: 11 April 2025).

McKergow, M. and Jackson, P.Z. (2002) *The solutions focus: making coaching and change SIMPLE*. London: Nicholas Brealey International.

MHFA. (2023) *What is a mental health first aider?* Available at: https://mhfaengland.org/mhfa-centre/blog/What-is-a-mental-health-first-aider/ (Accessed: 17 November 2024).

MIND. (no date) Available at: https://www.mind.org.uk/ (Accessed: 17 November 2024).

Morley, C. and Aston, S. (2023) 'Overcoming isolation with community based digital writing initiatives', *Journal of University Teaching and Learning Practice*, 20(2). doi: 10.53761/1.20.02.03

Nacif, A.P., Giraldez-Hayes, A., Finn, K. and Valdivielso-Martínez, E. (2023) 'Online group coaching: the experience of postgraduate students during the COVID-19 pandemic', *Coaching: An International Journal of Theory, Research and Practice*, *16*(2), pp. 190–204. doi: 10.1080/17521882.2023.2205598

Neves, J. and Hillman, N. (2017) *Student academic experience survey, HEA-HEPI*. Available at: https://www.hepi.ac.uk/wp-content/uploads/2017/06/2017-Student-Academic-Experience-Survey-Final-Report.pdf (Accessed: 20 December 2024).

Passmore, J. (ed.) (2021) *Excellence in coaching: theory, tools and techniques to achieve outstanding coaching performance*. 4th edn. London, New York: Kogan Page.

Patfield, S., Gore J. and Fray, L. (2022) 'Degrees of "being first": toward a nuanced understanding of first-generation entrants to higher education', *Educational Review*, 74(6), pp. 1137–1156. doi: 10.1080/00131911.2020.1740172

Phillips, N. (2020) *Navigating the tensions of undergraduate life: an existential phenomenological analysis of personal growth and the role of coaching at a UK university*. PhD thesis, Birkbeck. Available at: https://eprints.bbk.ac.uk/id/eprint/41732/1/Natalie%20Phillips%20Thesis%20Navigating%20the%20tensions%20of%20undergraduate%20life%20September%202020.pdf (Accessed: 30 November 2024).

Quinn, N., Wilson, A., MacIntyre, G. and Tinklin, T. (2009) 'People look at you differently': students' experience of mental health support within higher education', *British Journal of Guidance and Counselling*, 37(4), pp. 405–418. doi: 10.1080/03069880903161385

Rothenberg, A. (2006) 'Essay: creativity—the healthy muse', *The Lancet*, 368. doi: 10.1016/S0140-6736(06)69905-4

Samaritans. (no date). Available at: https://www.samaritans.org/ (Accessed: 17 November 2024).

Samuels-Hylton, J. and Wilton, M. (2023). 'Sharing stories of resilience: Open University partnership work with Shelayna Oskan-Clarke', *Learning Development Magazine* (July), pp. 12–13. Available at: https://online.fliphtml5.com/lwhvl/xgpp/#p=12 (Accessed: 6 October 2024).

Scullin, M.K. (2019) 'The eight hour sleep challenge during final exams week', *Teaching of Psychology*, 46(1), pp. 55–63.

Short, E., Kinman, G. and Baker, S. (2010) 'Evaluating the impact of a peer coaching intervention on well-being amongst psychology undergraduate students', *International Coaching Psychology Review*, 5(1), pp. 27–35.

Slack, H.R. and Priestley, M. (2023) 'Online learning and assessment during the Covid-19 pandemic: exploring the impact on undergraduate student well-being', *Assessment and Evaluation in Higher Education*, 48(3), pp. 333–349. doi: 10.1080/02602938.2022.2076804

Sontag-Padilla, L., Dunbar, M.S., Ye, F., Kase, C., Fein, R., Abelson, S., Seelam, R. and Stein, B.D. (2018) 'Strengthening college students' mental health knowledge, awareness, and helping behaviors: the impact of active minds, a peer mental health organization', *Journal of the American Academy of Child and Adolescent Psychiatry*, 57(7), pp. 500–507. doi: 10.1016/j.jaac.2018.03.019

St-Hilaire, E., Hillman, J. and Lochtie, D. (2023) *Closing the awarding gap: the role of the Personal Learning Advisor (PLA) service at the Open university*. Available at: https://www.ukat.ac.uk/media/u2fn0mj0/ukat-equity-inclusion-sig-case-study-2.pdf (Accessed: 10 November 2024).

Style, C. and Boniwell, I. (2012) 'The effect of group-based life coaching on happiness and well-being', *Groupwork*, 20(3), pp. 51–72. doi: 10.1921/gpwk.v20i3.708

Tinto, V. (1975) 'Dropout from higher education: a theoretical synthesis of recent research', *Review of Educational Research*, 45(1), pp. 89–125.

Universities UK. (2021a) *Suicide safer universities*. Available at: https://www.universitiesuk.ac.uk/sites/default/files/field/downloads/2021-07/guidance-for-sector-practitioners-on-preventing-student-suicides.PDF (Accessed: 17 November 2024).

Universities UK. (2021b). *Black, Asian and minority ethnic student attainment at UK Universities #closing the gap*. Available at: https://www.universitiesuk.ac.uk/sites/default/files/field/downloads/2021-07/bame-student-attainment.pdf (Accessed: 18 June 2024).

Universities UK. (2024). *Update – Black, Asian and minority ethnic student attainment at UK Universities #closing the gap*. Available at: https://www.universitiesuk.

ac.uk/what-we-do/policy-and-research/publications/black-asian-and-minority-ethnic-student (Accessed 17 November 2024).

Van Nieuwerburgh, C. and Barr, M. (2016) 'Coaching in education', in T. Bachkirova, G. Spence and D. Drake (eds.) *The SAGE handbook of coaching*. London: Sage, pp. 505–520.

Wang, Q. (2012) 'Coaching for learning: exploring coaching psychology in enquiry-based learning and development of learning power in secondary education', *Procedia – Social and Behavioral Sciences*, 69, pp. 177–186.

Watson, S. (2024) 'The other side of the coin: do the benefits of being a Christian postgraduate at a secular university in England contribute to student well-being?', *Journal of Beliefs and Values*. doi: 10.1080/13617672.2024.2380222

Whitmore, J. (2009) *Coaching for performance: growing human potential and purpose—the principles and practice of coaching and leadership*. 4th edn. London: Nicholas Brealey Publishing.

Whitten, S. (2018) *Why 'safe spaces' at universities are a threat to free speech*. Available at: https://theconversation.com/why-safe-spaces-at-universities-are-a-threat-to-free-speech-94547 (Accessed: 20 December 2024).

Winograd, G.W. and Rust, J.P. (2014) 'Stigma, awareness of support services, and academic help seeking among historically underrepresented first-year college students', *Learning Assistance Review*, 19(2), pp. 17–41.

Woloshyn, V., Savage, M.J., Ratkovic, S., Hands, C. and Martinovic, D. (2019) 'Exploring professors' experiences supporting graduate student well-being in Ontario faculties of education', *International Journal of Mentoring and Coaching in Education*, 8(4), pp. 397–411. doi: 10.1108/IJMCE-02-2019-0028

Zawada, C. (2024) 'Student drop out and feelings of belonging and mattering in UK undergraduate allied health students', *Journal of Learning Development in Higher Education*, 31. doi: 10.47408/jldhe.vi31.1172

5 Coaching, mentoring and the learning development toolkit

Jennifer Hillman and Mary-Jayne Wilton

Introduction

In the first chapters of this volume, coaching and mentoring have been situated within the ethical and professional frameworks which differentiate them from other 'helping' and therapeutic conversations, and from teaching or pedagogic interactions. The foundations of boundaried and equity-led practice have been set out and the key principles of contracting and confidentiality have been foregrounded. In this chapter, we begin to explore how – within the confines of these ethical codes of practice – coaching and mentoring techniques might map across to a specific forum for student support in the university: learning development (LD). Traditionally situated within a university's library services, but just as often positioned as part of a wider student support offering, a familiar (but reductive) rendering might use the shorthand of 'study skills' or 'academic skills' tuition to describe LD (Wingate, 2006; Richards and Pilcher, 2021; Richards and Pilcher, 2023). In this chapter, we begin from a more holistic view of LD which recognises both its broad social mission to widen participation and the specialist but varied skill of its practitioners in the Third Space (Whitchurch, 2003; Webster, 2022).

In this chapter, we make a case for the value of coaching and mentoring in the learning developers' specialist 'toolkit.' To do so, we begin by synthesising the origins and trajectory of LD itself as a space in the university and the commonalities between its mission to widen access to, and participation in, the academy, on the one hand, and the principles

DOI: 10.4324/9781003486015-6

of coaching and mentoring through an 'equity lens,' on the other hand (Clay *et al.*, 2023). Coaching and mentoring, we will seek to show, can help ensure alignment between our philosophies as learning developers, and how this translates into our practice with students. In the second part of the chapter, we go on to share, with a practical focus, how coaching and mentoring techniques have already been and could further be, usefully incorporated in LD interventions in both one-to-one tutorials and group settings. Finally, we offer practitioners working within LD teams and structures an opportunity for critical reflection on the place of coaching and mentoring in their own practice.

The congruence between coaching and mentoring, and learning development: insights from the literature

Before going on to explore the synergies between coaching and mentoring practices and the wider field of LD in the literature, let us first offer a note on terminology. The precise remit of a learning developer varies considerably but tends to include planning for and writing assessments, academic writing and 'learning to learn' skills such as critical thinking, note taking and time management (Webster, 2023, p. 1). 'Learning development' is, in many ways, a slippery term. Variations in where LD departments sit in organisational structures within universities, as well as a vast array of job titles ('advisers,' 'developers,' 'coaches,' 'mentors,' 'tutors,' to name a few), contribute to the enigma. Recognising that practitioners across a range of services and roles consider themselves engaged in LD work, in this chapter, we have deliberately adopted a fuzzier definition – recently offered from within the community of practice in the UK.

> a practitioner whose role is to help the student unpeel the layers of academic expectations and discourses, develop their skills and reflect on their learning. There is nothing predictable about that conversation; each Learning Developer will approach it differently, and each student will take away from it what they will. But what connects all these encounters is a love of learning, a deep need for scholarly engagement, and a set of values that foster spaces encouraging students to be the best they can be and to make the most of their learning.
>
> (Syska and Buckley, 2024, p. 1)

Other LD practitioners have pointed to the value of this diversity and continuing evolution of this area of practice:

> There remains a 'virtuality' to what we do –capacities that have yet to be actualised, or even anticipated. These are just as much a part of the reality of learning development and represent the space through which our practices might evolve, just as a fire burns in the space between the logs.
>
> (Eyre and Slawson, 2018, p. 10)

In this chapter (to extend the metaphor), we propose that coaching and mentoring is one example of the 'fire burning in the space between the logs' of LD (Eyre and Slawson, 2018, p. 10). In what follows in this prefatory discussion, we offer three observations about LD, and its origins, evolution and essence which demonstrate the synergies with coaching and mentoring – as shown in Table 5.1.

For clarity: we are suggesting *neither* that LD *is* coaching and mentoring (or can be subsumed by it!), *nor* that coaching and mentoring will always be the optimum approach. However, what we want to show here is the fundamental congruence between the essence and mission of LD in higher education (HE), and the coaching and mentoring techniques being shared later in this chapter – and, indeed, across this volume.

As authors we recognise LD work as a core part of our professional identities. Certainly, it is one component of our combined experience in educational guidance, student success coaching, personal development coaching, mentoring, advising and tutoring. Yet, as others have noted, learning developers may legitimately 'oscillate' between the roles of 'interpreter, coach, dialogue partner, listener, and intermediary' in order to meet the needs of students (Gravett and Winstone, 2019, p. 727, cited in Johnson and Bishopp-Martin, 2024, p. 19). Here, we draw upon our practice working across the coaching and mentoring continuum to help distance-learning students 'learn to learn' (Rawson, 2000) and fulfil their potential. Our discussions are rooted in the wider evidence base for

Table 5.1 The synergies between learning development, coaching and mentoring

Observation one	The origins of LD are rooted in the mission to widen access and participation through student-centred support.
Observation two	LD has been a key driver in the move away from 'remedial' support for students.
Observation three	The LD community of practice has evidenced both the value and impact of coaching and mentoring approaches on student learning experiences.

the impact of coaching and mentoring on students' academic outcomes, executive functioning and other soft skills.

Like other contributors to this volume, we regard coaching and mentoring as distinct practices but existing on a continuum where support is offered through questioning techniques and active listening (Passmore, Peterson and Freire, 2012). We use 'coaching and mentoring' to denote that relationship but identify the differences in how they manifest in practice later in the chapter. Essential to our conceptualisation of both coaching and mentoring, are the principles of the 'equity lens' proposed by Clay *et al.* (2023) and set out in full in Chapter 2 of this volume. It is non-judgemental, person-centred and, through dialogue, seeks to create a space which values the lived experiences of students.

The origins of learning development are rooted in the mission to widen access and participation through student-centred support

From its beginnings, LD has been driven by a social mission to truly widen participation (not just access) to university, to learning and ultimately to academia. It grew against the backdrop of mass expansion of programmes and diversification of the student population in the 1980s. In the UK, this was part of a political agenda to widen access, crystallised in the Dearing Report (National Committee of Inquiry into Higher Education, 1997). With a more diverse range of students, came greater differentiation in experiences. As a result, the need for tailored support became increasingly clear; initially, this was about an academic 'skills curriculum' (Cottrell, 2001; cited in Hilsdon, 2011, pp. 14–15), but it quickly grew into a wider movement of practitioners looking to develop a pedagogy of LD which could empower students and challenge damaging normative practices in teaching and assessment. Gradually, this was reflected in the creation of the Learning Development in Higher Education Network (LDHEN) in 2003 and the foundation of the Association for Learning Development in Higher Education (ALDinHE) in 2007 (Briggs, 2018). LD also coalesced in similar ways in Australia, New Zealand and Canada (Webster, 2023, p. 1).

What we have presented here is a highly condensed version of the narrative about the origins of LD and the rise in 'non-traditional' students at university and their need for enhanced, tailored support to truly 'access' the academy. LD is, in essence, based on a philosophy that all students – regardless of background and prior learning – have the capacity to succeed at university but may be disadvantaged by structural and institutional barriers and require core support. This is what Sandra Sinfield, Tom Burns and others have referred to as the 'socio-political' practice of empowering students (Sinfield *et al.*, 2010, p. 55) and what Helen Webster articulated as the 'person-centred' values which place learning developers 'at the more Rogerian, progressive end of the teaching spectrum' (Webster, 2023, p. 2). The starting point for coaching and mentoring is fundamentally aligned with this, resting on the belief in a student's capacity to determine their own goals, actions and futures and, with support, to overcome barriers. Sunny Dhillon has reminded us of the dangers of talking about the 'emancipation' of students via LD since 'emancipation' is itself a loaded concept, tied to colonialism (Dhillon, 2024, p. 114). They argue that, instead, practitioners should be reflecting on their 'complicity' and engaging with a 'pedagogy of discomfort' (Dhillon, 2022, 2024, p. 114). We acknowledge that from the outset and later in the chapter offer ways for practitioners to engage in that critical reflection.

Learning development has been a key driver in the move away from 'remedial' support for students

There has been a perceived tension between the interconnection of LD with widening participation (WP) because of the risk that it infers a skills 'deficit' for students from underrepresented groups. Yet, LD itself evolved in response to a move away from deficit-led 'study skills.' Gina Sherwood and Ian Johnson have discussed these theoretical underpinnings and LD view of 'systemically imposed deficits' (2024, p. 6). A recent community-sourced synthesis of the literature charts how Lea and Street's (1998) 'ethnographic' (or experiential) approach triggered a move towards recognising and validating diverse student experience in academic literacies; this is because it focused on how students learn to write and the intersections between writing, power and identity (Hilsdon, Malone and Syska, 2019, p. 4). In other words, learning developers were among the first to consider how the ways in which we teach and assess students in HE is essentially about measuring how well students can adapt to a system, rather than a genuine assessment of their learning. This is what Haggis articulated as how well students 'learn to function as is expected [...] the processes which are implicated are educational processes, not learning processes' (2006, p. 533).

The Learn Higher repository is an online collection of resources helping to facilitate LD activities in group and one-to-one tutorial settings – established in 2005 and reporting over 28,000 downloads in 2024 (Learn Higher, 2024).

In addition to the sharing of practice at an international annual conference and a regular programme of community of practice events, within LD there has also been – since 2008 – a peer-reviewed academic journal dedicated to publishing scholarship and sharing good practice (JLDHE, 2024). The LD movement has generated a wealth of evidence-based interventions, critical pedagogies and teaching resources which challenge the now-dated view of this support as remedial study skills provision.

LD has also helped to drive a move away from the pathologisation of students' need for learning support in its calls for changes to institutional approaches – for 'built-in' rather than 'bolt-on' support. In other words, learning developers have been advocates for the inclusion of academic literacies and learning skills as standard in the student journey through HE. In many institutions, there are now credit-bearing skills-based modules which support students as they transition to learning at university. A compelling case study on a first-year undergraduate module has shown, for example, how students can be supported to develop self-identified academic skills in spaces which recognise and validate their wider selves, experiences and identities (Abegglen, Burns and Sinfield, 2016). Here, they show that a 'dialogic rather than a didactic approach' (2016, p. 7) can develop students who may not have the social/academic capital to navigate HE (Abegglen, Sinfield and Burns, 2017).

In other settings, influenced by the North American approach, LD has been 'embedded' in the curriculum, where learning developers are aligned to a disciplinary area (Hill, Tinker and Catterall, 2010; Minogue, Murphy and Salmons, 2018). The embedding of learning developers within faculties has been seen as a more effective way of 'brokering' relationships between students and academic staff and 'negotiating power, access and transparency' by helping to demystify assessments and expectations about learning at university (Gornall, 2019, p. 14). 'Embedding' has thus been positioned as one solution to bolt-on, remedial study skills.

One of our starting premises for this chapter is that, whether embedded in programmes or not, person-centred coaching and mentoring helps us as practitioners to strengthen our opposition to the deficit model which casts students, rather than HE systems and spaces as 'problematic' (Hilsdon, 2011, p. 17). This is because coaching and mentoring both require practitioners to tap into and thus help to validate, the lived experiences of their students. There are, for example, some initial indications from qualitative studies that coaching and mentoring can help students from some underrepresented groups to 'reframe' their experiences, lift limiting beliefs and apply their skills and experiences to their studies (Hillman, Lochtie and Purcell, 2024, p. 254). Certainly, coaching students to adapt to broken HE systems is not the long-term solution for equity in HE. There has been a slow recognition of the way normative teaching and assessment practices have been detrimental to students from underprivileged backgrounds and the evidence for a continued need for deeper, systemic change is abundant (Børte, Nesje and Lillejord, 2020; Arday, Belluigi and Thomas, 2020). Yet what coaching and mentoring can do is to challenge the myth that WP has generated skills-deficient or 'problem' students by helping instil powerful 'counter narratives' in students themselves. Later in this chapter, we look at examples of how this translates in practice.

The learning development community of practice has evidenced both the value and impact of coaching and mentoring approaches on student learning experiences

As well as providing evidence of LD's sustained challenge to remedial study skills, scholarship from within the LD community has also begun to demonstrate some of the ways in which coaching and mentoring approaches have been successfully integrated into LD practice. In making a case for coaching and mentoring tools to be part of the learning developers' toolkit in this chapter, then, we are building upon the evidence-based research that LD has already generated for the value of coaching and mentoring approaches in harnessing the varied skills and experience of a diverse student population.

It is worth acknowledging here that the integration of coaching into interventions which support student LD has matured outside of the UK. In the international context, we can look to student support variously referred to as 'academic coaching' or 'student success coaching' to see examples of this. As noted in the introduction to this volume, in the United States, academic coaching programmes are well established at many institutions as distinct from other forms of support such as peer mentoring, academic advising and personal tutoring (Capstick *et al.*, 2019, p. 221). Academic coaching has also been provided to college students across the United States by external organisations such as 'Inside Track' which offers telephone, email and virtual one-to-one support for students at risk of withdrawal or poor outcomes focused on goal setting, self-organisation and study skills (Bettinger and Baker, 2014). There is demonstrable, causal evidence that college students coached by Inside Track were retained by their institutions at a higher rate than students in the control group (Bettinger and Baker, 2014, p. 10). Other studies in the United States have found comparable results for the impact of academic coaching on student learning – including models where students were targeted for support (Field *et al.*, 2013; Alzen *et al.*, 2021). Internationally, there is evidence of the efficacy of coaching on the types of intervention delivered in LD around academic literacies, self-organisation, time management and active learning skills from Europe and Asia (Rodríguez Fuentes *et al.*, 2023, pp. 13–14). In the Personal Learning Advice (PLA) Service 96 percent of 135 students respondents to our survey stated their PLA had a positive impact on their study related achievements (see Figure 1.4).

Academic or student success coaching is, in theory, based on the principles of person-centred coaching, using approaches such as co-active coaching (Howlett *et al.*, 2021b) and familiar coaching models such as GROW (Whitmore, 2002) discussed in further detail in Chapters 4 and 7 of this volume. However, it is also largely driven by, and towards, student grades rather than some of the more holistic and non-directive forms of coaching being described in other chapters in this volume. Equally, academic coaching is not a straightforward synonym for LD, either. One important distinction to make is that academic coaching does not always operate in the 'Third Space,' because is often delivered by faculty (Howlett *et al.*, 2021b). It also very often continues to be a targeted or specialist support offer, rather than mainstream and embedded, like LD. Academic coaching is enigmatic in the sense that it is 'not-quite-coaching' and 'not-quite-learning development.' What it does offer us, though, are examples of successful cross-fertilisation of approaches between coaching and LD. Let us now turn to look at some examples of this from across the literature on UK LD and wider, international approaches to academic success coaching. We have synthesised these into three themes which demonstrate just some of the ways in which coaching and mentoring approaches have already been used to positive effect.

Student-led goal setting and action planning

Coaching techniques offer practitioners another tool to help ensure that students' academic skills development is a personalised learning process owned by them and not prescribed by staff. We deliberately position coaching here as a 'another' or supplementary tool because student-led interactions are, in theory, part of the 'signature pedagogy' of LD which is 'non-directive, non-prescriptive, Rogerian (Webster, 2020). Student-led discussions are also part of the '5 Ps' framework recently proposed as a way of capturing what learning developers do to avoid directive and prescriptive skills sessions (Webster, 2023). This is a compelling and highly relevant case for the ways in which formulation – borrowed from the clinical therapeutic context – can help practitioners to co-construct learning plans rather than diagnose problems. Others have similarly noted the need for practices which ensure student agency in their interactions with learning developers (Caldwell, Stapleford and Tinker, 2018; Rooney, 2024).

There is clear evidence that where students have agency and ownership of the goals they are pursuing, they become autonomous and develop confidence and self-belief (Lancer and Eatough, 2018). There are helpful examples from the literature on LD about how coaching can enable this approach. In one study which tested coaching with two small cohorts of undergraduate health students, both GROW and the SIMPLE coaching models were used to help foster goal setting around deeper (rather than surface) learning (Gurbutt and Gurbutt, 2015, p. 15). In this piece, it is acknowledged that whilst a student might come to a one-to-one appointment expecting to be directed to very specific actions or solutions to a perceived problem or challenge, there is considerable value in using coaching to nurture them to take 'ownership' of their learning goals and identify interim steps towards achieving these (Gurbutt and Gurbutt, 2015, p. 10). Similarly, evaluation of an intervention at the University of North Carolina has demonstrated how strengths-based coaching helped students to direct their sessions based on their own reflection, facilitated by the coach (Howlett *et al.*, 2021a). In this case, it is argued that the coaching approach prevents practitioners being too directive which 'contrasts with more traditional academic support services, such as remedial and probationary services, that use a prescriptive expert approach to target student deficits through explicit skills-based instruction' (Howlett *et al.*, 2021a, p. 194). Building upon these, later in this chapter, we offer some practical examples of the way coaching approaches can be used to support student-led goal setting in relation to assessment feedback.

Creating student-centred spaces for active learning

Coaching and mentoring through an 'equity lens' means that practitioners aim to create a space which values, and centres, students' lived experiences. In the context of our work coaching and mentoring students from underrepresented backgrounds, we have learned from the literature on privileging experiential knowledge and counter-stories which disrupt traditional narratives about 'non-traditional' students (Quigley and Mitchell, 2018, p. 82). As practitioners in a coaching and mentoring service, we also strive to be critically reflexive about our practice and our positionalities – as practitioners in a position of power and relative privilege, when we invite students to share their experiences. Learning developers have similarly noted the importance of the skills and approaches used in one-to-one interactions between a learning developer and student. In one recent commentary on approaches to maths skills tutorials, for example, coaching and mentoring techniques such as open questioning, neutral language, holding silence and non-verbal cues such as mirroring body language were vital in creating 'a calm and purposeful working atmosphere' (Delderfield and McHattie, 2018, pp. 4–5). In this study, it was argued that student learning was also deepened as a result of the space being conducive to them taking time to sufficiently rework a task, to ask questions and to share frustrations and failures (p. 7). Steven White addressed this dynamic in a paper at the ALDinHE conference in 2023, with reference to the concept of 'brave' (not necessarily 'safe) spaces where students are supported to see that 'challenges will pass' (White, 2023, p. 3).

There is, then, already an awareness of the 'Rogerian person-centredness' that is more conducive to students' active learning in LD tutorials where students feel more at liberty to bring their whole selves to appointments. This is informed by, and extends to, some of the wider literature on student-centred pedagogy which has stressed that in its origins, being student centred meant consciously creating a space which takes into account the whole person. As Blackie, Case and Jawitz, put it well over a decade ago:

> If we are to take the idea of the person of the student seriously, we need to begin to pay attention to the emotional side of education. Knowledge may be emotionally neutral. There is no obvious emotional content to the concept of chemical bonding, for example. However, the manner in which an individual interacts with knowledge is emotionally charged.
>
> (2010, p. 641)

In related work, this is about facilitating a student's process of 'becoming' and not just a given piece of knowledge or particular skill (Barnett, 2009). In our case study scenario exemplifying person-centred questioning and its use in LD appointments below, we aim to contribute some practical examples to this discussion.

Taking down barriers to help-seeking

A final theme in the literature on coaching, mentoring and LD which we want to acknowledge in this discussion is the impact of coaching and mentoring approaches on staff-student relationships and, in turn, how this can help take down barriers to students seeking help in their studies. Chapter 6 in this volume demonstrates the way *peer* mentoring might be instrumental in engaging students in wider support mechanisms and learning developers have also noted similar things (Pritchard, 2015). There are also studies which show that one-to-one staff–student mentoring can create positive supportive and 'ongoing' relationships with staff, whether in faculties or professional services. In their study of one-to-one mentoring among Mechanical Engineering students at a Caribbean university, for example, Maharaj, Blair and Burns posited that implementing mentoring itself 'conveys the implicit message to students that they are valued and should be supported' and may be more important than the content of mentoring itself (2021, p. 16). Elsewhere, discussions in the LD community have revealed practitioner experiences of integrating empathy and compassion into their teaching and the impact this can have on students' continuing access to support, among other things (de Silva and Dempsey, 2022). Learning developers have also argued for the importance of reflecting on their own positionality, sharing their learning with students and facilitating students sharing in their relational practice to help eliminate barriers (Bohlmann, 2022, p. 3). Later in this chapter, we offer recommendations for ways to further enhance this 'relational practice' using coaching-informed approaches in both group and one-to-one settings.

In the first half of this chapter, we have charted some of the ways in which learning developers have already begun to incorporate coaching and mentoring techniques into their practice and the evidence of the impact this has on students. We have argued for the relevance of person-centred coaching and mentoring to the 'signature' pedagogy of learning developers. In what remains of this chapter we turn to consider some practical ways that learning developers can use coaching in their work with students.

Using coaching and mentoring techniques in learning development

Other contributors to this volume have set out the coaching and mentoring continuum as used in practice by the PLA Service. As authors here, we have so far used 'coaching and mentoring' together to reflect how we work across this continuum in a way which does not position either approach as optimum but offers a fluidity for meeting student needs. As learning developers, we are (perhaps?) more accustomed to approaches which might sit at, or towards, the mentoring end of the continuum because of the nature of the support. For instance, in an appointment on time management and study habits, we might legitimately expect a member of staff supporting a less experienced student to share insights, give advice and signpost to resources. What we want to show here is that being cognisant of this and recognising occasions where it might be more impactful to stop sharing and suspend our advice and, to instead, tap into a student's own knowledge, experience and resources. This does not require us to fundamentally change our approach, but it does require us to be conscious and purposeful. In his well-known TED Talk, Stanier described this as 'taming' our 'advice monsters' (Stanier, 2020).

As practitioners on our own journey with this, we are not seeking to be either exhaustive or prescriptive in what we offer here. We have (necessarily) limited our focus to three areas or types of scenario where selecting appropriate modes of interaction from across the coaching and mentoring continuum might enhance student learning and experience:

- Challenging barriers to engagement in group sessions;
- Supporting students to action plan using assessment feedback; and
- Questioning techniques for person-centred conversations.

Challenging barriers to learning and engagement in group sessions

Coaching and mentoring often take place in a one-to-one setting and we often associate these techniques as appropriate for work with individual students. However, lots of LD work takes place in group settings that are either 'embedded' or not (as we have seen above) in formal teaching sessions. Firstly, then, let us turn to consider how coaching techniques can add value to 'relational practice' (Bohlmann, 2022) in a group setting.

The context for our shared experience as learning developers delivering group sessions in the PLA Service was in the design and delivery of 'Study Success' and 'Learn, Grow, Connect' workshops for distance-learning students. These were part of a pilot trialling a targeted group support offer which were, like the 1:1 provision, aimed at students from backgrounds which are more generally underrepresented in HE. This included sessions for students with disabilities and / or mental health needs, students from areas with high levels of deprivation and students from racially minoritised backgrounds (and intersections of the three) (UK Government, 2024). In the Study Success programme, there were 15 standalone workshops across five themes: study focus, study hacks, study assessment, study know-how and study reflection. In the Learn, Grow, Connect series, there were six workshops on themes such as study vision, mindset, reflection and creating a support network and insights from staff have been shared elsewhere (Wilton and Samuels-Hylton, 2023, pp. 12–13). These workshops were delivered across 2022–2024 in parallel to existing forms of LD support at the university which include specialist one-to-one English for Academic Purposes tutorials delivered by Lecturers, and 'Student Hub Live' online skills sessions (Foley and Marr, 2019).

Both our planning and facilitation in the workshops were informed by our learning from the literature on the impact that integrated coaching approaches can have on students. The value that coaching brings to teaching is not a new observation. There have been several studies on how coaching has been used across the education system to enhance student behaviour and outcomes for some time (Devine, Meyers and Houssemand, 2013). However, the type of student-centred pedagogy which is the 'gold standard' for learning developers also has much in common with what some scholars in coaching psychology describe as 'coaching for learning' (Wang, 2012, p. 182). In coaching for learning, instructors talk less and spend less time 'transmitting information' and more time working towards the co-construction of knowledge with their students (Wang, 2012, p. 181). There is also some overlap between coaching for learning and group coaching in that group coaching seeks to 'leverage' the experience and subject expertise of the group (Britton, 2010, 2013). Studies of group coaching among student populations have also shown that it can help to build peer support and accountability (Canaan, 2022).

As learning developers, we discovered from this that there was something to learn from both group coaching interventions and coaching for learning principles. We recognised that we were not 'coaching' in the sense that we were (necessarily) being directive in setting learning objectives, writing content and delivering instructional information to students. But our aspiration was that our workshops – even those on skills-related areas such as reading and note-taking, writing paragraphs or time management – met some of the principles that 'coaching for learning' had taught us. We aimed to find a way to explore students' strengths and integrate lived experience into the workshops to help students to recognise and harness their own experiential learning and apply it to study. Below, we share some approaches based on our experience of doing so.

Contracting and 'soft starts'

Chapter 3 of this volume demonstrates the value of contracting with students in a one-to-one setting, but it also extends to workshops or group tutorials. In a classroom or online workshop setting, contracting might be impacted by policy documents such as codes of conduct, teaching and learning agreements and even individual instructor approaches. Our team approach has been to use two main mechanisms: shared ways of working and 'soft' starts to support our contracting with students. Below, we have shared our 'ways of working' template which is circulated to workshop registrants and is also used as part of an introductory slide in online workshops. It invites students to a 15-minute (optional) informal period before the session content formally begins – a 'soft start' – which we have found creates an opportunity for students to settle into the session, meet the facilitators and introduce themselves using the chat function. This was designed to set the tone for workshops, validate the many ways that students might participate and also grow confidence for engagement.

Shared ways of working: an example

What you can expect from us:

- We will treat you with respect and handle anything you share with us sensitively.
- We will not share anything you tell us outside of the session, however, we are obliged to report any safeguarding concerns as per the confidentiality statement.
- We want to create a safe, trusting, supportive and encouraging learning space.
- In these sessions there will be a similar structure in each session. This will include a welcome, introduction to the topic of the workshop, a deeper look at the topic, an activity and time for questions.
- We will start the sessions on time but will open the room 15 minutes early if you would like to join and meet us before the session starts.

What we would like from you:

- Please make every effort to turn up to sessions on time. We will start promptly.
- To be in a quiet and confidential space during the sessions.
- To not share any information/personal disclosures outside of the sessions.

- Everyone has their own level of comfort with on-line sessions. We respect this. Please feel free to have your camera on/off and your mic on/off and contribute to the chat as little or as much as you like. We welcome contributions and participation but equally if you are happier to take a more observer approach, we trust that this is the right decision for you.
- We want these sessions to be a safe, trusting learning space where we champion and support each other. All your questions or comments are valid and therefore we do ask that you always respect each other's comments and contributions.
- If at any time you need/decide to leave the session, please feel free to leave. We ask that before you do leave the workshop, you drop one of us a quick goodbye in the chat and that way we know you are OK before you leave the session. Thank you.

Using this approach is simple but fundamental to creating 'safe' (or maybe 'brave'?) spaces which are conducive to sharing (and validating) the range of experience within a group and is one way for us as facilitators to work proactively and consciously towards creating that environment. The value of this for students was broadly reflected in our student experience survey findings shown in Figure 1.4 of the introductory chapter to this volume, 86 percent of respondents to this opt-in evaluation who had attended group sessions across our programmes either strongly agreed or agreed with the statement that 'It was important for me to see and hear students with similar lived experiences AND/OR shared challenges to me at PLA Service group sessions.'

Strengths-based discussions

We have noted in this chapter how learning developers regularly face the challenge of teaching academic skills and literacies, in a way which does not emphasise the skills 'deficit' of students. Using a strengths-based approach (Peterson and Seligman, 2004; Driver, 2011) derived from group coaching can help facilitators to tease out and harness relevant experiences that student participants bring to a workshop. There are relevant examples in the literature on group coaching, such as an intervention reported on by McDowall and Butterworth (2014) who use questions such as: 'What are you particularly good at?' and 'What do you find comes naturally to you?' before guiding participants to reflect on how the identified strengths apply to their study goals. This can be harder to achieve where learning developers are delivering workshops where lived experiences and personal skills and attributes may feel less relevant, but it can be used as a starting point for approaching topics which feel unfamiliar or challenging for students. In the example below, we share some activities used to facilitate a workshop on reading, making notes and paraphrasing which is designed to help students make connections between their 'real world' and academic experiences.

Strengths-based activities for academic reading

The facilitator begins by encouraging students to recognise and acknowledge that active reading and note making are two important academic skills to being a successful, independent learner. Like any skill they need to be practiced and can take time to master.

Create awareness about the ways in which students already vary their reading techniques depending on the text they are using and the purpose they have.

1. We often take different approaches to reading depending on the text in front of us. Take a moment to reflect on your approach to reading when:
    - Scrolling through social media;
    - Skimming a newspaper or magazine in a waiting room;
    - Feeling engrossed in a novel; and
    - Checking a bus timetable or work rota.

    Questions and prompts to extend students' thinking:
    - How does the purpose of your reading determine your approach?
    - What impact does the type of text have on your approach to reading?
    - How much of the text do you need to read? How does that vary?
    - What kind of environment do you need to be able to read a text? How does this differ depending on the type of text?

    Invite students to share their responses and draw comparisons between these to validate differences.

The second part of the workshop considers strategies in academic reading at university and how students will already possess skills and experience to adopt different reading techniques depending on the text and purpose of their reading. Initially, the facilitator begins by introducing reading techniques – in this case skimming and scanning.

2. A couple of active reading techniques that can be helpful at university are skimming and scanning. In order to make links with experiences students will already have and encourage them to reflect and explore how these experiences could translate to academic study, invite students to think of times when they might already and intuitively be using these reading techniques in their day-to-day lives, work or hobbies.

Prompts or examples to get students reflecting on when they might already use skimming techniques:

- Have you ever used this in a bookshop when deciding whether or not to buy a book?
- Or perhaps looking through a newspaper or magazine browsing for an article to read?
- Maybe when re-reading something quickly to find something you have already read?
- Think about your own context – home, work, family or caring responsibilities, hobbies – what other scenarios have you used this approach? How did it help you? Please share your ideas in the chat.

Prompts or examples to get students reflecting on when they might already use scanning techniques:

- Have you ever used a directory to look for an address or telephone number?
- Perhaps you have scanned a work rota to find a shift or looked at a bus timetable to plan a journey?
- Maybe you have been organising a visit or day out somewhere and needed to find answers to a question on a company FAQs page?

- Think about your own context – home, work, family or caring responsibilities, hobbies – what other scenarios have you used this approach? How did it help you? Please share your ideas in the chat.

Again, the facilitator might conclude the exercise by inviting students to share their responses and acknowledge differences.

Using reflective questions in the way we did in the activities above can help identify areas where the facilitators might need to provide more context and deliver something more informational and instructional. This is an adaptation of the 'accordion' approach used in group coaching in a corporate context (Britton, 2013). Here, coaches *prepare* to cover a variety of themes through questioning but if there is interest in particular area(s) within the group, then the accordion can be 'squeezed' and the direction adjusted. It also exemplifies the strengths-based approach derived from positive psychology coaching (Peterson and Seligman, 2004) which has been translated to education more widely. As it has been described elsewhere, this is fundamentally:

> identifying and nurturing what students value and are good at, helping them find ways to optimize their strengths, and helping them find niches where they can live out their strengths.
>
> (Devine, Meyers and Houseemand, 2013, p. 1386)

The student survey feedback responses for this workshop as it was delivered across the PLA Service pilot highlighted the particular value students placed on hearing from each other and the sense of community in sharing challenges. This lends support to related arguments within the literature on inclusive approaches to teaching international students that we need to be able to respond to the needs of students who may have experienced different pedagogical systems (Bartram, 2008) and avoid making assumptions about learned academic conventions (Kingston and Forland, 2008). Normalising the fact that academic conventions are something to learn but building student familiarity with them by helping them make connections to other relevant experiences appears to help and reassure students. This is clear in the free-text comments from the PLA Service's survey which were specifically about group support. One student commented on the impact this had on them:

> At the group workshops it was encouraging to note that there were others who had the same fears that you had. Others who sometimes felt they could give up but persevered.
>
> I felt like other students had the same issues as me and since they were pushing through it gave me the desire to keep on going.

This was also strongly reflected in our reading and note taking workshop feedback where students commented on the 'realisation' that they were already able to use many of the reading techniques and that this helped them to overcome a significant 'barrier.' Findings from the 'coaching for learning' approaches we adopted in the pilot have been used to inform recommendations for the design and delivery of virtual one-to-many (group) spaces across student services as part of the core offer of support at the university.

Supporting students to action plan using assessment feedback

The approaches we can adopt to being mindful and attuned to student perceptions and feelings about assessment feedback is a perennial and thorny issue in HE. The role that learning developers might (or might not) play in supporting feedback assessment has been discussed elsewhere (Bailey, 2009) and there is a vast field of scholarship on assessment and feedback within SoTL. Some of the most recent literature reviews draw attention to the concept of 'feedback literacy' and, within that, 'the conceptual shift from feedback as an external input to feedback literacy as capacities residing within the individual' (Nieminen and Carless, 2023, p. 1394). Therefore, we offer ideas here in full acknowledgement that there is a broader conversation taking place about feedback literacies and how HE can, in more radical ways requiring substantial changes to assessment systems and models, ensure students are critical partners in assessment feedback.

As learning developers, we are often facing the challenge of working alongside students to positively engage with their feedback and how we can help them to reframe their feedback as an opportunity to identify personal academic development goals, rather than focusing on the perception of tutor criticism. We know that students can often find the experience of receiving feedback challenging and this is well documented in the literature (Middleton *et al.*, 2023, p. 120). As authors, we decided to take a reflective approach to thinking about our shared experiences in supporting students with feedback and identified the following challenges:

- In our experiences working with distance-learning students, there can be difficulties in separating the experience of receiving feedback on their academic performance from their self-worth as a capable learner, and even further, their valuing of themselves as a person.
- The default stance for many students is to read through feedback focusing on what parts the tutor is telling them are 'good' and which parts of their work are 'bad,' 'not good enough' or 'require improvement.'
- There can be difficulty in separating emotions from the experience to form a productive approach that empowers them to feel both inspired to take action and capable of doing so.
- Feelings of perfectionism and imposter syndrome (which are often caused by structural and systemic disadvantage and therefore more likely to be experienced by students from marginalised groups).
- There is a tendency to focus disproportionately on areas we perceive as negative feedback (negativity bias).

Borrowing from strengths-based coaching can go some way to address these challenges. The 'Traffic Lights' exercise we share below is designed to address the tension between the importance of formative development and continuous improvement and the feeling of 'never good enough' that our students often describe. Using 'traffic lights' as a tool for self-reflection, evaluation, and 'RAG ratings' will be familiar to most. There are, for example, practical toolkits available to show the potential application in self-evaluation activities with students (Canterbury Christ Church University, 2018). What we have sought to do here is share the exercise for completion by students, supplemented by a guide for practitioners to support a coaching-informed dialogue. This is designed to be worked through in a one-to-one appointment with students.

Traffic lights exercise

For students to complete prior to/during the first part of a one-to-one

1. Choose three different highlighter colours, or three other ways of marking the text to separate your feedback into categories. (This could be circling the bit of text, drawing a box around it or underlining it, whatever feels right for you.)
2. Assign each colour or marking to a category, for example: Green if you understand the feedback AND how you can action it

moving forward; amber if you understand the feedback but are unsure of or undecided on how you could go about actioning it in future; red if you don't understand that part of the feedback and don't know what you could do to action it.

3. Create three lists for each category and consider your lists, asking yourself the questions below that feel most relevant.

Bank of reflective questions for a learning developer/practitioner to draw from during the one-to-one

- What areas do you feel are your strengths? Has this feedback confirmed this or is it highlighting different areas?
- How can you continue to build on and demonstrate these strengths in your next assignment?
- How did you develop these strengths previously? (Looking backwards to look forwards can be really useful!)
- Comparing this to previous feedback you have received, are there any themes that are similar? Any differences (or things that are no longer being commented on, e.g. things you have changed or improved on since then?)?
- What are the next areas you would like to develop? You might like to consider what areas might be 'quick wins,' e.g. revisiting previous learning; and which areas might require more investment of time.
- Which actions could have the biggest impact on your confidence as a learner? What actions could impact on other areas you have highlighted as important to you?
- Who and what can support you to develop in this area? What can you read, watch, revisit? Who can signpost you to resources to make the progress you would like to make?
- Is there anything you need clarification on from your tutor? How will you go about getting this? When will you take this action?
- What things do you want to prioritise? How realistic are your priorities (see the question about 'quick wins' and longer-term investment)?
- What thoughts and feelings have this mark and feedback brought up for you? How have you experienced using the traffic lights process for reflecting on the feedback? How does this compare to your previous experiences of reading and reflecting on feedback?

- Create an action plan for your next steps. What are you choosing to focus on? How can you make the goals you set for yourself SMART?

Post-session reflection for practitioners

- Going through this process, was there a piece of the feedback that seems contentious for the student? For example, are they 'stuck' on their interpretation of a particular piece of feedback? Can you challenge their interpretation through coaching?
- Considering the potential that development could have on future marks is a sensitive point. How do we know the extent to which the individual student considers their marks to be of importance? What impact could the discussion of marks have on things such as leading the student's priorities? A focus on marks could be unhelpful for those with perfectionist tendencies.
- To what extent might our own professional agenda influence the questions we ask students? For example, have I led the student to focus on marks (an institutional way of measuring 'success') rather than following the student's definition of success?
- What does success mean to the student, i.e. self-actualisation? How can I support them to explore and prioritise this?

Working through the traffic lights exercise, questioning techniques, and self-reflective questions after an appointment help to ensure our approach as practitioners is geared towards supporting a mindset shift away from 'is this aspect of my work good or bad?' and more towards 'how well do I understand this and what options I have to develop in this area?' Partly, this is a way to embrace the idea of 'discomfort' that Steven White has argued can be transformative for students when cultivated carefully in such 'brave spaces' (2023, p. 3). At a simpler level, we have found it is also a way to nurture the growth mindset students need for learning, self-efficacy and independence (Kolyda, 2023).

Questioning techniques for person-centred conversations

Across this chapter, we have alluded to centrality of questioning for positive, person-centred conversations – whether to create spaces for learning, or to tap into students' experience and existing expertise in group sessions. In the final section of this chapter, we offer some examples of how questioning can help to drive a person-centred LD conversation, using the scenario below. This is intended as an illustration of authentic scenarios in which person-centred conversations may play out.

Scenario: Part one

PRACTITIONER: What is your main motivation for studying?
STUDENT: I wanted to study so I could support my career. I have this ambition to work in an area of public health and I know I need to enhance my qualifications as part of my development.
PRACTITIONER: What inspires you to do this kind of work?
STUDENT: I want to make a difference to people.
PRACTITIONER: Let's imagine that you achieve that goal, and you are in a role where you are working at your best, making a difference to people. [Pause] What would that be like?
STUDENT: It would be reflected in the equitable outcomes for my community, where Black women are not experiencing inadequate maternity care and infant death rates are not affected by racism and institutional racism.
PRACTITIONER: I'm hearing that your motivation is not just about your own career. It has a much wider purpose?
STUDENT: Developing my career is what will allow me to contribute to this but it's much more than my career, really.
PRACTITIONER: How can you hold on to that motivation in your day-to-day studies?

Post-session reflection suggestions for practitioners

- When might it be helpful in your role to understand what is really motivating a student?
- How do you currently find out about this?
- What depth of answers do you receive (think about extrinsic motivators such as career goals, intrinsic motivators such self-actualisation, and being their best version of themselves)?
- How can you explore and further understand a student's motivations?
- What questions could you ask?

Scenario: Part two

PRACTITIONER: You have shared with me some examples of what went well as you were preparing to submit this assignment. What challenges did you encounter, if any?

STUDENT: I usually hand in all of my assignments early but I just felt overwhelmed with this one. I worked up to the deadline as I didn't want to ask for an extension.

PRACTITIONER: You usually hand in your assignments early, so you find deadlines manageable. What do you think was different this time?

STUDENT: This time it coincided with the kids being poorly and off-school, and work was just hectic, so I didn't have as much time.

PRACTITIONER: Was there anything else that was different this time?

STUDENT: I could not get everything I wanted to say into the word count.

PRACTITIONER: That can definitely be challenging for lots of students I talk to. Tell me more about that.

STUDENT: Well, the topic I chose was really personal to me in lots of ways because it was relating to the inequities of Black maternal and infant mortality. I suppose I felt more pressure to get it right. I just kept reading more and more and feeling pretty triggered and emotional.

PRACTITIONER: Thank you for sharing that with me. You have told me in previous appointments that it is this personal connection to the subject that motivates you, but it sounds like on this occasion it has been triggering and raised some difficult emotions. How do you think you could find a place of balance between those elements in the future so that you hold on to the motivation but protect your emotional wellbeing too?

STUDENT: I'm not sure.

PRACTITIONER: Another way to look at this could be to think about what advice would you give to a friend or family member or patient who was experiencing something like this. Could you apply this advice to your own situation?

Post-session reflection suggestions for practitioners

- How might this person-centred approach affect your practice?
- How might it impact students?

- How might you manage a conversation when a student does not respond to a particular question (like the 'I'm not sure' response in the above example)?
- How might these questioning techniques ensure you are supporting students to find their own solutions?
- What ethical implications might you need to consider in relation to open questioning?
- How can you support the student with prioritising their own well-being and support needs beyond this conversation?
- How might your positionality and the power dynamics of your role affect this conversation? How can you effectively manage these aspects within your coaching relationship with the student?

Summary

In this chapter, we began by synthesising some of the key themes from the (largely Anglo-American) literature on how coaching and mentoring has enhanced student experiences in LD. This informed three simple observations about the way LD has evolved over the last few decades and the alignment between its mission, on the one hand, and coaching and mentoring, on the other hand. We suggested that:

- The origins of LD are rooted in the mission to widen access and participation through student-centred support – rooted in a philosophy shared by coaches and mentors, that all students have the capacity to learn and overcome challenges.
- LD has been a key driver in the move away from 'remedial' support for students. Coaching and mentoring offer techniques to validate and harness the lived experiences of a diverse range of students and challenge limiting beliefs caused by harmful stereotypes about the needs of 'non-traditional' students.
- The LD community of practice has itself evidenced both the value and impact of coaching and mentoring approaches on student learning experiences in a range of ways but particularly in: student-led goal setting and action planning, creating student-centred spaces for active learning and taking down barriers to help-seeking.

In the latter part of this chapter, our aim was to share evidence-led practice when embedding coaching and mentoring techniques in LD work with students in both a one-to-one and group context.

As we were finalising this chapter in September 2024, the professional association for learning developers in the UK (ALDinHE) hosted an 'LD@3' (LD at 15:00) seminar entitled 'Why coaching? How learning developers might use or be interested in coaching' (Jewitt, 2024). In this, Jewitt shared coaching approaches for effective feedback, coaching for long-term behaviour change and a selection of student-wellbeing activities (Jewitt, 2024). In collating the resources from the LD@3, ALDinHE also featured the PLA Service's coaching handbook for practitioners (Lindsey, 2024). At the seminar itself, and in the sharing of resources afterwards, the conversation was rich. It told us that the LD community are indeed interested in coaching (in particular) but also its relationship to mentoring and the way it can enhance practitioner toolkits. What we hope to have offered in this chapter are some considerations for this ongoing conversation. Our aim has been to posit some deeper, pedagogic reasons that learning developers might be interested in adding coaching and mentoring to their practitioner toolkit, as well as some practical ideas and examples of how they might do so.

Further reflective questions

- What do I already know about coaching and mentoring techniques? What would I like to learn?
- What steps do I need to take to enhance how I use coaching and mentoring skills in my practice?
- What support and resources could I draw upon to learn more?
- How will I ensure I create opportunities for students to bring in/share lived experiences and knowledge that is relevant to them?
- How will I ensure I am validating students' thoughts and contributions to discussions, rather than making value judgements about content of these responses?
- How will I ensure I hold space and create opportunities to deepen learning, working with students as 'thinking partners' (Kline, 1999)?

Bibliography

Abegglen, S., Burns, T. and Sinfield, S. (2016) 'The power of freedom: setting up a multimodal exhibition with undergraduate students to foster their learning and help them to achieve', *Journal of Peer Learning*, 9, pp. 1–9. Available at: https://ro.uow.edu.au/ajpl/vol9/iss1/2 (Accessed: 12 July 2024).

Abegglen, S., Burns, T. and Sinfield, S. (2019) 'It's learning development, Jim – but not as we know it: academic literacies in third-space', *Journal of Learning Development in Higher Education*, 15. doi: 10.47408/jLearning Developmenthe.v0i15.500

Abegglen, S., Sinfield, S. and Burns, T. (2017) ''Really free!': strategic interventions to foster students' academic writing skills', *The Journal of Educational Innovation, Partnership and Change*, 3(1), pp. 251–255. Available at: https://journals.studentengagement.org.uk/index.php/studentchangeagents/article/view/589 (Accessed: 12 July 2024).

Alzen, J.L., Burkhardt, A., Diaz-Bilello, E., Elder, E., Sepulveda, A., Blankenheim, A. and Board, L. (2021) 'Academic coaching and its relationship to student performance, retention, and credit completion', *Innovative Higher Education*, 46, pp. 539–563. doi: 10.1007/s10755-021-09554-w

Arday, J., Zoe Belluigi, D. and Thomas, D. (2020) 'Attempting to break the chain: reimaging inclusive pedagogy and decolonising the curriculum within the academy', *Educational Philosophy and Theory*, 53(3), pp. 298–313. doi: 10.1080/00131857.2020.1773257

Arthur, R. (2024) 'Closing the gap: learning development and race', in A. Syska and C. Buckley (eds.) *How to be a Learning Developer in higher education: critical perspectives, community and practice*. 1st edn. Abingdon: Routledge, pp. 126–134.

Bailey, R.A. (2009) 'Undergraduate students' perceptions the role and utility of written assessment feedback', *Journal of Learning Development in Higher Education*, 1. doi: 10.47408/jLearning Developmenthe.v0i1.29

Barnett, R. (2009) 'Knowing and becoming in the higher education curriculum', *Studies in Higher Education*, 34(4), pp. 429–440. doi: 10.1080/03075070902771978

Bartram, B. (2008) 'Supporting international students in higher education: constructions, cultures and clashes', *Teaching in Higher Education*, 13(6). doi: 10.1080/13562510802452384

Bettinger, E. and Baker, R. (2014) 'The effects of student coaching: an evaluation of a randomized experiment in student advising', *Educational Evaluation and Policy Analysis*, 36(1), pp. 3–19. doi: 10.3102/0162373713500523

Blackie, M.A.L., Case, J.M. and Jawitz, J. (2010) 'Student-centredness: the link between transforming students and transforming ourselves', *Teaching in Higher Education*, 15(6), pp. 636–646. doi: 10.1080/13562517.2010.491910

Bohlmann, J. (2022) 'Decolonising learning development through reflective and relational practice', *Journal of Learning Development in Higher Education*, (24). doi: 10.47408/jLearning Developmenthe.vi24.913

Børte, K., Nesje, K. and Lillejord, S. (2020) 'Barriers to student active learning in higher education', *Teaching in Higher Education*, 28(3), pp. 597–615. doi: 10.1080/13562517.2020.1839746

Briggs, S. (2018) 'Moving from learning developers to learning development practitioners', *Journal of Pedagogic Development*, 8(3). Available at: https://www.beds.ac.uk/jpd/volume-8-issue-3-november-2018/moving-from-learning-developers-to-learning-development-practitioners/ (Accessed: 30 October 2024).

Britton, J.J. (2010) *Effective group coaching: tried and tested tools and resources for optimum group coaching skills*. 1st edn. Mississauga: J. Wiley.

Britton, J.J. (2013) *From one to many: best practices for team and group coaching*. Newark, NJ: John Wiley and Sons, Incorporated. Available at: https://proquest.libguides.com/ebookcentral (Accessed: 8 October 2024).

Brown, S.M. and Grant, A. (2010) 'From GROW to GROUP: theoretical issues and a practical model for group coaching in organisations', *Coaching: An International Journal of Theory, Research and Practice*, 3(1), pp. 30–45. doi: 10.1080/17521880903559697

Caldwell, E., Stapleford, K. and Tinker, A. (2018) 'Talking academic writing: a conversation analysis of one-to-one Learning Development tutorials', *Journal of Academic Writing*, 8(2), pp. 124–136. doi: 10.18552/joaw.v8i2.464

Canaan, S., Fischer, S., Mouganie, P. and Schnorr, G.C. (2022) 'Keep me in, coach: the short- and long-term effects of targeted academic Coaching', IZA Discussion Papers, No. 15469, Institute of Labor Economics (IZA), Bonn, Available at: https://www.econstor.eu/bitstream/10419/265690/1/dp15469.pdf (Accessed: 04 October 2024).

Canterbury Christ Church University. (2018) *The traffic lights toolkit*. Available at: https://www.canterbury.ac.uk/learning-and-teaching-enhancement/docs/traffic-light-toolkit/The-Traffic-Lights-Toolkit-A-guide-for-practitioners-in-Higher-Education.pdf (Accessed: 07 October 2024).

Capstick, M.C., Harrell-Williams, L.M., Colton, D., Cockrum, D. and Steven, L. (2019) 'Exploring the effectiveness of academic coaching for academically at-risk college students', *Innovative Higher Education*, 44, pp. 219–231. doi: 10.1007/s10755-019-9459-1

Clay, E.-M., Williams, H., Blissett, J., Lindley, J. and O'Neil, L. (2023) 'Developing an equity lens: the experience of creating a professional framework for coaches and mentors', *Journal of Learning Development in Higher Education*, 26. doi: 10.47408/jLearning Developmenthe.vi26.932

Cottrell, S. (2001) *Teaching study skills and supporting learning*. Basingstoke: Palgrave Macmillan.

Delderfield, R. and McHattie, H. (2018) 'The person-centred approach in maths skills development: examining a case of good practice', *Journal of Learning Development in Higher Education*, 13. doi: 10.47408/jLearning Developmenthe.v0i13.447

de Silva, D. and Dempsey, E. (2022) 'Empathy and compassion: towards wellbeing in learning development', *Journal of Learning Development in Higher Education*, 25. doi: 10.47408/jLearning Developmenthe.vi22.988

Devine, M., Meyers, R. and Houssemand, C. (2013) 'How can coaching make a positive impact within educational settings?' *Procedia – Social and Behavioral Sciences*, 93, pp. 1382–1389. doi: 10.1016/j.sbspro.2013.10.048

Dhillon, S. (2022) *Podcast episode, Sunny Dhillon: pedagogies of discomfort and the neoliberal university: the learning development project*. Available at: https://open.spotify.com/episode/19xwyaS4UHH9cieH5TLJsx (Accessed: 31 October 2024).

Dhillon, S. (2024) 'Critical self-reflection in learning development', in A. Syska and C. Buckley (eds.) *How to be a Learning Developer in higher education: critical perspectives, community and practice*. 1st edn. Abingdon: Routledge, pp. 109–117.

Driver, M. (2011) *Coaching positively: lessons for coaches from positive psychology*. Maidenhead: McGraw-Hill Education. Available at: https://proquest.libguides.com/ebookcentral (Accessed: 31 October 2024).

Eyre, J. and Slawson, T. (2018) 'Dramatising learning development: towards an understanding without definition', *Journal of Learning Development in Higher Education*. doi: 10.47408/jLearning Developmenthe.v0i0.472

Field, S., Parker, D., Sawilowsy, S. and Rolands, L. (2013) 'Assessing the impact of ADHD coaching services on university students' learning skills, self-regulation, and well-being', *Journal of Postsecondary Education and Disability*, 26(1), pp. 67–81. Available at: https://files.eric.ed.gov/fulltext/EJ1026813.pdf (Accessed: 27 July 2024).

Foley, K. and Marr, L. (2019) 'Scaffolding extracurricular online events to support distance learning university students', *Journal of Interactive Media in Education*, 17, pp. 1–6. doi: 10.5334/jime.525

Gornall, L. (2019) 'Brokering academic literacies in a community of practice', *Journal of Learning Development in Higher Education*, 15. doi: 10.47408/jLearning Developmenthe.v0i15.536

Gravett, K. and Winstone, N.E. (2019) '"Feedback interpreters": The role of learning development professionals in facilitating university students' engagement with feedback', *Teaching in Higher Education*, 24(6), pp. 723–738. Available at: https://doi.org/10.1080/13562517.2018.1498076.

Gurbutt, D.J. and Gurbutt, R. (2015) 'Empowering students to promote independent learning: A project utilising coaching approaches to support learning and personal development', *Journal of Learning Development in Higher Education* [Preprint], (8). Available at: https://doi.org/10.47408/jldhe.v0i8.225

Haggis, T. (2006) 'Pedagogies for diversity: retaining critical challenge amidst fears of 'dumbing down'', *Studies in Higher Education*, 31(5), pp. 521–535. doi: 10.1080/03075070600922709

Hill, P., Tinker, A. and Catterall, S. (2010) 'From deficiency to development: the evolution of academic skills provision at one UK university', *Journal of Learning Development in Higher Education*, 2. doi: 10.47408/jLearning Developmenthe.v0i2.54

Hillman, J., Lochtie, D. and Purcell, O. (2024) 'Black students' experiences of coaching and mentoring in higher education: a case study', *International Journal of Mentoring and Coaching in Education*, 13(2), pp. 246–257. doi: 10.1108/IJMCE-01-2023-0011

Hilsdon, J. (2011). 'What is learning development?' in P. Hartley, J. Hilsdon, C. Keenan, S. Sinfie and M. Verity (eds.) *Learning development in higher education*. Basingstoke: Palgrave Macmillan, pp. 13–27.

Hilsdon, J., Malone, C. and Syska, A. (2019) 'Academic literacies twenty years on: a community-sourced literature review', *Journal of Learning Development in Higher Education*, 15. doi: 10.47408/jLearning Developmenthe.v0i15.567

Howlett, M.A., McWilliams, M.A., Rademacher, K., Conor O'Neill, J., Maitland, T.L., Abels, K.M., Demetriou, C. and Panter, A.T. (2021a) 'Investigating the effects of academic coaching on college students' metacognition', *Innovation Higher Education*, 46, pp. 189–204. doi: 10.1007/s10755-020-09533-7

Howlett, M.A., McWilliams, M.A., Rademacher, K., Conor O'Neill, J., Maitland, T.L., Abels, K.M., Demetriou, C. and Panter, A.T. (2021b) 'An academic coaching training program for university professionals: a mixed methods examination', *Journal of Student Affairs Research and Practice*, 58(3), pp. 335–349. doi: 10.1080/19496591.2020.1784750

Jewitt, K. (2024) *Why coaching? How learning developers might use or be interested in coaching*. Available at: https://drive.google.com/file/d/1TXu3M6ARkw_C6J-eeAVRVzXwMzJadpUK/view (Accessed: 01 October 2024).

JLDHE. (2024) *Journal of learning development in higher education*. Available at: https://journal.aldinhe.ac.uk/index.php/jldhe (Accessed: 01 October 2024).

Johnson, I. and Bishopp-Martin, S. (2024) 'Conceptual foundations in learning development', in A. Syska and C. Buckley (eds.) *How to be a learning developer in higher education: critical perspectives, community and practice*. 1st edn. Abingdon: Routledge, pp. 15–24.

Kingston, E. and Forland, H. (2008) 'Bridging the gap in expectations between international students and academic staff', *Journal of Studies in International Education*, 12(2), pp. 204–221. doi: 10.1177/1028315307307654

Kline, N. (1999) *Time to think: listening to ignite the human mind*. London: Ward Lock, Cassell.

Kolyda, F. (2023) 'Fostering a growth mindset in higher education for inclusive learning for all', *Journal of Learning Development in Higher Education*, 27. doi: 10.47408/jldhe.vi27.929

Lancer, N. and Eatough, V. (2018) 'One-to-one coaching as a catalyst for personal development: an interpretative phenomenological analysis of coaching undergraduates at a UK university', *International Coaching Psychology Review*, 13(1), pp. 72–88.

Lea, M. and Street, B. (1998) 'Student writing in higher education: an academic literacies approach', *Studies in Higher Education*, 23(2), pp. 157–172.

Learn Higher. (2024) Available at: https://aLearning Developmentinhe.ac.uk/learnhigher/ (Accessed: 01 October 2024).

Leanne Lindsey. (2024). Coaching Handbook: Personal Learning Advice Service. Unpublished Resource for Students.

Maharaj, C., Blair, E. and Burns, M. (2021) 'Reviewing the effect of student mentoring on the academic performance of undergraduate students identified as 'at risk'', *Journal of Learning Development in Higher Education*, 20. doi: https://doi.org/10.47408/jldhe.vi20.605

McDowall, A. and Butterworth, L. (2014) 'How does a brief strengths-based group coaching intervention work?', *Coaching: An International Journal of Theory, Research and Practice*, 7(2), pp. 152–163. doi: 10.1080/17521882.2014.953560

Middleton, T., ahmed Shafi, A., Millican, R. and Templeton, S. (2023) 'Developing effective assessment feedback: academic buoyancy and the relational dimensions of feedback', *Teaching in Higher Education*, 28(1), pp. 118–135. doi: 10.1080/13562517.2020.1777397

Minogue, L., Murphy, C. and Salmons, K. (2018) 'Embedding learning development; a model for collaborative practice', *Journal of Learning Development in Higher Education*, 13. doi: 10.47408/jLearning Developmenthe.v0i13.443

National Committee of Inquiry into Higher Education. (1997) *Dearing report*. Available at: https://education-uk.org/documents/dearing1997/dearing1997.html (Accessed: 07 August 2024).

Nieminen, J.H. and Carless, D. (2023) 'Feedback literacy: a critical review of an emerging concept', *Higher Education*, 85, pp. 1381–1400. doi: 10.1007/s10734-022-00895-9

Passmore, J., Peterson, D. and Freire, T. (2012) *The Wiley-Blackwell handbook of the psychology of coaching and mentoring*. Chichester: Wiley-Blackwell. doi: 10.1002/9781118326459 (Accessed: 25 June 2024).

Peterson, C. and Seligman, M.E.P. (2004) *Character strengths and virtues: a handbook and classification*. 1st edn. Washington, DC: American Psychological Association.

Pollard, E. (2023) 'On academia, critical pedagogy and 'coming out' as a third space practitioner', *Journal of Learning Development in Higher Education*, 27. doi: https://doi.org/10.47408/jldhe.vi27.927

Pritchard, C. (2015) 'Mentoring in the writing café: identity, belonging and ownership', *Journal of Learning Development in Higher Education*. doi: 10.47408/jLearning Developmenthe.v0i0.305

Quigley, M.W. and Mitchell, A.B. (2018) '"What works": applying critical race praxis to the design of educational and mentoring interventions for African American males', *Journal of African American Males in Education (JAAME)*, 9(2), pp. 74–102.

Rawson, M. (2000) 'Learning to learn: more than a skill set', *Studies in Higher Education*, 25(2), pp. 225–238. doi: 10.1080/713696137

Richards, K. and Pilcher, N. (2021) *Study skills are not the answer to students' academic woes, WonkHE*. Available at: https://wonkhe.com/blogs/study-skills-are-not-the-answer-to-students-academic-woes/ (Accessed: 03 June 2024).

Richards, K. and Pilcher, N. (2023) 'Study skills: neoliberalism's perfect Tinkerbell', *Teaching in Higher Education*, 28(3), pp. 580–596. doi: 10.1080/13562517.2020.1839745

Robinson, C.E. (2015) *Academic/success coaching: a description of an emerging field Learning Development in higher education*. PhD thesis. University of South Carolina Scholar Commons. Available at: https:// scholarcommons.sc.edu/etd/3148 (Accessed: 23 June 2024).

Rodríguez Fuentes, A., Navarro Rincón, A., Carrillo López, M.J. and Navarro, I.L. (2023) 'University coaching experience and academic performance', *Education Sciences*, 13(248), pp. 1–18. doi: 10.3390/educsci13030248

Rooney, S. (2024) 'The mess we're in: LD pedagogies and the question of student agency', in A. Syska and C. Buckley (eds.) *How to be a Learning Developer in higher education: critical perspectives, community and practice*. 1st edn. Abingdon: Routledge, pp. 25–33.

Samuels-Hylton, J. and Wilton, M.-J. (2023) 'Sharing stories of resilience: Open university partnership work with Shelayna Oskan-Clarke', *Learning Development Magazine*, July, pp. 12–13. Available at: https://online.fliphtml5.com/lwhvl/xgpp/#p=12 (Accessed: 6 October 2024).

Sherwood, G. and Johnson, I. (2024) 'Exploring the engagement of students who identify as Black, indigenous (and/or) people of colour (BIPoC) with Learning Development practitioners: reviewing the value, impact, and recommendations for future practice', *Journal of Learning Development in Higher Education*, 31. doi: 10.47408/jldhe.vi31.1169

Sinfield, S., Holley, D., Burns, T., Hoskins, K., O'Neill, P. and Harrington, K. (2010) 'Raising the student voice: learning development as socio-political practice', in P. Hartley, J. Hilsdon, C. Keenan, S. Sinfield and M. Verity (eds.) *Learning Development in higher education*. Basingstoke: Palgrave Macmillan, pp. 53–63.

Stanier, M.B. (2020) *How to tame your inner advice monster*. Available at: https://ideas.ted.com/how-to-tame-your-inner-advice-monster/ (Accessed: 12 August 2024).

Syska, A. and Buckley, C. (2024) 'Introduction', in A. Syska and C. Buckley (eds.) *How to be a learning developer in higher education: critical perspectives, community and practice*. 1st edn. Abingdon: Routledge, pp. 1–4.

UK Government. (2024) *Equality of access*. Available at: https://commonslibrary.parliament.uk/research-briefings/cbp-9195/ (Accessed: 12 August 2024).

Wang, Q. (2012) 'Coaching for learning: exploring coaching psychology in enquiry-based learning and development of learning power in secondary education', *Procedia – Social and Behavioral Sciences*, 69, pp. 177–186.

Webster, H. (2020) *LD@3: does learning development have a signature pedagogy?* Available at: https://www.slideshare.net/slideshow/Learning Development3-does-learning-development-have-a-signature-pedagogy/234504118 (Accessed: 12 August 2024).

Webster, H. (2022) 'Supporting the development, recognition and impact of third space professionals', in E. McIntosh and D. Nutt (eds.) *The impact of the integrated practitioner in higher education: studies in third space professionalism*. Abingdon: Routledge, pp. 178–187.

Webster, H. (2023) 'The five Ps of LD: using formulation in learning development work for a student-centred approach to 'study skills', *Journal of University Teaching and Learning Practice*, 20(4). doi: 10.53761/1.20.4.07

Whitchurch, C. (2003) *Reconstructing identities in higher education: the rise of third space professionals*. 1st edn. Oxford: Routledge. doi: 10.4324/9780203098301

White, S. (2023) 'Why inclusive learning shouldn't always be fun', *Journal of Learning Development in Higher Education*, 29. doi: 10.47408/jldhe.vi29.1100

Whitmore, J. (2002) *Coaching for performance – GROWing people, performance and purpose*. 3rd edn. London: Nicholas Brealey Publishing.

Wingate, U. (2006) 'Doing away with study skills', *Teaching in Higher Education*, 11(4), pp. 457–469.

Peer mentoring in higher education

6

Catherine Comfort and Chris Kubiak

Introduction

Other chapters in this volume have discussed practice in coaching and mentoring services and how these 'helping' skills might be developed among a wider population of student support and teaching practitioners (Asgari and Carter, 2016). This chapter focuses on a different type of service and considers formal programmes in which students support other students. Peer mentoring programmes – in which a more experienced student offers advice and support to less experienced students – have become ubiquitous in higher education (HE) and there is evidence that they offer significant value in relation to a wide range of outcomes (Snowden and Hardy, 2013; Seery *et al.*, 2021). This chapter explores this evidence by reviewing the existing literature in relation to peer mentoring and, using evidence-based practice from a case study at The Open University (OU), UK offers recommendations for the design and review of peer mentoring schemes.

What is peer mentoring?

In Homer's epic poem *The Odyssey*, Odysseus entrusts his friend Mentor with the care of his son Telemachus. It was by taking the form of Mentor that the Goddess Athena offered the wisdom and guidance necessary to support Telemachus's development into a capable leader (Irby *et al.*, 2020). Divine intervention aside, there are two core ideas from this story which still reflect

DOI: 10.4324/9781003486015-7

the practice of mentoring today. The first is that a mentor offers insight, wisdom and support in order to enable the growth of another. The second idea is that the most appropriate mentor is not simply defined by what they do but also by who they are. As will be argued below, guidance and support provided by those who have recently experienced the struggles of academic study is the crucial success factor in peer mentoring programmes.

While there is broad agreement on the purpose of mentoring, precise definitions of peer mentoring can be elusive. A survey of peer mentoring practice across HE reveals a multifaceted and highly context dependent field (Snowden and Halsall, 2016). A wide range of terms are employed to describe the process of one student supporting another: peer assisted learning (Bermingham, Boylan and Ryan, 2023), buddying (Simpson *et al.*, 2023), mentor-assisted learning, coaching (Snowden and Halsall, 2016), peer tutoring (Colvin and Ashman, 2010) and peer support (Osborn *et al.*, 2022), for example. Even when the term peer mentoring is settled upon, it too has its own variations; 'telementoring' and 'e-mentoring' imply telephone-based and online relationships, respectively (Single and Single, 2005). In addition to the terminological variety, there are a wide range of practices, purposes and configurations in the relationships associated with mentoring. Individual or group-based, online or on-campus and between those of equivalent experience or involving the more experienced supporting less experienced (Simpson *et al.*, 2023).

As such, for either faculty or professional services staff developing such a programme it is important that they establish the terms under which peer mentoring will operate. This chapter will work with the definition adapted from Nuis, Segers and Beausaert's (2023) systematic review: mentoring is a formalised process in which more experienced students offer less experienced students support in order to enhance their learning experience. There are two other dimensions of mentoring which also need to be established. First, how the mentoring relationship will be configured and second, the precise nature of the support offered.

The dimensions of peer mentoring

Mentoring primarily focuses on supporting the transitions associated with HE. That is, adapting to the social, academic, emotional or even career-related demands of university life. In essence, peer mentoring involves two core functions – the provision of task-based and/or psychosocial support (Terrion and Leonard, 2007):

- **Task-related support** usually refers to various forms of practical help or guidance. This might include academic support (Boyer *et al.*, 2010; Gunn, Lee and Steed, 2017), help with curriculum content (Colvin and Ashman, 2010), writing (Bakhshi, Harrington and O'Neill, 2009) or the provision of tips for study (Fayram *et al.*, 2018). Some mentoring programmes have a broader purpose. Colvin and Ashman's (2010) mentors directed students towards the resources on campus, helped with time management and even helped their group of students to prepare for an exam.
- **Psychosocial support** relates to the provision of psychological and emotional support (Risquez and Sanchez-Garcia, 2012; Thomas *et al.*, 2017). Having someone who listens, shows understanding and lends moral support can be important in reducing the stress of university (Gunn, Lee and Steed, 2017). Indeed, some mentoring programmes are primarily concerned with maintaining student mental health. Osborn *et al.*'s (2022) programme, for example, trained students to have supportive conversations with fellow students.

While logically separate domains, task and psychosocial support are indivisible in practice. Learning is hard and students often need emotional support. A skilled mentor is one who can offer useful advice while also communicating empathy and understanding. There are caveats here, however. While peer mentoring might offer some forms of academic support, it cannot replace tutoring from academic staff. Similarly, while being supportive and understanding is important, peer mentoring is not counselling or therapy. As such, it is essential that mentoring programmes establish a clear sense of boundaries for both mentors and students, similar to the way in which staff establish these – as outlined in Chapters 1 and 3 of this volume).

Characterising the relationship

In designing such programmes, decisions need to be made concerning how the mentor and student will interact and how the relationships will be structured. One broad distinction in approaches to the mentoring relationship is between individual, one-to-one relationships and group mentoring (Nuis, Segers and Beausaert, 2023). For the most part, different approaches appear to be predicated on organisational practicalities and resource availability. Group mentoring enables programmes to reach more students with fewer mentors, demands fewer training sessions and reduces organisational overhead. There are trade-offs, however. While group mentoring might enable mutual learning among students, individual mentoring is potentially more effective at addressing individual concerns (Gehreke, Schilling and Kauffeld, 2024). There is, however, little conclusive evidence of the superiority of either approach. Indeed, systematic reviews are often incurious about this issue though it could be argued that the sheer variety in programme types and objectives limit meaningful comparison. Pointon-Hass *et al.*'s (2024) work is an exception, however, and they note there is more evidence showing that individual peer mentoring is an effective method to support student mental health.

E-mentoring has become more prominent in the twenty-first century and during the 2020–2021 pandemic was sometimes used to offer students additional support in the absence of on-campus learning events. Like campus-based alternatives, e-mentoring can take place in dyads or groups (Goodrich, 2021). Mentor and student might meet at the same time through video or audio-conferencing tools such as Zoom, Skype or Microsoft Teams, or correspond asynchronously (Hixenbaugh *et al.*, 2006). Threaded discussion forums were used by Fayram *et al.* (2018) and similarly in the case study scenario cited later in this chapter to mentor groups of students by more experienced students.

One advantage of peer mentoring through virtual learning environments (VLE) compared to face-to-face approaches is that they represent a safe, supervised and managed environment for communication, are often connected to students' email accounts and other communication tools and offer accessible data for evaluation purposes (Risquez and Sanchez-Garcia, 2012). Smailes and Gannon-Leary (2011) suggest, however, that VLEs can often be seen as unengaging environments and in contrast, highlight the potential of non-institutional social media sites. Such platforms might be more likely to be used by students – they are popular, independent of the institution and accessible to most.

Arguably, thinking of a programme as either online or on-campus is a false dichotomy. Digital communication among students has become ubiquitous and many, if not all, campus-based courses are supplemented with the use of VLEs (JISC, 2022). Many peer e-mentoring schemes are hybrids which use several different mediums of communication (Goodrich, 2021). Indeed, Smailes and Gannon-Leary (2011) report that when they surveyed students about preferences for mentoring, 75 percent considered virtual contact the most suitable. Many mentoring programmes are therefore likely to be a blended experience.

Setting up for success: define the service

In summary then, those setting up mentoring programmes might want to consider the following issues:

1. **Clearly define the purpose of the mentoring programme and specify it as explicitly as possible**. What problem(s) will mentoring address? What outcome for students is intended? What type of support will the mentor offer? What activities are not included?
2. **Define the relationship between mentor and student:** will the purpose of the programme require the mentor to be more experienced than the student? What type of relationship will best achieve the service aims? Are dyads or group mentoring more suitable?
3. **Online, in person or both?** What is the most suitable communication medium for the support provided by the mentor?

Establishing a mentoring programme

Having defined peer mentoring, let us now move on to explore the planning and implementation phase of a mentoring programme. At this stage, the purpose(s) will need to be aligned with the type of mentoring required. This will inform a specification for prospective mentors and what training and support they may require.

Finding the right fit: mentor recruitment and placement

Finding students to serve as mentors should be cornerstone of the programme (Robinson and Niemer, 2010). Many accounts refer to recruiting students with certain personal characteristics. Terrion and Leonard (2007), for example, list things like communication skills, enthusiasm and flexibility. But does that rest on a fairly neurotypical view of what constitutes positive attributes? Are these even sufficient for effective mentoring? Other programmes are premised on the principle that only high performing students should be mentors (Robinson and Niemer, 2010; Deshler, Fuller and Darrah, 2019). Certainly, those programmes supporting academic skill or knowledge development would need mentors with a good grasp of the topic area. However, good grades alone are unlikely to be enough. In their mentoring programme aimed at developing maths skills, Morales, Ambrose-Roman and Perez-Maldonado (2016) not only targeted students with excellent grades but also those with a high degree of academic resilience and who were active on campus. Conversely, Deshler, Fuller and Darrah (2019) suggests that academically high performing students may be less likely to relate to the problems experienced by students struggling with their studies.

Targeted recruitment and selection of 'near-peers' is a more common approach. In essence, mentors are those who have completed the same programme of study as the students they are supporting (Fayram *et al.*, 2018; Schee, Andrews and Stovall, 2021). Such mentors would be better equipped to help students access the insider knowledge of the discipline which is often a core goal of the mentoring relationship (Fox *et al.*, 2010; Schee, Andrews and Stovall, 2021; Snowden, 2019). Those students with more recent experience might make more suitable mentors. Tout, Pancini and McCormack (2013) suggest that second year students may make more effective mentors than those further on in their studies as they have more vivid memories of the challenges of first-year study, strengthening their credibility.

Many programmes foster relationships through careful matching of mentor and student on the basis of background, personal characteristics or experience (Cornelius, Wood and Lai, 2016; Thomas *et al.*, 2017; Snowden and Hardy, 2013). There have been accounts of pairing on the basis of personal qualities or outlook (Putsche *et al.*, 2008), gender and race (Terrion and Leonard, 2007) or interests (Raposa *et al.*, 2019). For programmes focusing on supporting students from marginalised groups, having a mentor to whom the student can relate is imperative (Taylor *et al.*, 2023). Such similarity is assumed to foster a degree of congruence between mentor and student necessary for a relationship characterised by authenticity and empathy.

Other studies have demonstrated that the significance of matching can be somewhat equivocal. Gafni-Lachter *et al.* (2021) argue that surface-level similarities (such as age, race and gender) is not associated with relationship quality or positive outcomes and that deeper-level matching should be based on similarity in attitudes, values, beliefs and personality. Of course, external measures of similarity should not be confused with what participants consider important and the choices they make. What is valued in relationships varies from person to person. Furthermore, Bierema and Merriam (2002) argue that both mentor and student need to make frequent contact, share background information and work to establish familiarity. In short, establishing a trusting relationship takes effort and, consequently, fostering a sound match may take several attempts. Relationships take time and effort to develop (Comfort, 2023).

Training and supervision

Given the responsibilities and skills required to provide mentoring, formal training is usually required. Terrion (2012) argues that the development of the training programme should start by identifying the necessary skills and competencies. The accounts of training programmes across the literature often refer to some of the following topics:

- Guidelines for frequency of communication (Goodrich, 2021);
- Basic communication skills including giving feedback (Leidenfrost *et al.*, 2011); and
- Awareness of possible danger signs, safeguarding and ethical issues (Hixenbaugh *et al.*, 2006).

This list is not exhaustive. The topics covered will vary depending on the focus of the mentoring programme. For example, e-mentoring programmes might also train students to use the online communication environment (Noorodien-Fataar, 2016). Training format varies too. In addition to traditional on-campus training sessions, online modes have become prevalent. Single and Single (2005) describe the use of training via facilitated asynchronous discussion forums within which participants work through information about mentoring and share their responses to specific scenarios.

Given the challenges of mentoring, ongoing support is vital but often overlooked. There is evidence, for example, that regular supervision and support might address the emotional labour required of mentors. Seery *et al.* (2021) note that mentors can find their role challenging to manage, especially if they struggle to develop a constructive relationship with the student. They argue that programme coordinators need to create a safe and non-judgemental space for mentors to access support for the challenges and emotions they are facing. These meetings need not be in person but, as the scenario in the next section shows, can take place online and asynchronously. Such group supervision sessions also provide a valuable feedback mechanism for the programme itself and enable any iterative improvements while the programme is 'live.' Supervision in the context of coaching and mentoring is discussed in greater depth in Chapter 8.

Setting up for success: the recruitment and training of student peer mentors

1. **Establish the essential skill set needed for mentors.** Do you have a person specification aligned to the purpose of the mentoring programme? What attributes, skills and competencies do they need?
2. **Develop your recruitment strategy.** Which target group could offer necessary skills? What incentives could be offered to motivate a high number of applications in a selective process?
3. **How will you pair mentors with students?** If you are working with dyads, do you have a strategy to establish pairings who are most suited? Are some mentors most suited to working in groups?
4. **Plan essential training which is aligned with the programme focus and the skills listed in the person specification.** What medium will you use for training? Online for greater reach and flexibility or face-to-face? Synchronous or asynchronous?
5. **Design in ongoing support.** What support is necessary through the programme?

Peer mentoring in practice

In the next part of this chapter, we consider operational aspects once peer mentoring has been set up. We refer to a scenario exemplifying group mentoring in operation, as well as examples of other peer mentoring programmes to illustrate the realities of peer mentoring in practice.

Scenario one: many-to-many online mentoring

This peer mentoring programme was run by Catherine on a first-year undergraduate Business course offered by The OU. Many of the approximately 2,500 students studying the module were new to distance learning, in full- or part-time work, first in family and/or later life applicants. The programme's aims were to:

- Retain and progress students;
- Help students succeed by learning from the hints and tips of more experienced students;
- Facilitate supportive student-mentor relationships (sense of belonging and a sense that you matter to the university); and
- Enable mentors to develop employability skills and confidence.

Fifteen mentors who had previously studied the course were selected by written application. The openness of the selection process in which applicants outlined their experience of helping others and overcoming challenges enabled the inclusion of students facing barriers in participation in extra-curricular activities, an important consideration for Bovill (2023). Mentors were offered a voucher, to recognise their time and expertise as well as the effects of the pressures on their resources and to enable applications outside the 'socioeconomic elite' (Mercer-Mapstone and Bovill, 2020, p. 2552). Mentors attended two half days of online training, covering: what mentoring is, safeguarding, identifying topics to cover, how to use the online forum and when mentors should refer students to tutors or student support.

Day-to-day programme administration was carried out by an experienced tutor with a particular interest in providing alternative methods of support to students. The tutor developed a relationship with the mentors by delivering the training, moderating a dedicated forum, running mentor drop-in sessions and contacting mentors by email. Tutor and the programme lead met weekly to review the programme.

Mentoring was carried out online, on a many-to-many basis with all the mentors supporting all the students via forum threads. They responded to direct queries and offered one-to-one mentoring. Mentors chose which activities to participate in and were free to adapt their roles at different stages, which Bovill (2023) sees as beneficial. Students could join the programme and access the forum throughout the module's nine-month duration and over 50 percent chose to do so, some more than ten times. The tutor noted that students were often more forthcoming about their study challenges and triumphs to their peer mentors than they were on other forums.

A relationship based on trust

The scenario raises an important aspect of mentoring: how students can be encouraged to discuss their difficulties and successes. For Gaddis (2012) and Sipe (2002), trust is fundamental to effective mentoring relationships because it allows students to reveal themselves, their hopes and insecurities. At the start of the mentoring relationship, students are likely to have 'on trust,' or pre-existing trust, because mentors share their student identity and are offered and endorsed by their institution (Cox, 2005).

In our experience in the scenario above, most students reported that they applied suggestions and found them helpful. However, a few students were dubious about trusting guidance offered by those they considered fellow students rather than tutors.

A further concern of students is the fear that they will be judged negatively if tutors know that they need help. As other authors in this volume have shown, this can disproportionately affect students from racially minoritised groups, or first in family students (Payne, Muenks and Aguayo, 2023).

To build trust it is therefore important to establish ground rules at the beginning of mentoring, setting out how the relationship is to be conducted – or, in other words, formal contracting. Having a formal document containing guidance for contracting can reinforce the scheme's confidentiality. Boundaries may be outlined such as mentors not having personal relationships with mentees outside of the mentor/mentee relationship both for the duration and after the mentoring ends, including no contact on social media, or socialising outside of university spaces. The contracting document or the description of the mentoring programme should make clear the intentions of the higher education institution (HEI) organising the peer mentoring. This may help to mitigate concerns where mentoring is carried out through online, written communication which can then be monitored by the university. Otherwise, vigilance and wariness can be experienced (Cox, 2005). Further discussion about contracting, in a coaching and mentoring context, is covered in Chapter 3 in this volume.

Practical considerations about format

Given the importance of confidentiality, as discussed above, and its impact on what may be shared and discussed, one of the considerations when setting up a peer mentoring programme is the match between the format selected and the level of confidentiality possible. Where highly confidential, highly individualised support is appropriate, such as mental health focused mentoring (Osborn *et al.*, 2022) or the Specialist Peer Mentoring Program for students living with autism (Thompson *et al.*, 2018), one-to-one mentoring may be the best approach. Individualised support can increase student satisfaction, allowing the mentor to empower students and increase their confidence and self-esteem (Hillier *et al.*, 2019), particularly for students with autism (Thompson *et al.*, 2018).

Students in our case study seemed to prefer sharing learning via forum threads rather than having one-to-one relationships which were rarely taken up. Topics suggested by one student were often further developed by other students. Being able to attend on the fringes of a programme (either in person or online) but not actively participate, may allow those who do not trust the confidentiality of the scheme to still benefit from its advice. However, in such cases mentors who work hard at creating an inclusive and supportive relationship or space may be disappointed in the seemingly low take up of their mentorship. The benefits that students gain from less proactive participation should therefore be explained to mentors at training and reiterated regularly if they are not to become discouraged and disengage (Fayram *et al.*, 2018).

Setting up for success: building trust

1. **Think about how you can reassure students of the validity of peer mentors' advice**. How might you emphasise to students that your mentors' expertise from experience complements formal course guidance? Does your training explain to mentors that they may need to reassure students about their experience?
2. **Establish and communicate the guidelines about what can and cannot be discussed with mentors**. How will you cover contracting and confidentiality in your mentor training? What is the best way to clarify contracting and confidentiality to students?
3. **Consider the most appropriate format of your programme**. Which format or mix of formats offer the best fit to encourage disclosure and/or benefit from group learning?
4. **Encourage mentors**: how can you ensure mentors know that their support is useful, even if there seems to be little interaction? What feedback or research can you provide them to help them see the value of their work?

Deciding what to discuss and when

Programmes typically describe themselves as responding to student needs but the level of input by students and mentors about what these needs are can differ. In the programme described by Hillier *et al.* (2019), for example, participants were directed to attend structured activities which had been proposed by the programme coordinator rather than by students and mentors. Indeed, the extent to which the activities and foci of the mentoring relationship should be determined by the programme or students is a matter of some debate.

Ownership of the discussion may play out in one of three broad approaches: programme-led (which may be at discipline or institutional level), (student) mentor-led and student-mentee-led. In the programme-led approach, the programme coordinator may provide a curriculum of topics that the mentors should raise with students such as where to go for help or which study skills to focus on. In the programme described by Leidenfrost *et al.* (2011), mentors received guidelines on the structure and content of the meetings with students. Single and Single (2005), describe 'coaching' of the mentor and student by the programme coordinator through weekly emails. These included educational and motivational information, discussion topics and encouragement for participants to get in touch should interaction decrease.

In other cases, the programme may expect mentors to develop their own curriculum based on their lived experience, training and support. In the MaGE (Mega and Gigas Educate) mentoring programme for computer science mentors, for example, mentors received detailed training via online modules. These were research-based and designed to increase mentor knowledge of developing and supporting learners in an inclusive manner, as well as providing opportunities to practise and refine their skills with fellow mentors (Pon-Barry *et al.*, 2019).

These approaches contrast with an alternative view that the focus of the mentoring relationship should be self-determining. Here, the premise is that coordinators should not interfere at all and instead only offer support if needed. The role of the mentor in such programmes is to respond to student-mentee queries. The programmes examined by Hill and Reddy (2007) and Andrews and Clark (2011), for example, were based on this approach.

Finally, a programme may have a combination of approaches with some programme guidance, some mentor-led activity and some opportunity for students to suggest topics of interest to them. In our case study, mentors received two half-day training sessions where they identified initial foci for student help. However, after the first few weeks, they sought guidance from the programme coordinator about what to post on the student forum. Mentors also encouraged students to suggest the topics that they wanted help with, but students seemed to prefer to respond to topics suggested by mentors or to ask individual questions. The programme envisaged that mentors would develop and lead all discussions themselves, but experience showed that a suggested structure was helpful.

Duration and timing of mentoring advice

As well as determining roles in setting the agendas for mentoring, programme coordinators should also consider the appropriate timing and duration of peer mentoring sessions. In one-to-one relationships, meetings may be regular such as weekly, or on an ad hoc basis responding to student requests as they arise (Robson and Forbes, 2016). In the programme examined by Fayram *et al.* (2018), support was offered at a time when the programme knew that students might require additional support – specifically, two weeks before an assignment was due. Other programmes offer mentoring throughout a course or the academic year, such as in our case study.

Collings, Swanson and Watkins (2014) found that most students using a peer mentoring service did so only at the beginning of their studies, although almost 20 percent were using the service for at least an hour a week. Other studies have found that students seek support periodically in response to assessment deadlines. For example, Boyle *et al.* (2010) found that students most frequently seek support at the start of the course/before the first assignment, at the second assignment/mid-course and pre-examination/final assignment. Targeting support when it is most likely to be needed may thus be an efficient way to use resources.

Additionally, Fayram *et al.* (2018) found that although a third of students eligible for a peer mentoring online programme did not feel they needed the service, almost as many were unaware of the service or stated they did not have time to engage with it. Similar statistics have been found in other studies (Boyle *et al.*, 2010). In our case study, the student survey revealed similarly that around a third of students decided that their time was better spent focusing on their studies than using the peer mentoring services. Regular communications that help students to understand better the benefits of mentoring, and how to make use of it, might encourage them to reprioritise time to their advantage. In our case study, communications were sent via personally addressed emails before and during the module, with messages posted by tutors on their module forums and by posting on individual student home pages. Despite this communications campaign which led to over 50 percent of students accessing the programme, a third were still unaware of its existence. This suggests that students who do not sign up immediately may still be interested and communications should continue beyond the early stages.

Setting up for success: structure and timescales

1. **Consider the appropriate level of structure for your programme**. Should coordinators, mentors or students decide on topics, or a mix? What materials and training do you need to support the approach you have taken?
2. **Identify the most appropriate timescale for your programme**. Should the programme support students for a whole year or at specific times only? Do you have the resource to support this approach?
3. **Think about how best to publicise your programme**. At what points in your programme should you advertise it to students? What direct and indirect mechanisms can you use to reach potential users of the service?

Power and positionality

Having considered some of the practicalities of running a peer mentoring scheme, it is useful to consider the peer mentor's role and positionality. For Seery *et al.* (2021) a mentor is a leader, providing both emotional support and a link between students and faculty. The relationship between the HEI and the peer mentors might thus be described as a partnership. However, seeing mentors as partners and leaders may understate the complexity of their position within the organisation. They straddle a boundary between being agents of the university and members of the current student body with its incumbent pressures and challenges. Seery *et al.* (2021) report that peer mentors sometimes felt pressured by their university's expectations and suggest that this indicates a lack of comfort with a partnership dynamic with the university.

In our case study, a distributed form of leadership emerged with different mentors taking charge at different times as the programme progressed. Decision making such as agreeing the topic and nature of posts was cooperative, with no one student consistently being a leader. Mentors appreciated the fact that spreading the load of running the programme reduced pressure on them. This allowed them to contribute to different degrees of intensity as their time allowed and thus to continue to act as mentors. Interestingly, when mentors were offered additional compensation to act as coordinating spokespeople, none came forward.

Mentors can be leaders but also followers. Ruane and Lee (2016) talk of students as learner-participants who create content for learning based on their experience and who move from novice to expert in a peer mentoring setting. In our case study, mentors endorsed responses given by students to fellow students' questions, blurring the boundaries between 'novice' and 'master' as the course progressed. Mentors also acknowledged the expertise of other mentors' alternative approaches to student issues, reporting that they learned from each other and fellow students.

Positionality

Programme coordinators may see their mentors as 'insiders' of the university (Schee, Andrews and Stovall, 2021), able to help students understand how the university works and to speak knowledgeably about how to thrive. However, mentors are also students and so occupy a similar position to those they mentor. Unlike tutors or support staff, they have no power over decisions which impact on students. Despite being in the employ of the HEI, they may feel their loyalties lie with other students. Fayram *et al.* (2018) found evidence of a reduced power imbalance between students and their peer mentors who are also, like them, studying. This is indicated for example in the informal nature of communications on their forum. Seery *et al.* (2021) talk of peer mentors as disrupting power relationships and co-creating learning. The unique 'insider/outsider' status of mentors allows students to confide their anxieties and confusion about instructions around course material, providing responses confidentially, in a safe environment. After all, mentors are, themselves, learners too.

Blurred boundaries

For Hillier *et al.* (2019), mentors provide support for academic success – time management, study tips, how to talk to academics – rather than academic support per se. This support may include how to make friends and talk to people, how to get involved in university life and build social contacts. In practice, the boundary between 'support for academic success' and 'academic support' may be less clearcut than suggested. Fayram *et al.* (2018) found that students confused the peer mentor and tutor roles and were not always clear about who to approach for support. They suggest training for mentors which emphasises the distinction. The student mentors in our case study were trained to tell students that academic queries should go to tutors. When surveyed, most students were satisfied but some expressed frustration that responses were generic and did not always provide the support they wanted.

Mentors may also experience challenges with the blurring of boundaries in peer mentoring relationships. Seery *et al.* (2021) suggest that, perhaps surprisingly, student mentees may hold the power in interactions with mentors in that they decide the terms of engagement. Mentors almost have a greater need for interaction with the student. Mentors make themselves vulnerable by showing where they struggled and anticipating the needs of new students in the topics they propose. In fact, mentors may find that developing relationships and partnerships with faculty members is easier than with the students they mentor and increases their sense of institutional belonging. This may help counteract the lack of relationships with students (Seery *et al.*, 2021). However, although mentors in our case study appreciated the benefits of contact with programme coordinators who were faculty staff, their main relationships seemed to be with each other. These relationships were facilitated by their 'WhatsApp' group where they reported discussing issues and supporting each other, rather than using the forum provided and managed by the institution for communication.

Reflective questions – setting up for success

1. **Consider the relationship between the programme and its mentors**: do your programme aims match mentor expectations in terms of responsibility and input required? Is your training and recruitment literature realistic about the responsibilities, time and energy commitments of the role? Can your training programme develop students sufficiently to take the level of responsibility they aspire to? There are many ways and different times at which students can engage as partners (Bovill, 2023). Which is most appropriate for your programme?
2. **Clarify the boundaries between tutor and mentor support**: how can you help mentors reinforce differing mentor and tutor expertise and roles, so it is clear to students?

3. **Communication with your mentors**: how will you keep contact with your mentors – individually and/or collectively? How will you let them know what your expectations are about responding to you?
4. **Support mentors in their interactions with students**: how will you help them form relationships with the programme and/or each other if there is not much interaction with students?

Assessing outcomes

Given that mentoring programmes require institutional resources and an investment of time from students, evaluating the effectiveness of these programmes is essential. Getting started with evaluation should happen at the same time as the planning for the programme itself. Both programme design and evaluation depend on a well-established 'logic chain' (Jones-Devitt and Austen, 2021) or Theory of Change (TASO, no date). This logic chain establishes the problem or issue the programme wishes to address and clearly identifies its desired impact. It is this precision of identified impact which should lead a programme to determine what outcomes the students should achieve, the activities required to achieve those and how the mentors should be selected and prepared to offer that service. Indeed, establishing the logic chain could even determine that peer mentoring is not the most suitable method to use.

However, many evaluative accounts of mentoring programmes do not set out to demonstrate impact. Indeed, the literature is characterised primarily by accounts of testimonial and opinion (Terrion, 2012). It is not surprising then that the UK HE context at least, there has been a marked drive towards establishing 'what works' in addressing the issues currently challenging the higher education sector. In pursuit of 'what works,' the regulator for HE in England, the Office for Students (OfS) (2019), for example, distinguishes between type one, type two and type three evaluations. Type one evaluations might be drawn from systematic reviews of peer mentoring schemes and are useful to generate the logic chains discussed above. Pointon-Haas *et al.*'s (2024) systematic review of peer support for student mental health is one such example of a systematic review. They demonstrate the challenges here in that they found that the field was characterised by a huge variety of terminology, making it difficult to amass a large body of studies showing that a particular type of intervention was demonstrably effective or had replicable results.

Type two evaluations are concerned with demonstrating impact of some kind for the (precisely defined) target group. This approach might require collecting pre and post mentoring data from participants or even benchmarking using external data (Jones-Devitt and Austen, 2021). Andrews and Clark's (2011) comparative study of peer mentoring, for example, benchmarked the favourably low attrition rates of three institutions in the study with the national average and concluded that mentoring really 'does work' in reducing student drop out. They did, however, offer a caveat: there are many other factors in play and undoubtedly other student-focused programmes on offer which will have shaped the student experience.

Type three evaluations demonstrate that a causal link exists between those receiving mentoring and a control group who is not being mentored. The randomised controlled trials associated with this type of evaluation are very demanding to carry out (Jones-Devitt and Austen, 2021). It might be that many mentoring programmes work with such small numbers that they do not have a large enough sample size to demonstrate a statistically significant effect (Pointon-Haas *et al.*, 2024). Certainly, the ethical concern of providing some students with a service but not those in the control group could be offset somewhat by putting some on a waiting list for the service. Yet the length of time needed to demonstrate an effect might make this approach impractical.

The danger here is that evaluations of mentoring programmes fall foul of what is termed the McNamara fallacy – in that quantitative and metric-based studies such as improved student grades oversimplify the complexities behind these. Consequently, those intangible factors which make a difference are overlooked (Robertson, Cleaver and Smart, 2019). Qualitative methods such as in-depth case studies with participants which provide indications of the kind of impacts experienced and which factors made that difference can be very powerful. Andrews and Clarke (2011) conducted detailed interviews to this end, which documented both students' concerns and how mentoring met these. Pointon-Hass *et al.*'s (2023) interviews with staff leading peer support programmes revealed more practical challenges with evaluation. Staff struggled with knowing what outcomes they should measure, identifying what successful impact looks like and the ability to capture long term impacts. There were other factors too which might affect evaluation including the under resourcing of mentoring programmes and that low levels of student engagement over time make meaningful sample sizes elusive.

Reflective questions – setting up for success

1. **The empirical basis for the programme design**: how well evidenced is the programme design? Are there studies showing it will have an effect?
2. **Clearly establishing the problem to be addressed and the outcomes students should achieve**: is mentoring the most suitable method to achieve these outcomes? Are those outcomes measurable?
3. **Establish the evaluation strategy at programme start**: what resources are necessary to conduct the evaluation? What type of evaluation is necessary to convince management of the programme's effectiveness? Are the demands of evaluation proportionate to the size of the programme?

Conclusion

This chapter has considered the theory and practice of peer mentoring for students transitioning in and through HE. Synthesising both the existing literature and practical experience, it discusses the many ways in which peer mentoring is delivered to meet the needs of universities and their students. Whilst the variety of institutional programmes and culture, student needs and expectations of interested parties is varied, the literature shows that there are some common underpinning principles to consider which we have highlighted in the 'setting up for success' reflective questions punctuating this chapter.

The popularity and success of peer mentoring programmes indicate that the benefits to students, mentors and universities can often justify the effort they require. Our aim in this chapter has been to provide practical guidance informed by the literature which we hope will contribute to other successful peer mentoring programmes. In the context of this book, this chapter shows how coaching and mentoring practices can be implemented, not only by specialists and by wider teaching or guidance practitioners but also by students themselves as part of a holistic and comprehensive offering of student support.

Bibliography

Andrews, J. and Clark, R. (2011) *Peer mentoring works! How peer mentoring enhances student success in higher education*. Aston University. Available at: https://publications.aston.ac.uk/id/eprint/17968/1/Peer_mentoring_works.pdf (Accessed: 13 June 2024).

Asgari, S. and Carter, F. (2016) 'Peer mentors can improve academic performance: a quasi-experimental study of peer mentorship in introductory courses', *Teaching of Psychology*, 43(2), pp. 131–135. doi: 10.1177/0098628316636288

Bakhshi, S., Harrington, K. and O'Neill, P. (2009) 'Psychology students' experiences of academic peer mentoring at the London Metropolitan University Writing Centre', *Psychology Learning and Teaching*, 8(1), pp. 6–13. doi: 10.2304/plat.2009.8.1.6

Bermingham, N., Boylan, F. and Ryan, B. (2023) 'The 4C's of PAL – an evidence-based model for implementing peer assisted learning for mature students', *Innovations in Education and Teaching International*, 60(3), pp. 401–411. doi: 10.1080/14703297.2022.2050779

Bierema, L.L. and Merriam, S.B. (2002) 'E-mentoring: using computer mediated communication to enhance the mentoring process', *Innovative Higher Education*, 26(3), pp. 211–227.

Bovill, C. (2023) 'A framework to explore roles within student-staff partnerships in higher education: which students are partners, when, and in what ways?', *International Journal for Students as Partners*, 1(1). doi: 10.15173/ijsap.v1i1.3062

Boyer, K., Thomas, E., Rorrer, A., Cooper, D. and Vouk, M. (2010) 'Increasing technical excellence, leadership and commitment of computing students through identity-based mentoring', *Technical Symposium on Computer Science Education*. doi: 10.1145/1734263.1734320

Boyle, F., Kwon, J., Ross, C. and Simpson, O. (2010) 'Student–student mentoring for retention and engagement in distance education', *Open Learning: The Journal of Open, Distance and e-Learning*, 25(2), pp. 115–130.

Collings, R., Swanson, V. and Watkins, R. (2014) 'The impact of peer mentoring on levels of student wellbeing, integration and retention: a controlled comparative evaluation of residential students in UK higher education', *Higher Education*, 68(6), pp. 927–942. doi: 10.1007/s10734-014-9752-y

Colvin, J.W. and Ashman, M. (2010) 'Roles, risks, and benefits of peer mentoring relationships in higher education', *Mentoring and Tutoring: Partnership in Learning*, 18(2), pp. 121–134. doi: 10.1080/13611261003678879

Comfort, C. (2023) *Relationships, assets and social capital: a case study review of youth mentoring*. PhD Thesis. The Open University. Available at: https://oro.open.ac.uk/87092 (Accessed: 6 September 2024).

Cornelius, V., Wood, L. and Lai, J. (2016) 'Implementation and evaluation of a formal academic-peer-mentoring programme in higher education', *Active Learning in Higher Education*, 17(3), pp. 193–205. doi: 10.1177/1469787416654796

Cox, E. (2005) 'For better, for worse: the matching process in formal mentoring schemes', *Mentoring and Tutoring*, 13(3), pp. 403–414. doi: 10.1080/13611260500177484

Deshler, J., Fuller, E. and Darrah, M. (2019) 'Supporting students through peer mentoring in developmental mathematics', *The Learning Assistance Review*, 24, pp. 87–112.

Eby, L.T., Allen, T.D., Hoffman, B.J., Baranik, L.E., Sauer, J.B., Baldwin, S., Morrison, M.A., Kinkade, K.M., Maher, C.P. and Curtis, S. (2013) 'An interdisciplinary meta-analysis of the potential antecedents, correlates, and consequences of protégé perceptions of mentoring', *Psychological Bulletin*, 139(2), p. 441.

Fayram, J., Boswood, N., Kan, Q., Motzo, A. and Proudfoot, A. (2018) 'Investigating the benefits of online peer mentoring for student confidence and motivation', *International Journal of Mentoring and Coaching in Education*, 7(4), pp. 312–328. doi: 10.1108/IJMCE-10-2017-0065

Fox, A., Stevenson, L., Conelly, P., Duff, A. and Dunlop, A. (2010) 'Peer–mentoring undergraduate accounting students: the influence on approaches to learning and academic performance', *Active Learning in Higher Education*, 11(2), pp. 145–156. doi: 10.1177/1469787410365650

Gaddis, S.M. (2012) 'What's in a relationship? An examination of social capital, race and class in mentoring relationships', *Social Forces*, 90(4), pp. 1237–1269. doi: 10.1093/sf/sos003

Gafni-Lachter, L., Niemeyer, L., Doyle, N., Norcross, J. and Jacobs, K. (2021) 'Equal peer e-mentoring for online graduate students: a case study and mediation model', *Mentoring and Tutoring: Partnership in Learning*, 29(5), pp. 545–564. doi: 10.1080/13611267.2021.1986799

Gehreke, L., Schilling, H. and Kauffeld, S. (2024) 'Effectiveness of peer mentoring in the study entry phase: A systematic review', *Review of Education*, 12(1), pp. 1–32. doi: 10.1002/rev3.3462

Goodrich, A. (2021) 'Online peer mentoring and remote learning', *Music Education Research*, 23(2), pp. 256–269. doi: 10.1080/14613808.2021.1898575

Gunn, F., Lee, S.H. and Steed, M. (2017) 'Student perceptions of benefits and challenges of peer mentoring programs: divergent perspectives from mentors and mentees', *Marketing Education Review*, 27(1), pp. 15–26. doi: 10.1080/10528008.2016.1255560

Hill, R. and Reddy, P. (2007) 'Undergraduate peer mentoring: an investigation into processes, activities and outcomes', *Psychology Learning and Teaching*, 6(2). doi: 10.2304/plat.2007.6.2.98

Hillier, A., Goldstein, J., Tornatore, L., Byrne, E. and Johnson, H.M. (2019) 'Outcomes of a peer mentoring program for university students with disabilities', *Mentoring & Tutoring: Partnership in Learning*, 27(5), pp. 487–508. doi: 10.1080/13611267.2019.1675850

Hixenbaugh, P., Dewart, H., Drees, D. and Williams, D. (2006) 'Peer e-mentoring: enhancement of the first year experience', *Psychology Learning and Teaching*, 5(1), pp. 8–14. doi: 10.2304/plat.2005.5.1.8

Irby, B.J., Abdelrahman, N., Lara-Alecio, R. and Allen, T. (2020) 'Epistemological beginnings of mentoring', in B.J. Irby *et al.* (eds.) *The Wiley international handbook of mentoring: paradigms, practices, programs and possibilities*. Hoboken, NJ: Wiley Blackwell, pp. 19–28.

JISC. (2022) *Student digital experience insights survey 2021/22: UK higher education (HE) survey findings*. JISC. Available at: https://repository.jisc.ac.uk/8850/1/2022-07%20%28iDFltdP024.11%29%20DEI%20HE%20%26%20FE%20Reports%202022%20%28HE%29%20v1-05.pdf (Accessed: 6 June 2024).

Jones-Devitt, S. and Austen, L. (2021) *A guide to basic evaluation in higher education (why needed and how to do it)*. Staffordshire University. Available at: https://www.enhancementthemes.ac.uk/docs/ethemes/about-us/eval-guide_qaas_pdf.pdf?sfvrsn=fff7d781_12 (Accessed: 26 July 2024).

Kasprisin, C.A., Single, P.B., Single, R.M. and Muller, C.B. (2003) 'Building a better bridge: testing e-training to improve e-mentoring programmes in higher education', *Mentoring and Tutoring: Partnership in Learning*, 11(1), pp. 67–78. doi: 10.1080/1361126032000054817

Leidenfrost, B., Strassnig, B., Schabmann, A., Spiel, C. and Carbon, C.-C. (2011) 'Peer mentoring styles and their contribution to academic success among mentees: a person-oriented study in higher education', *Mentoring and Tutoring: Partnership in Learning*, 19(3), pp. 347–364.

Mercer-Mapstone, L. and Bovill, C. (2020) 'Equity and diversity in institutional approaches to student–staff partnership schemes in higher education', *Studies in Higher Education*, 45(12). doi: 10.1080/03075079.2019.1620721

Morales, E.E., Ambrose-Roman, S. and Perez-Maldonado, R. (2016) 'Transmitting success: comprehensive peer mentoring for at-risk students in developmental math', *Innovative Higher Education*, 41(2), pp. 121–135.

Noorodien-Fataar, N. (2016) 'An account of student mentors modes of reflexivity during an e-mentoring programme at a university', *South African Journal of Higher Education*, 26(3). doi: 10.20853/26-3-175

Nuis, W., Segers, M. and Beausaert, S. (2023) 'Conceptualizing mentoring in higher education: a systematic literature review', *Educational Research Review*, 41, pp. 1–22. doi: 10.1016/j.edurev.2023.100565

Office for Students (OfS). (2019) *Standards of evidence and evaluating impact of outreach*. Available at: https://www.officeforstudents.org.uk/publications/standards-of-evidence-and-evaluating-impact-of-outreach/ (Accessed: 26 July 2024).

Osborn, T.G., Town, R., Ellis, R., Buckman, J.E.J., Saunders, R. and Fonagy, P. (2022) 'Implementing peer support in higher education: a feasibility study', *SSM – Mental Health*, 2, pp. 1–11. doi: 10.1016/j.ssmmh.2022.100175

Payne, T., Muenks, K. and Aguayo, E. (2023) '"Just because I am first gen doesn't mean I'm not asking for help": a thematic analysis of first-generation college students' academic help-seeking behaviors', *Journal of Diversity in Higher Education*, 16(6), pp. 792–803.

Pointon-Haas, J., Byrom, N., Foster, J., Hayes, C. and Oates, J. (2023) 'Staff perspectives: defining the types, challenges and lessons learnt of university peer support for student mental health and wellbeing', *Education Sciences*, 13(9). doi: 10.3390/educsci13090962

Pointon-Haas, J., Waqar, L., Upsher, R., Foster, J., Byrom, N. and Oates, J. (2024) 'A systematic review of peer support interventions for student mental health and well-being in higher education', *BJPsych Open*, 10(1), pp. 1–16. doi: 10.1192/bjo.2023.603

Pon-Barry, H., John, A.S., Packard, B.W.-L. and Rotundo, B. (2019) 'A flexible curriculum for promoting inclusion through peer mentorship', in *Proceedings of the 50th ACM technical symposium on computer science education*. Minneapolis, MN. doi: 10.1145/3287324.3287434 (Accessed: 06 September 2024).

Putsche, L., Storrs, D., Lewis, A.E. and Haylett, J. (2008) 'The development of a mentoring program for university undergraduate women', *Cambridge Journal of Education*, 38(4), pp. 513–528. doi: 10.1080/03057640802482322

Raposa, E.B., Ben-Eliyahu, A., Olsho, L.E.W. and Rhodes, J. (2019) 'Birds of a feather: is matching based on shared interests and characteristics associated with longer youth mentoring relationships?', *Journal of Community Psychology*, 47(2), pp. 385–397. doi: 10.1002/jcop.22127

Risquez, A. and Sanchez-Garcia, M. (2012) 'The jury is still out: psychoemotional support in peer e-mentoring for transition to university', *The Internet and Higher Education*, 15(3), pp. 213–221. doi: 10.1016/j.iheduc.2011.11.003

Robertson, A., Cleaver, E. and Smart, F. (2019) *Beyond the metrics: identifying, evidencing and enhancing the less tangible assets of higher education*. QAA Scotland. Available at: https://www.enhancementthemes.ac.uk/docs/ethemes/evidence-for-enhancement/beyond-the-metrics-identifying-evidencing-and-enhancing-the-less-tangible-assets-of-higher-education.pdf?sfvrsn=ca37c681_14 (Accessed: 27 July 2024).

Robinson, E. and Niemer, L. (2010) 'A peer mentor tutor program for academic success in nursing', *Nursing Education Perspectives (National League for Nursing)*, 31(5), pp. 213–221.

Robson, J.M. and Forbes, T. (2016) *Vertical peer to peer mentoring in the faculty of social sciences: a pilot study.* Unpublished report. Milton Keynes: The Open University.

Ruane, R. and Lee, V. (2016) 'Analysis of discussion board interaction in an online peer-mentoring site', *Online Learning*, 20(4). doi: 10.24059/olj.v20i4.1052

Schee, B.A.V., Andrews, D. and Stovall, T. (2021) 'Enhancing first-year course student experience with virtual team support from senior marketing majors', *Journal for Advancement of Marketing Education, suppl. Special Issue*, 29, pp. 21–28.

Seery, C., Andres, A., Moore-Cherry, N. and O'Sullivan, S. (2021) 'Students as partners in peer mentoring: expectations, experiences and emotions', *Innovative Higher Education*, 46(6), pp. 663–681.

Simpson, D., Pearson, B., Kelly, M., Mendum, I., Lockwood, A. and Fletcher, S. (2023) 'Buddy up! Student mentoring in a social work undergraduate programme', *Social Work Education*, 42(5), pp. 747–768. doi: 10.1080/02615479.2022.2057465

Single, P.B. and Single, R.M. (2005) 'E-mentoring for social equity: review of research to inform program development', *Mentoring and Tutoring*, 13(2), pp. 301–320. doi: 10.1080/13611260500107481

Sipe, C.L. (2002) 'Mentoring programs for adolescents: a research summary', *Journal of Adolescent Health*, 31(6, Supplement), pp. 251–260. doi: 10.1016/S1054-139X(02)00498-6

Smailes, J. and Gannon-Leary, P. (2011) 'Peer mentoring – is a virtual form of support a viable alternative?' *Research in Learning Technology*, 19(2). doi: 10.3402/rlt.v19i2.10351

Snowden, M. (2019) 'Peer mentoring. Guaranteed gold?' in M. Snowdon and J. Halsall (eds.) *Mentorship, leadership and research: their place within the social science curriculum.* Basel: Springer International Publishing AG, pp. 117–128.

Snowden, M. and Halsall, J.P. (2016) 'Self-determined approach to learning: a social science perspective', *Cogent Education*, 3(1), pp. 1–9. doi: 10.1080/2331186X.2016.1247608

Snowden, M. and Hardy, T. (2013) 'Peer mentorship and positive effects on student mentor and mentee retention and academic success', *Widening Participation and Lifelong Learning*, 14(1), pp. 76–92.

TASO. (no date) *Our approach to evaluation.* Available at: https://taso.org.uk/evidence/our-approach-to-evaluation/ (Accessed: 26 July 2024).

Taylor, L., Mastrogiovanni, M., Lakin, J.M. and Davis, V. (2023) 'Give and gain: Black engineering students as near-peer mentors', *Journal of Engineering Education*, 112(2), pp. 365–381. doi: 10.1002/jee.20520

Terrion, J.L. (2012) 'Student mentors as a navigational resource in higher education', in S.J. Fletcher and C.A. Mullen (eds.) *The SAGE handbook of mentoring and coaching in education*. Los Angeles, CA: SAGE Publications, pp. 383–396.

Terrion, J.L. and Leonard, D. (2007) 'A taxonomy of the characteristics of student peer mentors in higher education: findings from a literature review', *Mentoring and Tutoring: Partnership in Learning*, 15(2), pp. 149–164. doi: 10.1080/13611260601086311

Thomas, L., Hill, M., O' Mahony, J. and Yorke, M. (2017) *Supporting student success: strategies for institutional change*. Available at: https://s3.eu-west-2.amazonaws.com/assets.creode.advancehe-document-manager/documents/hea/private/hub/download/what_works_2_-_full_report_1568037360.pdf (Accessed: 7 May).

Thompson, C., Falkmer, T., Evans, K., Bölte, S. and Girdler, S. (2018) 'A realist evaluation of peer mentoring support for university students with autism', *British Journal of Special Education*, 45(4), pp. 412–434. doi: 10.1111/1467-8578.12241

Tout, D., Pancini, G. and McCormack, R. (2013) 'Using mobile peer mentors for student engagement: student rovers in the learning commons', *Higher Education Research & Development*, 33(3), pp. 595–609. doi: 10.1080/07294360.2013.841645

7

Developing coaching skills in student support practitioners

Jane Dudeney and Georgina Durley

Introduction

When considering coaching provisions for students at university, there are a range of models that higher education (HE) providers might implement – from centralised coaching services delivered by professional services staff to coaching services that are embedded in teaching and academic support. Importantly, there needs to be consideration for where and when the delivery of coaching is best positioned in order to get the best outcomes for students, and for practitioners to use it most effectively. Having focused on the practices of student coaching and mentoring specialists (including trained student peers) throughout this book, we now turn our attention to how the principles of coaching – specifically – might be adapted and utilised by a wider range of student support practitioners and academic staff.

This chapter shares our experiences of embedding coaching within an existing student support service at The Open University (OU), UK, a large distance-learning provider which maintains its Matrix accreditation into 2024. The project was based on developing coaching skills in guidance practitioners who work with students. Using our own institutional case study, alongside a wider repository of evidence for the ways coaching can enhance student support provision, we will explore the differences between guidance and coaching and the types of scenarios where a student might benefit from coaching. We will look at different coaching methods and how these impact planning when embedding coaching into existing support

DOI: 10.4324/9781003486015-8

offerings, before moving on to show approaches for demonstrating coaching in action. After discussing these practical elements, we share feedback from practitioners who have adopted coaching practices in their discussions with students, as well as what they feel is helpful when making this change. We will critically review the implementation of coaching into existing support services from a leadership perspective. We make recommendations which seek to aid decision-making and plan the implementation of coaching. Finally, we signpost to additional resources and reading.

We acknowledge that embedding coaching provision into student support will necessarily depend upon institutional structures (and budget), the profile of the student body, and the skills and interests of staff but we suggest it is translatable to a variety of different settings. Rather than offering a prescriptive step-by-step guide, this chapter is written with the intention that readers will reflect on and consider adapting this approach to their own environment. As such, it may also be of interest to personal tutors, or institutions with faculty-based personal tutoring, who can also utilise coaching as part of their toolkit in supporting students (Lochtie et al., 2018; Lochtie, Stork and Walker, 2022).

Coaching as a mechanism of student support

Student support services vary by institution but typically include provision such as careers guidance, wellbeing and disability support and learning development. At our own institution, the main 'hub' of support is the student support team (SST). The SST is organised into an IAG structure. Students contact their SST for a range of reasons relating to personal and academic challenges. The more complex cases are referred to the 'G' (guidance teams) within the service. It was in this part of the service where we identified coaching as a potential enhancement.

Guidance is related to, but distinct from, coaching. At The OU, Guidance is considered in the university IAG framework to be an exploratory form of support, but one which is focused on a particular task or decision. Guidance may also involve offering a solution, or range of solutions, to an issue that is impacting academic progress, then helping a student navigate this issue according to the available options. The benefits of this support are timely resolution and directive support that can provide efficient and much-needed outcomes for the student, within policies, that are relevant to their specific situation at that particular time.

As other authors in this volume have outlined, coaching provision (in an educational context) is student-centred and inspires the student to find their own answers, facilitated by a coach. Whereas guidance can be offered as a one-off interaction, coaching is typically ongoing and with a specific goal in mind. Coaching is often more holistic than guidance, in the sense that it is not necessarily driven by academic goals and may lead to longer-term changes and development (Inside Track, 2022). Whilst coaching may take longer than one guidance conversation would, there is the ability to build more substantial trust and growth over time and for students to be facilitated in finding a solution for themselves. Let us consider how these two approaches to supporting students might differ in practice.

Scenario one: Guidance

Guidance – A student contacts their student support service as their health is impacting their ability to complete their assignments on time and to the standard they usually complete them. Here, a guidance practitioner might ask them more about their health and let them know what support and reasonable adjustments can be made to either keep them on track, or how to go about pausing their studies.

STUDENT: I need help with my studies. I have had a recent diagnosis of generalised anxiety disorder (GAD). I can't keep on top of my assignments.

GUIDANCE PRACTITIONER: There are several options we can explore with you to support you to stay on track with your studies, or to take a break if you wish. Can you start by telling me a little more about your health and what you're experiencing?

STUDENT: I have two young children and my employer is talking about a restructure, I'm now waking in the night with sweats and struggling to catch my breath. My doctor has given me some medication and signposted to some local therapy support too but the lack of sleep is affecting my ability to concentrate, and looming deadlines are adding more pressure and I don't think I can continue studying.

GUIDANCE PRACTITIONER: OK, I'd like to explore several options with you before you decide on the best way forward for you, is that ok? Firstly, we can discuss the possibility of getting an extension to your assignment ... [conversation continues].

Scenario two: Coaching

Coaching – A student has been out of education for a number of years, is the first in their family to study at HE level and is struggling with time management. A coach might set up a number of planned sessions with the student and over the course of these, invite the student to explore and uncover the reasons why they are struggling with their time, what it might look like if they took a different approach and how it might feel if they did.

COACH: Thank you for meeting with me today. We have 45 minutes today to discuss some of the challenges you're facing and some of the goals you would like to achieve by the end of these six sessions. Do you want to start by telling me what you'd like to get from these coaching sessions?

STUDENT: I just can't seem to work well with deadlines, I hate the pressure that comes with an upcoming deadline, and it makes me freeze, like I don't know how to move forward or get anything done. I'd like to be able to feel calm and organised so there is less pressure on me.

COACH: If you were to put yourself in the end goal, having achieved it, what do you think that would feel like?

STUDENT: I guess I would feel relieved, less pressure, who knows, I might even enjoy the process of learning! That is what I started all of this for, my passion for history.

COACH: Is there a time when you felt the pressure you've described in past? What has worked for you before?

[Conversation continues]

As these scenarios demonstrate, there are clear similarities between guidance and coaching. The mechanics of guidance and coaching conversations are, for example, closely related. Both will begin with contracting and boundary setting in order to keep the conversation focussed and ensure the remit of the practitioner remains clear. Also, both guidance and coaching practitioners will likely use comparable skills – such as open questioning techniques, active listening and summarising.

It is also useful to consider the distinctions between mentoring and guidance. While both make use of expert power unlike coaching, which is non-directive, a crucial difference is that mentoring is often a sustained relationship over a longer period with the mentor using their expert power to aid the development of the mentee. In contrast to mentoring, guidance is often short term and for the purpose of navigating specific tasks or challenges with the guidance practitioner focusing on supporting the individual in understanding information and offering advice or direction.

While using a hybrid approach to coaching and mentoring has been explored in this volume, this chapter examines how embedding coaching approaches in guidance spaces can support IAG provision.

Case study: developing a guidance service using coaching

The rationale for embedding coaching within the guidance service at our own institution was informed by the value a centralised coach-mentoring service, the Personal Learning Advice (PLA) Service demonstrated in its four-year pilot at the university (Hillman, Lochtie and Purcell, 2024; Wilton and Samuels Hylton, 2023). Incorporating some of the approaches used within the PLA service into core forms of IAG was an important way for student support services to innovate and respond to learning from the pilot, as well as continue to invest in the development of staff through continuing professional development (CPD). We have already seen, above, the connections between guidance and coaching, and the development of practitioners in the guidance space was where we chose to start. In what follows below, we share our experiences of introducing coaching to an existing service, our considerations and the steps that were taken to implement this across two phases:

1. Exploring coaching with staff to establish existing knowledge, skillset and training needs – led by a manager, experienced in coaching skills, Georgina Durley. Georgina is currently a Senior Manager for a group of guidance practitioners who offer support to students navigating complex barriers to study.
2. Designing and delivering two workshops to address these training needs – led by a qualified coach and learning and development specialist, Jane Dudeney. Jane is a Training and Development Specialist with a particular interest in fostering personal and professional growth, particularly in areas of mindset and self-awareness.

Part one: exploring coaching with guidance practitioners

The first step was to establish the team's current understanding of coaching. This involved exploratory conversations, reflective tasks and a review of existing working practices and techniques. Our experience showed the value of instigating learning with an initial workshop rather than as formal training to account for individual development needs and offer differentiation for varying levels of practitioner experience (Guccione and Hutchinson, 2021). Team discussions required senior leaders in the service to create awareness about coaching as a tool, whilst providing evidence of its effectiveness. This helped to glean investment from practitioners that coaching is a meaningful and beneficial approach to diversify their practice. Seraj and Leggett (2023) have evidenced in their research with personal tutors that the longer-term impact of coaching with students is improved resilience, self-reliance and self-confidence, for example. Other chapters in this volume contribute to the wider evidence base. As demonstrated in the introductory chapter, for example, there is evidence for the impact of coaching over time to students (examples include Dias, Foster and Zunszain, 2019; Kaper, Graafeiland and Vogelaar, 2024; van der Baan *et al.*, 2024), but it is also important to note the benefits to the coach themselves. It is in offering support over a longer period, and with specific goals in mind, that a relationship is formed and so too are 'feedback loops' that promote iterative, long-term progression (Carless, 2019). Coaches will be able to see what works, and what perhaps does not, and therefore adjust their practice of support overall. Each interaction will inform the evolution of the service they, and the team more widely, provide.

Our approach was to pilot this in one service initially before evaluating it, making improvements and later rolling out across all of the core IAG services. As we have noted, these are known as SST and support students in the four faculties respectively. The pilot was carried out in the SST within the Faculty of Business and Law (FBL) within the guidance service. The team consisted of seven established guidance practitioners who were led by their line manager (Georgina) to reflect on the coaching and mentoring (PLA Service) pilot, and how they could adopt some learnings and examples of best practice.

Part of the initial exploration involved self-reflection and we found it helpful to use an exploratory exercise, in this case, the Johari window (Luft and Ingham, 1955, quoted in NHS, no date) which explores several perceptive angles of the self. This exercise provides a useful demonstration of self-reflection that can be utilised and encouraged in coaching with students. As part of this reflection, we asked practitioners where they might see coaching being relevant to their practice – particularly where they were engaged with a student in navigating longer-term processes such as 'academic progress' (following a pause in study). Reflective questions to support practitioners to identify where coaching might add value to their practice include the following:

- How do you identify the essential core competencies and key skills that are needed to effectively support your students?
- How, when and where do you demonstrate these core competencies and key skills? How do you ensure that these core competencies and key skills meet the needs of all your students?
- What training, support or professional qualification(s) might you / others need to further develop your core competencies or key skills?
- How frequently will you review your core competencies and key skills, and how much time and resources can you commit to their development?

Importantly, it was crucial to begin this foundational work from the premise that adopting coaching techniques in a guidance service did not make guidance practitioners 'coaches.' Essential to this was raising awareness through discussion about the fact that there would be times when it is appropriate to employ coaching and times when it is not. As Guccione and Hutchinson (2021) highlight, it is vital to consider the students (or learners) and their uniqueness of experience and context. For example, if a student has a same day deadline which they cannot meet and needs to know their options, coaching will not be appropriate. If, however, a student is demonstrating patterns of behaviour, such as repeatedly not submitting assignments, a longer-term approach such as coaching could be valuable. Additionally, we needed to take steps to ensure that coaching did not become the 'default' approach or be regarded as the optimum intervention, but rather as an additional technique to empower individuals to have greater autonomy over their learning experiences. These practice-based conversations with a guidance team informed the scenario below which serves as an example of where a blended approach of coaching alongside or within existing support might benefit students.

Scenario three: guidance and coaching

Context: A personal tutor contacts the support service as one of their students has had a recent diagnosis of ADHD and would like to know what can be done to support the student.

GUIDANCE: A practitioner will likely discuss the diagnosis from an academic progress viewpoint, for instance, by exploring what reasonable adjustments can be made for the student, and what additional support the student may now be entitled to, for example, the UK disabled students allowance.

COACHING: Following on from the initial guidance, this student could have several follow up sessions in which the practitioner uses coaching skills to explore with the student what impact their recent diagnosis has had on their studies, and what strategies, techniques and support networks the student can develop and employ to enhance their ability to study independently as they adjust to their recent diagnosis. Coaching would also be used to explore with the student what they perceive as their own challenges now that they have a confirmed diagnosis.

Having explored coaching with our guidance practitioners and considered where and how it might complement their work with students, we turned to the design and delivery of more formal workshop training. The next part of this chapter outlines our learning and insights from this process.

Part two: training and development in coaching

While the first part of this project consisted of establishing with the practitioners in the team how coaching could enhance the guidance service, we then needed to move to the second part which involved planning, delivering and evaluating the more formal training and development workshops.

Coaching methods and approaches

When creating workshops to embed coaching skills within academic and support services, it is important not only to consider the practitioners' level of knowledge and abilities but also which model of coaching may work best with potential coachees. The context for how coaching will be used is critical. At our institution, prospective students (known as 'enquirers') and current students will not consider themselves 'coachees' and so we do need to be concrete and explicit when engaging students in this way.

In designing coaching skills training for guidance practitioners, it was crucial to return to the simple principle that – whatever approach is used – coaching is sought out by individuals who want to look forward and focus on enhancing their life and create change (Starr, 2008). Coaching is an enabling process and can be used in many different contexts. With this mind, we chose to focus on two models to help our guidance practitioners put coaching into practice: GROW (Whitmore 2009) and a solutions-focused model known as OSKAR (McKergow and Jackson, 2002). GROW and OSKAR are also discussed in Chapter 4 of this volume.

In our context, it was crucial to remember that the guidance practitioners were not being trained to be coaches – rather, the rationale was supporting them to develop and embed coaching skills (where appropriate) within their existing practice. Our design was based on using the GROW model (Whitmore, 2009) to establish some of the foundations of coaching questions first, and then using OSKAR to develop skills thereafter. An advantage of using the GROW coaching model in CPD for student support staff is that it is an adaptable and flexible model which can enhance many different types of solution-focused conversations. There is also evidence that the GROW model helps to provide processes designed to increase the likelihood of change (Whitmore, 2009).

Our selection of GROW and OSKAR was also informed by our knowledge of the guidance role, and explorations of how coaching could enhance interactions in certain scenarios gleaned from the discussions covered in part one, above. Many of the guidance practitioners in student support services are working to help a student move through some kind of challenging situation. Some students might feel stuck about what steps to take, or may be bringing their personal history, emotions and subjectivities into their study. This can be so fundamental to them that they then struggle to separate it from the facts of their situation. The reason a student appears to be fixed on one route when, objectively, a guidance practitioner might see a positive alternative, could also be linked to pragmatic rational decision-making (Hodkinson and Sparkes, 1997). This suggests that choices are often context-related and based on the partial information people hold about the topic. Using the correct coaching approach and open questions would allow guidance practitioners to navigate this. In other instances, it was clear that students may become 'stuck' because of their own blind spots (Egan, 2012). Blind spots are the areas that we might struggle to see (or sometimes even choose to ignore) that are holding us back and making it harder for us to identify and resolve problematic situations. Blind spots are also obstacles to effective decision-making

(Hecke, 2007). Through implementing specific coaching techniques, guidance practitioners can help a student overcome these barriers.

In addition to practitioner perspectives on how coaching could enhance conversations in particular scenarios, our approach to designing skills workshops was also informed by the wider literature on solution-focused coaching. Solution-focused coaching has two main goals: changing the viewing and changing the doing (O'Hanlon and Beadle, 1996, cited in Yates, 2022, p. 119). This is where the coach can help the student reframe their problem and see the situation in a new light (the viewing), which hopefully goes some way towards shifting the student's focus away from ruminating on their problem and instead they begin to consider potential solutions. Students can frequently be caught in a loop of despair when seeking support so this area of solution-focused coaching would be extremely beneficial to start to break that cycle. Once this is done, the coach and student can move onto changing the doing, which involves supporting the coachee to focus on times in the past where they have succeeded before and working collaboratively together to build upon this for their current problem (Yates, 2022).

The GROW coaching model uses both a reflection and solution-focused approach, empowering the student-as-coachee to come up with their own solutions, brought out via the coach's questioning (South of Scotland Coaching Model, 2023). Self-determination theory also suggests that people are more likely to follow through with their next steps towards a goal when they feel they have been allowed some autonomy and ownership over their decisions (Sheldon, 2014). Therefore, this method seemed supportive for the range of students the guidance practitioners would be speaking to and help to better align a student's unconscious thoughts and what they want, as well as their need for change (Seraj and Leggett, 2023).

Similarly, the evidence for solution-focused models such as OSKAR is linked to the idea that solution-focused coaching sees 'coachees as the experts in their lives' (O'Connell and Palmer, 2019, p. 271). This complements the non-directive tone of the GROW model. Using solution-focused approaches can help students to secure a pathway towards the academic achievements they may have struggled to reach otherwise (Lindsay, 2023).

Connecting coaching and guidance

Having established the coaching models that would be the focus of our training and development and using insights from our initial explorations with guidance practitioners in one SST, our next step was to run the skills development workshops. Firstly, we wanted to ensure the training workshops offered more opportunities to unpick the relationship between coaching and other student support techniques. Through discussion, we developed practitioner understanding of the connections between coaching and guidance approaches and that they are not always mutually exclusive.

We also raised awareness that whilst our staff may not be qualified coaches themselves, they would have been utilising related skills in guidance. With coaching and guidance sitting on a continuum, it is not unusual for guidance practitioners to move between the two, adopting a coaching or mentoring approach at different times and being aware of the different boundaries around and within each. Support staff can be viewed as experts, by students, for their study issues and as students are often looking for, and expecting, to be mentored a little more and have suggestions made about what they should do. According to Irby (2012), while the role of coaching or mentoring is related, they are also quite different. She argues that mentors can coach, but coaches rarely mentor owing to the non-directive nature of coaching, and this was a distinction which it was important to draw attention to. This notion of working along a coaching and mentoring continuum as a way to enhance equitable practice is further discussed in Chapter 2 of this volume, while an exploration on how one can contract effectively in scenarios where offering an alternative approach within the same relationship or interaction is beneficial is outlined in Chapter 3.

Mindset

Exploring mindset is foundational in developing coaching skills because it supports practitioners to consider how they can prepare for a coaching conversation. Unconditional positive regard (UPR) is a concept developed by Carl Rogers (1957). In the context of coaching, UPR is the idea that a coach is able to be completely accepting and non-judgemental of their coachee no matter what they say (Yates, 2022). It is one of the fundamental mindsets that a coach should hold. Although the guidance practitioners we were training do not always work over a long-term period with students, UPR still applies in single interactions and single-session coaching (Dryden, 2020).

Within the workshop, the delegates were split into smaller groups and asked to discuss one question – 'What mindset and beliefs do you bring to the conversation about the students you support?' This generated conversation about the importance of recognising practitioner mindset when going into a call with students and how it could impact ability to hold students in UPR. Staff acknowledged challenges that arise when a student's situation is reminiscent of other student cases, and they feel predisposed to guide the student in a certain way. There is a clear power imbalance when a practitioner 'holds' information about the student (through their student profile, record of grades, for example) whereas the student does not necessarily know anything about the practitioner. We felt it was important to encourage practitioners to consider how to build connection authentically with students while balancing the responsibility and power of a guidance role. This might be usefully seen as 'walking alongside' rather than 'guiding.'

Unconscious bias was also an area to be scrutinised because it can unfairly influence our first impressions of someone. Research suggests that it is within the initial moments of meeting a new person that we are most likely to be influenced by our unconscious biases (Keane, 2017). If we consider the type of personal or sensitive details a student may reveal right from the start of a conversation, it is important to try to stay aware of any unconscious biases by questioning reactions as they happen rather than allowing inappropriate judgements. As demonstrated in Chapter 2 of this volume, student support advisers and practitioners must ensure that they take time to reflect effectively on any unconscious biases they may hold, and what shapes or triggers these thoughts for them, or it may impact on them holding the student in UPR.

The training workshop also aimed to revisit and reinforce the concept of holding a growth mindset about students, and how that should inform interactions with them. Growth mindset is a familiar concept for most practitioners; the idea that abilities are not innate and can be improved through effort and persistence; this contrasts with a fixed mindset where they might believe that there is nothing they can do to make improvements in their activities (Dweck, 2015).

Creating a safe and supportive space

Other authors in this volume have discussed the components that help to create safe spaces in coaching – such as contracting, chemistry and rapport – and many of the same principles apply in guidance. As discussed in Chapter 3, rapport is the foundation of any effective coaching relationship, and it means building a connection based on respect, empathy and mutual understanding. Rapport might be established by showing genuine interest in the other person, using their preferred name and communication style, acknowledging their strengths and achievements and finding common ground. Rapport also involves being attentive, responsive, supportive and avoiding distractions, interruptions and judgements. Reflective practice such as summarising, paraphrasing and restating the students' words can also support with building rapport (Knowles, 2021), as it helps to avoid misunderstanding and demonstrates active listening, ensuring the student will feel heard.

Rapport-building and contracting are both skills that guidance practitioners use habitually. However, their use in coaching is distinct and required exploration with our staff. While a coach may traditionally have the option of holding a 'chemistry call' with a potential coachee to explore compatibility factors between them before going into a more 'formal' coaching relationship (Koh, 2020), interactions in student support services tend to be reactive conversations in response to a situation or challenge and may be time sensitive. This means a rapport with the student needs to be established quickly. Students will generally contact a guidance practitioner with a specific issue and expect to be given a solution to their problem, so the contracting would need to be explicit. There is also the fact that even if the situation the student presents would suit a coaching approach, the student may not be in the right frame of mind to engage with this method of support, and the contracting and rapport building will help to expose this early on.

The use of open-ended questions and active listening can also be key to establishing psychologically safe spaces. Our approach to building upon these skills in the guidance context was to invite our practitioners to reflect on an interaction with a student and discuss why they used the questions they did, and which active listening skills worked best for them. Active listening allows them to listen not only to the story the student is bringing but also how they are telling the story (for example, focusing not just on the words they use, but also the intensity of the words). In our context, guidance is provided by remote teams via a telephony system with recorded calls. Reflection can therefore be supported by call listening. In the absence of this, the following questions can still be explored from memory and any notes taken during the interaction:

- What types of questions were most effective in eliciting information from the student?
- How did active listening skills contribute to building rapport and trust?
- Were there any instances where active listening broke down? Why might this have happened?

For a full analysis of the interaction, some practitioners might benefit from using a formal reflective model such as Gibbs' reflective cycle (1988) to support the structure of this process. However, if we want to encourage reflexivity on top of standard reflection, practitioners will also need to find the strategies that work best for them in questioning their own attitudes, assumptions and thought processes. It may well be that working with trusted peers and garnering honest feedback, may be a simple way for practitioners to establish the part they have played in an interaction and make changes towards their next student exchange. The value of peer (and other forms of) supervision is explored in greater detail in Chapter 8.

Accountability

Accountability in coaching helps support a coachee to build relevant strategies for taking responsibility for their own growth. Developing independent learners who take responsibility for their own progress is something that we strive for in support roles in HE and one of the key reasons that coaching is increasingly used across the sector. Focusing on powerful open questions and letting the students look within and come up with their own solutions to their problems will build confidence and give the students enough space for them to make meaningful and lasting changes in their lives. According to Clutterbuck (2020), the powerful questions that most effectively prompt coachees to stop and think all shared the same characteristics, forming the acronym PRAIRIE. These are:

- Personal – often using the word 'you.'
- Resonant – having an immediate, sometimes emotional, impact.
- Acute and Incisive – being succinct and getting straight to the point.
- Reverberant – these trigger long-term reflection and cannot always be answered in the moment.
- Innocent – not being asked with the intention of pushing forward a particular solution, focused solely on the coachee's agenda.
- Explicit – stating clearly and leaving no room for doubt, but still triggering answers other than yes or no.

In our experience, developing powerful questioning techniques in student support staff can be achieved by inviting reflection on the potential value of moving away from closed questions and towards coaching questioning techniques, and contrasting the two. An example exercise in Table 7.1 below demonstrates how to support that in a training or staff development setting.

By contrast, a less effective approach to questioning is where statements are disguised as questions. For example: 'Have you tried asking your boss if you could have any time off to work on your studies since they are linked to your job?' This is a closed question, and the person choosing to ask this likely has a 'right' answer in mind. Phrasing a question like this makes it a

Table 7.1 Comparison of open and closed questioning styles

Question type	Example	Observations
Open	What is stopping you from achieving this goal?	• Asked with genuine curiosity • No 'right answer' in mind • Seeks to uncover what the student feels is their barrier.
Closed	Have you tried asking your boss if you could have any time off to work on your studies since they are linked to your job?	• A suggestion rather than a question • Asked with the 'right' answer in mind • Seeks to direct student to take a particular action.

suggestion, and while suggestions may have a place within guidance practice, it is important to rephrase for powerful, coaching questions.

Student support practitioners work differently across institutions. Where they do not take on caseloads of regular students, they may not have ongoing contact with students in the same way a coach-mentor may have with a student. In these cases, empowering the student to manage accountability is even more crucial. A standalone conversation with clear actions can have a considerable impact on student confidence and the way they view their situation. If psychological safety has been established, the student may feel comfortable being challenged to explore accountability for their next steps and not relying on directive instructions from an adviser.

Introducing GROW to our staff

The GROW model is a framework that contains all the core elements of an effective coaching session; it is results-oriented, always ending in the client choosing actions to take. The mnemonic makes it memorable and accessible for those new to coaching. In our experience, it was important to preface the training with five acknowledgements to help guide our practitioners in their use of GROW:

- GROW does not have to be followed in a linear format and the order of each phase of GROW can be adapted.

- Each stage of the model can require a different amount of time and focus, and this could vary from student to student. It may not always be possible to use the GROW model in its entirety or in a pure coaching form and guidance practitioners need to be able to spot what is a coachable moment and what is not.
- Trust must be present between the guidance practitioner and the student, and rapport must have been effectively built.
- The student should have shown signs that they are open to being asked challenging questions, and the best way to know for sure is to check directly.
- The student must have enough time to talk, as a coaching conversation will generally take a bit longer than a typical interaction over the telephone, to allow for exploration.

  These principles helped reinforce the flexibility of the GROW model and that guidance practitioners can, and should, switch approaches in the moment, following the needs of the student. We used coaching video resources to demonstrate the GROW model in action and highlight the questions asked at each stage. For example:
- GOALS – What is the aim of the discussion? What areas do you want to work on?
- REALITY – What skills/knowledge/attributes do you have? What progress have you made so far?
- OPTIONS – What are your options? What else/anything else? What could you do differently?
- WILL/WAY FORWARD – On a scale of 1–10 how committed/motivated are you to doing it? How will you know you have been successful?

Our guidance practitioners were also given a copy of a checklist of coaching skills that they would be asked to demonstrate in the next workshop. This included describing the process to the coachee, taking steps to build rapport, using the GROW model to bring insight and learning, and checking the use of open and probing questions as opposed to multiple or leading questions. After attending this introductory workshop, our practitioners were invited to a second development session which would focus on the application of these techniques.

Putting theory into practice: GROW

Having established some of the foundational principles for coaching using the GROW model, our second skills workshop for guidance practitioners focused on putting the GROW model into practice. The session aimed to cover:

- The importance of spending time with a student to get the goal setting right. This requires practitioners to consider the goals students present with; these goals may lack specificity, or be dependent on a third party or external resource. In these cases, it is vital that the coach supports the student to explore their own autonomy in such a situation. Goal setting may also necessitate reframing in instances where students position goals in a way that is moving away from (rather than towards) something. For example, a student might say that they do not want to fail their exams, rather than they would like to perform well in them.
- A practical opportunity to trial GROW. To practice their skills, our practitioners were placed in pairs or triads and invited to think of an issue they would be open to discuss with their colleague – either professional or personal. In a triad, one colleague would act as coach and the other as observer. Roles were rotated so that each practitioner had the opportunity to be observed, with time allowed for the delegates to discuss feedback. Alternative peer support models are explored in Chapter 8.

The learning design process for these activities was considered carefully, and this was about creating an educational setting where the session would be learner-centred (rather than teacher- or trainer-centred). The goal was to implement an authentic activity that would engage learners. Role playing (or scenario-based learning) is a good example of such an active learning and teaching strategy (Caltabiano *et al.*, 2018; Erturk, 2015). While in many role-playing activities, scenario-based situations are provided for people to 'act out' how they would respond to a situation, we felt that bringing a real situation to the session would provide a more authentic environment for developing coaching skills. Following the scenario-based learning activity, the group were invited to discuss how using a 'purer' coaching approach felt, and at this point, the group was also able to delve more deeply into reflection on how these skills may work in student-based scenarios.

Evaluating the impact of coaching skills development on guidance practitioners

In this case study, we have shared our experience of planning and then implementing skills development for student support services staff in coaching. The final element of this pilot was to evaluate the initiative by surveying staff participants. In total, 53 student support staff opted to attend the workshops, and out of these participants, 30 opted-in to complete the evaluation form. The evaluation was sent out four weeks after the first coaching workshop had taken place.

Ninety percent of the guidance practitioners who opted in to the development workshops stated that they felt the training had enabled them to identify circumstances where coaching methods could enhance their guidance. Sixty-seven percent said that they already felt this training had enabled them to start using coaching skills consciously in their practice. In the free-text responses it was clear that the development had helped staff to be more self-reflexive about their practice and when to adapt it, mentioning that they now recognised during calls when a coaching question or approach may be more beneficial to the student, as well as understanding times that a coaching approach may not be as helpful within guidance work. Our practitioners referenced feeling more confident about using coaching questions in combination with other techniques when interacting with students; they reported thinking more carefully about the questions they are using and finding that this has worked well with goal setting conversations with students and encouraging them to be more proactive in finding their own solutions. By being more mindful about coaching questions, the practitioners also commented that it helped them avoid potential 'leading' of students when offering guidance.

It is worth noting that the development of coaching skills is a long-term investment/commitment rather than a quick 'fix.' Indeed, our evaluation found that 33 percent of trainees were not yet feeling able to consciously use these coaching skills within their practice at the time of the survey. It would be prudent to consider evaluating whether using a coaching approach in certain situations has positively affected the student experience when they interacted with the guidance practitioner, perhaps through student feedback after their call. However, the current evaluation from the guidance practitioners does support a case for developing further opportunities to strengthen coaching skills in student support services at our institution, for those moments where it will benefit a student by empowering them to find solutions.

Recommendations

When considering the role of coaching in HE, we urge leaders and practitioners to keep the student at the centre of their plans. As other authors in this volume have posited, students are not a single homogenous group that require generic levels of support but rather individuals, with specific needs, experiences and preferences. If we are truly to impact their chances for continuation and progression, and in an equitable way, then consideration for a personalised and tailored approach is needed. Equipping practitioners with various tools to draw upon, and with the skills to evaluate when certain approaches are needed, will be essential to offering a more equitable service that prioritises individual student need.

To successfully embed and work with staff on their development requires engaged line managers who can prioritise development amidst the familiar operational pressures of a university student support service. Our hope is that the workshop approach we have shared in this chapter can be adapted and utilised according to team dynamics and preferences. Our evaluation provides some initial, indications that coaching skills can enhance practitioner confidence.

To ensure that the student experience is always at the centre of staff development, encouraging practitioners to look for safe, coachable moments with students is important. To support this, we have identified ongoing CPD opportunities for our guidance practitioners, such as coaching circles. Coaching circles are based on the work of Otto Sharmer (2018). They are a confidential form of small group coaching which can allow those dealing with emotionally challenging situations to feel supported. It encourages deep reflection on practice, as well as the sharing of multiple perspectives. Within these coaching circles, a facilitator-coach guides a small group of 'coaches' towards supporting a colleague, who is acting as a client, or 'case giver.' These groups should be kept small (between five and six participants). During each session, the case giver has dedicated time to explore the challenging situation they have presented to the group. The coaches should avoid offering advice or solutions and remain in the coaching mindset, asking appropriate questions to support the case giver towards finding their own solutions and next steps (Brassard, 2019). Our aspiration is that coaching circles will provide a safe space for guidance practitioners to hone their coaching skills and also allow them to deepen their professional relationships with each other. Additional models of peer coaching support are explored in Chapter 8.

Reflective questions

We invite leaders within SST and practitioners in student guidance, wellbeing, careers and other related services to consider some of the reflective questions below to help identify the potential value of coaching skills development in their own context.

- What resources are required to effectively introduce and integrate coaching skills into your own context?
- What opportunities for continuing reflective practice and development will you make available to staff?
- How can practitioners be supported to navigate situations where they may feel uncomfortable using their newly developed coaching skills with students?
- will you measure the effectiveness of the coaching approach as a whole (including staff training and student impact)?

Next steps

This chapter has built upon the principles and practice of coaching in HE and shows how this can be used to develop staff and enhance support for students in alternative contexts, such as in guidance. Becoming a qualified coach takes time and there is no expectation for staff trained in other 'helping' professions to pivot to this professional route. However, what we have described in this chapter is the value of coaching skills development for delivering the more holistic support universities are increasingly (and duly) expected to provide for students. It is with this in mind that the authors continue to work on embedding coaching skills within the IAG services at The OU. We look forward to learning more from others, across a range of academic and support services, about what this approach can offer as universities move more towards holistic support for students.

Bibliography

Brassard, C. (2019) *Coaching circles: leveraging coaching skills in a truly inspiring environment*. Available at: https://coachingfederation.org/blog/coaching-circles (Accessed: 16 June 2024).

Caltabiano, M., Errington, E., Ireland, L., Sorin, R. and Nickson, A. (2018) 'The potential of role-play in undergraduate psychology training', *Asian Journal of University Education*, 14(1), pp. 1–14, Available at: https://files.eric.ed.gov/fulltext/EJ1207768.pdf (Accessed: 25 July 2024).

Carless, D. (2019) 'Feedback loops and the longer-term: towards feedback spirals', *Assessment and Evaluation in Higher Education*, 44(5), pp. 705–714. doi: 10.1080/02602938.2018.1531108 (Accessed: 10 May 2024).

Clutterbuck, D. (2020) 'Questions in coaching', in J. Passmore (ed.) *The coaches' handbook: the complete practitioner guide for professional coaches*. London: Routledge, pp. 92–103.

Dias, G.P., Foster, J. and Zunszain, P.A. (2019) 'Time to flourish: designing a coaching psychology programme to promote resilience and wellbeing in postgraduate students', *European Journal of Applied Positive Psychology*, 3(7), pp. 1–12.

Dryden, W. (2020) *Single session coaching and one-at-a time coaching: distinctive features*. Abingdon: Routledge.

Dweck, C. (2015) *Carol Dweck revisits the 'Growth Mindset'*. Available at: https://www.edweek.org/leadership/opinion-carol-dweck-revisits-the-growth-mindset/2015/09 (Accessed: 9 June 2024).

Egan, G. (2012) *The skilled helper. A problem-management and opportunity-development approach to helping*. 10th edn. Pacific Grove, CA: Brooks/Cole.

Erturk, E. (2015) 'Evaluation of role play as a teaching strategy in a systems analysis and design course', *International Journal of Learning, Teaching and Educational Research*, 13(3), pp. 150–159. Available at: https://www.ijlter.org/index.php/ijlter/article/view/487 (Accessed: 25 July 2024).

Gibbs, G. (1988) *Learning by doing: a guide to teaching and learning methods*. Oxford: Further Education Unit. Available at: https://thoughtsmostlyaboutlearning.wordpress.com/wp-content/uploads/2015/12/learning-by-doing-graham-gibbs.pdf (Accessed: 31 August 2024).

Guccione, K. and Hutchinson, S. (2021) *Coaching and mentoring for academic development (surviving and thriving in academia)*. Bingley, Leeds: Emerald Publishing Limited.

Hecke, M. (2007) *Blind spots: why smart people do dumb things*. Amherst, NY: Prometheus.

Hillman, J. Lochtie, D. and Purcell, O. (2024) 'Black students' experiences of coaching and mentoring in higher education: a case study', *International Journal of Mentoring and Coaching in Education*, 13(2), pp. 246–257. doi: 10.1108/IJMCE-01-2023-0011.

Hodkinson, P. and Sparkes, A.C. (1997) 'Careership: a sociological theory of career decision making', *British journal of sociology of education*, 18(1), pp. 29–44. doi: https:// 10.1080/0142569970180102.

Inside Track. (2022) *Knowing the differences between coaching and advising creates a collaborative road to success*. Available at: https://assets.website-files.com/6488cf617d767c69391c1167/6529ab7982740c62c5544ed6_Coaching-vs-Other-Student-Support-Roles_InsideTrack.pdf (Accessed: 18 April 2024).

Irby, B.J. (2012) 'Editor's overview: mentoring, tutoring, and coaching', *Mentoring and Tutoring: Partnership in Learning*, 20(3), pp. 297–301. doi: 10.1080/13611267.2012.708186

Kaper, S., Graafeiland, N. and Vogelaar, B. (2024) 'Effects of coaching on well-being, perception of inclusion, and study-interest', *Nordic Journal of Vocational Education and Training*, 14(1), pp. 1–30. doi: 10.3384/njvet.2242-458X.241411 (Accessed: 10 May 2024).

Keane, A. (2017) 'Unconscious bias—its impact on the coach and the organisation', *The OCM Coach and Mentor Journal*, pp. 19–21. Available at: https://www.theocm.co.uk/sites/default/files/2019-01/Unconscious%20bias%20-%20Angela%20Keane.pdf (Accessed: 9 June 2024).

Knowles, S. (2021) *Positive psychology coaching*. 1st edn. Cham: Springer.

Koh, J.A. (2020) *How to create powerful chemistry coaching calls*. Available at: https://coachingfederation.org/blog/create-powerful-chemistry-calls (Accessed: 9 June 2024).

Lindsay, J. (2023) 'Out of the shadows: the coaching space in education', *International Coaching Psychology Review*, 18(2), pp. 112–115.

Lochtie, D., McIntosh, E., Stork, A. and Walker, B. (2018) *Becoming an effective personal tutor: supporting learners through personal tutoring and coaching*. 2nd edn. Norwich: Critical Publishing.

Lochtie, D., Stork, A. and Walker, B. (2022) *The higher education personal tutor's and advisor's companion translating theory into practice to improve student success*. Norwich: Critical Publishing.

Luft, J., and Ingham, H. (1955). *The Johari window, a graphic model of interpersonal awareness*. Proceedings of the western training laboratory in group development. Los Angeles: University of California.

McKergow, M. and Jackson, P.Z. (2002). *The solutions focus: making coaching and change SIMPLE*. London: Nicholas Brealey International.

NHS. (no date) *Johari window*. Available at: https://www.hee.nhs.uk/sites/default/files/documents/Johari%20window.pdf (Accessed: 13 December 2024).

O'Connell, B. and Palmer, S. (2019) 'Solution-focused coaching', in S. Palmer and A. Whybrow (eds.) *Handbook of coaching psychology: a guide for practitioners*. 2nd edn. Abingdon: Oxon, pp. 270–281.

O'Hanlon, B. and Beadle, S. (1996) *A field guide to possibility land: possibility therapy methods*. London: BT Press.

Rogers, C.R. (1957) 'The necessary and sufficient conditions of therapeutic personality change', *Journal of Consulting Psychology*, 21, pp. 95–103. doi: 10.1037/h0045357

Seraj, S. and Leggett, R. (2023) 'The challenges of personal tutoring in higher education: applying a coaching approach at a UK higher education institution', *International Journal of Evidence Based Coaching and Mentoring*, 21 (1), pp. 85–98. Available at: https://radar.brookes.ac.uk/radar/items/2d391475-00a6-44b4-b81f-8f1b284d10e9/1/ (Accessed: 26 April 2024).

Sharmer, C.O. (2018) *The essentials of theory U. Core principles and applications*. 1st edn. Oakland: Berrett-Koehler Publishers.

Sheldon, K.M. (2014) 'Becoming oneself: the central role of self-concordant goal selection'. *Personality and Social Psychology Review*, 18(4), pp. 349–365. doi: 10.1177/1088868314538549

South of Scotland Coaching Model. (2023) *5. The GROW model of coaching*. Available at: https://plh.napier.ac.uk/ (Accessed: 9 June 2024).

Starr, J. (2008) *The coaching manual: the definitive guide to the process, principles and skills of personal coaching*. London: Pearson Prentice-Hall.

van der Baan, N., Nuis, W., Beausaert, S., Gijselaers, W. and Gast, I. (2024) 'Developing employability competences through career coaching in higher education: supporting students' learning process', *Studies in Higher Education*, pp. 1–20. doi: 10.1080/03075079.2024.2307976.

Whitmore, J. (2009) *Coaching for performance: growing human potential and purpose—the principles and practice of coaching and leadership*. 4th edn. London: Nicholas Brealey Publishing.

Yates, J. (2022) *The career coaching handbook*. 2nd edn. Abingdon: Routledge.

Coaching supervision **8**

Supporting staff development and wellbeing

Julie Stock, Helen Williams and Richard Peat

Introduction

In the final chapter of this volume, we seek to show how effective and ethical coaching and mentoring support for students in higher education (HE) is contingent upon the provision of adequate professional support for the staff delivering it. Coaching supervision is not only a critical element of ethical practice for professional coaches, as outlined in the first chapter of this volume, but it is also a valuable tool for creating reflective spaces among staff in coaching, mentoring and other 'helping roles.'

The theoretical and conceptual development of coaching supervision is ongoing in the specialist literature but, in essence, it refers to the regular meeting of a coach (supervisee) and a supervisor to support coaching practice (Carroll, 2006). A fuller definition is offered by the Association for Coaching:

> Coaching supervision is a formal and protected time for facilitating a coach's in-depth reflection on their practice with a coaching supervisor. Supervision offers a confidential framework within a collaborative working relationship in which the practice, tasks, process and challenges of the coaching work can be explored. The primary aim of supervision is to enable the coach to gain in ethical competency, confidence and creativity so as to ensure best possible service to the coaching client, both coachees and coaching sponsors.

DOI: 10.4324/9781003486015-9

> Supervision is not a 'policing' role, but rather a trusting and collegial professional relationship.
>
> (Association for Coaching, 2018, p. 1)

A thread running through most definitions of coaching supervision is relevant for all staff involved in teaching, learning and support in HE: reflective practice. In coaching supervision, practitioners are supported to carry out 'in-depth consideration of events, situations, words and actions' to build understanding and self-awareness (Iordanou, Hawley and Iordanou, 2017, p. 94), as well as examine behaviours, outcomes and possible alternative approaches (Hay, 2007, p. 7).

The need to create reflective spaces for staff in coaching-related roles was the starting point for our work. In this chapter, we share our experiences in providing supervision at both a team and organisational level. In the first part of this chapter, Julie shares insights based on supervising staff-facing coaches staff in an Organisational Learning department at The Open University (OU), UK. In the second part, Richard and Helen write from the experience of supervising, and procuring supervision for, student-facing coach-mentors in the Personal Learning Advice (PLA) Service at The OU. Using the scholarly and professional literature alongside our own case studies, we present the case for supervision and evaluate its benefits.

Part one: supervision in theory and practice: developing organisational coaching

The growth of a coaching culture at any HE provider is not just about coaching students; it also extends to staff. Offering coaching and mentoring to staff in academic and professional services roles helps to embed the person-centred philosophies outlined in the introduction to this volume in our core work and services. This, we posit here, helps to develop staff and (indirectly) enhances the student experience.

At The OU, there has been a coaching service for staff for almost a decade, situated within Organisational Learning. Coaching is delivered by qualified coaches within the university who act as an internal coaching 'pool.' As a supervisor for the coaches, Julie has trialled different approaches to providing internal supervision drawn from three influential models: The Seven-Eyed Supervisor Model by Hawkins *et al.* (2020), Six Categories of Counselling Intervention (Heron, 2001) and Proctor's Model of Clinical Supervision (Proctor, 1987). In what follows in the first part of this chapter,

Julie offers insights from the application of these theoretical models to the supervision of coaching staff – sharing successes and challenges.

The Seven-Eyed supervisor model

The Seven-Eyed model of supervision was first developed by Peter Hawkins (1985) based on his work supervising counsellors and psychotherapists. The 'Seven-Eyed' model is described as an approach to supervision which allows consideration of both the relational and systemic (Hawkins *et al.*, 2020, p. 85). This means that it enables a supervisor to be aware of what is happening in the different relationships involved in coaching – between coachee and coach, as well as coach and supervisor. It then takes into consideration the relationship between each party and their wider systems. The model is comprised of seven 'lenses' (or what Hawkins *et al.* call 'modes,' 2020, p. 85) through which supervisors view these relationships. This is designed to help a coach explore different elements of their practice. Table 8.1 shows how this can be applied to the supervision of staff coaches.

Table 8.1 The application of the Seven-Eyed model (Hawkins and McMahon, 2020) to the supervision of staff coaches in HE

Lens of the Seven-Eyed model (Hawkins and McMahon, 2020)	How this shapes the focus of a supervision session
Lens 1	Supervision focuses on the needs and experiences of the staff member being coached (the 'coachee').
Lens 2	Supervision focuses on the approaches used by the staff member delivering the coaching (the 'supervisee').
Lens 3	Supervision focuses on the coaching relationship between the two members of staff and highlights any subtle or unconscious dynamics between them.
Lens 4	Supervision focuses on the wellbeing of the staff member delivering the coaching (the 'supervisee').

(*Continued*)

Table 8.1 (Continued)

Lens of the Seven-Eyed model (Hawkins and McMahon, 2020)	How this shapes the focus of a supervision session
Lens 5	Supervision focuses on the relationship between the coaching supervisor and the staff member delivering coaching (the 'supervisee').
Lens 6	Supervision focuses on the experiences of the supervisor and how that may be manifesting in supervision sessions.
Lens 7	Supervision focuses on the wider contexts for all members of staff involved in coaching (supervisor, supervisee and coachees).

As it has been noted, supervision rarely takes place through just one of these lenses (Hawkins *et al.*, 2020). Coaching in any organisation involves a complex interplay between coaches and line managers and other stakeholders, institutional policies and strategic agendas, as well as the coachee and their personal context and worldview. The Seven-Eyed model helps a supervisor to support their supervisee to navigate this in their coaching work. In the scenario below, we offer an example of how this might play out in supervision.

Scenario one: Using the Seven-Eyed model in supervision practice

A supervisor, supervisee and coachee work within in the same organisation. The supervisor is working with a supervisee over four sessions. The supervisee is delivering coaching to other members of staff within the university whilst completing a formal coaching qualification.

The supervisee finds the non-directive nature of coaching challenging and is keen to develop their practice so they are supporting the coachee to find their own solutions. Supervision is helping the supervisee to explore what they thought their role was. Using the Seven-Eyed model helps to generate the following insights:

- Lens 7: Viewing the relationships and their interplay through lens seven helps to highlight cultural differences between the supervisor and supervisee, supervisee and coachee and how this impacts on style and approach. The supervisee reflects on the way they were working in a second language and practicing their coaching skills in triads on their professional course with others also from a diverse range of cultural backgrounds.
- Lens 4: The challenge when a member of staff is struggling with the non-directive element of coaching is to explore the impact that the burden of a more directive, advice-giving approach might have on them. Lens 4 helps the supervisor to explore the supervisee's difficulty in being able to go deep and get to heart of issues for their coachee. The supervisee is nervous about holding up a mirror to the coachee so, through supervision, they rehearse how the conversation may go offering them reassurance.
- Lens 5: The supervisory relationship can be challenging where it seems to subtly 'parallel' (Hawkins and McMahon, 2020, p. 88) the coaching relationship. In this case, the supervisor wants to direct the supervisee in a way which mirrored the relationship between supervisee and coachee. Lens 5 helps the supervisor to see how the supervisee might be experiencing a confidence issue, with the consequential 'need' to find solutions for the coachee. The supervisor helps the coach recognise that people need to help themselves.
- Lens 2: The challenge in supervision is the temptation to simply re-coach the supervisee to show them what they should do. Initially in supervision, the supervisee would repeatedly ask, 'what can I ask them?' Viewing the coaching relationship through lens 2 in supervision helped to model questioning techniques and exploratory conversations. This raises the supervisee's awareness of how different the conversation could be for them and their coachee.

As this scenario shows, the Seven-Eyed model can be used in a non-linear way to address different dynamics of coaching practice. In the absence of supervision, it can also be used as a reflective tool by coaching and mentoring practitioners.

Six categories of counselling intervention

The six categories framework is based on Heron's work in counselling and was used to train health and education professionals (Heron, 2001). More recently, the model has been used in executive coaching where business professionals, including coaches and supervisors, have used the model to gain insights into how they interact with people when they are trying to help.

The framework is based on six categories – or styles – people used to help others. These are then each aligned to an overarching approach: either authoritative or facilitative. Heron describes the authoritative approaches as: prescriptive, informative and confronting (Heron, 2001, pp. 5–6). Heron considers 'facilitative' approaches as cathartic, catalytic and supportive (2001, pp. 5–6). There is no hierarchy here between the categories and neither should be regarded as more valuable than the other. A supervisor's approach and the decision on which category to use will be based on their role, the needs of the client and the focus for the session.

In scenario 2, we offer a scenario where a supervisor notices a directive approach being used by a recently qualified coach. This example illustrates how the model can support the ongoing development of a coach by highlighting areas that need further work and thereby improving their coaching practice. This example is based on one supervision session.

Scenario two: Using Heron's categories in supervision

A supervisor is working with a supervisee who is a recently qualified coach within their organisation. As the supervision session unfolds, the supervisor becomes increasingly aware that the coach is using a directive approach more aligned to mentoring, rather than the coaching they had contracted for. How could the supervisor employ the six categories model to explore these issues in a way which did not risk the relationship or the imposition of the supervisor's values?

In this situation, the role of the supervisor is arguably to name behaviour that falls outside of the standards expected of coaches. The supervisor might therefore usefully explore what is happening in coaching, firstly, by using Heron's (2001) three authoritative categories. This might begin with, 'what do you think coaching means?' Then moving into the three facilitative categories, for instance, by asking questions such as: 'so, tell me what happened in the session?,' 'how did that make you feel?,' 'how did you respond to that?,' 'now that you have had some time to reflect, what would you have done differently?,' 'what have your learned from this experience?,' 'how will you use that learning going forward?' and 'what does this mean for your coaching practice more holistically?.'

Asking the coach to restate what coaching means and moving into the facilitative categories helps the coach to reflect on what coaching is and is then able to compare that to what happened in the session. Then using the same facilitative categories, it can take the coach into a space where they are learning from that experience and applying that learning to their practice.

In doing so, Heron's model can help to distinguish between coaching and supervision. The authoritative (prescriptive, informative, confronting) might come more naturally in supervision in that they support the need to hold the standards of coaching, and the ethics of how coaches should be working. However, the facilitative categories can be helpfully used to explore and open the topic further before the authoritative categories can take the discussion beyond coaching and into supervision.

Practitioners responsible for supervision might use Heron's framework (2001) to explore how to 'show up' in supervision sessions. If a supervisor tends towards one or two styles only, the framework can help provide flexibility and enhance responsiveness to the situation and possibly change the focus of the supervision session to areas that haven't been explored before. In short, it can help supervisors to be more intentional about the categories being used.

Proctor's Model of Clinical Supervision (Proctor, 1987)

Proctor's Model of Clinical Supervision (Proctor, 1987) is recognised internationally, although mostly used in the UK and Europe. It is a model used in nursing practice and later adopted by other helping professionals, initially counselling. It has since been used more broadly including coaching supervision. The core focus of the model is to support the professional needs of the supervisee within the supervision session. Essentially the model has three areas of focus that should be addressed in the supervision session, to make the session effective; Proctor calls these three areas the formative, restorative and normative functions. The formative function focuses on the skills development of the practitioner; the restorative focuses on their wellbeing and personal development; the normative function addresses professional 'normative' standards (Litherland *et al.*, 2023).

To determine the focus in coaching supervision, practitioners can assess a supervisee's needs and agree which functions should be prioritised to deliver the desired outcomes. Most often, supervision will be a balance of all three functions. In the concluding scenario for part one of this chapter, we offer learning on the role this model can play in supporting ethical coaching practice in balance with the other functions of supervision.

Scenario three: Using Proctor's model of clinical supervision in coaching supervision practice

A supervisor is delivering sessions for a supervisee who is a newly qualified coach in their own organisation. They are struggling to balance in supervision the development of the individual coach and upholding professional standards and ethical practice required of professional coaches. Using Proctor's model helps the supervisor to support reflective practice, professional growth and wellbeing, without overemphasising standards, ethics and policies:

- Formative: The supervisor explores the supervisee's observations about their own skills and competence, as well as their ongoing continuous professional development. Focusing on the formative function in supervision enhances learning opportunities and lends itself to sharing knowledge and encouraging reflective practice.
- Restorative: The supervisor moves on to consider the wellbeing of the supervisee, as well as their personal development and growth. Focusing on the restorative function in supervision helps the supervisor to explore several emotional challenges the supervisee is experiencing.
- Normative: The supervisor asks questions about professional standards, ethical practice and the supervisee's accountability for these. As a supervisor for internal coaches, they are also able to raise awareness about institutional policies and procedures relating to safeguarding and data protection.

Summary

In the first part of this chapter, we have shared examples of how three influential models of supervision might apply to the supervision of coaches in a university. Before moving on to consider coaching supervision for student-facing staff, we invite readers to reflect on the approaches to supervision discussed thus far and consider what might be helpful for their own practice.

- Which supervision model resonates with you the most? Why is that?
- If you are a supervisor, what is your approach to supervision? What would happen if you used more authoritative or facilitative styles in your practice?
- Thinking about the Seven-Eyed model, which lenses can you identify with in your practice now? Which lenses could provide you with more insight and different perspectives?
- In supervision, how much time do you spend exploring the supervisee's ongoing professional development (formative)? What about the supervisee's wellbeing and personal growth (restorative)? What do you explore around the supervisee's ethical practice (normative)?
- In supervision, how might you balance authoritative and facilitative approaches to ensure psychological safety for supervisees?

Part two: using supervision to support student-facing staff

The evidence for the value of supervision in coaching practice is extensive. In the first part of this chapter, Julie has provided examples of how some of the theoretical models might translate to the supervision of staff-facing coaches and its value for staff development and quality, ethical coaching. In this part of this chapter, we turn our attention to the ways in which supervision can support student-facing staff. Our experiences here are based on the experience of providing and procuring supervision for coach-mentors in the centralised coaching and mentoring (PLA) service. However, what we also want to draw attention to, is the value and timeliness for considering supervision at a time when practitioners across student services portfolios are regularly delivering interventions relating to highly complex and sometimes traumatic situations. As other authors in this volume have observed, many support services in the UK are operating amidst a 'mental health crisis' (Times Higher Education, 2023) compounded by the global economic climate (British Sociological Association, 2024). In this environment, supervision is one way to safeguard staff and students by supporting ethical and quality coaching, guidance and support for students.

In our context, delivering a coaching and mentoring service for students who may experience considerable barriers, we recognised at an early stage the potential mental and emotional impact for practitioners in the team. Recognising the role of supervision in supporting staff, in this part of this chapter, we share insights from our experiences of trialling five approaches to supervision over a four-year period, considering the balance between effectiveness, value and cost throughout. Our aspiration is that this part of this chapter will support managers to evaluate existing forms of supervision and/or identify forms of supervision that might help support staff to support students.

Reaching a shared understanding about the role of supervision in a student support team

Before going on to outline the five approaches to supervision we piloted in the PLA Service, it is worth noting the value of having a shared understanding of what supervision is, the role of the supervisor and supervisee and how supervision could support our practice. An exercise which helped us to co-create this as a team is one which might easily be used in other student support services to explore the potential place for supervision. We asked practitioners to begin by reflecting on a student they had been working with and asked them to consider the following questions:

- What did the student choose to focus on or share with you?
- What was significant about their story?
- What interventions did you choose to use and why?
- How would you describe your relationship with this student?
- What thoughts and feelings did you experience within this interaction?
- Who does the student remind you of?
- What is an image of the session?
- What might you have held back in any way during the session?
- What 'residues' from the session did you experience in your thoughts and/or body?

This exercise was used an example of the gentle, constructive challenge that supervision might bring to enhance reflective practice. It also raised awareness about the potential value of hearing other practitioners reflect on the same issues, in a supported way. To extend this and consider the role of the supervisor in facilitating reflective spaces, we also explored how the Seven-Eyed model might apply to the supervision of coaching and mentoring work with students. In Table 8.2, we share the template used to outline this in a way which is relevant to the context of our work as a team.

Table 8.2 The application of the Seven-Eyed model (Hawkins and McMahon, 2020) to the supervision of student coaches in HE

Lens	Aim of viewing coaching through this lens	Supervisor thoughts/ responses/questions
1 The student and their context	To support the coach-mentor to pay attention to their student, the choices the student is making and the connections between the various aspects of the students life.	What was significant about their story? How did they 'present themselves'? Which area of their life/ studies did they want to explore?
2 Interventions made by the coach	To support the coach-mentor in their choices and skills in intervention and increase their range and knowledge.	What interventions did you choose to use? When did these interventions happen and what were the reasons the reason you chose them?
3 Relationship between coach and student	To support the coach-mentor to step out of their own perspective and develop greater insight and understanding of the dynamics of the working relationship with a particular student	What did you first notice in your interaction with this student? How would you describe the relationship? Who does this student remind you of? Can you identify an image or a metaphor to represent the relationship?

(*Continued*)

Table 8.2 (Continued)

Lens	Aim of viewing coaching through this lens	Supervisor thoughts/ responses/questions
4 What is happening for the coach in the interactions	To increase the capacity and efficacy of the coach-mentor in engaging with their clients.	What thoughts/feelings are arising in you when you are working with this student? How is this affecting your responses and interventions?
5 Relationship between the supervisor and coach	To role model the reflection/attention on 'self as practitioner' To uncover 'parallel processes'	Let's take a minute to ask how supervision is going for you and I today. Is there anything (possibly underlying) we are not discussing?
6 What is happening for the supervisor in the supervisory meeting	To use what is happening for the supervisor as a source of insight into what is happening for coach-mentor and student.	I am having thoughts about/I am feeling..... When you tell me about Student X being angry in the session, I am also beginning to feel angry. I wonder if that is how you felt?
7 Wider context – including organisational, social, cultural and ethical factors	To recognise the wider context in which all the above 'eyes' are taking place and how this context influences student, coach-mentor and supervisor.	How does your handling of this situation fit within the expectations of The OU and with relevant ethical standards? How does our work specifically with students from marginalised groups impact on our practice?

Using the reflective exercise and exploring the role of the supervisor helped establish a shared vision for supervision in the team. It also helped to highlight several important functions for supervision which included:

- Professional development and accreditation
- Maintaining ethical practice in a way which allowed practitioners to be constructively challenged on their beliefs and mindsets, uncovering unconscious biases and helping to maintain balance and neutrality.
- Provision of a safe space to share challenging and complex cases with colleagues, gain emotional support and perspective and engender deeper trust and relationships between colleagues.
- Safeguard staff wellbeing.

Creating this shared understanding of our needs and expectations of supervision meant that we knew what functions it needed to fulfil and how we would evaluate it. This informed the approaches we took to designing supervision for the team.

Five approaches to supervision in a student support service

Peer supervision

The first approach we implemented was to establish peer supervision pairings. Peer supervision is characterised by two essential elements: the mutual benefit to, and working relationship between, participants. As Turner, Lucas and Whitaker (2018) have shown, peer supervision occurs when there is 'reciprocity' as peers are not necessarily trained supervisors.

> Peer supervision is a collaborative learning environment created between fellow coaches, mentors or other professionals (practitioners). It is of mutual benefit to the practitioners involved as well as being of service to their clients and the wider system.
>
> (Turner, Lucas and Whitaker, 2018, np)

Our approach was to partner each coach-mentor with another 'peer' from the team for an hour-long supervision session at least once a month. After six months, the pairs would rotate unless the practitioners requested otherwise. Peer supervision pairs were provided with two potential structures that they could use for their conversations. The first was derived from Peter Hawkins' CLEAR model (Hawkins and McMahon, 2020, pp. 76–77). The CLEAR model is another example of a seminal model of supervision, in addition to the three which Julie discussed in the first part of this chapter. Table 8.3 shows how we adapted it to support peer supervision pairs.

Table 8.3 The CLEAR supervision model applied in peer supervision in the PLA Service

Stage of the CLEAR model	Application in peer supervision sessions
C = Contracting	Agree what your respective aims for supervision are together. Begin with the end in mind and agreeing how you are going to get there together.
L = Listening	Listen to each other and reflect what you each hear from the other to help facilitate the generation of personal insight.
E = Exploring	Explore together how you are working with students and the impact you might have as coaches.
	Challenge each other to create new possibilities for future action in resolving the situation.
A = Action	Action plan to agree each of your next steps in the short term and a longer-term way ahead.
R = Review	Take stock and reinforce the ground covered and commitments made. Review the experience and how it could be improved.

Adapted from Hawkins and McMahon (2020, p. 77).

The obvious benefit to peer supervision is that it can be easily resourced. In our case, the peers were all working within the same field with the same student groups and were able to share knowledge and experience from their different coaching backgrounds and styles. Turner, Lucas and Whitaker (2018, 2021) identify a similar range of benefits and limitations. The benefits they identified included feeling part of a wider community, building on each other's learning, understanding of the job role and client group, and the sharing of perspectives. Limitations included supervision taking place at a more superficial (rather than deep) level and avoiding challenging one's peers.

Ultimately, supervision – even among peers – is confidential and it can be difficult to evaluate its dynamics. Whilst feedback from all parties suggests the limitations observed by Turner, Lucas and Whitaker (2018, 2021) did not manifest, we did find some issues encountered including that team members differed in their understanding of the value and benefits of peer supervision for their development. As others have shown, the developmental function of supervision is often the important for most coaching practitioners (Lawrence and Whyte, 2014, p. 49).

Coaching triads

The developmental function of supervision and its importance for our practitioners informed the introduction of coaching triads. Our aim was to evaluate whether triads could better meet the needs of experienced coaches by providing each supervisee with the opportunity to work with two colleagues instead of one. Our team of practitioners were subdivided into triads and provided with comprehensive guidance about how to fulfil the roles of coach, coachee and observer.

In the model we used, each session was 45 minutes long with a skeleton structure provided. The team were directed to hold one session per month for seven months with a suggested theme for each. These included logistics, contracting, questioning, emotions, motivational interviewing, reflective practice and 'endings' (closing coaching relationships). Each triad was comprised of three colleagues to take the role of coach, coachee and observer respectively. Triads were encouraged to avoid extensive note-taking but keep personal, reflective notes. They were also asked to provide a scenario, maybe from their own experience as a coach, or a hypothetical 'role play' – where ethical and appropriate – to discuss in the triad.

Triads provided an opportunity to bring in new situations and where the potential is to 'trial run' a scenario before it has been experienced. Because there is the role playing of a part of a coaching session, it also provided the opportunity to actively share a problem, issue or concern. The realities were, however, that some practitioners found the element of 'role play' uncomfortable, artificial or otherwise difficult. Finally, we found that the structured nature of triads provided less opportunity for flexibility than other supervisory approaches which enable supervisors to respond to emergent concerns or issues in an organisation.

External supervision

The decision to procure an external supervisor for coaches working within an organisation is about the balancing of several considerations. As others have shown (Champion, Maxwell and Pinder, 2021, pp. 271–276), there are procedural, professional, psychological and power dynamics to consider when identifying a supervisor for any internal coaching programme. Table 8.4 demonstrates how we used these to evaluate the benefits and drawbacks of externally led supervision for our practitioners.

Table 8.4 Considerations for procuring external supervision for student-facing staff

Issues	Considerations	Reflective questions to aid decision making
Procedural	We recognised that an external supervisor may: • Offer more rigorous contracting than a peer. • Be less likely to make assumptions about coaching practice. However, they may also: • Be less aware of internal structures and stakeholder dynamics. • Cost more.	What outcomes should the provision of external supervision achieve? How long will the external supervisor work for? How many people require the supervision? Will the supervisor offer group or one to one supervision or both? What knowledge and/ or experience does the supervisor need to have? Does the Supervision need to be delivered face to face or can it be done virtually? What is the budget?
Professional	• Possess more experience/ qualifications in coaching field of supervision. • Be registered with a recognised Coaching/ Supervision body. • Have received positive feedback and/or endorsement from other organisations. • Have experience of adapting to different organisational settings.	What kinds of coach training is most relevant for our team? What value would affiliation with professional associations bring? Which supervisors have worked successfully at other universities? Which supervisors have worked at institutions with a similar ethos and/or social mission? What style of supervision would best suit our practitioners? What styles might challenge them?

(Continued)

Table 8.4 (Continued)

Issues	Considerations	Reflective questions to aid decision making
	• Offer a range of supervision styles and techniques o Have less relevant contextual knowledge about barriers affecting students in HE.	
Psychological	• Require induction to the organisation and/or team of coaches. • Offer a 'counter balance to group think' (Champion, Maxwell and Pinder, 2021, p. 274). o Take longer to build rapport and trust as an utsider.'	What level of induction will a supervisor require? Who will be responsible for this? How might this supervisor challenge any hegemonic or dominant views? How will this supervisor gain trust from the team? What relevant lived experiences might they be able to bring?
Power	• Have a reduced risk of conflict of interest. o Be less aware of power dynamics	What experience does this supervisor have of working with diverse teams, and diverse coachees?

Adapted from Champion, Maxwell and Pinder (2021, pp. 272–276).

In our experience, there have been clear advantages to using some externally led supervision in small groups. The external perspective which supervisors brought with them was valuable, as was their greater capacity for neutrality. However, we found that external supervision did not offer the same opportunities for creating a 'community of practice' (Wenger, 1999) among our coach-mentors as peer-led support.

Implementing internal supervision

Having evaluated two models of peer-led supervision in pairs and triads and trialled externally led group supervision, we decided to adopt an approach which combined the beneficial elements of a peer community of practice with the need for a trained and dedicated supervisor. Five practitioners in the team (including Richard and Helen) were selected to attend an experiential and interactive external training course on supervision and use this to develop principles of internal team supervision. These were:

- The need for alignment with relevant professional standards and frameworks such as those of the European Mentoring and Coaching Council (EMCC, 2022) and International Coaching Federation (ICF, 2024).
- The importance of a safe psychological space for supervisees in which confidentiality arrangements, boundaries and expectations are clear to all.
- The need to ensure psychological safety for supervisors who were also practitioners in the team and not line managers.
- The need for the supervisors and the supervisees to understand the confidentiality arrangements within this model of internal supervision.
- The need to share and be transparent about the 'supervisor learning journey' and be clear about the 'novice' status of supervisors.
- The need to discuss confidentiality, expectations and level of involvement with the Senior Management of the service.
- The need to agree our 'keystones' as a supervisory group and within these be able to develop our own supervisory style.
- The need to gain feedback and evaluate the effectiveness of supervision.
- The need to plan the practical aspects of the supervision, including communications to the team, times, dates and frequency.
- The need to plan the content of the supervision sessions, including a 'launch' session, a 'first' session and subsequent sessions.

A critical tool for delivering on these principles was our 'Shared Ways of Working' agreement for participants and supervisors. It provided a basis from which all supervisors and supervises worked from and within and is shown in Table 8.5.

Table 8.5 Shared Ways of Working in supervision

Aims	– To ensure evaluation of continual improvements for the student experience – To provide an important and safe space for reflective practice and in doing so to bring awareness to the surface of any issues affecting individuals in their day-to-day practice – To promote and support positive practitioner wellbeing based on ethical practice across the service.
Expectations	– To be respectful and supportive of all colleagues in attendance – To strictly adhere to the guidelines on confidentiality. To maintain confidentiality to create a trusting, respectful and safe space where colleagues can share openly – To give priority to these appointments and arrive at all sessions on time – To review the Supervision contract (Shared Ways of Working) before a session if this helpful
Role of supervisee	– To prepare for each session by bringing a question or a real scenario to the session upon which they would like to reflect on with the group. – To be open to insight, wisdom, reflections and questions from others in the group and the supervisor. – To develop the ability to discriminate what feedback is useful and how you may use any learning gained in group supervision to support and enhance your practice.
Role of supervisor	– The supervisor in the role of supervisor, not coach/mentor in this context – To prepare for each session and commit to continuing professional development within the role. – To facilitate a fair environment for all supervisees to participate – To provide a space for awareness of how supervisees see themselves as a coach and where they are with their coaching.

(*Continued*)

Table 8.5 (Continued)

	– To develop and nurture a safe, respectful group environment to promote within colleagues an increased awareness of their own of strengths, talents and further potential within their practice.
Confidentiality	– Discussions within the group should remain within the group and not be shared elsewhere by any attendee. – None of the content will be shared with senior managers other than general emerging themes that may require training and development input across the team or for parts of the team. – Conversations and discussions taking place in supervision are confidential and remain 'within the supervision space' to ensure a foundation of trust and create a safe environment in which group members can share openly.
Evaluation/ feedback	– Supervisors will welcome feedback about both their facilitation of the session and how effective group members feel the supervision is for them and others. – Feedback will be invited at the end of the session and via a feedback form. – Any group member who wishes to feedback their experience of supervision to their line manager is invited to do so. – Supervisors will agree with group members at the end of the session what 'theme' feedback (if any) is required to be passed onto Senior Management. – Feedback to senior managers will relate only to attendance and any emerging themes but within the bounds of confidentiality mentioned before.

We planned to send to all team members the 'Shared Ways of Working' document two weeks before the first session to provide time for supervisees to read and digest the information and come to the first session with any questions, thoughts or observations. We also agreed a loose structure for subsequent supervision sessions which is shown in Table 8.6.

The evaluation of this approach to supervision was carried out 12 months after the programme began, via staff survey with participants and through

Table 8.6 Session plan for supervision sessions

Grounding or settling	Open	Check-in	Sharing	Insight and wisdom	Summary and feedback
Time to gather thoughts, decide what is meaningful and important to bring to the session today.	Supervisor 'opens' the session. Reference to the agreed 'Shared Ways of Working'	Wellbeing 'check-in' and each group member shares briefly the case, scenario or questions they are interested in exploring further.	Each group member in turn shares what they have brought to supervision.	Other group members and supervisor listen deeply, ask clarifying questions and shares what feelings, images and thoughts may arise for them.	Supervisor summarises session and the themes and asks for feedback.

reflective discussions among supervisors. The evaluation survey, completed by practitioners, sought to capture how effective they found the supervision to be and highlighted the impact of the space supervisors created for reflection and the sense of 'safety' in working with peers. Importantly, it also highlighted the impact supervision had on staff wellbeing – specifically having a place to explore emotions, process experiences, thoughts and feelings about student interactions, and wider experiences in the role.

As new supervisors we reflected on the vital importance of having supervision ourselves, to ensure ethical practice and our own professional development, in line with the recommendations in the literature (Hawkins and McMahon, 2020). In particular, we wanted to ensure that we developed the coaching supervisor skills set out by British Psychological Society (BPS) (2007) and gained support with the supervision of more complex coaching situations and issues of power in both coaching and supervision. Given the context in which we work and that ourselves and our supervisees are engaged in making a difference through coaching students from marginalised groups, we believe this supervision needed careful procurement. We wanted to ensure that we had a raised awareness of the seventh lens within the Seven-Eyed model, were addressing any systemic inequalities and the need for equity, and that we look at ourselves through the lens of what it means to take an anti-racist stance and engage in compassionate, critical self-reflection (Roche and Passmore, 2021). This would be an ongoing area of development for us, and our colleagues, as supervisors.

Practice forums

The final form of supervision for staff we trialled was intended as a way of strengthening the 'community of practice' which had developed in peer supervision and triads. Providing opportunities for reflective practice is crucial for coach-mentors – especially in the context of work with students with complex barriers. There are other examples in the literature where structures such as Action Learning Sets has been successfully used to create reflective spaces for coaches as part of a peer supervision model (Turner, Tee and Crompton, 2017). Modelled on this approach, we developed 'Practice Forums.'

Like Action Learning Sets, the main premise of Practice Forums was social learning in small groups, enabled by a facilitator (Brockbank and McGill, 2004, pp. 12–13). Similarly, Practice Forums were designed to facilitate the sharing of best practice and problem solving. Forums with small groups of four to six members of staff. Practice Forums successfully engaged our whole team of practitioners – reflected in high levels of attendance and engagement. They also enabled some in-depth sharing and problem solving. It is undoubtable that having a qualified coaching supervisor (Richard) facilitate all the Practice Forums contributed to the effective maintenance of the reflective space. Borrowing from supervision models ensured the Practice Forums fulfilled some of the core functions of supervision in coaching and attentiveness to the seventh 'lens' ensured the Practice Forums retained the reflexivity our team needed to develop their own anti-oppressive coaching practice.

However, the anecdotal impact we were observing of the introduction of Practice Forums, alongside earlier initiatives such as the Peer Supervision pairings and Triads suggest that there is also a place for a more 'innately egalitarian' approach to supervision than is afforded by the 'central dyad of supervisor and supervisee' which has been 'imported into coaching' from therapeutic settings (Turner, Tee and Crompton, 2017, p. 55). In addition to these benefits, this model may also offer a more cost-effective and sustainable approach to meeting the developmental needs of large student-facing teams in HE.

Summary

In this chapter, we have explored the ways in which supervision can help to sustain an effective and ethical coaching culture in an organisation. Firstly, Julie shared her experiences about how supervision can be used to support the professional coaching practice of internal coaches working with staff. Secondly, Richard and Helen discussed supervision for student-facing support staff. One emerging theme which is beyond the scope of this chapter, but which we continue to explore (and invite others to do the same), is the role that Generative AI might play in supervision, helping practitioners to review their practice and consider biases.

What we hope to have foregrounded in this chapter is the utility of supervision for the support of staff in HE – whether for coaches (or line managers) working with other staff, or student-facing support teams. Like other authors in this volume, we share the view that a coaching culture enhances the student experience at university, but we also lend support to the range of literature which attests to the criticality of supervision for practitioners. Our experiences show that there may not be a singular or definitive model which we can adapt to meet the needs of all staff, but rather that institutions consider what might be gained from implementing different modalities of supervision in their own contexts.

Reflective questions

- How might the supervision models discussed in this chapter be adapted in your own context?
- How might supervision enhance the developmental and well-being support available to yourself and others at your institution?
- What 'checks' on ethical practice might supervision help to provide?
- How might supervision support the progress of anti-racist and anti-oppressive student support at your institution?
- How will you gain feedback and evaluate the effectiveness of any supervision you provide?
- How could generative AI or other technologies be used in supervision?

Bibliography

Association for Coaching. (2018) *Supervision guide*. Available at: https://cdn.ymaws.com/www.associationforcoaching.com/resource/resmgr/accreditation/coach_accreditation/supporting_documentation/ca_supervision_guide.pdf (Accessed: 18 November 2024).

Bachkirova, T., Clutterbuck, D. and Jackson, P. (2021) *Coaching and mentoring supervision: theory and practice*. 2nd edn. London: Open University Press.

Bachkirova, T., Jackson, P., Hennig, C. and Moral, M. (2020) 'Supervision in coaching: systematic literature review', *International Coaching Psychology Review*, 15(2), pp. 31–53. doi: 10.53841/bpsicpr.2020.15.2.31

British Psychological Society. (2007) *Guidelines for supervision in coaching psychology*. Available at: https://www.bps.org.uk/member-networks/division-coaching-psychology (Accessed: 20 November 2024).

British Sociological Association. (2024) *HE students: the neglected voices of the cost of living crisis*. Available at: https://es.britsoc.co.uk/he-students-the-neglected-voices-of-the-cost-of-living-crisis/ (Accessed: 20 November 2024).

Brockbank, A. and McGill, I. (2004) *The action learning handbook: powerful techniques for education, professional development and training*. 1st edn. Oxford: Routledge. doi: 10.4324/9780203416334

Carroll, M. (2006). 'Supervising executive coaches', *Therapy Today*, 17(5), pp. 47–49.

Champion, C.K., Maxwell, A. and Pinder, K. (2021). 'Supervising internal coaches', in T. Bachkirova, P. Jackson and D. Clutterbuck (eds.) *Coaching and mentoring supervision: theory and practice.* 2nd edn. London, England: Open University Press, pp. 266–278.

Clutterbuck, D., Whitaker, C. and Lucas, M. (2016) *Coaching supervision: a practical guide for supervisees.* 1st edn. Oxford: Routledge. doi: 10.4324/9781315687070

EMCC. (2022) *Supervision guidelines.* Available at: https://emccdrive.emccglobal.org/api/file/download/HVoMoKnzpKAi6gPyLjHsTqS57aRuRJpNIacHGmSl (Accessed: 18 November 2024).

Hawkins, P. (2006) 'Coaching supervision', in J. Passmore (ed.) *Excellence in coaching: the industry guide.* London: Kogan Page, pp. 203–216.

Hawkins, P., McMahon, A., Ryde, J., Shohet, R. and Wilmot, J. (2020) *Supervision in the helping professions.* 5th edn. London: Open University Press.

Hawkins, P. and Smith, N. (2006) *Coaching, mentoring and organizational consultancy: supervision and development.* Maidenhead: Open University Press.

Hawkins, P., Turner, E. and Passmore, J. (2019) *The manifesto for supervision.* Available at: https://centaur.reading.ac.uk/83810/1/The%20Manifesto%20for%20Supervision-%20Hawkins%20Turner%20%20Passmore%202019.pdf (Accessed: 20 November 2024).

Hay, J. (2007) *Reflective practice and supervision for coaches.* 1st edn. Maidenhead: McGraw-Hill Education.

Heron, J. (2001) *Helping the client: a creative practical guide.* 5th edn. London: Sage.

ICF. (2024) Coaching supervision. Available at: https://coachingfederation.org/credentials-and-standards/coaching-supervision (Accessed: 18 November 2024).

Iordanou, I., Hawley, R. and Iordanou, C. (2017). *Values and ethics in coaching.* London: Sage.

Lawrence, P. and Whyte, A. (2014) 'What is coaching supervision and is it important?', *Coaching: An International Journal of Theory, Research and Practice,* 7(1), pp. 39–55. doi: 10.1080/17521882.2013.878370

Litherland, G., Schulthes, G., Cowles, C. and Ewe, E. (2023) 'The proctor model of clinical supervision: an introduction for professional counselors', *The Journal of Counselor Preparation and Supervision,* 17(5). Available at: https://digitalcommons.sacredheart.edu/jcps/vol17/iss5/4 (Accessed: 20 November 2024).

Passmore, J. and McGoldrick, S. (2009) 'Super-vision, extra-vision or blind faith? A grounded theory study of the efficacy of coaching supervision', *International Coaching Psychology Review,* 4(2), pp. 145–161. doi: 10.53841/bpsicpr.2009.4.2.145

Proctor, B. (1987) 'Supervision: a co-operative exercise in accountability', in M.C. Marken and M. Payne (eds.) *Enabling and ensuring supervision in practice.* Leicester: National Youth Bureau and Council for Education and Training in Youth Community Work, pp. 21–23.

Roche, C. and Passmore, J. (2021) *Racial justice, equity and belonging in coaching.* Available at: https://assets.henley.ac.uk/v3/fileUploads/Racial-Justice-Equity-and-Belonging-in-Coaching.pdf (Accessed: 19 November 2024).

Times Higher Education. (2023) *How to combat the mental health crisis on campus.* Available at: https://www.timeshighereducation.com/campus/how-combat-mental-health-crisis-campus (Accessed: 20 November 2024).

Turner, T., Lucas, M. and Whitaker, C. (2018) *Peer supervision in coaching and mentoring: a versatile guide for reflective practice.* 1st edn. London: Routledge. doi: 10.4324/9781315162454

Turner, T., Lucas, M. and Whitaker, C. (2021) 'Peer supervision', in T. Bachkirova, P. Jackson and D. Clutterbuck (eds.) *Coaching and mentoring supervision: theory and practice.* 2nd edn. London, England: Open University Press, pp. 240–253.

Turner, A., Tee, D. and Crompton, S. (2017) 'Critical action learning: a method or strategy for peer supervision of coaching practice', *Action Learning: Research and Practice,* 14(1), pp. 53–61. doi: 10.1080/14767333.2017.1282640

Wenger, E. (1999) *Communities of practice: learning, meaning, and identity.* Cambridge: Cambridge University Press.

Postscript

What might the future hold for coaching and mentoring in higher education?

Martin Ousley

The story so far: coaching and mentoring at The OU

In this volume, we have a set of practical, evidence-based recommendations for the design and implementation of coaching and mentoring in higher education (HE). There are approaches which could be adapted variously for a centralised service, a student-led model, or through integration in existing student support/IAG services. Together, the contributors offer us a picture of coaching and mentoring at one institution through the lens of the Personal Learning Advice (PLA) Service pilot. This picture is not a static one, however. Within The Open University (OU), UK, the value of coaching and mentoring for both staff and students continues to be recognised – as outlined in the introduction to this volume – and the PLA Service, in particular, is seeing a welcome 'ripple' effect as part of its legacy at the university.

Acknowledging then that what we have here is the beginning (not the end) of the story, this postscript offers a further invitation to ponder what might lie ahead for coaching and mentoring services more widely in the sector. It considers, too, ongoing financial challenges in the provision of 1:1 student support, concerns about measuring and proving demonstrable 'impact,' and the potential for artificial intelligence (AI) to shape how we support students (and staff) in HE.

DOI: 10.4324/9781003486015-10

Reflections on key themes in coaching and mentoring in HE

Before looking forward, let us take a moment to briefly look back at some of the key themes in this volume and what we hope readers will take away for further discussion.

Ethics, equity and contracting

The first three chapters of the book demonstrate the foundational principles for establishing any coaching and mentoring service or culture. A common thread in all three pieces is the pivotal role that practitioner self-awareness plays in how ethical and equity-centred coaching and mentoring is in practice. In Chapter 1, we see this in the discussion of 'ethical maturity.' Lynden cites (Smith *et al.*, 2023) in defining ethical maturity as: 'a way of being which, by cultivating a sensitivity and self-awareness of the motivations for behaviour and its consequences, seeks to facilitate positive outcomes and avoid harm.' This is closely related to some of the personal characteristics, experience and abilities required by a coach.

Practitioner self-awareness and positionality are central to the 'equity lens' chapter. Here, we have a metanarrative of approaches to anti-oppressive practice and, within that, the development of a practitioner-led professional framework in the PLA Service. Person-centred approaches can, as the authors show, help to avoid a 'deficit' approach, providing flexibility and adaptiveness to individual needs. However, we should also be aware that coaching is not a neutral act, and practitioners should engage in critical self-reflection to expose their own privilege and bias. More broadly, this reflexive approach to positionality is in many ways exemplary. Frontline student support staff, as well as lecturers and tutors, are the 'face' of the university. Their interface with students has the potential to cement or undermine student belonging and success, as is well known. There is, of course, a wider structural role for universities in the decolonisation of the curriculum and policy reviews regarding things like assessment. Yet the degree to which staff are able to view their roles and their work with students through an equity lens may well determine how successfully universities can take down barriers experienced by students.

There is a wealth of evidence in this volume about the ways in which coaching and mentoring can help enhance student engagement and experience. Chapter 3, in particular, reminds us how pivotal effective contracting and rapport building is in that. In essence, contracting creates the first foundation stone of a coaching relationship, but we can also see in this chapter how contracting (even informally) can enhance staff-student interactions. The approaches to rapport building and contracting offered in this chapter and the importance of practitioner reflexivity might have something to offer for wider forums for staff-student engagement in HE – including the potential value of adopting similar approaches within student engagement and partnership work.

Supporting students to 'flourish'

The middle three chapters of the book demonstrate – in very different ways – how coaching and mentoring might variously support students to 'flourish.' In positive psychology coaching, 'flourishing' refers to the fulfilment of potential that comes when a client is effectively managing their wellbeing and using their strengths to overcome challenges and achieve their goals (Seligman, 2011, p. 26). In the context of HE, as Chapter 4 illustrates, whether a student can 'flourish' often hinges upon holistic wellbeing support involving a combination of person-centred services such as IAG, coaching, peer support and where relevant, access to specialist mental health provision. At a time when mental health and community services outside of HE in the UK are incredibly over stretched, practitioners and tutors are seeing the impact in student mental health and wellbeing. In this context, as the authors show, proactive coaching is one tool to prevent students reaching crisis in many cases. In other scenarios, it can help a student successfully return to study following a break in learning because of a mental health challenge.

Coaching may therefore offer institutions one approach to provide that holistic support – whether it is working with students on coping strategies and raising self-awareness or offering strengths-based exercises. This does, however, come with significant caveats. As noted in Chapter 4, student wellbeing is often profoundly impacted by structural barriers – especially pronounced for racially minoritised students – and without a whole-institutional approach to removing these, there is a risk that the safe space offered by coaching becomes just a temporary reprieve.

Supporting students 'learning to learn' in the context of supported open learning is the focus in Chapter 5, which makes the case for coaching and mentoring strategies as a tool for Learning Developers to support student flourishing in that space. The background to Learning Development and indeed its philosophy is grounded in the idea that all students have the capacity to succeed but, in many cases, may be hampered by structural and institutional barriers. As M. N. Roy posits in his work on Radical Humanism, the only limitation on human potential is the limitation placed by societal or structural barriers (Roy, 2004). Coaching and mentoring can – in different ways – help to create the culture to support students to navigate 'insider' spaces associated with things like academic conventions, writing and assessment. More broadly, the process of students 'learning to learn' requires practitioners who know how to hold silence, use open questions, consider their body language and – in essence – create a calm, safe space.

Creating peer-led models to support student flourishing is the focus of Chapter 6, where the authors make a case for the value of peer mentoring for both student mentors and their mentees. Peer-led support is often an integral part of university life, and in this chapter, the authors show how this might translate into a distance- or hybrid-learning context.

Staff learning and development and support

The final two chapters of this volume speak to two related aspects of building a broader coaching culture within an organisation. The case study in Chapter 7 demonstrates one of the ways that learning from the PLA Service pilot has been used to help inform staff development. There is a strong focus here on taking an approach led by staff – from an initial exploration about the benefits, the CPD opportunities and potential impact on job satisfaction. Coaching skills can help to support frontline staff, particularly those in IAG roles, with the management of boundaries with students, as well as tools for supporting their own wellbeing.

The authors of both chapters in this section of the book acknowledge that developing coaching skills does not equate to generating coaches. Universities seeking to build a coaching culture need to consider longer-term, substantive training programmes to ensure ethical practice and quality assure coaching. The provision of appropriate supervision is also critical for underpinning this, as the authors of Chapter 8 argue. The multi-modal, cost-effective approach to supervision described in this chapter illustrates how investment in supervision can serve to protect staff wellbeing whilst at the same time develop professional skills and identities.

The practitioners who have contributed to this volume have helped to strengthen the case for coaching and mentoring in HE, using insights from both operational and strategic perspectives, with practical and experiential case studies, as well as scholarship. Let us now turn to a 'horizon scan' to identify further considerations for readers, practitioners and leaders exploring coaching and mentoring in their own institutions.

What does the future hold for coaching and mentoring in higher education?

The evidence that coaching and mentoring work is strong – as the chapters in this volume exemplify. Yet the reality is that providing dedicated one-to-one (or small group) coaching and mentoring for students requires investment. In an increasingly challenging economic landscape for the sector, cost is an obvious challenge. In this volume, authors have been sensitive to these realities. As noted in the introduction to this volume, evaluation of impact on student outcomes is vital and that remains a clear recommendation for pilot projects. How we measure causal 'impact' using quantitative data is not straightforward, of course, and much of the evidence for coaching and mentoring in this volume is centred on self-reported student experience and stories of coach-mentors supporting them to 'flourish.' The extent to which universities can justify investment in coaching and mentoring will rest upon the evidence that it works. Our aspiration is that this volume makes a contribution to this.

Beyond fiscal challenges, a further consideration to the future of one-to-one and small group support is the development of AI. AI is clearly no longer a technological, indeed societal, prospect on the horizon; it has well and truly 'arrived' and at some pace, impacting almost every facet of our everyday lives. Using generative AI for content creation in writing, music, images and computer code, is of particular interest in HE. Most universities now have dedicated steering groups creating frameworks to encourage and oversee ethical and appropriate use of generative AI and advance HE has commissioned colloquia and related projects (Advance HE, 2023, 2024).

The use of AI across business, industry and public services has featured heavily in customer service functions with conversational AI techniques increasingly being used in the form of chatbots (IBM, no date) to deal with aspects such as enquiries and complaints, at least as a first point of contact. Clearly, the attraction to any organisation or business to the use of AI in this way is creating cost efficiencies and HE is no different in that respect. But as such automated systems become more sophisticated and more 'human-like,' a question is posed on how they can be used both effectively and ethically as an enhancement to person-centred interactions. Particularly relevant for coaching and mentoring practitioners, are considerations about how AI will shape student experiences of HE and by extension, student support services, and how this can be done ethically and equitably while maintaining duty of care and high standards of service and practice.

AI in coaching and mentoring outside of HE represents something much more significant than the simple implementation of automated chatbot systems. AI can support administrative and preliminary tasks, enhancing the overall coaching experience via coach matching, meeting coordination and preliminary interactions but beyond this point there are important ethical considerations (Lamb, 2024). Whilst the technology used in these functions has become more sophisticated and able to deal with more complex and in-depth enquiries and complaints, the increasing sophistication of AI in terms of being able to understand and replicate complex human behaviour poses significant questions about the human role within the field of coaching and mentoring.

If coaching, as noted in the introductory chapter, is on the way to becoming a more mature and regulated profession, the use of AI in its methods is in relative infancy. It has been suggested that 'Coaching bodies such as ICF, EMCC, and all others should develop AI coaching standards, guidelines, and best practices to help guide stakeholders on the responsible creation and use of AI coaching' (Terblanche, 2024, p. 636). This process has begun (ICF, 2023) and there is a body of literature and research swiftly developing (Passmore and Woodward, 2023; Diller, 2024; Passmore *et al.*, 2025) which highlights both the potential benefits and risks.

In the developing intersection of AI in coaching the authors of this volume do not claim to be experts but suggest this context highlights some of the deeper, ethical issues student support services will need to confront. The difficulties that could stem from such non-human services going wrong have potentially far more wide-reaching consequences than those of human error, and any institution should consider fully the ethical considerations and potential risks involved.

Reflective questions: ethical use of AI in coaching

- How would contracting and rapport be established between a non-human coach driven by AI and a student?
- How can AI be used to enhance the logistical elements of coaching practice (for example, diary management) without decentralising or diminishing human elements of coaching?
- How can equitable practice be embedded within the use of AI, and how can this be monitored and measured effectively?
- What approaches would be needed to ensure AI coaches are not vulnerable to hackers, dubious algorithms or technical glitches?

- How would institutions offset the significant impact that AI is forecasted to have upon the climate (Delort *et al.*, 2023; Ren and Wierman, 2024)?

Some concluding observations

In sharing stories from the PLA Service and related coaching and mentoring projects from one institution, this volume offers the beginnings of a toolkit for practitioners and senior leaders interested in coaching and mentoring in HE. What is clear is the value of the person-centred approach described by all the contributors to this volume. Coaching and mentoring start with unconditional positive regard but, translated to HE, are rooted in a pedagogy of care and compassion (Gibbs, 2017). This allows us to support students in navigating aspects of student life such as intersectional disadvantage, academic conduct, bereavement and grief, homelessness and poverty, domestic violence or abuse and the many other stories student support staff hear on a regular basis.

AI services could not replicate this because, fundamentally, they lack humanity and heart. In the world of education, particularly as student support strives to become increasingly holistic while meeting the challenges of scalability and economisation, humanity and heart remain indispensable.

Bibliography

Advance HE. (2023) 'Member Project 23–24- Generative AI: beyond assessment'. Available at: https://advance-he.ac.uk/membership/all-member-benefit-projects/Generative-AI-Beyond-Assessment (Accessed: 3 October 2024).

Advance HE. (2024) 'Artificial Intelligence Symposium 2024: AI journeys – being human'. Available at: https://www.advance-he.ac.uk/programmes-events/events/AI-Symposiums-2024/AI-Journeys-Being-Human (Accessed: 3 October 2024).

Delort, A., Riou, L. and Srivastava, A. (2023) 'Environmental impact of artificial intelligence', *HAL Open Science*. Available at: https://inria.hal.science/hal-04283245/document1/12/24 (Accessed: 1 December 2024).

Diller, S.J. (2024) 'Ethics in digital and AI coaching', *Human Resource Development International*, 1–13. Available at: https://coachingfederation.org/blog/navigating-bias-in-the-age-of-ai (Accessed: 1 December 2024).

Gibbs, P. (2017). 'Higher education a compassion business or edifying experience?', in P. Gibbs (ed.) *The pedagogy of compassion at the heart of higher education*. London: Springer, pp. 1–18.

Hullinger, A. (2023) *The importance of maintaining your coaching ethics in an AI-driven world*. ICF. Available at: https://coachingfederation.org/blog/navigating-bias-in-the-age-of-ai (Accessed: 18 December 2024).

IBM. (no date) 'What is a chatbot?'. Available at: https://www.ibm.com/topics/chatbots (Accessed: 1 November 2024).

Köbis, L. and Mehner, C. (2021) 'Ethical questions raised by AI-supported mentoring in higher education', *Frontiers in Artificial Intelligence*, 4, 624050.

Lamb, A. (2024) *AI in coaching: key ethical considerations for HR leaders for 2025 and beyond*. Available at: https://boldly.app/blog/ai-in-coaching-key-ethical-considerations-for-hr#:~:text=While%20AI%20can%20enhance%20coaching,remains%20central%20to%20coaching%20processes (Accessed: 1 December 2024).

Passmore, J. and Woodward, W. (2023) 'Coaching education: wake up to the new digital and AI coaching revolution!', *International Coaching Psychology Review*, 18(1), pp. 58–72.

Passmore, J., Olafsson, B. and Tee, D. (2025). *A systematic literature review of artificial intelligence (AI) in coaching: insights for future research and product development*. Available at: https://www.emerald.com/insight/content/doi/10.1108/jwam-11-2024-0164/full/pdf (Accessed: 11 April 2025).

Ren, S. and Wierman, A. (2024) *The uneven distribution of AI's environmental impacts*. Available at: https://hbr.org/2024/07/the-uneven-distribution-of-ais-environmental-impacts (Accessed: 1 December 2024).

Roy, M.N. (2004) *Radical humanist – selected writings*. Amherst, NY: Prometheus.

Seligman, M.E.P. (2011) *Flourish: a visionary new understanding of happiness and well-being*. London: Free Press.

Smith, W.-A., Passmore, J., Turner, E., Lai, Y.-L. and Clutterbuck, D. (2023) *The ethical coaches' handbook: a guide to developing ethical maturity in practice*. Abingdon: Routledge.

Terblanche, N.H.D. (2024) 'Artificial intelligence (AI) coaching: redefining people development and organizational performance', *The Journal of Applied Behavioral Science*, 60(4), pp. 631–638. doi: 10.1177/00218863241283919

Appendices

Appendix A: Student experience survey questions

I feel confident that I can cope with my studies. How would you have answered this before the Personal Learning Advisor (PLA) session(s)? How do you feel now?

I feel I belong at The Open University (OU). How would you have answered this before the PLA session(s)? How do you feel now?

I feel I matter to The OU. How would you have answered this before the PLA session(s)? How do you feel now?

I am more confident about accessing help when I need it as a result of the support I received from the PLA Service.

I have already done/or intend to do things differently as a result of the support I received from the PLA Service.

Please tell us about anything you have done differently and give examples if you can.

Did you attend one or more one-to-one appointments with a PLA?

Individualised, personal support from my PLA helped me to complete my module/studies.

I felt comfortable sharing any barriers and/or challenges to my success I may have faced at The OU in one-to-one appointments with my PLA.

Please state what, if any, types of barriers and/or challenges to your success you have faced (and may have shared with your PLA).

Thinking about any study-related achievements, please say how much you think these are a result of working with your PLA.

Thinking about any achievements or positive changes in your personal life, please say how much you think these are a result of working with your PLA.

I have achieved the goals I set during one-to-one appointments with my PLA.

Did you attend Group Workshops or Study Together Sessions with other students?

It was important for me to see and hear students with similar lived experiences AND/OR shared challenges to me at PLA Service group sessions.

Please take this opportunity to expand on any of your answers. You might like to share your suggestions for improving the PLA Service, or for completing this feedback questionnaire.

Appendix B: Peer networks

AdvanceHE – global charity seeking to improve higher education for all
https://www.advance-he.ac.uk/

Association of Higher Education Professionals
https://ahep.ac.uk/

Association for Coaching
https://www.associationforcoaching.com/

Association for Learning Development in Higher Education (ALDinHE) – ALDinHE supports and champions the work of learning developers through community building and practice-sharing, facilitating research and dissemination and providing professional development opportunities:
https://aldinhe.ac.uk/

British Psychological Society, Division of Coaching Psychology Peer Practice Groups
https://www.bps.org.uk/peer-practice-groups

CIPD – professional body for HR and people development
https://www.cipd.org/en/

Coaching in Higher Education Network – established in 2024, this network aims to bring together coaches across higher education to connect, collaborate, develop their coaching practices and contribute to enhancing student experience of learning and teaching.
(website forthcoming at the time of publication)

European Mentoring and Coaching Council Higher Education Special Interest Group (UK)
https://emcc-sandbox.uk/higher-education-special-interest-group/

European Mentoring and Coaching Council Networks
https://emcc-sandbox.uk//networks/

International Coaching Federation
https://foundationoficf.org/

NEON – professional organisation supporting those involved in widening access to higher education (HE)
https://www.educationopportunities.co.uk/

Researching, Advancing and Inspiring Student Engagement (RAISE) – a worldwide network of staff and students in Higher Education who work or have an interest in the research and promotion of student engagement:
https://www.raise-network.com/

Staff and Educational Development Association (SEDA) – SEDA is the professional association for staff and educational developers in the UK, promoting innovation and good practice in higher education:
https://www.seda.ac.uk/

UK Advising and Tutoring Association (UKAT) – a learned society of professional practitioners and researchers interested in advancing the scholarship and practice of student advising and personal tutoring in higher education in the UK:
https://www.ukat.ac.uk/

Appendix C: Support and wellbeing resources

Alcohol Change UK
Information on accessing support if you are concerned about your own or another's alcohol use.
https://alcoholchange.org.uk/help-and-support/get-help-now

Campaign Against Living Miserably (CALM)
0800 58 58 58
thecalmzone.net
Provides a helpline and online chat, as well as information and support, for anyone affected by suicide or suicidal thoughts.

Equality Advisory and Support Service (EASS)
0808 800 0082 (helpline)
18001 0808 800 0084 (textphone)
equalityadvisoryservice.com
Advice on issues relating to equality and human rights, including guidance for disabled people.

Mind
Support in all areas of mental health including helplines, in-person branches across the UK, useful contacts, resources, training and mental health advocacy.

https://www.mind.org.uk/

Samaritans
Support available through a phone call, email, letter, or regional branches as well as resources for people experiencing emotional distress

https://www.samaritans.org/

Tommy's
Charity to support those affected by pregnancy and infant loss. Includes specialist support helpline for Black and Mixed Black women and birthing people.

https://www.tommys.org/

Victim Support
0808 168 9111
victimsupport.org.uk
Provides emotional and practical support for people affected by crime and traumatic events.

Appendix D Personal Learning Advisor (PLA) core competencies and key skills

Overview of the PLA coaching and mentoring framework

PLA AND STUDENT COACHING/MENTORING JOURNEY				
PLA AND STUDENT COACHING/MENTORING SESSION(S) PLA coaching and mentoring is focused on fostering student agency and empowerment among learners in underrepresented groups which, in turn, seeks to enhance their overall learning experience and academic performance.				
ESTABLISHING THE APPROACH	CO-CREATING THE RELATIONSHIP	COMMUNICATING EFFECTIVELY	EMPOWERING ACTION	REVIEWING RESULTS
Demonstrates PLA professional practice Embodies a coaching / mentoring mindset Demonstrates cultural awareness and sensitivity	Builds and fosters trust and safety Establishes a working agreement (contracting) Maintains presence	Employs active/ deep listening Encourages and increases awareness	Facilitates growth Encourages accountability and autonomy	Encourages recognition of all achievements Supports reflection

Details of Key Skills within the PLA Coaching and Mentoring Framework

All PLA coaching/mentoring work is developed and delivered through an Equity Lens. This involves exploring the individual needs of a student to provide the right support at the right time. PLA coaching/mentoring seeks to remove barriers to student opportunity, advancing anti-oppressive practice and promoting diverse and inclusive practice – **treating students differently to treat them fairly.**				
ESTABLISHING THE APPROACH	CO-CREATING THE RELATIONSHIP	COMMUNICATING EFFECTIVELY	EMPOWERING ACTION	REVIEWING RESULTS
Demonstrates PLA professional practice	**Builds and fosters trust and safety**	**Employs active/deep listening**	**Facilitates growth**	**Encourages recognition of achievements**
Works within The OU Access and Participation Strategy and The OU Access and Participation Plan. Uses language appropriate and respectful to students and relevant OU parties.	Intentionally creates and holds a space for under-represented students. Recognises intersectionality and respects the student's decision whether to share aspects of their identity.	Listens to encourage self-directed coaching/mentoring sessions and to foster student agency. Considers the student's context, identity, experiences, environment,	Facilitates the student's growth by transforming learning and insight into action. Partners with the student to design goals, actions and accountability measures. Invites the student to consider	Encourages recognition of ALL achievements, celebration of outcomes/success, completion of aims or goals. Empowers the student to feedback their experiences

(Continued)

(Continued)

Demonstrates PLA professional practice	Builds and fosters trust and safety	Employs active/deep listening	Facilitates growth	Encourages recognition of achievements
Displays personal integrity, compassion, authenticity, honesty and sincerity. Demonstrates empathetic respect and sensitivity for the student's identity, experiences, environment, situation, perceptions, concerns, values, beliefs, emotions, approach and personal being. Maintains student confidentiality within The OU Safeguarding guidelines.	Adapts coaching/ mentoring approach to respect the student's identity, perceptions, style and language and needs. Meeting the student 'where they are.' Encourages the student to share their lived experience and acknowledges the student's truth. Acknowledges and respects the student's unique strengths, insights and participation in the coaching/ mentoring process.	situation, concerns, values and beliefs to enhance understanding of what the student is communicating. Listens actively and clarifies understanding. Hearing emotion/ emotive phrases. Noticing non-verbal cues, other behaviours and what is not said. Uses a range of powerful questioning, silence, metaphor and analogy – where appropriate. Uses reflection, paraphrasing,	how to move forward, including resources, support and potential barriers.	through appropriate routes/forums. Partners with the student to close the coaching/ mentoring session(s).

(Continued)

Demonstrates PLA professional practice	**Builds and fosters trust and safety**	**Employs active/deep listening**	**Facilitates growth**	**Encourages recognition of achievements**
	Acknowledges and supports the student's expression of feelings, emotions, perceptions, concerns and beliefs. Shows support, empathy and concern for the student.	summarising to ensure clarity and to acknowledge and demonstrate understanding. Notices trends in the student's behaviours and emotions during/across sessions to help discover themes or patterns.		
Embodies a PLA coaching/mentoring mind-set	**Establishes a working agreement (contracting)**	**Encourages and increases awareness**	**Encourages accountability and autonomy**	**Supports reflection**
Provides a person-centred approach which considers the student holistically, as an individual, and not a homogenous group.	Explains what coaching/mentoring is and is not and describes the process to the student and relevant OU parties.	Considers the student's lived experience as part of tailored support. Helps the student identity factors that influence current and	Works with the student to create options and possibilities to solve challenges. Empowers the student to access the support available to them.	Enables the student to reflect on their personal growth, areas of development and the whole coaching journey. Commits to organisational

(*Continued*)

(Continued)

Embodies a PLA coaching/mentoring mind-set	Establishes a working agreement (contracting)	Encourages and increases awareness	Encourages accountability and autonomy	Supports reflection
Acknowledges and appreciates the power of language and dominant, Western discourse. Prepares mentally and emotionally for coaching/mentoring sessions. Remains open, curious, flexible and person centred. Is comfortable working with the student in a space of not knowing. Acknowledges limitations of PLA role and seeks help from other OU resources/support when necessary.	Reaches agreement on how the coaching/mentoring works, making any necessary adjustments to support the student's needs. Provides clarity on the responsibilities of the PLA and those of the student such as confidentiality, scheduling/duration and follow-up activity/actions. Encourages the student to set the coaching/mentoring focus and to be heard.	future patterns of behaviour, thinking or emotion. Supports the student's self-discovery around new thoughts, beliefs, perceptions, emotions and strengths for greater understanding, awareness and clarity. Asks questions/deeper questions that help the student explore beyond their current thinking. Encourages the student to explore 'accepted norms';	Encourages student accountability and autonomy moving forward. Partners with the student to summarise learning and insight within or between session(s).	change by sharing the student voice/experience with relevant OU parties. Identifies themes, barriers to study and case studies to share with relevant internal and external parties to inform meaningful, long-term change in The OU and where possible across HE.

(Continued)

(Continued)

Embodies a PLA coaching/mentoring mind-set	Establishes a working agreement (contracting)	Encourages and increases awareness	Encourages accountability and autonomy	Supports reflection
	Partners with the student to establish and maintain an agreed outcome for each coaching/mentoring session or across all the sessions offered. Reconfirming where necessary.	reframing/offering an alternative view. Where appropriate, challenges the student to increase their awareness or insight. Offers feedback to the student on the strengths heard/observed (that they themselves may not recognise). Potential to create new learning for the student.		

(Continued)

(Continued)

Demonstrates cultural awareness and sensitivity	**Maintains presence**			
Thinks beyond race and ethnicity. Thinks beyond disability and circumstance. Appreciates the student's values, customs and beliefs and meets them without judgement or prejudice. Learns by asking and being curious.	Remains present, focussed, observant and empathetic throughout the coaching/mentoring experience, without an agenda. Allows the student to direct the discussion and responds as needed. Demonstrates curiosity during the coaching/mentoring process.			

Adapted from: International Coaching Federation (2022) and International Coaching Federation (ICF).

Bibliography

International Coaching Federation. (2022) 'A resource guide on diversity and inclusion for coaching education providers'. Available at: https://coachingfederation.org/app/uploads/2021/07/ICF-Coach-Training_DEIJB-Resource-Guide.pdf

International Coaching Federation (ICF). (2019) 'Core competencies'. Available at: https://www.coachingfederation.org.uk/credentialing/icf-core-competencies

Index

abuse *see* trauma
academic coaching 7, 20, 193, 194
access and participation plan 10, 71, 81, 167, 307; *see also* widening participation
accessibility 73, 75, 85–89, 91, 96, 134, 150, 174; *see also* inclusion
active/deep listening 45, 59, 76, 190, 248, 257, 306–309
addiction 22, 39, 168, 169, 174, 304
ADHD 125, 251; *see also* neurodiversity
advising 4, 6, 189, 193, 304; *see also* student support services; tutor
anti-oppressive approaches 8, 20, 24, 70–71, 75, 92–94
artificial intelligence 21, 131, 290, 291, 294, 298
associate lecturers *see* tutors
association for coaching (AC) 35, 118, 268–269, 303
association for learning development in higher education 18, 190, 196, 212, 303
autism 156, 230; *see also* neurodiversity
awarding gaps 10–11, 75, 141

barriers (*to and within higher education*) 8, 10, 11, 17, 41, 43, 80, 82, 84, 86, 87, 101, 104–106, 123, 130, 150–152, 166–167, 174, 175, 177, 190, 191, 196–199, 211, 228, 249, 254, 277, 284, 289, 295, 296
belonging (*student sense of*) 6, 16, 17, 73, 75, 83, 89, 92, 96–98, 138, 141, 157, 158, 172, 175, 228, 235, 295
boundaries (*professional practice*) 6, 32, 35–37, 39, 41, 44, 62, 64, 89, 116, 119–121, 125, 127, 129, 131, 139–140, 144, 150, 158, 169, 176–177, 222, 229, 234–235, 255, 285, 297
British Psychological Society (BPS) 35, 36

careers and employability 50, 51, 87, 88, 115, 128, 136, 168, 209, 228
causal evaluation 7, 8, 18–19, 193, 237, 298
clear model 76; in supervision 280–281
coaching and mentoring (*distinction between*) 5–6; coaching and mentoring scenarios 22, 50, 54, 58, 122, 123, 126, 134, 135, 141, 160, 164, 168, 209–211, 227–228, 247, 248, 251, 271–275; continuum 3, 5, 9, 72–74, 77–80, 115, 119–121, 129, 189, 197–198, 255; framework 72–74, 78, 79, 84, 106, 295, 306–312; by telephone or video call 9, 12, 13, 88, 124, 130, 134, 143, 193, 221, 260

coaching, (*origins of the term*) 3; chemistry 115, 128, 136–144; culture 21, 269, 290, 297; distinction from counselling 2, 4, 120–121, 124; distinction from student support 6, 71, 119–120, 245–249, 251, 254–255, 263–264; group coaching and mentoring 10, 12, 32, 88, 158, 165–166, 199–201, 298; relationship with teaching 6, 199; *see also* ethics, evaluation; supervision
confidentiality (*in coaching and mentoring*) 14, 32, 35–37, 41, 42, 44, 51, 53–55, 58, 64, 89, 93, 103, 125, 126, 128, 129, 131, 229, 230, 308; in supervision 285–288
contracting 20, 32, 34–36, 38–41, 43, 47, 50, 53, 54, 58, 62, 64, 77, 78, 89, 93, 114–115, 169, 248, 256–257, 295–296, 299, 306; approaches to inclusive contracting 124–125; creative contracting 133–135; definitions of 116–119, 127–129, 136–137; group contracting 199–201; in peer mentoring 229–230; re-contracting 32, 38–39, 121, 132–133, 140; in supervision 281, 283; tools for contracting 136
critical race theory 75, 81
cultural competence 42–43, 82, 103, 141, 142

data protection (UK GDPR) 36, 41–43, 64, 275
decolonisation 8, 70, 71, 106; of student support 102–103
disability 10, 16, 36, 38, 52, 86, 88, 134, 169, 246, 312
distance learning 2, 9, 12, 13, 19, 43, 58, 164, 227; *see also* neurodivergence, mental health
duty of care 33, 51, 53, 62, 119, 135, 152, 298
dyslexia 58; *see also* neurodiversity

Equality Act (UK) 81; *see also* protected characteristics
equity 7, 10, 20, 36, 141, 188, 193, 289, 295; equity lens approach to coaching and mentoring 20, 70–107, 188, 190, 195, 307
ethics 19, 20, 31–64; definition of 33–34; ethical standards 35–37; global code of 35–36; role of reflective practice 34, 44
European Mentoring and Coaching Council (EMCC) 4, 35, 50, 58, 118, 129, 285, 299, 304
evaluation (*of coaching and mentoring programmes in higher education*) 6–8, 11, 14, 16–19, 124, 153, 155, 158, 175, 195, 201, 236–238, 298; *see also* student feedback

flourishing 20, 31, 33, 37, 42, 296–298; *see also* positive psychology

goals and goal setting 2, 7, 9–10, 17, 31, 40, 50, 54, 57, 58, 75, 104, 116, 118–120, 122, 127–128, 131–134, 136–137, 139, 140, 156, 158–163, 191, 193–195, 202, 205, 208, 209, 211, 225, 247, 248, 250, 254, 259–261, 296, 303, 307
GROW model in coaching 76, 158–160, 194, 195, 253, 254; developing skills in using GROW 259–261

helping relationships 2, 4–6, 9, 20, 114–116, 119, 121, 126, 136, 138, 144, 168
hybrid learning 2, 7, 19, 130, 297

inclusion/inclusive practice 4, 73, 80, 81, 85, 87, 88, 91, 93, 94, 101, 105–107, 124, 150, 152, 172, 173, 204, 230, 231, 307; *see also* equity, equity lens and accessibility
independent learners/independence in learning 1–2, 7, 88, 89, 202, 208, 258
information, advice and guidance *see* student support services
International Coaching Federation (ICF) 35, 36, 54, 79, 100, 104, 119, 129, 285, 299, 304, 312
intersectionality 13, 21, 71, 73, 79–85, 92, 95, 99, 152, 300, 307

learning development 18, 20, 87, 103, 187–212, 246, 296, 303
lecturer *see* tutor
lived experiences (*of students*) 17, 74, 78, 82, 84, 99, 152, 158, 172, 174, 195, 199, 201, 202, 211, 212, 231, 303, 308–309; of staff in higher education 12, 14, 21, 22, 98, 99, 139, 142, 152, 158, 172, 177; in supervision 284; *see also* positionality and representation

mattering (*student sense of*) 16, 83, 157; *see also* belonging
mental health 7, 10–12, 16, 20, 32, 39, 41, 50–54, 64, 87, 88, 130, 136, 149–177, 198, 222, 223, 230, 236, 276, 296, 305; *see also* wellbeing of students and wellbeing of staff
mentoring (origins of the term) 3, 4, 220; distinction from guidance 249; *see also* peer mentoring; and coaching and mentoring; coaching and mentoring distinction between; and coaching and mentoring continuum

NEON–National Education Opportunities Network 18, 304
neurodiversity 12, 32, 38, 43, 83, 156, 230, 251

obsessive compulsive disorder (OCD) 168; *see also* mental health
office for students 10, 18, 81, 82, 85, 236
The Open University (UK) 2, 7–10, 15, 17, 71, 74, 79, 151, 220, 245, 246, 264, 269, 294, 302
OSKAR model in coaching 76, 159, 253, 254

peer mentoring 20, 220–238
personal academic tutor *see* tutor
Personal Learning Advice (PLA) Service–*introduction to* 9–14, 71–74; approach to coaching and mentoring 76–80; evaluation of 11, 16–19; *see also* evaluation
person-centred 1, 2, 5, 9, 14, 20, 21, 70, 71, 74, 77, 78, 116, 190, 192, 194, 196–198, 208–210, 269, 295, 296, 298, 300, 309
positionality 32, 38, 40, 42–43, 73, 114–115, 140, 141, 144, 197, 211, 233, 234, 295; *see also* lived experience and representation
positive psychology 204, 296; *see also* flourishing; strengths-based approaches
postgraduate students 31, 50, 153, 158
post-traumatic stress disorder 39, 174, 304–305; *see also* mental health; and trauma
protected characteristics 21, 80, 81, 93, 95, 174; *see also* Equality Act UK
psychological safety 32, 47, 89, 93, 125, 127, 128, 166, 259, 276, 285; *see also* safe spaces

questioning techniques 196, 202–204, 209–211, 258, 259, 308

re-contracting *see* contracting
referrals 51
reflective exercises for coaching and mentoring practitioners 64, 85, 91, 102, 103, 105, 130, 144, 175, 212, 235, 238, 263, 291, 299
representation in higher education 12, 21, 31, 172, 177
Researching and Inspiring Student Engagement (RAISE) x, 304
retention 13, 16–19, 31, 81
rogers, carl 3–5, 78, 255

safe spaces 89, 94, 99, 138, 141, 166, 176, 263, 280, 286, 296, 297; *see also* psychological safety
safeguarding 125, 126, 129, 135, 169, 177, 200, 226, 228, 275, 308
self-harm 22, 50, 51, 53; *see also* mental health, and suicide
Seven Eyed model (in supervision) 269–273, 276, 278, 289
solution-focused approaches 40, 120, 158–160, 163, 253, 254

Staff and Educational Development Association–SEDA UK 6, 304
staff development 14–15, 20, 35–38, 47, 48, 76, 104, 249, 259–261, 275, 276, 280, 286, 289, 303, 304
strengths-based approaches 88, 195, 201, 202, 204, 206, 296
student experiences of coaching and mentoring 1–2, 16–17, 83, 84, 205; survey 302–303
student support services 1, 6, 12, 19, 21, 70, 71, 82, 87, 103, 106, 116, 152, 245–264, 277, 298, 299
study skills *see* learning development
suicide 22, 169, 174, 177, 305; *see also* mental health
supervision 21, 38, 43, 44, 46–49, 51–57, 60, 99, 104, 119, 125, 126, 174, 226, 258, 268–293; definition of supervision in coaching 268–269 *see also* seven eyed model; peer supervision 280–282, 289–290

trauma 39, 40, 152, 169, 174, 276, 300, 304–305; *see also* mental health; post-traumatic stress disorder
tutor 1–3, 6, 9, 14–15, 19, 31, 40, 41, 51, 54, 58, 60, 61, 84, 116, 117, 122–124, 131, 156, 205–207, 228, 235, 251

UK Advising and Tutoring Association (UKAT) 304
universal design 70, 80, 85–86, 91; *see also* accessibility

video coaching *see* coaching and mentoring by telephone or video call

wellbeing (*of students*) 4, 7, 15, 16, 20, 31, 40, 44, 49, 50, 52, 58, 77, 82, 87, 98, 135, 136, 149–177, 210–211, 246, 263–264, 296, 304–305 *see also* mental health; definition of 150
wellbeing of staff 15, 22, 32, 38, 54–57, 63, 99, 157, 297; role of supervision 268–291, 304–305
wheel of life 136, 164–165
Whitmore, John 3; *see also* GROW model
widening participation 9, 18, 20, 31, 92, 114, 304; deficit approach to 20, 74, 86, 135, 172, 191–192, 201, 295

For Product Safety Concerns and Information please contact our EU
representative GPSR@taylorandfrancis.com Taylor & Francis Verlag GmbH,
Kaufingerstraße 24, 80331 München, Germany

Printed and bound by CPI Group (UK) Ltd, Croydon, CR0 4YY
11/07/2025
01915257-0016